OXFORD EARLY CHRISTIAN STUDIES

General Editors
Gillian Clark   Andrew Louth

THE OXFORD EARLY CHRISTIAN STUDIES series includes scholarly volumes on the thought and history of the early Christian centuries. Covering a wide range of Greek, Latin, and Oriental sources, the books are of interest to theologians, ancient historians, and specialists in the classical and Jewish worlds.

Titles in the series include:

Gregory of Nyssa and the Grasp of Faith
Union, Knowledge, and the Divine Presence
Martin Laird (2004)

The Suffering of the Impassible God
The Dialectics of Patristic Thought
Paul L. Gavrilyuk (2004)

Cyril of Alexandria and the Nestorian Controversy
The Making of a Saint and of a Heretic
Susan Wessel (2004)

The Byzantine Christ
Person, Nature, and Will in the Christology of St Maximus the Confessor
Demetrios Bathrellos (2004)

The Doctrine of Deification in the Greek Patristic Tradition
Norman Russell (2004)

The Body in St Maximus the Confessor
Holy Flesh, Wholly Deified
Adam G. Cooper (2005)

The Asketikon of St Basil the Great
Anna M. Silvas (2005)

Marius Victorinus' Commentary on Galatians
Stephen Andrew Cooper (2005)

Asceticism and Christological Controversy in Fifth-Century Palestine
The Career of Peter the Iberian
Cornelia B. Horn (2006)

Marcellus of Ancyra and the Lost Years of the Arian Controversy 325–345
Sara Parvis (2006)

The Irrational Augustine
Catherine Conybeare (2006)

Clement of Alexandria and the Beginnings of Christian Apophaticism
Henny Fiskå Hägg (2006)

The Christology of Theodoret of Cyrus
Antiochene Christology from the Council of Ephesus (431)
to the Council of Chalcedon (451)
Paul B. Clayton, Jr. (2006)

Ethnicity and Argument in Eusebius' *Praeparatio Evangelica*
Aaron P. Johnson (2006)

Marriage, Celibacy, and Heresy in Ancient Christianity

The Jovinianist Controversy

DAVID G. HUNTER

OXFORD
UNIVERSITY PRESS

OXFORD
UNIVERSITY PRESS

Great Clarendon Street, Oxford OX2 6DP

Oxford University Press is a department of the University of Oxford.
It furthers the University's objective of excellence in research, scholarship,
and education by publishing worldwide in

Oxford New York

Auckland Cape Town Dar es Salaam Hong Kong Karachi
Kuala Lumpur Madrid Melbourne Mexico City Nairobi
New Delhi Shanghai Taipei Toronto

With offices in

Argentina Austria Brazil Chile Czech Republic France Greece
Guatemala Hungary Italy Japan Poland Portugal Singapore
South Korea Switzerland Thailand Turkey Ukraine Vietnam

Oxford is a registered trade mark of Oxford University Press
in the UK and in certain other countries

Published in the United States
by Oxford University Press Inc., New York

© David G. Hunter 2007

The moral rights of the author have been asserted
Database right Oxford University Press (maker)

First published 2007

All rights reserved. No part of this publication may be reproduced,
stored in a retrieval system, or transmitted, in any form or by any means,
without the prior permission in writing of Oxford University Press,
or as expressly permitted by law, or under terms agreed with the appropriate
reprographics rights organization. Enquiries concerning reproduction
outside the scope of the above should be sent to the Rights Department,
Oxford University Press, at the address above

You must not circulate this book in any other binding or cover
and you must impose the same condition on any acquirer

British Library Cataloguing in Publication Data

Data available

Library of Congress Cataloging in Publication Data

Data available

Typeset by SPI Publisher Services, Pondicherry, India
Printed in Great Britain
on acid-free paper by
Biddles Ltd., King's Lynn, Norfolk

978–0–19–927978–4

3 5 7 9 10 8 6 4 2

For Lynn

...coniugi incomparabili et amantissimae

Preface

In the later years of the fourth century an intense theological controversy occurred in Western Christianity over the issue of celibacy and marriage. At the centre of this debate stood a monk named Jovinian, who earned ecclesiastical condemnation for asserting that celibate and married Christians were equal in God's sight. Jovinian was opposed by some of the foremost churchmen of his day, among them Ambrose, Jerome, and Augustine (all later named 'doctors' of the Latin Church). This book tells the story of Jovinian and the conflicts generated by his teaching.

A word about the scope of my discussion is in order, for much of this book deals with figures and ideas that appeared prior to the time of Jovinian. Chapter 3, for example, begins with Jesus and Paul and concludes with Origen of Alexandria, and Chapter 4 ranges widely across the East and West in the fourth century. I deemed this approach necessary because I wished to place Jovinian within the context of the broader history of early Christian teaching on marriage and celibacy. One of the central arguments I develop is that although Jovinian was condemned as a 'heretic', he actually had much in common with previous Christian writers of impeccably 'orthodox' stripe. Conversely, I considered it necessary at times to trace the prehistory of ideas opposed by Jovinian (e.g. my discussion of Mary's *virginitas in partu* in Chapter 5), if only to demonstrate the marginal status of such ideas within the earlier tradition.

Scholars of Christianity in late antiquity have produced an abundance of studies of ascetic behaviour, and especially sexual renunciation, in recent decades. But no one has yet directed comparable attention to the reverse phenomenon, that is, to the ways in which Christians questioned and challenged aspects of the ascetic ideal. My aim has been to retrieve some of these anti-ascetic tendencies in early Christianity and to demonstrate their place within the broader Christian tradition. The result, I believe, is a revised and more nuanced account of the development of Christian thought on asceticism in late antiquity.

As my friends know, I have been at work on this project for much too long and have accumulated more than the usual share of debts. Over the years many scholars have heard, read, or responded to pieces of the present work, especially at meetings of the North American Patristics Society, the Oxford International Conference on Patristic Studies, the American Academy of Religion and Society of Biblical Literature, and the American Society of Church History. I apologize to those I have unwittingly omitted from the following acknowledgements.

Several dear friends have graciously read the entire manuscript and offered their expert criticism: Elizabeth A. Clark, J. Patout Burns, Peter Iver Kaufman, Robert A. Markus, and Robert Louis Wilken. One could not ask for more learned or more generous readers. Special thanks are owed to my colleague at Iowa State University, Eric Northway, who unselfishly (perhaps imprudently) took time from his own dissertation to read the entire text and to encourage me along the way.

Conversations with colleagues in the United States and abroad have often enlightened me and always delighted me, among them: Gillian Clark, Kate Cooper, Jack Davidson, Thomas Fisch, Carol Harrison, Susan Ashbrook Harvey, Madeleine Henry, Mathijs Lamberigts, Conrad Leyser, Bill Klingshirn, Neil McLynn, Susan Marks, Thomas Martin, Kim Power, Richard Price, Michael Rackett, Michele Salzman, Dennis Trout, and Mark Vessey. In the spring of 2001 a lecture for the Early Christian Studies programme at The Catholic University of America and for the Group for the Study of Late Antiquity at Princeton University gave me the opportunity to present material later incorporated into Chapter 6. I wish to thank Philip Rousseau of Catholic University and Peter Brown of Princeton for their kind invitations and gracious hospitality. In attendance at Princeton were Virginia Burrus, Susanna Elm, and Brent Shaw. Their encouragement contributed more than they know to the completion of this book.

Grants from the National Endowment for the Humanities supported my research at several points, and the Leverhulme Trust of Great Britain enabled me to spend a year as a Visiting Fellow at the University of Nottingham, where I pursued some of the initial work on this project. Colleagues at Nottingham were always warmly receptive to the foreigner in their midst. I thank Ed Ball, Richard Bell, Maurice Casey, Douglas Davies, John Heywood Thomas, Hugh Goddard, Wolf Liebeschuetz, Sr. Mary Charles Murray, and Gerard O'Daly. Sabbatical grants from the University of St. Thomas in Minnesota and Iowa State University provided the freedom from teaching needed to complete this work.

At Oxford University Press Lucy Qureshi has been a model editor and graciously tolerant of my delays. I am grateful to Dorothy McCarthy, Jenny Wagstaffe, and Rachel Woodforde for guiding the typescript through production, and to Jack Sinden for his careful copy-editing. I must acknowledge, as well, the editors of the Oxford Early Christian Studies series, Gillian Clark and Andrew Louth, for accepting the book into their series. I owe a special debt to Professor Robin Margaret Jensen of Vanderbilt University Divinity School for providing the photograph on the jacket.

Finally, I am grateful that my sons, Gregory and Robert, who having grown up in the shadow of Jovinian, have emerged no worse for it. And to my wife, Lynn, who has provided her skill as an editor and her support as a spouse, the dedication says it all.

D. G. H.

Contents

List of Abbreviations	x
Introduction	1

PART I. JOVINIAN AND HIS WORLD

1. Reconstructing Jovinian	15
2. Jovinian and Christian Rome	51

PART II. JOVINIAN, HERESY, AND ASCETICISM

3. Asceticism, Heresy, and Early Christian Tradition	87
4. Jovinian, Heresy, and Fourth-Century Asceticism	130
5. Mary Ever-Virgin? Jovinian and Marian Heresy	171

PART III. JOVINIAN AND HIS OPPONENTS

6. Against Jovinian: From Siricius to Jerome	207
7. After Jovinian: Marriage and Celibacy in Western Theology	243
Conclusion	285
References	288
Index	308

Abbreviations

1. Periodicals and series

Abbreviations of the names of periodicals and series have been adapted from Patrick H. Alexander, John F. Kutsko, James D. Ernest, Shirley A. Decker-Lucke, and David L. Petersen (eds.), *The SBL Handbook of Style for Ancient Near Eastern, Biblical, and Early Christian Studies* (Peabody, Mass.: Hendrickson, 1999); supplemented by Siegfried Schwertner (ed.), *Internationales Abkürzungsverzeichnis für Theologie und Grenzgebiete* (Berlin and New York: Walter de Gruyter, 1974).

AB	Anchor Bible
ACW	Ancient Christian Writers
AJA	*American Journal of Archaeology*
ANRW	*Aufstieg und Niedergang der römischen Welt*
ATR	*Anglican Theological Review*
Aug	*Augustinianum*
AugStud	*Augustinian Studies*
BA	Bibliothèque Augustinienne
BJRL	*Bulletin of the John Rylands Library*
BLE	*Bulletin de littérature ecclésiastique*
CAH	Cambridge Ancient History
CBQ	*Catholic Biblical Quarterly*
CH	*Church History*
CIL	*Corpus Inscriptionum Latinarum*
CCSA	Corpus Christianorum, Series Apocryphorum
CCSL	Corpus Christianorum, Series Latina
CSEL	Corpus Scriptorum Ecclesiasticorum Latinorum
CQ	*Classical Quarterly*
CSCO	Corpus Scriptorum Christianorum Orientalium
C.Th.	*Codex Theodosianus*, in T. Mommsen and P. M. Meyer (eds.), *Theodosiani libri XVI cum constitutionibus Sirmondianis* (Berlin, 1905)

CWE	Collected Works of Erasmus
CWS	Classics of Western Spirituality
DOP	*Dumbarton Oaks Papers*
DSp	*Dictionnaire de spiritualité, ascétique et mystique*
EphMar	*Ephemerides Mariologicae*
ETL	*Ephemerides theologicae lovanienses*
FC	Fathers of the Church
FZPhTh	*Freiburger Zeitschrift für Philosophie und Theologie*
GCS	Die griechischen christlichen Schriftsteller der ersten drei Jahrhunderte
Greg	*Gregorianum*
HTR	*Harvard Theological Review*
ILCV	E. Diehl (ed.), *Inscriptiones latinae christianae veteres*, 3 vols. (Berlin, 1925–31)
JAC	*Jahrbuch für Antike und Christentum*
JECS	*Journal of Early Christian Studies*
JEH	*Journal of Ecclesiastical History*
JBL	*Journal of Biblical Literature*
JMEMS	*Journal of Medieval and Early Modern Studies*
JRS	*Journal of Roman Studies*
JSPSup	Journal for the Study of the Pseudepigrapha: Supplement Series
JTS	*Journal of Theological Studies*
LCC	Library of Christian Classics
LCL	Loeb Classical Library
MFC	Message of the Fathers of the Church
Mus	*Muséon: Revue d'études orientales*
NHMS	Nag Hammadi and Manichaean Studies
NPNF[1]	Nicene and Post-Nicene Fathers, Series 1
NPNF[2]	Nicene and Post-Nicene Fathers, Series 2
NTS	*New Testament Studies*
OECS	Oxford Early Christian Studies
OECT	Oxford Early Christian Texts
PG	Patrologia Graeca
PL	Patrologia Latina
PLS	A. Hamman (ed.), *Patrologiae Latinae Supplementum*, 5 vols. (Paris, 1958–74)

PLRE	A. H. M. Jones, J. R. Martindale, and J. Morris (eds.), *The Prosopography of the Later Roman Empire*, 4 vols. (Cambridge: Cambridge University Press, 1980–92)
PMS	Patristic Monograph Series
PTS	Patristische Texte und Studien
RAC	*Reallexikon für Antike und Christentum*
RBen	*Revue Bénédictine*
REAug	*Revue des études augustiniennes*
RechAug	*Recherches augustiniennes*
REL	*Revue des études latines*
RHE	*Revue d'histoire ecclésiastique*
RHR	*Revue de l'histoire des religions*
RQ	*Römische Quartalschrift für christliche Altertumskunde und für Kirchengeschichte*
RTAM	*Recherches de théologie ancienne et médiévale*
RTL	*Revue théologique de Louvain*
RTP	*Revue de théologie et de philosophie*
SacEr	*Sacris erudiri: Jaarboek voor Godsdienstwetenschappen*
SAEMO	Sancti Ambrosii Episcopi Mediolanensis Opera
SC	Sources chrétiennes
StPatr	*Studia Patristica*
TAPA	*Transactions of the American Philological Association*
TaS	Texts and Studies
TS	*Theological Studies*
TU	Texte und Untersuchungen zur Geschichte der altchristliche Literatur
VetChr	*Vetera Christianorum*
VC	*Vigiliae Christianae*
VL	Vetus Latina: Die Reste der altlateinischen Bibel
WGRW	Writings from the Greco-Roman World
WSA	The Works of Saint Augustine: A Translation for the 21st Century
ZKG	*Zeitschrift für Kirchengeschichte*
ZNW	*Zeitschrift für die neutestamentliche Wissenschaft*
ZTK	*Zeitschrift für Theologie und Kirche*

2. Ancient sources

Abbreviations of the titles of Latin sources have been adapted from Albert Blaise and Henri Chirat (eds.), *Dictionnaire Latin–Français des auteurs chrétiens* (Turnout: Brepols, 1954); titles of Greek patristic texts from G. W. H. Lampe (ed.) *A Patristic Greek Lexicon* (Oxford: Clarendon Press, 1961). Full publication information is not given for editions that have appeared in the most common series: CSEL, CCSL, CSCO, GCS, PL, PLS, PG, and SC.

Ambrose of Milan

Cain	*De Cain et Abel* (CSEL 32.1)
Ep.	*Epistulae* (CSEL 82.1-3)
Exh. virg.	*Exhortatio virginitatis*, in F. Gori (ed.), *Verginità e vedovanza* ii (SAEMO 14.2; Milan and Rome, 1989)
Fid.	*De fide* (CSEL 78)
Inst.	*De institutione virginis*, in F. Gori (ed.), *Verginità e vedovanza* ii (SAEMO 14.2; Milan and Rome, 1989)
Luc.	*Expositio evangelii secundum Lucam* (CCSL 14)
Myst.	*De mysteriis* (SC 25bis)
Off.	*De officiis*, in Ivor Davidson (ed.), *Ambrose: De officiis* i (OECS; Oxford, 2001)
Paen.	*De paenitentia* (SC 179)
Sacr.	*De sacramentis* (SC 25bis)
Vid.	*De viduis*, in F. Gori (ed.), *Verginità e vedovanza* i (SAEMO 14.1; Milan and Rome, 1989)
Virg.	*De virginibus*, in F. Gori (ed.), *Verginità e vedovanza* i (SAEMO 14.1; Milan and Rome, 1989)
Virgin.	*De virginitate*, in F. Gori (ed.), *Verginità e vedovanza* ii (SAEMO 14.2; Milan and Rome, 1989)

Ps-Ambrose

Laps. virg.	*De lapsu virginis* (PL 16)

Ambrosiaster

Comm. in Rom. (etc.)	*Commentarius in xiii epistulas Paulinas: ad Romanos* (etc.) (CSEL 81.1–3)
Quaest.	*Quaestiones veteris et novi testamenti* (CSEL 50)

Abbreviations

Anonymous authors

Cast.	*Epistula de castitate* (PLS 1)
Cent.	*De centesima, sexagesima, tricesima* (PLS 1)
Odes Sol.	*Odes of Solomon*, ed. J. H. Charlesworth (Oxford, 1973)
Prot. Jac.	*Protevangelium Jacobi*, in R. F. Hock (ed.), *The Infancy Gospels of James and Thomas* (Santa Rosa: Polebridge, 1995)
Zacch.	*Consultationes Zacchaei et Apollonii* (SC 401–2)

Aristides

Apol.	*Apologia*, ed. J. Armitage Robinson (TaS 1.1; Cambridge, 1893)

Arnobius the Younger

Praedest.	*Praedestinatus* (PL 53)

Ascension of Isaiah

Ascens. Is.	*Ascensio Isaiae* (CCSA 7)

Athanasius

Ep. Drac.	*Epistula ad Dracontium* (PG 25)
Ep. virg.	*Epistula ad virgines* (CSCO 150)
Vit. Ant.	*Vita Antonii* (SC 400)

Athenagoras

Leg.	*Legatio*, ed. W. R. Schoedel (OECT; Oxford, 1972)

Augustine of Hippo

Adim.	*Contra Adimantum* (BA 17)
Bon. conjug.	*De bono conjugali* (CSEL 41)
C. du. ep. Pel.	*Contra duas epistulas Pelagianorum* (CSEL 60)
C. Jul. op. imp.	*Contra Julianum opus imperfectum* (PL 45)
Civ.	*De civitate dei* (CSEL 40)
Conf.	*Confessiones* (BA 13–14)
Doct. chr.	*De doctrina christiana* (BA 11.2)
Ep.	*Epistulae* (CSEL 34, 44, 57, 58, 88)
Faust.	*Contra Faustum Manichaeum* (CSEL 25.1)

Fel.	Contra Felicem Manichaeum (BA 17)
Gen. litt.	De Genesi ad litteram (CSEL 28.1)
Haer.	De haeresibus (CCSL 46)
Jul.	Contra Julianum (PL 44)
Leg.	Contra adversarium legis et prophetarum (CCSL 49)
Man.	De moribus Manichaeorum (CSEL 90)
Mon.	De opere monachorum (CSEL 41)
Mor. eccl.	De moribus ecclesiae catholicae (CSEL 90)
Nupt.	De nuptiis et concupiscentia (CSEL 42)
Pecc. or.	De peccato originali (BA 22)
Psal.	Enarrationes in psalmos (PL 36–7)
Retract.	Retractationes (CCSL 57)
Secund.	Contra Secundinum (BA 17)
Ser.	Sermones (PL 38, 39; PLS 2)
Vid.	De bono viduitatis (CSEL 41)
Virg.	De sancta virginitate (CSEL 41)

Basil of Caesarea
Ep. Epistulae, in Yves Courtonne (ed.), *Saint Basile: Lettres*, 3 vols. (Paris: 'Les Belles Lettres', 1957–66)

Clement of Alexandria
Paed. Paedagogus (SC 70, 108)
Strom. Stromata, ed. Otto Stählin (GCS 15, 17); 2nd edn, revised by L. Früchtel (GCS 52)

Clement of Rome
1 Clem. Epistula Clementis ad Corinthios, ed. B. Ehrman (LCL)

Cyprian of Carthage
Hab. virg. De habitu virginum (CSEL 3)

Didache
Did. Didache xii apostolorum, ed. B. Ehrman (LCL)

Epistle to Diognetus
Diogn. Epistula ad Diognetum, ed. B. Ehrman (LCL)

Epiphanius of Salamis
Exp. fid.   *Expositio fidei* (GCS 34)
Haer.   *Panarion (Adversus haereses)*, ed. K. Holl (GCS 25, 31, 37); revised by J. Dummer, 3 vols. (1976–85)

Eusebius of Caesarea
Hist. eccl.   *Historia ecclesiastica* (SC 31)

Filastrius of Brescia
Haer.   *Diversarum haereseon liber* (CSEL 38)

Hermas
Mand.   *Mandata pastoris*, ed. B. Ehrman (LCL)

Hippolytus of Rome
Haer.   *Refutatio omnium haeresium*, ed. M. Marcovich (PTS 25; Berlin and New York, 1986)

Ignatius of Antioch
Eph.   *Epistula ad Ephesios*, ed. B. Ehrman (LCL)
Pol.   *Epistula ad Polycarpum*, ed. B. Ehrman (LCL)
Smyr.   *Epistula ad Smyrnaeos*, ed. B. Ehrman (LCL)

Irenaeus of Lyons
Demon.   *Demonstratio praedicationis apostolicae* (SC 406)
Haer.   *Adversus haereses* (SC 100, 152, 153, 210, 211, 263, 264, 293, 294)

Jerome
Adv. Jo. Hier.   *Adversus Johannem Hierosolymitanum* (PL 23)
Chron.   *Chronicon Eusebii* (PL 27)
Did. spir.   *Liber Didymi de Spiritu sancto* (PL 23)
Ep.   *Epistulae* (CSEL 54–6)
Ephes.   *Commentariorum in ep. ad Ephesios libri iii* (PL 26)
Gal.   *Commentariorum in ep. ad Galatas libri iii* (PL 26)
Helv.   *Adversus Helvidium de Mariae virginitate perpetua* (PL 23)
Jer.   *Commentariorum in Jeremiam libri vi* (CSEL 59)

Jov.	*Adversus Jovinianum libri ii* (PL 23)
Matt.	*Commentariorum in Matthaeum libri iv* (SC 242, 259)
Qu. Heb. Gen.	*Quaestionum Hebraicorum liber in Genesim* (PL 23)
Ruf.	*Adversus Rufinum libri iii* (SC 303)
Tit.	*Commentariorum in epistulam ad Titum liber* (PL 26)
Vigil.	*Contra Vigilantium liber* (PL 23)
Vir. ill.	*De viris illustribus* (PL 23)

John Chrysostom

Compunct.	*De compunctione* (PG 47)
Oppugn.	*Adversus oppugnatores vitae monasticae* (PG 47)
Sac.	*De sacerdotio* (SC 272)

Justin the Martyr

1 Apol.	*Apologia I*, ed. A. Wartelle (Paris, 1987)
Dial.	*Dialogus cum Trypho*, ed. M. Marcovich (PTS 47; Berlin and New York, 1997)

Liber pontificalis

Lib. pont.	*Liber pontificalis*, in L. Duchesne (ed.), *Le Liber pontificalis: Texte, introductione et commentaire*, 2nd edn., revised by C. Vogel (Paris, 1955–7)

Minucius Felix

Oct.	*Octavius* (CSEL 2)

Origen of Alexandria

Comm. Jo.	*Commentarii in Johannem* (SC 120)
Comm. Matt.	*Commentarii in Matthaeum libri x–xi* (SC 162)
Comm. Rom.	*Commentarii in epistulam ad Romanos*, in C. P. Hammond Bammel (ed.), *Der Römerbriefkommentar des Origenes: Kritischer Ausgabe der Übersetzung Rufins* (VL 16, 33, 34; Freiburg: Herder, 1990–8)
Fr. in 1 Cor.	*Fragmenta ex commentariis in 1 Cor*, ed. C. Jenkins (*JTS* 9–10 [1908])
Hom. in Lc.	*Homiliae in Lucam* (SC 87)
Hom. in Lev.	*Homiliae in Leviticum* (SC 286, 287)
Or.	*De oratione* (PG 11)

Abbreviations

Princ.	*De principiis* (SC 252, 253, 268, 269, 312)

Pacian of Barcelona

Bapt.	*Sermo de baptismo* (SC 410)

Palladius of Helenopolis

H. Laus.	*Historia Lausiaca*, ed. C. Butler (TaS 6; Cambridge, 1904)

Paulinus of Nola

Carm.	*Carmina* (CSEL 30)
Ep.	*Epistulae* (CSEL 29)

Pelagius

Exp. Rom. (etc.)	*Expositiones xiii epistularum Pauli*, ed. A. Souter (TaS 9.1–2; Cambridge, 1926)
Dem.	*Epistula ad Demetriadem* (PL 30)
Virg.	*Epistula ad Claudiam de virginitate* (CSEL 1)
Cel.	*Epistula ad Celantiam matronam* (CSEL 56.1)

Polycarp of Smyrna

Phil.	*Epistula ad Philippenses*, ed. B. Ehrman (LCL)

Priscillian of Avila

Can.	*Canones in Pauli apostolic epistulas* (CSEL 18)
Tract.	*Tractatus* (CSEL 18)

Proba

Laud. Chr.	*Cento Virgilianus de laudibus Christi* in Elizabeth A. Clark and Diana F. Hatch, *The Golden Bough, The Oaken Cross: The Virgilian Cento of Faltonia Betitia Proba* (Chico, Ca.: Scholars Press, 1981)

Rufinus of Aquileia

Apol.	*Apologia adversus Hieronymum* (CCSL 20)

Siricius, bishop of Rome

Ep.	*Epistulae* (PL 13)

Socrates Scholasticus

Hist. eccl.	*Historia ecclesiastica* (PG 67)

Sozomen
Hist. eccl.   *Historia ecclesiastica* (PG 67)

Sulpicius Severus
Chron.   *Chronicorum libri ii* (CSEL 1)
Ep.   *Epistulae* (CSEL 1)
Dial.   *Dialogi* (CSEL 1)

Tatian
Orat.   *Oratio ad Graecos*, ed. M. Whittaker (OECT; Oxford, 1982)

Tertullian
An.   *De anima*, ed. J. H. Waszink (Amsterdam, 1947)
Apol.   *Apologeticus* (CCSL 1)
Carn. Chr.   *De carne Christi* (CCSL 2)
Exh. cast.   *De exhortatione castitatis* (SC 319)
Marc.   *Adversus Marcionem* (CCSL 1)
Mon.   *De monogamia* (SC 343)
Praescr.   *De praescriptione haereticorum* (CCSL 1)
Pud.   *De pudicitia* (SC 394)
Ux.   *Ad uxorem* (SC 273)
Virg.   *De virginibus velandis* (SC 424)

Theodoret of Cyrrhus
H. rel.   *Historia religiosa* (SC 234, 257)

Theophilus of Antioch
Autol.   *Ad Autolycum*, ed. R. M. Grant (OECT; Oxford, 1970)

Zeno of Verona
Tract.   *Tractatus* (CCSL 22)

Introduction

'A NEW HERESY AND BLASPHEMY'

'Our religion has invented a new dogma against nature', wrote the monk Jovinian, thus characterizing the exaltation of celibacy and asceticism in the late fourth-century church.[1] The target of Jovinian's polemic was the notion that a life spent in fasting, self-denial, and sexual renunciation merited for the Christian a higher or better reward in heaven. No, Jovinian argued, Christian sanctity does not depend on an individual's ascetic merit. Christ promised holiness to the Church as a whole, and all baptized Christians share in that holiness. Therefore, distinctions based on celibacy, fasting, or other ascetic practices have no relevance in this world or the next. All the faithful are one in Christ, and all will receive the same reward in the kingdom of heaven.

The official ecclesiastical response to Jovinian was swift and unambiguous. Siricius, bishop of Rome, called his clergy into synod and condemned Jovinian's teaching as a diabolical perversion of scripture, 'a new heresy and blasphemy'. Ambrose of Milan responded likewise, praising Siricius' initiative in protecting Christ's flock from savage attack by the 'wolves' and accusing Jovinian of propagating the 'Manichaean' heresy. From his monastery in Bethlehem, Jerome, the prominent biblical scholar and ascetic teacher, issued two scathing books which characterized Jovinian as 'the Epicurus of the Christians', 'rutting in his gardens among young men and young women', 'slippery as a snake and like another Proteus'. By the early fifth century the continued spread of Jovinian's ideas (and the excesses of Jerome's *Adversus Jovinianum*) led Augustine in North Africa to compose two treatises on marriage and virginity in an effort to find a mean between Jovinian and Jerome.

My aim in this book is to examine the 'heresy' of Jovinian and the controversy sparked by the spread of his ideas. In recent decades the study of early Christianity and late antiquity has been dramatically transformed. Arguably the most prominent feature of that transformation has been a new appreciation of the centrality of asceticism, and specifically sexual renunciation, in shaping the contours of church and society in the late ancient

[1] Cited in Jerome, *Jov.* 1.41 (PL 23, 282).

world.[2] Early Christian monasticism and asceticism have been a major focus of scholarly research and publication for the past twenty years, and yet few scholars have acknowledged the degree to which some Christians opposed the spread of ascetic piety. As a voice of resistance to the ascetic ideal, Jovinian expressed sentiments that were shared by many of his contemporaries. A reassessment of his 'heresy', therefore, will add an important dimension to the contemporary discussion of early Christian asceticism.

Another issue I intend to engage here is the formation of orthodoxy and heresy in early Christianity. Although Jovinian was condemned as a heretic, it is clear that he was motivated by anti-heretical concerns and directed accusations of heresy against his opponents. Indeed, one of the central arguments I will advance throughout this book is that Jovinian drew on a long-standing tradition of anti-heretical discourse. On many specific points Jovinian echoed the arguments of Christian heresiologists who engaged in polemic against what they called the 'Encratite' heresy. Although, as we shall see, encratism was, in many respects, a heresiological fiction, it remained a potent rhetorical label in late antique theological polemics, and one that Jovinian did not hesitate to employ. One aim of this book, then, is to reconstruct this anti-heretical tradition and to demonstrate Jovinian's affinity with it.

Another matter I wish to examine is the process by which Jovinian was condemned as a 'heretic' by the leading figures of the fourth-century Western Church. When Pope Siricius characterized Jovinian's teachings as 'a new heresy and blasphemy', he inadvertently acknowledged that such ideas had not previously been regarded as 'heresy' in the prior Christian tradition. In other words, new boundaries were being drawn in the late fourth century, and Jovinian's condemnation marked a decisive turning point in the making of orthodoxy and heresy on the matter of asceticism. These two purposes, therefore, characterize the overall aim of this study: to elucidate the anti-heretical features of Jovinian's own thought and to explain why his views came to be regarded as 'heresy', at least by the clerical leadership of the Western Christian Church.

In Part I ('Jovinian and His World') I offer two preliminary chapters to set the stage for the later examination of the issues of heresy and orthodoxy. Chapter 1 will provide an initial overview of Jovinian's teaching. Here I will identify the main biblical and theological foundations of Jovinian's arguments, to the extent that these can be reconstructed from the refutations written by his opponents. Moreover, since Jovinian appealed frequently to Christian baptism as the basis of the equality of all Christians, at the end of Chapter 1 I will present a brief excursus on the early Christian ritual of

---

[2] The indispensable starting point is the work of Peter Brown, especially *The Body and Society: Men, Women, and Sexual Renunciation in Early Christianity* (New York: Columbia University Press, 1988).

baptism. Attention to the fourth-century baptismal ritual and the theology underlying it will shed light on several of Jovinian's theological arguments and helps to explain the strong influence that his teaching exerted among Christians in his day.

In Chapter 2 I explore more fully the social context of Jovinian's activity by examining the phenomenon of resistance to asceticism, especially as it appeared in the Western Church in the later years of the fourth century. There is considerable evidence of popular Christian hostility to ascetics, especially at Rome, and Jovinian's initial success is readily comprehensible in this environment. Furthermore, Jovinian's activity at Rome can be correlated with the increasing adoption of Christianity by late Roman aristocrats at the end of the fourth century. The emergence of a 'Christianized' Roman aristocracy, and the resulting culture of 'assimilation and accommodation'[3] it produced, does much to explain the popularity of Jovinian's views that is attested in the sources. And yet, it seems, the definition of Jovinian as 'heretic' ultimately did prevail within the Western Church. One reason for this, I will suggest, was the gradual acceptance of ascetic piety among Christian aristocrats. The rhetoric of ascetic superiority proved to be a valuable commodity in the traditional aristocratic search for status and acclaim and thus facilitated the condemnation of Jovinian and the decline of his influence.

Part II ('Jovinian, Heresy, and Asceticism') contains three chapters which focus on the issue of heresy and orthodoxy. In Chapter 3 I review Christian discussion of marriage and celibacy from the first three centuries. Here I reconstruct a tradition of early Christian discourse that was engaged in the refutation of—and, indeed, the creation of—what came to be called the 'Encratite' heresy. In many specific details Jovinian's arguments echoed a heresiological tradition which can be documented in sources from the Pastoral Epistles to the writings of Clement of Alexandria. By the early third century, however, other views began to predominate. A number of third-century authors, such as Tertullian, Cyprian, and Origen, developed ascetical theologies that reflected specifically 'encratite' ideas, though in a more moderate form. These authors exerted direct influence on some of the most notable teachers of the late fourth century, among them Ambrose and Jerome, the opponents of Jovinian.

In Chapter 4 I turn to Jovinian's more immediate context and examine the persistence and permutation of this anti-heretical tradition in the late fourth century. The spread of monasticism, the emergence of Manichaeism, and the imperial persecution of heresy were factors that conspired to render some

---

[3] I borrow the expression from Michele Salzman, *On Roman Time: The Codex Calendar of 354 and the Rhythms of Urban Life in Late Antiquity* (Berkeley: University of California Press, 1990), *passim*.

forms of ascetic piety liable to accusations of heresy. This development is especially evident in the case of the Spanish bishop and ascetic teacher Priscillian, who was executed around the year 386 on a charge of sorcery and suspicion of 'Manichaeism'. Furthermore, in the writings of several fourth-century heresiologists, such as Epiphanius of Salamis, Filastrius of Brescia, and Ambrosiaster, we find a blurring of the boundaries between 'Encratism' and 'Manichaeism'. Jovinian's anti-heretical concerns and the accusations of heresy that he directed against his opponents were consistent with this broader heresiological effort.

Chapter 5, which concludes Part II, offers a test-case of my hypothesis that Jovinian was engaged in an anti-heretical effort that sought to counter what he perceived as encratite features in the ascetical teaching of Ambrose and Jerome. Among the doctrines being popularized by ascetic writers in the late fourth century, the notion of the perpetual virginity of Mary stands out. Jerome and, especially, Ambrose presented Mary as the model of the consecrated virgin, particularly in her state of physical integrity. Conversely, Jovinian, as well as a near-contemporary Helvidius, sought to restrain ascetic piety by opposing these new forms of Marian doctrine. Helvidius attacked the notion of Mary's *virginitas post partum* ('after the birth' of Jesus), and Jovinian rejected the doctrine of her *virginitas in partu* ('during the birth' of Jesus). This chapter will survey the origins and development of these Marian doctrines, particularly the *virginitas in partu*. Jovinian's resistance to this teaching, I will argue, is yet further evidence of the anti-heretical aims that dominated his teaching on the equality of all baptized Christians.

In Part III ('Jovinian and his Opponents') I turn to a question that inevitably follows from Part II: If Jovinian's theology was, in many respects, compatible with the prior Christian tradition, and if his views were regarded with sympathy by a significant number of his contemporaries, why did so many prominent leaders of the Western Church condemn his ideas as heresy? My final chapters address this question by examining the perspectives on asceticism of those who condemned Jovinian. Chapter 6 discusses the three authors who initially responded to Jovinian's propaganda: Siricius, Ambrose, and Jerome. Close analysis of the sources reveals that each of these Western churchmen had a somewhat different view of Jovinian's 'heresy'. Siricius, Ambrose, and Jerome each had his own reasons for condemning Jovinian and for construing his views as heresy, and they did not always agree with each other. Moreover, in the case of Jerome, there is evidence that he bore considerable animosity towards both Siricius and Ambrose. This chapter examines both the personal rivalries that were being expressed in the controversy around Jovinian, as well as the rival visions of asceticism and ecclesiastical authority that were being negotiated.

In Chapter 7 I examine what might be considered a second phase of the Jovinianist controversy. This phase included the widespread rejection of Jerome's treatise *Adversus Jovinianum* at Rome and the entry into the debate about ten years later by Pelagius and Augustine. One of the striking features of the Jovinianist controversy is the extent to which Jerome himself became the object of attack for his excessive polemic against Jovinian. Augustine was not alone in his effort to correct Jerome's excesses and to provide a more satisfactory resolution to the issues raised by Jovinian. Moreover, Augustine went to great lengths to accommodate many of the central emphases of Jovinian's teaching and to counteract what he saw as dangerous (even heretical) elements in the ascetical theology of Jerome. The aim of these final two chapters, therefore, is to examine the disparate perspectives on Jovinian presented by his main opponents, and to determine why they all agreed in regarding him as a heretic.

In short, my purpose here is to present a comprehensive study of the conflict between Jovinian and his opponents. This book is unique in its effort to understand and interpret both sides of the debate within the context of the social and theological history of late ancient Christianity. The Jovinianist controversy marked a decisive turning point in the history of Western asceticism (or, to be more precise, in the development of ascetic discourse in the West). By officially declaring the ascetic life—celibacy, in particular—to be an intrinsically higher form of Christianity, Jovinian's opponents established what I will call a 'new orthodoxy', one that inscribed an ascetical hierarchy onto the structures of ecclesial authority. But the very existence of resistance to the ascetic ideal by Jovinian and others reveals that alternative visions were not lacking in the Western Church. Moreover, the diversity of responses to Jovinian evinced by Western churchmen reflects something of the broad diversity of ascetic perspectives in Christian late antiquity. A critical and historical study of the debate surrounding Jovinian provides a unique opportunity to examine these conflicting tendencies in Western Christianity at a crucial moment in its formation.

JOVINIAN IN PROTESTANT AND CATHOLIC HISTORIOGRAPHY

Any reader approaching the Jovinianist controversy for the first time should be made aware of the curious place held by Jovinian in the modern discipline of church historiography. Like many issues in the study of Christian origins, the early Christian debates on marriage and celibacy have not escaped the shadow of Protestant and Catholic polemics.[4] Because monasticism, marriage, and clerical celibacy were contentious issues during the Protestant Reformation, Protestants have tended to see Jovinian as a forerunner of the Reformation (and hence to praise him), while Catholics have tended to condemn Jovinian as an anti-ascetic heretic.

Ironically, this partisan line of interpretation may have begun with the reform-minded Catholic humanist Desiderius Erasmus. In his *Encomium matrimonii* ('In Praise of Marriage') first published in 1518, Erasmus presented an argument for the superiority of marriage over celibacy that drew largely from the remains of Jovinian present in Jerome's *Adversus Jovinianum*. Although Erasmus did not mention Jovinian by name, he did refer to Jerome's hostile refutation of Jovinian. 'I am not unaware', Erasmus wrote, 'that the praise of virginity has repeatedly been sung in huge volumes by the early Fathers, among whom Jerome admires it so much that he all but abuses marriage, and was summoned to recant by some orthodox bishops.'[5] Erasmus was later censured for his views on marriage by theologians at Louvain and the Sorbonne; in response he protested that his treatise was originally meant to be part of a book of rhetorical exercises (the same excuse, Erasmus must have known, that Jerome had proffered for the excesses of his *Adversus Jovinianum*). Nonetheless, it is impossible to read Erasmus's treatise, as John Oppel has noted, 'without recognizing that Erasmus is setting himself up as "Jovinian" reincarnated—that is, as a heretic'.[6]

Later Protestant Reformers were even more outspoken about the errors of Jerome's refutation of Jovinian, although they stopped short of trying to rehabilitate Jovinian himself. For example, in his book, *A Judgment on Monastic Vows*, published in Latin in 1522, Martin Luther complained that some of his critics regarded him as a new Jovinian:

Indeed, just as one disputation gives rise to another, these ungodly people will shout that I am a Jovinian and they will bring Jerome's argument against Jovinian, in which he defended celibacy, to bear against me. They will think that I have never read Jerome. They think that it is enough just to have read him; they never think it necessary to form some opinion about what they have read. Whatever they read is an article of faith.

---

[4] For a stimulating discussion of this problem, primarily in New Testament studies, see Jonathan Z. Smith, *Drudgery Divine: On the Comparison of Early Christianities and the Religions of Late Antiquity* (Chicago: University of Chicago Press, 1990).

[5] 'An example of a letter of persuasion', in J. K. Sowards, *Erasmus: Literary and Educational Writings*, iii (CWE 25; Toronto: University of Toronto Press, 1985), 138.

[6] 'Saint Jerome and the History of Sex', *Viator*, 24 (1993), 5. Erasmus's treatise had first appeared as one of four declamations titled *Declamatio in genere suasorio de laude matrimonii*. Although Erasmus's views received formal condemnations from theologians at Louvain and the Sorbonne, he later issued a tract, *Institutio christiani matrimonii*, which reiterated his views on marriage.

I myself do not know what Jovinian really meant. Perhaps he did not handle the argument properly. What I do know, however, is that Jerome has not handled it properly. He treats virginity as a thing existing in its own right. He neither relates it to faith nor uses it to build up faith. If this kind of teaching goes on—it is only human teaching—no good work or virtue can be taught without disaster and danger.

Although Luther did not speak explicitly in favour of Jovinian's views, he plainly found fault with Jerome's ardent defence of asceticism. For Luther, Jerome's attack on Jovinian failed because it made a good work, that is, celibacy, the basis of justification, rather than faith.[7]

Luther's associate, Philip Melanchthon, issued a similar evaluation of Jerome's *Adversus Jovinianum*. In his essay, 'The Church and the Authority of the Word of God', Melanchthon took Jerome to task for the opinions expressed in *Adversus Jovinianum*:

In writing against Jovinian he strongly confirms false and superstitious opinions about human traditions. He disparages marriage and rails at it with abusive language, which is by no means worthy of a Christian. He collects badly distorted passages of Scripture as if they disparage marriage, such as: 'If you live according to the flesh, you shall die', and similar passages. He expressly states that there is no difference between one who marries a second time and a prostitute. Likewise, he says that we must observe not what God allows, but what he wills, as though God does not will marriage.[8]

In short, Melanchthon concluded, 'it is clear that there are many errors in Jerome's writings, and those errors are not small.' Like Luther, Melanchthon stopped short of defending Jovinian himself, but it is clear that his sympathies do not lie with Jerome.

It did not take long for Catholic apologists to respond to these criticisms of Jerome's *Adversus Jovinianum* and to reiterate the condemnation of Jovinian as heretic. In its decree on the sacrament of matrimony, the Council of Trent condemned the teaching of Jovinian on the equality of marriage and celibacy, although it did not mention him by name.[9] However, in his anti-Protestant

---

[7] 'The Judgment of Martin Luther on Monastic Vows', in James Atkinson, *The Christian in Society* (Luther's Works, 44; Philadelphia: Fortress Press, 1966), 305–6. Further discussion in Robert C. Gregg, 'Die Ehe: Patristische und reformatorische Fragen', *ZKG* 96 (1985), 1–12.

[8] 'De ecclesia et de auctoritate verbi dei: De Hieronymo', in Charles Leander Hill, *Melanchthon: Selected Writings* (Minneapolis, Minn.: Augsburg, 1962), 161. Melanchthon went on to note that Jerome's treatment of women was excessively severe. Cf. Eugene F. Rice, *Saint Jerome in the Renaissance* (Baltimore, Md.: The Johns Hopkins University Press, 1985), 141–2.

[9] Session XXIV, 11 Nov. 1563, *Doctrina de sacramento matrimonii*, can. 10: 'If anyone says the married state is to be preferred to that of virginity or celibacy, and that it is no better or more blessed to persevere in virginity or celibacy than to be joined in marriage: let him be anathema.' Text and translation in Norman P. Tanner, *Decrees of the Ecumenical Councils*, ii, *Trent to Vatican II* (London and Washington, DC: Sheed & Ward and Georgetown University Press, 1990), 755.

history, the *Annales Ecclesiastici*, which began to appear in 1588, Caesar Baronius provided an extensive discussion of Jovinian 'the heresiarch' and his condemnation. He also drew an explicit parallel between the preaching of Jovinian and the 'more recent heretics' (that is, the Protestants) of his own day who questioned the value of celibacy and monastic vows. After praising Pope Siricius, Ambrose, and Jerome for their interventions against Jovinian's *nefanda haeresis*, Baronius concluded:

> We have said these things, so that the more recent heretics may be covered with shame (if they still know how to feel shame), those who, as I have said, have dug up again the sewer of Jovinian's filth that had been dammed up for a long time and that soils people with its very stench. They should know, even if they don't want to, that they were already condemned along with Jovinian twelve hundred years ago by the judgment of the Roman pontiff, by the Council of Milan, and by the private consent of holy men, such as Jerome, Ambrose and Augustine, and others; and, we might add, by imperial decrees.[10]

For Baronius, the appearance of Jovinian's heresy in the fourth century had led to all manner of moral corruption (including sodomy) that required imperial intervention.[11] The Protestant refusal to grant that celibacy was superior to marriage, Baronius argued, showed that Jovinian's heresy had reappeared in the sixteenth century and brought with it the same pernicious effects as its predecessor.

These polarized viewpoints of Protestant and Catholic continued in the nineteenth- and early twentieth-century scholarship on Jovinian. Modern critical study of Jovinian was inaugurated by the German dissertation of Wilhelm Haller (1897), a student of the distinguished Protestant church historian, Adolf von Harnack.[12] Haller's book provided the important service of collecting all the known sources on Jovinian's life and teaching. As a student of Harnack, however, Haller followed his teacher's view that Jovinian should be considered the 'first Protestant'. He argued that by equating married people with virgins, as well as by rejecting ascetical fasting, Jovinian had declared the priority of faith and grace over any form of 'works-righteousness'. For example, Haller concluded his study of Jovinian with this quotation from Harnack: 'In the entire history of Paulinism in the ancient church, no one has restored to grace and faith their rightful place as has

---

[10] *Annales Ecclesiastici*, anno 390, ch. 47 (Venice: S. Monti, 1740), vi, 84.

[11] *Annales Ecclesiastici*, anno 390, ch. 63, vi, 88. Baronius complained that the spread of Jovinian's ideas had led to widespread moral corruption in fourth-century Rome, leading to the imperial decree of 390 that condemned those who engaged in passive homosexual activity to be publicly burned: *C.Th.* 9.7.6.

[12] W. Haller, *Iovinianus: Die Fragmente seiner Schriften, die Quellen zu seiner Geschichte, sein Leben und seine Lehre* (TU 17.2; Leipzig: Hinrichs, 1897).

Jovinian.' In his opposition to all justification based on works and in his assertion of the priority of faith, Harnack (and Haller) argued, Jovinian was 'a Protestant of his time' and 'a witness of truth in antiquity'.[13]

In the fifty years or so that followed the publication of Haller's book, Catholic scholars tended to accept the Harnack–Haller interpretation of Jovinian as a 'proto-Protestant' and hence to adopt an attitude of hostility towards him. We see this approach, for example, in the influential biography of Jerome published in 1922 by Ferdinand Cavallera. In *Saint Jérôme. Sa vie et son oeuvre* Cavallera emphasized the grave danger posed by Jovinian's teaching to 'Catholic morality and to morality *tout court*'. By proclaiming the equality of all the baptized faithful, Cavallera argued, Jovinian had replaced moral effort by a fideism that led inevitably to moral laxity. 'Whether he wished to or not', Cavallera complained, 'Jovinian became the apostle of mediocrity and thereby prepared the paths to corruption and disorder.'[14] Cavallera's critique is typical of the Catholic rejection of Jovinian conceived as a 'proto-Protestant' that prevailed in the first part of the twentieth century.

The publication of Francesco Valli's *Gioviniano* in 1953, by contrast, signalled a new development in Catholic historical scholarship.[15] His book marked the definitive move away from the Protestantizing interpretation of Jovinian and introduced a more historically nuanced interpretation of Jovinian. Valli recognized correctly that the Harnack–Haller thesis did not do justice to the categories of Jovinian's own thought. Faith and grace, as opposed to good works, were not the focus of Jovinian's arguments. On the contrary, Valli demonstrated that Christian baptism, and the consequent equality of all the baptized within the one body of Christ, was the starting point and determinative category in Jovinian's thought. The Protestant opposition between faith and works in achieving justification was simply not the primary issue for Jovinian.[16]

Valli's critique of the Protestant approach to Jovinian was essentially correct. The efficacy of baptism was central to Jovinian's thought, and, as we shall see in Chapter 1, Jovinian mentioned baptism explicitly in three out of the four 'propositions' treated by Jerome. But despite his historical insights,

---

[13] Cited in Haller, *Iovinianus*, 159. He refers to Harnack, 'Geschichte der Lehre von der Seligkeit allein durch den Glauben in der alten Kirche', *ZTK* 1 (1891), 152. In his *Lehrbuch der Dogmengeschichte*, however, Harnack qualified these remarks: 'We may call Jovinian actually a "witness of antiquity to the truth", and a "Protestant of his time", though we must not mistake a point of difference: the indwelling of God and Christ in the baptized is more strongly emphasized than the power of faith.' See Harnack, *History of Dogma*, v, trans. Neil Buchanan (New York: Dover Publications, 1961), 58, n. 1.

[14] Cavallera, *Saint Jérôme*, 155–6. Cavallera cites Haller on 155.

[15] F. Valli, *Gioviniano: Esame delle fonti e dei frammenti* (Urbino: Università di Urbino, 1953).

[16] Valli, *Gioviniano*, 78–9, 95–101.

Valli continued the Catholic tradition of regarding Jovinian with hostility. While he did not develop a full-scale critique of Jovinian's ideas, Valli displayed his antipathy to Jovinian by referring to him throughout his study simply as 'the heretic' (*l'eretico*). As a result of this polemical attitude, Valli had difficulty accounting for the popularity and influence of Jovinian that is attested in the sources. He assumed, for example, that Jovinian found support only among 'that amorphous mass of Christians who had lost their primitive fervor and to certain malcontents who despised Roman monasticism'. If any morally upright persons were attracted to Jovinian, Valli claimed, they were 'simple souls who had been seduced by Jovinian's syllogisms'.[17] Because he remained hostile to Jovinian on theological grounds, Valli was unable to acknowledge that Jovinian may have appealed to any authentic Christians in the fourth century, or that his arguments may have possessed any theological validity in their own context.

This pejorative perspective on Jovinian and his followers has persisted, among some Roman Catholic scholars, down to the present day. For example, in a brief abstract of a Catholic University of America dissertation on the *Adversus Jovinianum* published in 1956, John Gavin Nolan portrayed Jovinian as a laxist and heretic in terms that virtually echoed Jerome's polemic against him: 'In his personal life Jovinian the heretic was all one might expect of an ex-monk who preached a philosophy of no restraint.' Although Nolan acknowledged that Jerome's caricature of Jovinian could not be taken literally, he insisted that 'there is no doubt that Jovinian in his new life did not live as a monk should live, that he did give reasons for complaint.'[18] Similarly, in an otherwise excellent article on fourth-century opposition to monasticism, Gian Domenico Gordini has characterized Jovinian as an 'ex-monk', whose views appealed to 'lukewarm Christians seeking an easy way of life'.[19] Up to the present day, some Roman Catholic scholars have continued to perpetuate the view that Jovinian found little support at Rome, and then only among lax and lukewarm Christians.[20]

---

[17] Valli, *Gioviniano*, 26–7.

[18] John Gavin Nolan, *Jerome and Jovinian* (Washington, DC: The Catholic University of America Press, 1956), 27. Nolan was aware that Jovinian did not marry and remained a monk, but he attributed this to Jovinian's 'fear of public opinion'.

[19] 'L'opposizione al monachesimo a Roma nel IV secolo', in M. Fois, V. Monachino, and F. Litva (eds.), *Dalla chiesa antica alla chiesa moderna* (Rome: Università Gregoriana Editrice, 1983), 30 and 33. Gordini's views are contradicted by Jerome who complained that Jovinian had (inconsistently) remained a monk and that he was supported by 'clerics, monks, and continent married men'.

[20] This error is continued by Stefan Heid, *Celibacy in the Early Church*, trans. Michael J. Miller (San Francisco: Ignatius Press, 2000), 253: 'In Rome, at any rate, [Jovinian's] views met with little or no enthusiasm.' An important exception is the valuable theological retrieval of Jovinian's ideas by Allan J. Budzin, 'Jovinian's Four Theses on the Christian Life: An Alternative Patristic

A central aim of this book is to move beyond these partisan readings of Jovinian by earlier Protestant and Catholic scholars. Rather than interpret Jovinian in the light of the later Reformation controversies, I will attempt a more historical approach, locating him (and his opponents) within the context of the events and concerns of their own time and place. The time is right for such a reinterpretation. As noted above, recent decades have witnessed a remarkable transformation in the study of Christianity in late antiquity. Not only have scholars come to appreciate more deeply the impact of sexual renunciation on late Roman society, but significant advances have occurred in the study of the Roman family and marriage as well. Judith Evans Grubbs, to cite but one important example, has stressed the deep continuities that existed between a traditional Roman marital ethos and that promoted by fourth-century emperors, such as Constantine.[21] It is now possible to place Jovinian within a moderate Christian tradition that differed significantly from the shrill asceticism of a Tertullian or a Jerome.[22]

Other scholars have emphasized the extent to which a traditionalist blend of marital piety and civic duty continued to attract the loyalties of Christian and pagan alike, especially within the Roman aristocracy. Kate Cooper, in particular, has argued persuasively that the late fourth-century debates on marriage and celibacy at Rome—at the heart of which stood the Jovinianist controversy—were rooted in a conflict between 'separatist' and 'civic' views of the relationship between Christianity and the social order.[23] Likewise, as John Curran has suggested in a recent examination of the 'Christianization' of the city of Rome, 'the vigorous resistance of moderate Christian nobles to extreme asceticism laid the foundation of a Christian nobility which took its urban Christian piety very seriously indeed. The Christians whom Jerome

Spirituality', *Toronto Journal of Theology*, 4 (1988), 44–59. Budzin argued that Jovinian's theology was compatible with the emphasis of the Second Vatican Council on the shared holiness of all baptized Christians.

[21] Judith Evans Grubbs, *Law and Family in Late Antiquity: The Emperor Constantine's Marriage Legislation* (Oxford: Clarendon Press, 1995). As Peter Brown has recently summarized these developments: 'Nothing is more impressively ambiguous than is the legislation on social *mores*, and on marriage and the family, issued by the Christian emperors in this period. The more closely it is studied, the less it seems to betray direct Christian influence.' See his essay, 'Christianization and Religious Conflict', in Averil Cameron and Peter Garnsey (eds.), *The Late Empire A.D. 337–425* (CAH 13; Cambridge: Cambridge University Press, 1998), 659.

[22] See also Judith Evans Grubbs, '"Pagan" and "Christian" Marriage: The State of the Question', *JECS* 2 (1994), 361–412. This book was nearly completed when the following study appeared: Yves-Marie Duval, *L'affaire Jovinien: D'une crise de la société romaine à une crise de la pensée chrétienne à la fin du IVe et au début du Ve siècle* (Rome: Institutum Patristicum Augustinianum, 2003). I have attempted to take account of Duval's work in the footnotes, although the text of my study has remained substantially unchanged.

[23] *The Virgin and the Bride: Idealized Womanhood in Late Antiquity* (Cambridge, Mass.: Harvard University Press, 1996), esp. chs. 4–5.

dismissed as frauds, had, in fact, a coherent Christian view of their role as part of the social elite of Rome.'[24] Studies such as these have now made it possible to view the Jovinianist controversy within the broader context of the transition from a 'pagan' to a 'Christian' culture in late antiquity.[25]

Another new perspective in late antique historiography that informs this book is a changed appreciation of the significance of the notion of 'heresy' in the early church. Since the middle of the twentieth century, largely owing to the pioneering work of Walter Bauer and the discovery of the Nag Hammadi library, scholars have become increasingly dissatisfied with a model of 'orthodoxy' (itself the product of early Christian heresiology) that presumed an original, pristine truth that was later compromised by the deviations of 'heresy'. To put the matter simply, scholars of early Christianity now tend to see the act of defining a 'heresy' as an essential moment in the creation of 'orthodoxy' itself. Moreover, the work of Alain Le Boulluec and others has illuminated the various literary and theological strategies by which the early Christian heresiologists went about constructing their notions and images of 'heresy'.[26] These newer approaches will help us to analyse both Jovinian and his opponents, insofar as both sides made abundant use of the rhetorical devices of traditional heresiology.

This study of the Jovinianist controversy, then, aims to shed new light on the rise of both asceticism and heresy in late antiquity. By examining the views of Jovinian and his opponents, I hope to elucidate in new ways the complex processes by which ascetic piety came to prevail in Western Christendom and the role which accusations of 'heresy' played in that development. At the same time, I intend to challenge the picture of an inevitable and thoroughgoing 'triumph' of asceticism in late antiquity. The protests of Jovinian and his supporters demonstrate the persistence of an alternative tradition of Christian thought and practice. Moreover, as I will show, the views of Jovinian exerted a moderating effect on some advocates of asceticism, such as Augustine and Pelagius. Like the ideas of many heretics, therefore, Jovinian's 'new heresy' influenced the development of a 'new orthodoxy' on the matter of asceticism in ways that he could not have anticipated and perhaps would not have intended. The Jovinianist controversy provides a unique lens through which to view these varied dynamics at a crucial moment in the history of Western culture.

---

[24] *Pagan City and Christian Capital: Rome in the Fourth Century* (Oxford: Clarendon Press, 2000), 319–20.

[25] Many of these developments were anticipated by Robert Markus, *The End of Ancient Christianity* (Cambridge: Cambridge University Press, 1990), esp. 27–43.

[26] The essential starting point is the writings of Walter Bauer, *Orthodoxy and Heresy in Earliest Christianity*, ed. and trans. Robert Kraft and Gerhard Krodel (Philadelphia: Fortress Press, 1971) and Alain Le Boulluec, *La notion d'hérésie dans la littérature grecque IIe–IIIe siècles*, 2 vols. (Paris: Études Augustiniennes, 1985). See also Susanna Elm, Éric Rebillard and Antonella Romano (eds.), *Orthodoxy, Christianity, History* (Rome: École Française de Rome, 2000).

Part I

Jovinian and his World

1

Reconstructing Jovinian

The writings of ancient heretics have rarely survived in their entirety, and Jovinian's are no exception. We are fortunate, however, that Jerome composed an extensive refutation of Jovinian, in which he preserved numerous extracts from his writings, as well as lengthy summaries of his treatment of biblical texts. Moreover, Jerome claimed to have reproduced arguments and illustrations that Jovinian had adduced 'in the very same order' (*eodemque ordine*) that Jovinian had followed.[1] There is no reason to doubt the basic accuracy of Jerome's quotations, though of course we must be sceptical of the interpretations that Jerome placed on these writings. As a polemicist, Jerome naturally tended to present his opponents' views in the worst possible light. But when supplemented by other sources, the *Adversus Jovinianum* provides a basis on which a reliable portrait of Jovinian can be reconstructed.

My aim in this chapter is to sketch the main outlines of Jovinian's views and to offer an initial interpretation of them. For the sake of methodological clarity, I will begin with a survey of the relevant sources and a discussion of the chronology of the controversy. It will become apparent that Jovinian's various opponents did not always see eye to eye on the details of his teaching, nor did they all have the same information available to them regarding his views. It will be important, therefore, to discuss each source separately and to distinguish each author's knowledge of and attitude towards Jovinian. This information will be especially important in the later chapters of this book, where the stance of Jovinian's opponents will be analysed in greater depth. But it is also important for an accurate portrait of Jovinian's teaching to know who opposed him when, and why.

1. SOURCES AND CHRONOLOGY

I will focus on the writings of Pope Siricius, Ambrose, and Jerome, the three authors who were the first to respond to Jovinian. The reason for this choice is simple: each of these three men had direct access to Jovinian's writings and

[1] *Jov.* 1.4 (PL 23, 225).

can therefore be regarded as, in some sense, 'primary' sources. There were other fourth- and fifth-century writers who mentioned Jovinian and referred to his views, including Augustine, Pelagius, Julian of Eclanum, and Vincent of Lérins. Some, such as Julian, may even have had direct acquaintance with Jovinian's writings, though none of them provides an extensive discussion of his teaching. Occasionally evidence from one of these authors will be significant, but it will be adduced only when it corroborates or clarifies what we know about Jovinian from the writings of Siricius, Ambrose, or Jerome.

i. Siricius

The earliest source of information on Jovinian is the letter of Pope Siricius reporting the condemnation of Jovinian and his followers by a synod of the Roman clergy. Addressed to various western bishops, among them Ambrose of Milan, Siricius' letter alerted his episcopal colleagues to the danger of Jovinian's heresy out of fear that it might spread to the regions under their jurisdiction. Siricius stated that Jovinian's 'horrifying writing' (*scriptura horrifica*) had been brought to his attention 'by the most faithful Christians, men of the highest lineage, distinguished for religion' (*a fidelissimis Christianis viris genere optimis, religione praeclaris*).[2] Siricius must be referring to certain Roman aristocrats, and one of them was surely Pammachius, husband of Paulina, the daughter of Jerome's dear friend Paula. In a letter to Pammachius written in 394 Jerome stated that Jovinian had been condemned at Rome through the agency of Pammachius.[3] It is likely, therefore, that Pammachius was one of the Roman noblemen who first alerted Siricius to the spread of Jovinian's views.

The date of the Roman synod and of Siricius' letter has received considerable discussion in the scholarly literature. Baronius was the first to suggest a date of 390 for the Roman condemnation of Jovinian, and some scholars still believe this.[4] Since the early twentieth century, however, most scholars have held that the synods at Rome and Milan occurred in the year 393.[5] The most

[2] *Ep.* 7.5 (CSEL 82.3, 300).
[3] Jerome, *ep.* 49.2 (CSEL 54, 351). Cf. Valli, *Gioviniano*, 28.
[4] The most extensive argument for the date of 390 was developed by Charles William Neumann, *The Virgin Mary in the Works of Saint Ambrose* (Paradosis, 17; Fribourg: The University Press, 1962), 142–54; the most recent advocate is Stefan Heid, *Celibacy in the Early Church*, 240.
[5] The most thorough discussion is that of José A. de Aldama, 'La condenación de Joviniano en el sínodo de Roma', *EphMar* 13 (1963), 107–19, whose chronology I have followed here. The following also support the date of 393: J. Brochet, *Saint Jérôme et ses ennemis* (Paris, 1905), 69–71; Jean-Rémy Palanque, *Saint Ambroise et l'empire romaine* (Paris: Boccard, 1933), 545–6;

cogent argument for 393 is the fact that Jerome did not mention the ecclesiastical condemnations of Jovinian when he composed his *Adversus Jovinianum* in the spring of 393.⁶ By contrast, in the following year, when he wrote his lengthy apologetic letter to Pammachius regarding the reception of *Adversus Jovinianum*, Jerome referred explicitly to the Roman condemnation.⁷ It is highly likely that Jerome would have mentioned the Roman and Milanese synods, had he known of them when he wrote *Adversus Jovinianum*. It also is likely that Jerome would have been informed of Jovinian's condemnation, had it occurred prior to his writing *Adversus Jovinianum* in 393. The best explanation of this omission is that the synods occurred (and Jerome was informed of Jovinian's condemnation) only after he had composed *Adversus Jovinianum* and dispatched it to Rome. Therefore, the most likely date for the synods at Rome and Milan is approximately the same as the date of the composition of *Adversus Jovinianum*, that is, the spring of 393.

Siricius did not discuss Jovinian's views in any detail, nor did he attempt to refute them at length. The closest he came to a description of Jovinian's teaching was when he referred to its inspiration by the devil, the 'ancient enemy', the 'adversary of chastity', the 'teacher of luxury', 'who hates fasting'. Siricius' only attempt to respond directly to Jovinian's teaching occurred when he stated his own view of the relation between marriage and celibacy: 'Surely we do not treat the vows of marriage with contempt, for we are present at the [nuptial] veiling. But we bestow a greater degree of honour on virgins who are consecrated to God and who are produced by marriage.'⁸ Siricius' comment implies that Jovinian had directed his critique of ascetic piety against members of the Roman clergy, probably even against Siricius himself. Jovinian appears to have accused them of treating marriage with contempt by giving preference to celibacy. Such an attack would help to explain the harsh tone Siricius adopted in his letter. Otherwise, we learn little from Siricius regarding the precise content of Jovinian's teachings.

Despite his failure to discuss the specifics of Jovinian's error, Siricius did provide important information about Jovinian and his activity in the church

---

F. Holmes Dudden, *The Life and Times of St. Ambrose*, 2 vols. (Oxford: Clarendon Press, 1935), 397–8; Valli, *Gioviniano*, 30–5; Angelo Paredi, *Saint Ambrose: His Life and Times*, trans. M. Joseph Costelloe (Notre Dame, Indiana: University of Notre Dame Press, 1964), 355–6; J. N. D. Kelly, *Jerome: His Life, Writings and Controversies* (New York: Harper & Row, 1975), 18. See now the thorough discussion in Duval, *L'affaire Jovinien*, 11–21.

⁶ The date of the *Adversus Jovinianum* is secure. See Pierre Nautin, 'Études de chronologie hiéronymienne (393–397): IV. Autres letters de la période 393–396', *REAug* 20 (1974), 253–5.

⁷ *Ep.* 49.2 (CSEL 54, 351). By 394 Jerome also seems to have become aware of Jovinian's rejection of the doctrine of Mary's *virginitas in partu*. See *ep.* 49.21 (CSEL 54, 386–7). Siricius, likewise, did not mention Jovinian's attack on Mary's virginity; Ambrose was the first to report it.

⁸ *Ep.* 7.5 (CSEL 82.3, 300).

at Rome. It is clear, for example, that Jovinian's teaching had influenced a large number of Christians at Rome. Siricius complained that Jovinian and his followers had infiltrated the church 'unrecognized' because they hid their teaching 'under the cover of a pious name' (*sub velamento pii nominis*) and 'under a religious name' (*sub religioso nomine*). Siricius mentioned several times that Jovinian's preaching had entered 'the church' or 'the house of prayer', which suggests that Jovinian and his followers may have initially received support from some members of the Roman clergy who allowed them to preach.[9] Siricius also claimed that, unlike previous heretics who erred by misunderstanding individual points of doctrine, Jovinian and his allies had completely perverted the examples of continence found in both the Old and New Testaments. Through their diabolical interpretation of scripture, he claimed, 'they have begun to destroy no small number of Christians and to win them over to their own insanity.'[10] According to Siricius, Jovinian's ability to offer plausible evidence from the scriptures enabled him to garner significant support within the church at Rome.

Siricius' testimony concerning the popularity of Jovinian at Rome can be confirmed from a variety of other sources. Jerome, for example, who was informed on the matter by Pammachius and other friends at Rome, such as the priest Domnio, complained in a letter to Pammachius that Jovinian had received support even from monks and members of the clergy who lived in celibacy: 'If worldly men are indignant that they are in a lower grade than virgins, I am amazed that clerics and monks and those who live in continence do not praise that which they do. They separate themselves from their wives in order to imitate the chastity of virgins, and yet they want married people to be what virgins are.'[11] Similarly, Augustine, though writing at some distance from the controversy, reported that Jovinian's arguments had caused many professed ascetics at Rome, male and female alike, to abandon celibacy and to marry. Augustine even pointed out that some of these converts to Jovinian's teaching were ascetics of advanced age, 'about whose chastity there had previously been no suspicion'.[12] Although Siricius claimed that his action against Jovinian had been supported unanimously by the 'presbyters, deacons, and the entire clergy', there is no doubt that Jovinian's preaching met with considerable success at Rome, and not merely among lax Christians.[13]

---

[9] *Ep.* 7.2–3 (CSEL 82.3, 297–8). Siricius condemned the following along with Jovinian: Auxentius, Genialis, Germinator, Felix, Plotinus, Marcianus, Januarius, and Ingeniosus (*ep.* 7.6 (CSEL 82.3, 301)).
[10] *Ep.* 7.4 (CSEL 82.3, 299).
[11] Jerome, *ep.* 49.2 (CSEL 54, 352).
[12] Augustine, *Retract.* 2.22 (48) (CCSL 57, 107–8); cf. *Haer.* 82 (CCSL 46, 337).
[13] *Ep.* 7.6 (CSEL 82.3, 300–1).

Siricius' letter also indicated that Jovinian had put his preaching into written form. As we have seen, Siricius spoke of Jovinian's *scriptura horrifica*; elsewhere he stated that Jovinian and his followers 'had issued their blasphemies publicly in a rash document' (*conscriptio temeraria*).[14] Was this the same document known to Jerome, to which he responded in Adversus Jovinianum? In Adversus Jovinianum Jerome referred to certain 'books' (*libri*) of Jovinian that discussed his four 'propositions' and contained his extensive proofs from scripture; Jerome also characterized Jovinian's writing as 'commentaries' (*commentarii*) and 'little commentaries' (*commentarioli*).[15] Because of this difference in terminology Haller believed that the writings Jerome possessed must have been different from the document mentioned by Siricius. After the first *scriptura horrifica* or *conscriptio temeraria* was condemned at Rome, Haller suggested, Jovinian felt the need to explain his condemned writing and to expand on its positions with further arguments and therefore composed the *commentarii*.[16]

There is no compelling reason, however, to conjecture two distinct sets of writings by Jovinian. Although Siricius did not provide much information about Jovinian's writings, he did allude to Jovinian's alleged opposition to celibacy and fasting. These comments correspond to several of the 'propositions' of Jovinian listed by Jerome. Siricius also mentioned Jovinian's prominent use of scriptural arguments from both the Old and New Testaments, and this corresponds to what Jerome presented in Adversus Jovinianum. Although Jerome discussed all of these points in much greater detail than Siricius did, there is no need to assume that Jerome had before him a different account of Jovinian's teaching than Siricius possessed. The differences between Siricius' presentation of Jovinian and that of Jerome can be accounted for by their different aims in writing: Siricius was concerned only to alert Ambrose and the other bishops to Jovinian's activity and to the Roman condemnation, whereas Jerome was attempting a full-scale refutation.[17]

Finally, Siricius' letter stated that Jovinian's preaching at Rome may have appealed to pagans or even stimulated pagan opposition to Christianity in some way. In the passage cited above, Siricius expressed his dismay that Jovinian and his followers 'had issued their blasphemies publicly in a rash document and, aroused by the madness of a desperate mind, published them everywhere to the benefit of the pagans' (*in favorem gentilium*). Siricius' comment is intriguing, and it would be easy to dismiss as mere slander,

---

[14] *Ep.* 7.4 (CSEL 82.3, 299).
[15] Jerome, *Jov.* 1.1 (*commentarioli, libri*), 1.41 (*commentarii*).
[16] Haller, *Iovinianus*, 1, 18–19; followed by Nolan, *Jerome and Jovinian*, 25.
[17] See Valli, *Gioviniano*, 51–6, for the position taken here; also Duval, *L'affaire Jovinien*, 43–4.

were it not for the fact that Jerome also stated that Jovinian's writings contained citations from pagan literature that attested to the high respect for marriage in traditional Greco-Roman culture.[18] Moreover, as we shall see below, in addition to his criticisms of the Roman clergy, Jovinian also accused some Christian ascetics, such as Ambrose and Jerome, of adhering to the 'Manichaean' heresy. It is possible that these accusations may have led Siricius to characterize Jovinian's propaganda as an asset to pagan criticism of Christianity.

There is yet another factor that may have led Siricius to observe that Jovinian's teachings were a 'benefit' to the pagans. If Jovinian's condemnation at Rome took place in the spring of 393, as we have argued, then it occurred in the midst of the revolt of Arbogastes and Eugenius against the regime of Theodosius. Although he was a Christian and an acquaintance of Ambrose, the rhetor Eugenius displayed some sympathy towards the proponents of paganism among the Roman aristocracy. For example, after rejecting several requests from prominent pagans to restore the famous Altar of Victory at Rome, Eugenius finally agreed to provide his personal funds for the restoration of pagan ceremonies. It is well known that there was a resurgence of pagan activities and sympathy at Rome during the years 392–394, although the extent of this 'pagan revival' has been much disputed.[19] In such a highly charged atmosphere Jovinian's critique of ascetic piety and his recourse to pagan literature could easily have been construed by his opponents as unduly assisting pagan criticism of Christianity.

ii. Ambrose

The second major source for the reconstruction of Jovinian's teaching is the letter of Ambrose written to Siricius reporting the condemnation of Jovinian by a group of bishops at Milan. Ambrose stated that Jovinian had fled to Milan after the Roman condemnation, so the Milanese synod must have taken place shortly after the Roman synod, that is, in the spring or early summer of 393. It is not entirely clear why Jovinian went to Milan at this time.

---

[18] *Jov.* 1.4, 1.41.

[19] A balanced discussion of the revolt of Eugenius and the 'pagan revival' at Rome can be found in John Matthews, *Western Aristocracies and Imperial Court A.D. 364–425* (Oxford: Clarendon Press, 1975), 238–47. In numerous publications Alan Cameron has raised questions about the extent of the pagan resistance; see, most recently, 'The Last Pagans of Rome', in W. V. Harris (ed.), *The Transformations of Vrbs Roma in Late Antiquity* (Journal of Roman Archaeology, Supplementary Series 33; Portsmouth, R. I. 1999), 109–21. But stressing the religious dimension of the conflict is Charles W. Hedrick, *History and Silence: Purge and Rehabilitation of Memory in Late Antiquity* (Austin, Texas: University of Texas Press, 2000), 39–71.

J. N. D. Kelly has suggested that Jovinian may have fled to Milan to appeal the Roman condemnation before the emperor: '[Jovinian] must have expected short shrift from Ambrose, but he might reasonably have looked for sympathy from the usurper Eugenius, whose plans for moving from Gaul to Milan must have already been known.'[20] Given Siricius' comment regarding Jovinian's effect on pagan opinion at Rome, Kelly's suggestion is a likely one. Eugenius had entered Italy from Gaul in the spring of 393; when he arrived in Milan by the end of the summer, Ambrose abandoned his see for nearly a year in order to avoid committing himself to Eugenius' regime.[21] If, as Siricius suggested, Jovinian's views were well received by non-Christians, then Jovinian may have believed that Eugenius would be supportive of his cause.

Ambrose's letter presented a somewhat different perspective on Jovinian than did the letter of Siricius. It included, for example, a fuller account of Jovinian's teachings than Siricius had provided. Taking up the metaphor employed by Siricius—that Jovinian and his followers were wolves among the Lord's sheep—Ambrose proceeded to offer the following outline of Jovinian's views: 'It is wild howling to give no preference to virginity or any rank to chastity, to wish to mix together all things promiscuously, to destroy the degrees of different merits, and to suggest that there is a kind of poverty of heavenly rewards, as if Christ had only one palm to bestow and as if there were not an abundance of claims to reward.'[22] Like Siricius, Ambrose seems to have before him the same version of Jovinian's writing as Jerome. His account of Jovinian's teaching included two of the four 'propositions' of Jovinian presented by Jerome: that Jovinian denied any special merit to virginity or celibacy, and that he denied any special reward in the afterlife for the sexually abstinent.

Elsewhere in his letter, Ambrose also referred to Jovinian's alleged hostility to fasting. According to Ambrose, Jovinian and his followers once practiced strictness in diet, but now have capitulated to a life of luxury. Moreover, they claim to have the apostle Paul on their side as a 'teacher of luxury' (*luxuriae magistrum*).[23] Ambrose may have in mind a passage from 1 Timothy 4: 4 that Jovinian is known to have quoted: 'For everything created by God is good, and nothing is to be rejected, provided it is received with thanksgiving, for it is sanctified by God's word and by prayer.'[24] Jovinian's third proposition, as

---

[20] For this suggestion, see Kelly, *Jerome*, 182, n. 15.

[21] See Ambrose, *ep. extra collectionem* 10, addressed to Eugenius, and the discussion in Neil McLynn, *Ambrose of Milan: Church and Court in a Christian Capital* (Berkeley: University of California Press, 1994), 341–53.

[22] Ambrose, *ep. extra collectionem* 15.2 (CSEL 82.3, 303).

[23] Ambrose, *ep. extra collectionem* 15.10 (CSEL 82.3, 308).

[24] See *Jov.* 2.16, where Jerome responded to Jovinian's interpretation of this text.

reported by Jerome, also contained an allusion to 1 Timothy 4: 4: 'There is no difference between abstinence from food and receiving it with thanksgiving.'[25] It seems likely, therefore, that Ambrose also was aware of the third proposition of Jovinian.

The most significant difference between Ambrose's version of Jovinian's teaching and that of Siricius and Jerome is Ambrose's claim that Jovinian had denied the perpetual virginity of Mary. According to Ambrose, Jovinian taught that although Mary had conceived the child Jesus while still a virgin, she had not remained physically intact during Jesus' birth: *Virgo concepit, sed non virgo generavit*, Jovinian had claimed.[26] This was an opinion of Jovinian's that had not been mentioned by Siricius; nor was it included in Jerome's *Adversus Jovinianum*. But roughly half of Ambrose's letter was devoted to his defence of this doctrine and to a rebuttal of Jovinian's views. For Ambrose, Jovinian's rejection of the doctrine of Mary's *virginitas in partu* was one of the primary features of his heresy.

Why did Jovinian's teaching on Mary play such a prominent role in Ambrose's response, but not in that of Siricius or Jerome? The answer is connected to another feature of Ambrose's letter that differs significantly from the other sources in the controversy. Ambrose was the only author to accuse Jovinian of holding the 'Manichaean' heresy. Moreover, he directly connected this charge, which contradicts everything else that we know about Jovinian, to Jovinian's denial of Mary's virginity. As Ambrose put it:

And they proved that they were Manichaeans in truth by not believing that [Christ] came forth from a virgin. This madness is equal almost to that of the present-day Jews. If they do not believe that he came, neither do they believe that he took flesh. Thus he was seen only as an illusion and was crucified as an illusion.... A Manichaean is one who denies the truth, who denies Christ's incarnation.[27]

Ambrose even concluded his letter with an ominous reference to an imperial edict against the Manichaeans, implying that his action against Jovinian and his followers had been taken with imperial approval and that Jovinian had been condemned as a Manichaean.[28]

The manner in which Ambrose focused on Jovinian's teaching about the virginity of Mary and his accusation of 'Manichaeism' are important (and idiosyncratic) additions to the evidence of the Jovinianist controversy. Ambrose's claim that Jovinian was a Manichaean was a rather obvious and

---

[25] Jerome, *Jov.* 1.3 (PL 23, 224).

[26] Cited in Ambrose, *ep. extra collectionem* 15.4 (CSEL 82.3, 305).

[27] Ambrose, *ep. extra collectionem* 15.12–13 (CSEL 82.3, 310).

[28] There were numerous edicts against the Manichees issued in the late fourth century. Ambrose may be referring to *C.Th.* 16.5.18, issued by Theodosius on 17 June 389.

deliberate distortion of Jovinian's teaching. The real Manichaean position was precisely the opposite to Jovinian's. Manichaeans held a docetic Christology; that is, they did not believe that Jesus could have taken on flesh at all.[29] Jovinian's point in questioning Mary's *virginitas in partu*, as we shall see in Chapter 5, was a decidedly anti-Manichaean or anti-docetic one. For Jovinian, the genuinely physical character of Jesus' birth meant that Mary must have lost her physical integrity in the process of giving birth.

Augustine affirmed this point many years later during the Pelagian controversy when he was accused of being a 'Manichaean' by Bishop Julian of Eclanum. In his *Contra Julianum* Augustine noted: 'Jovinian also did the same thing with the name and charge of Manichaeism, when he denied that the virginity of holy Mary, which existed when she conceived, was preserved when she gave birth. He supposed that we believed along with the Manichaeans that Christ was a phantom, if we said that he was born with his mother's virginity remaining intact.'[30]

Ambrose's attempt to tar Jovinian with the brush of Manichaeism was a blatant falsehood, and it would be difficult to explain were it not for two salient facts. First, it was Ambrose himself who had pioneered in the West the notion of Mary's *virginitas in partu*. Secondly, it was Jovinian who had first attacked Ambrose as a 'Manichaean' for teaching Mary's perpetual virginity. Ambrose's accusation of 'Manichaeism', therefore, was simply an effort to turn the tables on Jovinian, so to speak, and to reverse the charge that Jovinian had made against him.

In Chapter 5 I will examine further Ambrose's role in the development of the doctrine of the *virginitas in partu* and Jovinian's opposition to it. On the question of Jovinian's attack on Ambrose, however, we have the explicit testimony of Augustine. In *De nuptiis et concupiscentia*, another writing against Julian, Augustine indicated that it was Ambrose specifically against whom Jovinian had directed his accusation of Manichaeism:

Will you, Pelagians and Caelestians, dare to call even this man [i.e. Ambrose] a Manichee? The heretic Jovinian called him that, when that holy man maintained that the virginity of holy Mary remained even after she gave birth. If, then, you do not dare to call him a Manichee, why do you call us Manichees, though on the same point we are defending the Catholic faith with the same line of thought?[31]

---

[29] Cf. the discussion in Augustine, *Conf.* 5.10.20 (CCSL 27, 69); and *Faust.* 30.6 (CSEL 25, 755). On the complexity of Manichaean Christology, see Majella Franzmann, *Jesus in the Manichaean Writings* (London and New York: T & T Clark, 2003).

[30] *Jul.* 1.2.4 (PL 44, 643); trans. Roland J. Teske, *Answer to the Pelagians*, ii (WSA I/24; Hyde Park, NY: New City Press, 1998), 269–70, slightly altered.

[31] *Nupt.* 2.5.15 (CSEL 42, 267); trans. Teske, 62. See also Augustine's comments in *C. Jul. op. imp.* 4.121–2 (PL 45, 1415–19).

Augustine clearly indicates that Jovinian had accused Ambrose of Manichaeism and that he had based this charge on Ambrose's teaching of the doctrine of Mary's *virginitas in partu*.

If the information provided by Augustine is accurate—and I know of no reason to doubt him on this matter—we have two possible explanations why Jovinian's rejection of the doctrine of Mary's *virginitas in partu* had not been mentioned by Siricius or by Jerome in *Adversus Jovinianum*. If Jovinian's rejection of Mary's *virginitas in partu* was present in his original writings, then Siricius and Jerome may not have mentioned it simply because the doctrine was not significant to them; perhaps they even shared Jovinian's doubts on the subject.[32] On the other hand, if Jovinian did not speak of the *virginitas in partu* in his written work, then he may have developed his polemic against the doctrine only when he went to Milan. In this case he would have been responding directly to the teaching of Ambrose, and Siricius and Jerome would have been unaware of Jovinian's rejection of Ambrose's Mariology. Whichever of these options is correct, it is clear that the doctrine of Mary's *virginitas in partu* was significant for Ambrose in a way that it was not for Siricius or Jerome.

iii. Jerome

By far the most important source for the reconstruction of Jovinian's teaching is the *Adversus Jovinianum* of Jerome. Composed by Jerome in the spring of 393, the work provided extensive selections from the 'books' (*libri*) of Jovinian to which Jerome had access. In addition to the *Adversus Jovinianum*, in the following year Jerome wrote three letters in defence of his treatise to friends at Rome: Letters 48 and 49 to Pammachius, and Letter 50 to Domnio. In the opening paragraph of *Adversus Jovinianum* Jerome stated that he had received copies of Jovinian's writings from 'the holy brothers at Rome' (*sancti ex urbe Roma fratres*) who asked him to write a refutation. Many commentators have assumed that Pammachius was the one who sent Jovinian's writings to Jerome. This view is based on the knowledge that Pammachius had been instrumental in Jovinian's condemnation at Rome and on the fact that Jerome and Pammachius later corresponded about the *Adversus Jovinianum*.[33]

---

[32] As we shall see in Chapter 5, there is serious question whether Jerome ever clearly adhered to the doctrine, and Siricius never mentioned it. See the thorough discussion in Neumann, *Virgin Mary*, 146–52. For Ambrose, by contrast, the perpetual virginity of Mary—before, during, and after the birth of Jesus—was central to his understanding of Christ, salvation and the Church.

[33] See, for example, Valli, *Gioviniano*, 36; Kelly, *Jerome*, 182; and Charles Pietri, *Roma Christiana: Recherches sur l'Église de Rome, son organization, sa politique, son idéologie de Miltiade à Sixte III (311–440)* (Rome: École Française de Rome, 1976), 434.

There are, however, serious obstacles to this view. First, Jerome never said that it was Pammachius who first alerted him to Jovinian's activity. On the contrary, Jerome's expression, that he had received Jovinian's writings from 'holy brothers at Rome', suggests that it was a group of monks or ascetics who originally requested his intervention and not the senator Pammachius. Moreover, a careful reading of Jerome's correspondence with Pammachius confirms that Pammachius could not have been responsible for initially sending Jovinian's writings to Jerome. Although Jerome and Pammachius had been acquainted since their school days, they had not been active correspondents prior to 394. Letters 48 and 49 of Jerome, in fact, are the earliest extant pieces of their correspondence. Several features of Jerome's letters indicate that Pammachius initiated contact with Jerome only after the arrival of the *Adversus Jovinianum* at Rome. In other words, Pammachius entered the Jovinianist controversy not only as an opponent of Jovinian, but also as a critic of Jerome.

For example, at the beginning of Letter 49, Jerome's lengthy apology for the *Adversus Jovinianum*, Jerome wrote as if his correspondence with Pammachius had only just begun with his response to Pammachius' criticism of *Adversus Jovinianum*:

> Your own silence was the reason that until now I have not written to you. For I was afraid that if I wrote to someone who was silent, you would think me troublesome, rather than dutiful. But now that I have been challenged by your most delightful letters—letters that call me to [defend] the philosophy of our teaching—I welcome my old fellow student and companion and friend with open arms, as they say, and hope to have in you a champion of my little writings. But first I must persuade you to give me a favourable judgement and instruct you on all the points where I have been criticized, if I am to have you as my advocate.[34]

It is clear from Jerome's opening remarks to Pammachius that he was responding to Pammachius' initiative, but the letter to which he responded must have been the (now lost) letter of Pammachius criticizing the *Adversus Jovinianum*.

The same conclusion is evident from Letter 48, the 'cover letter' Jerome composed to accompany the apologetic Letter 49, where Jerome wrote the following:

> Sometimes it is the mark of Christian modesty to be quiet even with our friends and to nurture our humility with silence rather than risk the accusation of self-seeking by renewing old friendships. As long as you kept silent, I kept silent, nor did I wish to criticize you for this, lest I appear to be seeking after a person of influence, rather than

---

[34] Jerome, *ep.* 49.1 (CSEL 54, 350–1).

looking for a friend. But now that I have been challenged by the duty of correspondence, I will try always to take the initiative and not so much to answer your letters than to write [my own]. Thus, just as until now I have been silent out of modesty, so I will start to be more modest by speaking.[35]

It is impossible that Jerome could have written these words if he had already exchanged letters with Pammachius the previous year and been requested by him to write against Jovinian. It is clear that Jerome began to correspond with Pammachius only in 394 in response to the latter's criticism of the *Adversus Jovinianum*. One can only conclude that it was someone other than Pammachius who had sent Jovinian's writings to Jerome.[36]

The most valuable feature of Jerome's *Adversus Jovinianum* for the reconstruction of Jovinian's teaching is its collection of direct quotations from Jovinian's writings. Although Jerome complained about the illogical, even 'barbarous', style of Jovinian's *libri*, his presentation suggests that there was a systematic unity to Jovinian's thought based on his 'four propositions'. These four propositions were as follows:

1. Virgins, widows, and married women, once they have been washed in Christ, are of the same merit, if they do not differ in other works.
2. Those who have been born again in baptism with full faith cannot be overthrown by the devil.
3. There is no difference between abstinence from food and receiving it with thanksgiving.
4. There is one reward in the kingdom of heaven for all who have preserved their baptism.[37]

After listing the four propositions above, Jerome stated that he would follow the organization of Jovinian's *libri* and discuss each of the four propositions in turn.[38] Several lines later Jerome asserted that he would 'discuss all of his arguments and examples concerning marriage in the very same order in which [Jovinian] has stated them'. Jerome followed this procedure and discussed the first proposition in book one of *Adversus Jovinianum* and the second, third, and fourth propositions in book two.

The organization of Jerome's *Adversus Jovinianum* raises the question of the number of books composed by Jovinian. Did Jovinian write two *libri*, just as Jerome did, the first devoted to the first proposition and the second devoted to the second, third, and fourth propositions? Or, did he compose four *libri*, one devoted to each of the four propositions? It is impossible to resolve this

---

[35] Jerome, *ep.* 48.1 (CSEL 54, 347).
[36] For a similar argument see Duval, *L'affaire Jovinien*, 40–1.
[37] Jerome, *Jov.* 1.3 (PL 23, 224).   [38] Jerome, *Jov.* 1.4 (PL 23, 225).

question with certainty. The only hint of a solution is the fact that both Jerome and Julian of Eclanum made reference to material treated in Jovinian's 'second book', and in both cases it is clear that the second proposition of Jovinian was under discussion in that book.[39] On the basis of this evidence, both Haller and Valli believed that Jovinian had composed four *libri*, each one devoted to one of the four propositions. Although this is the most likely hypothesis, certainty on the question is elusive.

In addition to providing the four propositions of Jovinian, Jerome also indicated that Jovinian had supported each of his propositions with an extensive dossier of scripture texts. Jerome cited many of the biblical passages used by Jovinian and occasionally presented Jovinian's interpretation of these passages. If Jerome's responses in *Adversus Jovinianum* accurately reflect the format of Jovinian's writings, then the biblical citations and explanations would have formed the greater part of Jovinian's *libri*. This would explain why Jerome could call them 'commentaries'. Virtually all of the sources connected with the Jovinianist controversy speak of Jovinian's extensive use of scripture, and it is reasonable to assume that these biblical citations figured prominently in Jovinian's defence of his four theses.[40] In order to interpret each of Jovinian's propositions properly, therefore, we must pay close attention to his use of scripture and to the connection between his propositions and the scriptural evidence he adduced in support of his arguments.

Jerome's account of Jovinian's *libri* also included the claim that Jovinian supported his positions with 'illustrations taken from secular literature' (*exempla saecularis quoque litteraturae*).[41] Towards the end of the first book of *Adversus Jovinianum*, Jerome began to cite examples of chastity from pagan literature. He said that he did so in response to Jovinian's challenge:

We have offered abundant (and more than abundant) evidence of Christian chastity and angelic virginity from the sacred books. But since I understand that in the commentaries of our adversary we are challenged to fight on the level of worldly wisdom—because [he claims] this kind of thing is never approved in the world and our religion has invented a new dogma against nature—I will briefly run through

---

[39] Jerome, *Jov.* 1.1 (PL 23, 222); Julian, cited in Augustine, *C. Jul. op. imp.* 1.98 (PL 45, 1114). Cf. Valli, *Gioviniano*, 56–7.

[40] Vincent of Lérins, for example, lists Jovinian among the heretics who used scripture most extensively. See *Commonitorium* 35, cited in Haller, *Iovinianus*, 111–12. As Benedetto Clausi has observed, Jerome's own extensive (and distorting) treatment of scripture in *Adversus Jovinianum* was a direct response to Jovinian's thorough use of biblical texts. See his detailed analysis in 'La parola stravolta: Polemica ed esegesi biblica nell'*Adversus Iovinianum* di Gerolamo', in Marcello Marin and Mario Girardi (eds.), *Retorica ed esegesi biblica: Il rilievo dei contenuti attraverso le forme* (Bari: Edipuglia, 1996), 87–126.

[41] *Jov.* 1.4 (PL 23, 225).

Greek, Latin, and barbarian histories and will demonstrate that virginity has always held the first place among the forms of chastity.[42]

Although Jerome did not preserve any specific examples of Jovinian's appeals to pagan literature, there is no reason to doubt his word on the matter. Jovinian's strategy, apparently, was to argue that examples of virtuous married men and women could be found not only within the texts of scripture, but also in the literature of Greek and Roman antiquity. Such an argument suggests that Jovinian may have directed his propaganda specifically to cultured, aristocratic Christians (and, perhaps, even pagans) at Rome, that is, to those most likely to respond to an appeal to 'secular literature'.

What sort of examples might Jovinian have cited? Illustrations of the virtues of married life would have lain close to hand. The subject of marriage and its value for both individual and civic morality (the ancients would not have separated the two) had long been a commonplace in Greco-Roman literature. For example, the Stoic philosopher Musonius Rufus, who taught at Rome in the first century C.E., directly addressed the question, 'Is Marriage a Handicap for the Pursuit of Philosophy?' Musonius cited the examples of Pythagoras, Socrates, and Crates to support his contention that marriage was not only *not* a hindrance to philosophy, but actually essential to the pursuit of virtue:

Now the philosopher is indeed the teacher and leader of men in all the things which are appropriate for men according to nature, and marriage, if anything, is manifestly in accord with nature. For to what other purpose did the creator of mankind first divide our human race into two sexes, male and female, then implant in each a strong desire for association and union with the other...? Is it not then plain that he wished the two to be united and live together, and by their joint efforts to devise a way of life in common, and to produce and rear children together, so that the race might never die?

Approaching the issue as a good Stoic, Musonius went on to argue that nature itself dictated that human beings should strive to preserve the common good, that is, to pursue not merely their private interests, but those of the city as well. Therefore, Musonius concluded, each person's duty is 'to take thought for his own city, and to make of his home a rampart for its protection. But the first step toward making his home such a rampart is marriage. Thus whoever destroys human marriage destroys the home, the city, and the whole human race.'[43]

Similar sentiments were voiced in the Greco-Roman rhetorical tradition. An Eastern contemporary of Jovinian, Aphthonius of Antioch, composed a

---

[42] *Jov.* 1.41 (PL 23, 282). On Jerome's counter-use of *exempla*, see Benedetto Clausi, 'Storia sacra e strategia retorica: Osservazioni sull'uso dell' *"exemplum"* biblico nell'*Adversus Iovinianum* de Gerolamo', *Cristianesimo nella Storia* 16 (1995), 475–84.

[43] Musonius Rufus, frag. 14, trans. Cora E. Lutz, 'Musonius Rufus: The Roman Socrates', *Yale Classical Studies*, 10 (1947), 93.

set of *progymnasmata* or preliminary exercises, which were part of the elementary stage of instruction in schools of rhetoric. As Kate Cooper has observed, Aphthonius regarded the discussion of marriage as a 'political thesis', since marriage was essentially a matter of civic conduct.[44] Like Musonius, Aphthonius portrayed marriage as the context within which a man might cultivate the virtues necessary for civic life: courage, justice, wisdom, and self-control. Aphthonius saw special significance in the way marriage blends the enjoyment of pleasure with the exercise of self-control. After defending marriage against several of the standard objections (e.g. it produces orphans and widows), Aphthonius concluded with the following tribute to the role of marriage in shaping civic virtue:

Wonderful is marriage, both for producing gods and for granting to mortals, for whom it devises a means of continuing life, that they seem to be gods. And it guides those needing strict rules, it urges a consideration of self-control, and it seeks after pleasures, as many as are obviously not worthy of blame. Wherefore, it is established among all that marriage should be reckoned of the greatest worth.[45]

Jovinian's appeal to the high regard in which marriage was held in 'secular literature' no doubt would have echoed the kind of views expressed by philosophers and orators such as Musonius and Aphthonius.

A final feature of Jovinian's preaching evident from Jerome's *Adversus Jovinianum* is its strongly anti-heretical character. We have already noted that Jovinian accused Ambrose of Manichaeism for his teaching on Mary's *virginitas in partu*, and that Ambrose had responded in kind. Jerome did not refer to Jovinian's view of Mary in *Adversus Jovinianum*, but he did indicate that Jovinian had accused some advocates of asceticism of being heretics. Early on in *Adversus Jovinianum* Jerome undertook to deflect Jovinian's accusation of heresy: 'We do not follow the teachings of Marcion and Manichaeus and condemn marriage. Nor, deceived by the error of Tatian, do we regard all intercourse as polluted.'[46] Several chapters later, after reviewing the collection of biblical texts that Jovinian had cited in favour of his first proposition, Jerome quoted the following passage from Jovinian's first book: 'From this it is clear that you follow the teachings of the Manichees who forbid marriage and the eating of foods which God has created for use, who have consciences seared with a hot iron.'[47]

---

[44] *The Virgin and the Bride*, 94–5, on which my discussion of Aphthonius depends.

[45] Trans. Ray Nardeau, 'The Progymnasmata of Aphthonius in Translation', *Speech Monographs*, 19 (1952), 283.

[46] *Jov.* 1.3 (PL 23, 223).

[47] *Jov.* 1.5 (PL 23, 227). Jovinian has paraphrased a passage from 1 Tim 4: 1–3, where the biblical writer predicted the end-times' appearance of 'hypocritical liars whose consciences are seared with a hot iron' and who 'forbid marriage and demand abstinence from foods which God created to be received with thanksgiving by those who believe and know the truth'.

Jerome's testimony has explicitly affirmed what Siricius and Ambrose had only implied. Jovinian had directed the charge of 'Manichaean' against anyone who opposed his first proposition, that is, who denied his claim that after baptism virgins, widows, and married women are 'of the same merit'. In Chapter 4 I will explore further the context of Jovinian's accusations and the precise connotations carried by the label of 'Manichaean' in the late fourth century. Here it is enough to note that whatever biblical or theological justification Jovinian may have offered for his views, his accusations of heresy would have earned him the enmity of Siricius, Ambrose, and Jerome. In the late fourth century, Christians who practised the ascetic life were an easy target for such charges. While the label of 'Manichaean' was often simply a term of abuse, it could sometimes have serious consequences.[48] Whatever merit there may have been in Jovinian's arguments, his impolitic attack on the orthodoxy of the Western clergy must have virtually assured his own condemnation.

2. JOVINIAN'S FOUR PROPOSITIONS

Jovinian's four propositions, as reported by Jerome, provided the basic framework of his books. We must, therefore, take a closer look at these statements in order to discern the main theological orientation of his critique of ascetic piety. Each proposition will be discussed individually, for each one addressed a specific feature of the ascetic agenda. I would stress, however, that a unified perspective informed (more or less explicitly) all of these propositions. J. N. D. Kelly has provided an incisive account of Jovinian's central theological position: 'Although Jerome fails to bring it out, what gave a theological basis and inner cohesion to these propositions was Jovinian's stress on the element of faith in baptism, and his conviction that the transformation effected by it not only rescued a man from the power of sin but created a unified, holy people in which considerations of merit were irrelevant.'[49] Kelly's account surely is correct. Jovinian spoke of baptism explicitly in three of his four propositions. Moreover,

---

[48] Jerome, *ep.* 22.13.3 (CSEL 54, 161), said that the accusation of 'Manichaean' was used against anyone who appeared to be pale from fasting. On the trial of the bishop Priscillian and the taint of Manichaeism, see Henry Chadwick, *Priscillian of Avila: The Occult and the Charismatic in the Early Church* (Oxford: Clarendon Press, 1976), 143–4, and my discussion in Chapter 4.

[49] Kelly, *Jerome*, 181; cf. Budzin, 'Jovinian's Four Theses', 52–3: 'All of Jovinian's theses demonstrate his keen awareness of the relationship between church and sacrament. Through baptism a person was initiated into the Christian community and transformed spiritually into a new creation by the grace of this sacrament.'

when Jovinian's propositions are read in conjunction with the biblical evidence he cited, it becomes clear that he stressed not only the efficacy of baptismal regeneration, but also the ecclesial dimensions of the sacrament. Jovinian regarded baptism as the source of all Christian sanctification and the fundamental principle of salvation. And, as Kelly has observed, Jovinian's emphasis on baptismal rebirth was inseparable from his stress on the *locus* of that rebirth, namely the womb of the Church, the true 'bride of Christ'.

i. First Proposition: 'Virgins, widows, and married women, once they have been washed in Christ, are of the same merit, if they do not differ in other works.'

Several features of Jovinian's first proposition are noteworthy. First, in no sense did Jovinian criticize the practice of celibacy in itself. The first proposition was neither a call to abandon celibacy, nor a licence for sexual indulgence, as Jerome extravagantly claimed. Rather, Jovinian affirmed that celibacy should not be used to create distinctions of merit among baptized Christians. This is a fundamental point to grasp about Jovinian's teaching. Although Siricius, Ambrose, and Jerome all concurred in characterizing Jovinian as an 'enemy of chastity', such a view cannot be sustained from any of the extant fragments of his writings. Jovinian did not oppose the practice of celibacy per se; indeed, he even remained a celibate monk himself. His argument pertained specifically to the elevation of celibacy over marriage. In his first proposition Jovinian simply maintained that celibacy did not, in itself, convey any higher 'merit' on the baptized Christian.[50]

Another feature of Jovinian's first proposition that deserves comment is its focus on Christian women. The first proposition addressed specifically the status of 'virgins, widows, and married women' (*virgines, viduas, et maritatas*). In book one of *Adversus Jovinianum* Jerome preserved additional fragments from Jovinian's first book, in which he referred explicitly to the status of women. For example, in one fragment Jovinian stated that after baptism there were no grounds for distinguishing between a virgin and a widow: 'Granted that there is a difference between marriage and virginity, what can you say to this: If a virgin and a widow were both baptized and then remained as they were, what difference would there be between them?'[51] Moreover, Jerome also asserted that the following statement could be found at the conclusion of Jovinian's first book: 'I do you no wrong, virgin. You have chosen chastity "on account of the present

---

[50] On this point both Haller, 151, and Valli, 85, agree. See *Jov.* 1.40 (PL 23, 280), where Jerome stated that Jovinian 'boasted' that he was still a monk.
[51] *Jov.* 1.33 (PL 23, 267).

distress" (1 Cor 7: 26). It pleased you to be "holy in body and spirit" (1 Cor 7: 34). Be not proud! You belong to the same Church as married women.'[52] It is clear from the foregoing quotations that Jovinian had a particular interest in the status of Christian women, and that he wished to emphasize their essential unity within the one Church. The 'pride' of Christian virgins appears to have been a matter of special concern to Jovinian.

Why would Jovinian have focused especially on Christian women, and on the problems associated with virgins in particular? The answer to this question must lie in the prominent position that women had come to assume in the ascetic discourse and practice of the late fourth-century church, especially in the West. The writings of both Ambrose and Jerome provide ample testimony to the high regard in which they held female ascetics, especially widows and virgins. Jerome, for example, often appealed to ascetic women and used them to denigrate his fellow clergymen. Such invidious comparisons did much to alienate Jerome from the Roman clergy and hastened his departure from the Roman scene upon the death of his patron Damasus. Jovinian's focus on women in his first proposition indicates that he, like many of his contemporaries, rejected the new status claims being made for ascetic women, especially virgins.

In the case of virgins, however, there was another factor that contributed to their special status in Jovinian's day. By the end of the fourth century, a special ritual, the 'veiling' (*velatio*) of virgins, had developed in which a young woman received official consecration and recognition as the 'bride of Christ' in a ceremony modelled after a Roman wedding. The consecration or veiling of virgins was a practice unique to Western Christianity in the late fourth century; in fact, Ambrose, Siricius, and Jerome provide the main evidence of this ritual. As Nathalie Henry has recently demonstrated, the rite of virginal consecration turned what had previously been a personal and private matter (i.e. the virgin's vow of celibacy) into a public act accompanied by a precise ritual, which included a sermon from the bishop, a nuptial blessing, the bestowal of a veil, and (most likely) the antiphonal chanting of the Song of Songs. As the writings of Ambrose demonstrate, the celebration of a virgin's *velatio* was also an occasion to affirm the unique status of the Christian virgin and to assert her superiority over married women.[53]

---

[52] *Jov.* 1.5 (PL 23, 228).

[53] Nathalie Henry, 'A New Insight into the Growth of Ascetic Society in the Fourth Century AD: The Public Consecration of Virgins as a Means of Integration and Promotion of the Female Ascetic Movement', *StPatr* 35 (2001), 102–9; see also her essay, 'The Song of Songs and the Liturgy of the *velatio* in the Fourth Century: From Literary Metaphor to Liturgical Reality', in R. N. Swanson (ed.), *Continuity and Change in Christian Worship* (Woodbridge: Boydell, 1999), 18–28. In Chapter 6 I will discuss further Ambrose's role in the development of the ritual of the *velatio* and in the promotion of consecrated virgins.

Jovinian's focus on virgins in his first proposition may have been a response to the ritual elevation of virgins in the ceremony of the *velatio*. Jerome suggested as much when he said that Jovinian wished to apply the words of 2 Corinthians 11: 2 ('I espoused you to one husband, so that I might present you as a pure virgin to Christ') not simply to Christian virgins, but to 'the whole Church of believers'. According to Jerome, Jovinian insisted that 'married women, and twice-married women, and widows, and virgins should all be included in this espousal.'[54] We know that the words of 2 Corinthians 11: 2 were spoken at a pivotal moment in the ritual of the *velatio*. In Letter 130, written to commemorate the consecration of the noble virgin Demetrias, Jerome stated that the bishop pronounced these words while placing the bridal veil on the virgin's head.[55] By insisting that the apostle's words applied to all women in the Church, and not merely to consecrated virgins, Jovinian was directly undermining the claims to elite status being made on behalf of the *virgo velata*.

Although Jovinian's first proposition attended specifically to the issue of ascetic women, the biblical citations he presented in his first book were not restricted to this issue. Jovinian's assemblage of biblical texts, in fact, was used to develop another side of his argument, namely that the biblical tradition itself, both the Old and the New Testaments, gave a prominent place to married persons and showed no preference for celibacy. In order to support this argument, Jovinian surveyed the history of salvation in order to demonstrate that sex and procreation played an intrinsic role in God's plan for the human race. Beginning with Genesis and continuing into the New Testament, Jovinian argued that the significance of married people in God's plan of salvation effectively precluded any preference for celibacy. From Adam to Enoch to Noah to Moses, Jovinian appealed to all of the great figures in the Hebrew Bible (and their wives) as examples of those who shared in the original blessing of God, 'Be fruitful and multiply, and replenish the earth.'[56]

One of the most prominent examples of marital sanctity cited by Jovinian was the pair of Abraham and Sarah. Jovinian's point in referring to the first patriarch and matriarch was not merely to attest to the presence of married people in the Hebrew dispensation. He also wanted to demonstrate the crucial role that their marital life itself played in the history of salvation. As Jovinian put it: 'By the merit of his faith Abraham received a blessing in the generation of children. Sarah, who was a type of the Church, when she was past the age of childbearing, exchanged the curse of sterility for the blessing of childbirth.'[57] For Jovinian, the coexistence of sanctity and sexual activity—indeed, the very

---

[54] *Jov.* 1.37 (PL 23, 275).   [55] *Ep.* 130.2 (CSEL 56, 176–7).
[56] Cited in *Jov.* 1.5 (PL 23, 225–6).   [57] *Jov.* 1.5 (PL 23, 226).

necessity of sex within the history of salvation—was a permanent reminder to celibate Christians that they did not merit any special status before God. As Augustine noted many years after Jovinian's condemnation, it was precisely Jovinian's appeal to the married saints in scripture that persuaded many consecrated virgins and celibate men at Rome to follow the patriarchal precedent and to marry.[58]

Nor did Jovinian restrict himself to examples from the Old Testament. What seems to have most infuriated Jerome was Jovinian's claim that the sanctity of married persons pertained not merely to the Hebrew *past*, but also to the Christian *present*. In his first book Jovinian had surveyed the New Testament for evidence of holy married people. He cited Zachariah and Elizabeth, Peter and his mother-in-law, and indeed most of the apostles.[59] Contrary to the view of Ambrose, Jerome, and other Christian ascetics, who believed that the time for procreation lay in the past when the earth still needed to be filled with people, Jovinian explicitly argued that sex and marriage still had a place in Christian times. In one lengthy fragment cited by Jerome, Jovinian articulated this point with an array of New Testament texts:

> But if [my opponents] wish to offer a vain defense and assert that the world needed an increase only in its early stages, let them hear the apostle Paul saying, 'I wish the younger widows to marry, to procreate children' (1 Tim 5: 14). And, 'Marriage is honorable and the marriage bed undefiled' (Hebrews 13: 4). And, 'A wife is bound only as long as her husband lives; but if he dies, she is free to marry whomever she wishes, but only in the Lord' (1 Cor 7: 39). And, 'Adam was not deceived, but the woman was deceived and became a transgressor. But she will be saved through childbearing, if they continue in faith and love and holiness, with modesty' (1 Tim 2: 14–15).[60]

Elsewhere we learn that Jovinian did not argue merely that Paul and the other apostles permitted marriage, but rather that most of the apostles themselves were married men. For example, Jovinian cited Paul's statement in 1 Corinthian 9: 5 ('Do we not have the right to be accompanied by a sister as wife, as do the other apostles and the brothers of the Lord and Cephas?') and noted that the apostles, 'the chief authorities of our teaching and the leaders of our way of life', were not virgins.[61] For Jovinian, the New Testament confirmed the Old Testament in its teaching that married persons played an essential role in the history of salvation.

---

[58] *Retract.* 2.22 (48) (CCSL 57, 107–8). According to Augustine, Jovinian pressed consecrated virgins with the question, 'Are you better than Sarah, better than Susanna or Anna?' Similarly, Augustine reported that Jovinian had 'destroyed' the celibacy of ascetic men by comparing them with the fathers and husbands of the Old Testament.

[59] *Jov.* 1.5, 26.   [60] *Jov.* 1.5 (PL 23, 227).   [61] *Jov.* 1.26 (PL 23, 256–7).

Jovinian's final example of the prominence of married Christians was taken from the successors of the apostles, namely the bishops, presbyters, and deacons of the Church. As Jovinian observed, the apostle Paul had recommended in his letters to Timothy and Titus that the bishop should be 'a man of one wife' and one who had raised his children to be proper and respectful Christians.[62] Jovinian does not seem to have rejected the requirement of sexual continence that was being imposed on the higher clergy of the West in the late fourth century; rather, his argument was that married men were often judged to be suitable for clerical life. For example, Jovinian noted that congregations often preferred to elect a married man to the clergy rather than a celibate monk. Although Jerome responded with a rather jaundiced view of the selection process, it is clear that Jovinian believed the choice of a married clergy was simply fidelity to the advice of the apostle and a sign that marriage was no obstacle to holiness.

In sum, then, the biblical arguments that appeared in Jovinian's first book were designed to stress the continuity between the Old Testament and the New Testament on the question of marriage. The importance of procreation in the Hebrew scriptures, the role of married apostles in the New Testament, and the presence of married men among the contemporary leaders of the Church confirmed Jovinian's view that distinctions of merit based purely on degrees of sexual renunciation were without foundation in the Bible or Christian tradition. These biblical and historical claims, therefore, supported Jovinian's more theological argument about baptism. Given the significant place of married persons in the history of salvation, and in the light of the baptismal transformation that was available to all Christians, Jovinian concluded that any attempt to claim an elevated status for Christian virgins was theologically suspect.

ii. Second Proposition: 'Those who have been born again in baptism with full faith cannot be overthrown by the devil.'

Like his first proposition, Jovinian's second proposition called attention to the efficacy of Christian baptism. In this case, however, he emphasized the role of baptism in protecting the Christian from the power of evil. There is, however, a question about the precise wording of the second proposition. In book one of *Adversus Jovinianum*, where Jerome listed all four propositions, the second one was phrased as follows: 'Those who have been born again in baptism with full faith cannot be overthrown by the devil' (*a diabolo non posse subverti*). But

---

[62] Jovinian had alluded to 1 Tim 3: 2, 4 and Titus 1: 6, according to *Jov.* 1.34.

at the beginning of book two, where Jerome began to discuss the second proposition, he phrased it differently: 'The second proposition of Jovinian is that the baptized cannot be tempted by the devil' (*a diabolo non posse tentari*).[63] There is clearly a significant difference between the two formulations.

Jerome's initial wording of Jovinian's second proposition was almost certainly the correct one. When he listed the four propositions in book one, Jerome must have been following Jovinian's own account. But when he came to respond to the second proposition in book two, Jerome seems to have paraphrased the proposition and altered the wording in order to refute it more easily. As J. N. D. Kelly has observed, Jerome 'had little difficulty in showing that the New Testament is full of warnings against sin, and that the saints of both Testaments had been tempted and sinned'.[64] It would have been much easier for Jerome to refute the proposition that baptized Christians could not be 'tempted' by the devil, whereas Jovinian's claim that baptized Christians could not be 'overthrown' by the devil required a more subtle approach. In fact, it is possible that Jerome did not fully understand Jovinian's second proposition as it was written.

What, then, did Jovinian mean when he proposed that 'those who have been born again in baptism with full faith cannot be *overthrown* by the devil'? First, we should say what Jovinian did not mean. As both Haller and Valli have observed, Jovinian's second proposition did not claim that baptized Christians could not sin. Indeed, it is apparent from a later section of *Adversus Jovinianum* that Jovinian acknowledged the importance of penance in restoring baptized Christians after they had sinned.[65] Although some of Jovinian's opponents portrayed him as teaching the possibility (or even necessity) of sinlessness, there is no clear evidence of this in his writing. Jovinian's authentic teaching, it seems, was that a person who had been truly transformed (i.e. 'born again') by the grace of baptism, and who had thereby come to receive the gift of faith, could not ultimately lose the benefits of that gift (i.e. be 'overthrown by the devil'). Strictly speaking, Jovinian's second proposition asserted the final *indefectibility* of baptized Christians, rather than their personal *impeccability*.

How are we to make sense of Jovinian's second proposition? Jovinian's argument, I suggest, is perfectly comprehensible when we consider both the biblical warrant he supplied for it and the sacramental interpretation he gave to the biblical evidence. According to Jerome, Jovinian relied especially on two passages from the First Letter of John. The first of these stated: 'Every

---

[63] *Jov.* 2.1 (PL 23, 295).   [64] Kelly, *Jerome*, 184.
[65] *Jov.* 2.37, cited in Haller, *Iovinianus*, 140, and Valli, *Gioviniano*, 98.

person who has been born of God does not sin, because God's seed abides in him. He cannot sin, because he has been born of God. In this the children of God and the children of the devil are revealed' (1 Jn 3: 9–10). The second passage read: 'Everyone who is born of God does not sin. But the one who was born of God protects him, and the evil one does not touch him' (1 Jn 5:18).[66] Jovinian interpreted these passages as an expression of the efficacy of baptism. For Jovinian it was baptism that provided the 'rebirth' described in the biblical texts. The 'seed' (*semen*) of God that gives birth to the Christian in baptism was nothing other than the Holy Spirit, whose presence in the baptized was seen as the source of their new identity as 'children of God'. Empowered by the Spirit, the baptized Christian was genuinely capable of living a new life. Protected by 'the one who was born of God' (i.e. by Christ), the baptized Christian was not only forgiven of past sins, but also freed from the malignant power of the devil.

The understanding of baptism that Jovinian presented in his second proposition, I would argue, was by no means an idiosyncratic one. As I will show in the excursus at the end of this chapter, the fourth-century ritual of baptism was oriented to convince the newly baptized that such a total transformation of the person was truly possible. In fact, Jovinian's image of 'rebirth' and even the notion of the Holy Spirit as the 'seed of God' were familiar concepts in the literature associated with baptismal practice. For example, in a sermon preached to the newly baptized, Pacian of Barcelona (a Spanish bishop whose son, Nummius Aemilianus Dexter, was a high-ranking official under Theodosius and a correspondent of Jerome) employed the same images in order to explain the regeneration produced by baptism.[67] For Pacian, the marriage between Christ and the Church—a marriage made possible by the prior union of the human and divine natures in Christ—led to the birth of the Christian people in baptism:

From this marriage is born the Christian people, with the Spirit of the Lord coming from above. And at once, with the heavenly seed (*semen caelestis*) being spread upon and mingled with the substance of our souls, we develop in the womb of our [spiritual] mother, and once we come forth from her womb, we are made alive in Christ.... And so the seed of Christ (*Christi semen*), that is, the Spirit of God, produces through the hands of the priests the new man, conceived in the womb of our [spiritual] mother and received at birth at the baptismal font, with faith still attending as the nuptial protectress. For neither will someone appear attached to the

---

[66] Both passages are cited in *Jov.* 2.1.
[67] On Pacian, see Jerome, *Vir. ill.* 106 (PL 23, 742). The son, Nummius Aemilianus Dexter (*PLRE* 1, 251), served as proconsul of Asia under Theodosius and later as Praetorian Prefect (395). See *Vir. ill.* 132 (PL 23, 755) on Dexter, to whom Jerome dedicated *De viris illustribus*.

Church who has not believed, nor will someone be born from Christ who has not received his Spirit. We must believe therefore that we can be born again.[68]

In this sermon Pacian has described precisely the kind of baptismal transformation that Jovinian envisioned in his second proposition. Born of the Holy Spirit in baptism and possessing the gift of faith, the Christian became a 'new man' (*novus homo*), freed from the power of sin. As Pacian put it,

all peoples who were once given over to the princes and powers of darkness are now set free through the victory of our Lord Jesus Christ.... Freed therefore from our chains, when through the sacrament of baptism we come unto the sign of the Lord, we renounce the devil and all his angels whom we served in the past, so that we should now not serve them any longer, having been liberated by the blood and name of Christ.[69]

For Pacian, no less than for Jovinian, baptism meant freedom from the power of evil.

A final observation regarding Jovinian's second proposition is in order. It is likely that Jovinian intended the ultimate triumph over evil that was granted to Christians in baptism to be understood primarily in a communal or ecclesial sense. There is evidence of this in a fragment of Jovinian's second book quoted by Jerome at the beginning of *Adversus Jovinianum*: 'We know that the Church through faith, hope, and charity is inviolable and impregnable. In it no one is immature; everyone is capable of learning. No one can force a way into it by violence or deceive it by craft.'[70] This passage, which Jerome said was taken from the *exordium* of Jovinian's second book, must have been concerned in some way with the second proposition. Since baptism was understood not simply as the regeneration of the individual, but also as the incorporation of the individual into the body of Christ, it is reasonable to conclude that Jovinian's emphasis on the indefectibility of the baptized Christian must have been rooted in a view of the Church itself as indefectible. As this passage from Jovinian's second book indicates, he spoke explicitly of the Church as 'inviolable' (*inaccessibilem*) and 'impregnable' (*inexpugnabilem*) when discussing the second proposition. Jovinian's stress on the power of baptism to protect the Christian from overthrow by the devil would have been simply an extension of his vision of the Church as sharing in the eschatological triumph of Christ.[71]

---

[68] *Bapt.* 6.2–4 (SC 410, 158); trans. Craig L. Hanson, *The Iberian Fathers* (FC 99; Washington, DC: The Catholic University of America Press, 1999), 91–2.

[69] *Bapt.* 7.3 (SC 410, 162); trans. Hanson, 93–4.

[70] *Jov.* 1.2 (PL 23, 222). In *Jov.* 1.1 (PL 23, 222) Jerome stated that this passage was taken from 'the opening of Jovinian's second book' (*secundi libri eius... exordium*).

[71] In his defence of the fourth proposition, Jovinian made a similar claim about the Church. See *Jov.* 2.19 (PL 23, 328): 'Unam habet fidem, nec constupratur dogmatum varietate, nec haeresibus scinditur. Virgo permanet. Quocumque vadit agnus, sequitur illum: sola novit Canticum Christi.'

iii. Third Proposition: 'There is no difference between abstinence from food and receiving it with thanksgiving.'

Jovinian's third proposition was the only one that did not refer explicitly to baptism. Nevertheless, there is a close similarity between this proposition and the others. Jovinian asserted that no moral preference was to be given to the act of fasting. Although Jerome and others accused Jovinian of preaching gluttony and excess, the evidence of Jovinian's own words does not support this accusation. Jovinian did not reject fasting in itself. Rather, he regarded fasting as equivalent to 'receiving food with thanksgiving'. Again Jovinian's use of the bible sheds light on the intent of his proposition. In a fragment cited by Jerome we read: 'What need of argument is there when scripture clearly teaches that "every moving creature, just like the herbs and vegetables", has been given to us as food (cf. Gen 9: 3). And the apostle cries out: "Everything is clean to the clean" (Rom 14: 20; Titus 1: 15), and "Nothing is to be rejected which is received with thanksgiving" (1 Tim 4: 4).'[72]

As this excerpt indicates, the key words of Jovinian's third proposition, 'received with thanksgiving', were derived from the text of 1 Timothy 4: 4. Further attention to this biblical text will help us to discern what was at stake in Jovinian's third proposition, namely the proper Christian attitude towards creation.

It will be helpful to cite the full text of 1 Timothy 4: 1–5 in order to assess the impact of this passage on Jovinian's third proposition:

Now the Spirit expressly says that in the last times some will renounce the faith by paying attention to deceitful spirits and teachings of demons, through the hypocrisy of liars whose consciences are seared with a hot iron. They forbid marriage and demand abstinence from foods, which God created to be received with thanksgiving by those who believe and know the truth. For everything created by God is good, and nothing is to be rejected, provided it is received with thanksgiving; for it is sanctified by God's word and by prayer (1 Tim 4: 1–5 NRSV).

Jovinian's third proposition clearly has been influenced by this Pauline text. While not rejecting fasting itself, Jovinian taught that a proper attitude towards creation—that is, acknowledging all creation as good and a gift from God—was essential for the Christian. Such an attitude of 'thanksgiving' made eating no less holy an activity than fasting.[73]

---

[72] *Jov.* 2.5 (PL 23, 304).

[73] Jovinian's use of First Timothy in his third proposition also links it to the first proposition. According to *Jov.* 1.5, Jovinian had cited 1 Tim 4: 1–2 in his first book, where he accused ascetics at Rome of being 'Manichaeans'. The Pauline text connects the rejection of marriage with the rejection of foods 'which God created to be received with thanksgiving'.

Further evidence of the theology of creation underlying Jovinian's view of fasting can be found in another fragment cited by Jerome. In the following passage Jovinian emphasized the place of human beings in the order of creation as grounds for approving the use of animals for food:

All things were created to serve for the use of human beings. And just as the human person, being a rational animal, who is so to speak the tenant and owner of the world, is subject to God and worships his Creator, so too all living things were created either to be food for mankind, or to be clothing, or to till the earth, or to carry the harvest or man himself. Hence they are called *jumenta* because they help (*juvent*) mankind.[74]

Jovinian then quoted Psalm 8: 4–8, where the Psalmist described human beings as 'a little lower than angels', who have been given dominion over all created things, including sheep, oxen, birds, and fish. 'If they are not eaten', Jovinian concluded, 'all these things were created by God in vain.'[75]

It is clear from the foregoing quotations that Jovinian's third proposition was based on theological considerations about the goodness of creation and about the place of human beings within that creation. Indeed, such considerations link Jovinian's concern about fasting with his ideas on marriage and sexual renunciation. In both cases, Jovinian maintained that the excessive practice of asceticism—or, to be more precise, the elevation of ascetic over non-ascetic practices—ran the risk of impugning the value and purpose of creation. In defence of the first proposition, for example, Jovinian had advanced the following argument: 'If everyone became a virgin, how would the human race survive? ... Why were the genitals created? Why were we fashioned by the all-wise Creator so that we experience a mutual desire for one another and long for natural intercourse?'[76] In addition to his emphasis on the efficacy of baptism and its power to bring spiritual rebirth, Jovinian also stressed the essential goodness of creation. To 'receive food with thanksgiving' was to acknowledge the beneficence of the Creator and the place of the human race within the order of creation.

The final biblical argument that Jovinian presented in defence of his third proposition was an appeal to the example of Jesus and the apostles. Pointing to the conspicuous lack of ascetic behaviour in Jesus' ministry, Jovinian remarked: 'The Lord himself was called a wine-bibber and a glutton by the Pharisees, and a guest of tax-collectors and sinners because he did not refuse a meal with Zachaeus and attended the wedding feast.'[77] Jovinian also noted that Jesus willingly provided wine for the feast and, later, offered wine (not water) as the sign of his blood at the last supper. Even after the resurrection,

---

[74] *Jov.* 2.5 (PL 23, 303). Jovinian's etymology was erroneous. *Jumenta* is derived from *jungo*, 'to put in a harness'.
[75] *Jov.* 2.5 (PL 23, 304).   [76] *Jov.* 1.36 (PL 23, 271).   [77] *Jov.* 2.5 (PL 23, 304).

Jovinian observed, Jesus ate fish, not merely nuts and berries. The apostles likewise are presented in scripture as eating freely, and Paul even advised Timothy to drink wine when his stomach was upset. In short, Jovinian argued, to eat with the proper attitude was the essential thing. The practice of Jesus and the apostles cohered with their teaching; they partook of creation with thanksgiving.

iv. Fourth Proposition: 'There is one reward in the kingdom of heaven for all who have preserved their baptism.'

Jovinian's fourth and final proposition turned on the question of eschatology, that is, the final end of the human race. As Jerome described it:

> His fourth proposition, which is the last, is that there are two classes, the sheep and the goats, the just and the sinners; the just stand on the right hand, and the others stand on the left. The just will hear these words: 'Come, blessed of my Father, inherit the kingdom prepared for you from the foundation of the world' (Mt 25: 34). But to sinners he will say: 'Depart from me, you accursed ones, into the eternal fire which has been prepared for the devil and his angels' (Mt 25: 41).[78]

The persistent theme in Jovinian's choice of biblical testimonies was that only one distinction ultimately mattered: that between the righteous and the unrighteous, between the saved and the damned. At the time of Noah the righteous were all saved and sinners all perished; at Sodom and Gomorrah no distinction was made except between the good and the bad; at the parting of the Red Sea, 'the righteous all passed over and the sinners were all overwhelmed'.[79]

Jovinian's fourth proposition was related to the previous ones in several ways. Like the first proposition, it asserted the essential equality of all baptized Christians; like the second proposition, it emphasized the crucial role of baptismal regeneration in determining a person's ultimate destiny; and like the third proposition it denied any special merit to forms of ascetic behaviour. What was new in Jovinian's defence of his fourth proposition was a more explicit discussion of the nature of salvation, one that confirmed both the sacramental and the ecclesial aspects of his previous propositions. For Jovinian it was baptism that determined the character of salvation for all Christians, not any form of ascetic merit. Once again, attention to Jovinian's use of biblical texts will bring to light these features of his argument.

Immediately following the passage cited above, Jovinian quoted John 8: 44 ('You are from your father the devil, and you wish to do the desires of your

[78] *Jov.* 2.18 (PL 23, 326).   [79] Ibid.

father'). For Jovinian, the Johannine text illustrated the biblical dictum that 'a good tree cannot produce bad fruit, nor can a bad tree produce good fruit.' These citations must be interpreted in the light of Jovinian's theology of baptism. As we saw above, Jovinian's second proposition had maintained that the reception of the sacrament of baptism entailed the making of a 'new man', that is, the rebirth of the Christian as a child of God through the descent of the Holy Spirit. Such regeneration entailed that the baptized, if they remained faithful to their baptism, would ultimately be preserved from evil. Jovinian's fourth proposition extended this argument to the final state of the baptized in heaven. Since the source of salvation was the work of God's Spirit, not ascetic merit, Jovinian reasoned, the quality or state of salvation also was to be determined solely by the reception of the Spirit and not by ascetic merit.

Jovinian articulated this point precisely in his citations and comments on several biblical passages. For example, he cited John 6: 56 ('He who eats my flesh and drinks my blood abides in me and I in him'), adding the following comment: 'Therefore, just as Christ is in us without any difference of degrees, so too we are in Christ without degrees.' In a similar vein he quoted John 14: 23 ('Everyone who loves me will keep my word, and my Father will love him, and we will come to him and make our home in him') and offered the following interpretation: 'The person who is righteous loves. And if a person loves, the Father and the Son come to him and dwell in him as in a guest-house. In my view, when the guest is such as this, there can be nothing lacking in the guesthouse.'[80] As Jovinian read it, John's Gospel stated clearly that God would dwell in all of the baptized faithful. Since salvation is accomplished by that indwelling of God, Jovinian argued, there is no reason to posit different degrees of that indwelling in this life or the next.

Jovinian also illustrated his fourth thesis with biblical quotations that stressed the unity of the Church and the permanence of the union between Christ and his heavenly bride. For example, he paraphrased the prayer from John 17: 20–3, where Jesus entreated the Father on behalf of the disciples and all future believers: 'I ask not only on behalf of these, but also on behalf of those who will believe in me through their word, that they may all be one. As you, Father, are in me and I am in you, may they also be in us.... The glory that you have given me I have given them.... I have loved them as you have loved me.' For Jovinian this prayer of Jesus guaranteed that the Church—'the whole Christian people'—would be 'one people in the Father, Son and Holy Spirit, that is to say, beloved children, participants in the divine nature'.[81]

---

[80] *Jov.* 2.19 (PL 23, 327).
[81] *Jov.* 2.19 (PL 23, 328); cf. *Jov.* 2.29 (PL 23, 340), where Jovinian indicated that this applied to 'omnis populus Christianus'.

This ecclesial emphasis is also evident in another fragment of Jovinian in which he presented the indwelling of the Trinity in the Church as the principle of the Church's ultimate indefectibility in grace: 'Bride, Sister, Mother, whatever words you wish to use, she is the gathering of one Church, which is never without her Bridegroom, Brother, Son. She possesses a single faith. She is not corrupted by a variety of doctrines nor divided by heresies. She remains a virgin. And wherever the Lamb goes, she follows. She alone knows the Canticle of Christ.'[82]

Once again, it is clear that Jovinian's critique of the theory of ascetic merits rested on a sacramental and ecclesial foundation. For Jovinian, the ultimate triumph of baptized Christians over the forces of evil and their final entry into the kingdom of God was nothing other than the gift of salvation promised to the Church. The spiritual marriage of Christ and the Church was a union into which all Christians entered at their baptism. As Jerome observed, Jovinian applied the titles 'Bride, Sister, Mother' to the 'one Church'.[83] Insofar as the whole Church is a faithful virgin, Jovinian insisted, the rewards of that virginity belong to all Christians alike.

3. JOVINIAN AND BAPTISM: AN EXCURSUS ON RITUAL

Baptism, as we have seen, was the foundation of Jovinian's theological argument on behalf of the equality of all Christians. But baptism in the early church was much more than a theological concept. It was, as Thomas Finn has described it, 'an extended, exacting, and dramatic ritual of conversion'.[84] In the late fourth century, preparation for baptism lasted several weeks; it involved intensive fasting, instruction, and repeated exorcism. The baptismal ceremony itself entailed several anointings, semi-public nudity, and a public repudiation of Satan. Moreover, the ritual itself was weighted with profound and moving symbolism. In short, baptism played a role in the life of a fourth-century Christian that can scarcely be imagined by anyone today. In order to appreciate the full force of Jovinian's argument, therefore, we must attend to specific features of the ritual of baptism as it was practised in the churches of Italy in the late fourth century. When the character of baptism as a ritual process is examined, and when patristic commentaries on that process are taken into account, the full import of Jovinian's appeal to Christian baptism will become apparent.

[82] *Jov.* 2.19 (PL 23, 328).   [83] *Jov.* 2.30 (PL 23, 341).
[84] Thomas M. Finn, *From Death to Rebirth: Ritual Conversion in Antiquity* (New York: Paulist Press, 1997), 168.

44   *Jovinian and his World*

We are fortunate to possess relatively abundant evidence of baptismal practice in the West in the time of Jovinian. It was common for bishops to preach catechetical sermons to newly baptized Christians during the week following their baptism. In these sermons the bishops explained to the neophytes the significance of the elaborate rituals they had just undergone. Ambrose of Milan produced two sets of such sermons, *De sacramentis* and *De mysteriis*. The former consisted of six sermons that were delivered in the late 380s during the period when Augustine underwent baptism at Milan. The latter was a carefully edited treatise, based on his previous sermons, that was published around 390. Moreover, other Western writers, such as Zeno of Verona, Pacian of Barcelona, and Augustine, preached sermons that commented on various aspects of the baptismal ritual. As a result both the form and the meaning of the Western baptismal ritual as it existed in the days of Jovinian can be reconstructed with considerable precision.[85]

The most striking feature of the fourth-century baptismal ritual—and the one most relevant to an interpretation of Jovinian's teaching—is that it aimed to effect the personal transformation of the new Christians and their incorporation into the community of the Church. From its inception the ritual process was drenched in symbolism that signified the new identity or radical reorientation that the new Christian was expected to undergo. Early Christian baptism was, in the classic anthropological sense of the term, a 'rite of passage' that involved the successive steps of separation from an alien and evil world, individual transformation, and incorporation into a new social reality.[86] Each step of the ritual process emphasized that the person was becoming a new creature or being 'born again'. Baptism effected a 'passage', a *transitus*, as Ambrose put it, 'the passage from sin to life, from fault to grace, from defilement to sanctification'.[87] It was just such an understanding of baptism, I contend, that provided a consistent logic and persuasive force to Jovinian's propositions.

---

[85] Thomas M. Finn has provided an accessible collection of primary sources in his volume, *Early Christian Baptism and the Catechumenate: Italy, North Africa, and Egypt* (MFC 6; Collegeville, Minn.: The Liturgical Press, 1992). I have relied here especially on Finn's collection of the evidence from Italy (29–110). In *Sacr.* 3.1.5 (SC 25bis, 94) Ambrose indicated that, with the exception of the post-baptismal foot washing, he followed the liturgical practice of Rome.

[86] The classic study is that of Arnold Van Gennep, *The Rites of Passage*, trans. Monika Vizedom and Gabrielle Caffee (Chicago: The University of Chicago Press, 1960), 10–11, 93–6 (on baptism).

[87] *Sacr.* 1.4.12 (SC 25bis, 66). Ambrose noted that the word *pascha* ('Passover') was equivalent to the Latin *transitus*.

i. Phase One: Pre-Baptismal Preparation

In order to make this point effectively, it is necessary to examine in detail the various stages in the early Christian ritual of baptism. Although the climax of the baptismal process occurred at the Easter Vigil when the candidates definitively renounced the devil and underwent immersion in the baptismal font, an ancient Christian's preparation for baptism began much earlier. In the late fourth century, adult baptism was still the norm, and a Christian might spend many years officially enlisted as a catechumen, that is, 'one undergoing instruction', before finally deciding to make the full Christian commitment (Augustine is a famous example). When the catechumens decided that they were ready to be baptized, they were formally enrolled as members of the *competentes*, that is, those 'seeking together' to be baptized. The candidates submitted their names at the rite of enrolment, which usually took place on the feast of Epiphany. At that time the bishop took mud and spread it over the eyes of the *competentes*. Reminiscent of the Gospel story of the healing of the blind man (John 9: 7), the ritual signified, according to Ambrose, the confession of sin that was implied in the desire to seek justification through baptism.[88]

Enrolment marked the beginning of an intensive period of preparation that lasted for the next forty days leading up to the feast of Easter. During this time the *competentes* met daily to receive instruction; at Milan these sessions (which may have occurred twice daily) focused on moral teaching, especially interpretation of the patriarchal narratives in Genesis and the precepts of Proverbs.[89] They fasted daily as well. A prominent feature of this stage of the ritual was a series of exorcisms and a physical 'scrutiny' of the candidates. As Finn has observed, the latter involved a ritualized physical exam to determine whether there were any physical or psychosomatic signs that Satan still clung to the *competentes*.[90] Describing the effect of the ritual of scrutiny, Quodvultdeus, a North African contemporary of Augustine, invoked Psalm 138: 3 ('Probe me, Lord, and know my heart'): 'He has probed, he has weighed, he has touched the hearts of his servants with fear of him; by his power he has caused the devil to flee, and he has freed his servant from the devil's dominion.'[91] The cumulative effect of these weeks of instruction, fasting, exorcism,

---

[88] *Sacr.* 3.2.12 (SC 25bis, 98–100); trans. Finn, *Early Christian Baptism*, 59, 76.
[89] *Myst.* 1.1 (SC 25bis, 156). The evidence for the twice-daily instructions is found in Paulinus of Milan, *Vita sancti Ambrosii*, cited in Finn, *From Death to Rebirth*, 223.
[90] Finn, *From Death to Rebirth*, 223.
[91] Quodvultdeus, *Ser.* 1, *De symbolo* i (CCSL 60, 305), cited in Finn, *From Death to Rebirth*, 223.

and scrutiny was to divest the prospective Christians of their attachments to the non-Christian 'world' and to free them from the influence of evil.

The culmination of this period of ritual preparation occurred on the night of the Easter Vigil when the *competentes* formally renounced Satan and publicly pledged their loyalty to Christ. Once again, this ritual was accompanied by a variety of actions heavily laden with potent symbolism. At the beginning of the vigil the bishop touched the ears and nostrils of the candidates for baptism with his spittle, recalling the gospel story of the healing of the deaf mute (Mark 7: 33–4). The word *Ephphatha*, that is, 'be opened', was pronounced so that, as Ambrose put it, the candidates might be receptive to the words of the bishop and open to the meaning of the rituals they were about to undergo.[92]

The *competentes* were then stripped naked and anointed head to foot with olive oil. Recalling the preparation of athletes for hand-to-hand combat, Ambrose described the ritual as preparing the candidates to be 'athletes for Christ', that is, 'to contend in the contest of this world'.[93] At this point there occurred one of the most dramatic parts of the pre-baptismal ritual, the renunciation of Satan. Standing naked and dripping with oil, one by one the candidates faced west and heard the bishop ask two questions: 'Do you renounce the devil and his works?' They responded, 'I do renounce them.' 'Do you renounce the world and its pleasures?' the bishop asked. 'I do renounce them,' they answered.[94] The *competentes* then turned eastward and addressed another profession to Christ, possibly in the form of a shortened creed.[95] Preparation for baptism was now complete. The candidates had been led, after weeks of instruction, fasting, and exorcism, to detach themselves from their former lives, symbolized by 'the devil and his works' and 'the world and its pleasures'. They were ready to enter a new world and receive a new identity. They were ready to be born again.

When Jovinian emphasized in his second proposition that 'those who have been born again in baptism with full faith cannot be overthrown by the devil,' his assertion would have fitted with the experience of anyone who had undergone the early Christian rites of initiation. The period of preparation for baptism focused intensively on the candidates' turning from sin and renunciation of evil. The exorcisms, scrutinies, anointings, and final renunciation of Satan would have brought home to the catechumens the seriousness

---

[92] *Sacr.* 1.1.2 (SC 25bis, 60); *Myst.* 1.3 (SC 25bis, 156).

[93] *Sacr.* 1.2.4 (SC 25bis, 62). Nakedness, of course, was a symbol that was multi-vocal. It might symbolize the innocence of childhood, the loss of status or distinction, or the divestment of one's former identity. No doubt it meant all of these at once.

[94] *Sacr.* 1.2.5 (SC 25bis, 62).

[95] For this suggestion, see Finn, *From Death to Rebirth*, 227.

of the new identity they were about to adopt. As Zeno of Verona urged those about to undergo baptism: 'Brethren, exult. Your own faith has given you birth. You have fled the snares of this world, its sin, its wounds, its death. You have invoked the assistance of your Father in majesty. Fly, then ... to the water of the saving font. Immerse yourselves with confidence. Fortunately, by the death of your old man, you are destined to be victorious.'[96]

As Jovinian emphasized, freedom from the influence of evil was precisely the promise that had been made to the *competentes* who had renounced 'the devil and his works' and approached the baptismal font.

ii. Phase Two: Baptismal Transformation

The second phase of the ritual process of baptism centred on the baptism proper, that is, the immersion of the candidates in the baptismal font full of flowing water.[97] Prior to their entry into the water, however, an exorcism and consecration of the font itself took place, thus ensuring (again through symbolic efficacy) that the waters themselves would be filled with power. As Ambrose observed, water alone was merely an *opus*; the presence of God was required to produce a divine *operatio*: 'water does not cure unless the Holy Spirit descends and consecrates that water.'[98] The blessing of the water 'in the name of the Father and of the Son and of the Holy Spirit', using the words of Jesus from Matthew 28: 19, ensured that the Holy Trinity itself would be present and operative in the baptismal font.[99]

Upon entering the baptismal waters, the *competentes* experienced the crucial moment of the entire ritual process, the three-fold immersion. They were asked three questions: 'Do you believe in God the Father Almighty?' 'Do you believe in our Lord Jesus Christ and his cross?' 'Do you believe in the Holy Spirit?' As they responded to each question, 'I do believe,' the candidates were immersed in the water. The three-fold immersion was the central turning point in the ritual process, the moment at which the baptized passed from death to life. As we saw above in the sermon of Pacian of Barcelona, the baptismal font was seen simultaneously as the *tomb* of Christ, where Christian were baptized into the death of the Lord (cf. Romans 6: 3), and the *womb* of

---

[96] *Tract.* 2.23, *De baptismo* (CCSL 22, 197), cited as 'Invitation 5' in Finn, *Early Christian Baptism*, 57.

[97] Annabel Wharton has observed that the baptismal fonts at Rome and Milan were outfitted with elaborate hydraulic systems in order to assure a continuous flow of fresh water into the font. See 'Ritual and Reconstructed Meaning: The Neonian Baptistery in Ravenna', *The Art Bulletin*, 69 (1987), 364. I thank Professor Wharton for alerting me to her study.

[98] *Sacr.* 1.5.15 (SC 25bis, 68); cf. *Myst.* 4.19 (SC 25bis, 164).

[99] *Sacr.* 2.5.14 (SC 25bis, 80).

the Church, out of which they emerged as newborn infants. Imitating ritually the burial and resurrection of Christ, the newly baptized exited the font having appropriated the merit of Christ's death and resurrection.[100]

Again, Jovinian's stress on the power of baptismal regeneration would have rested on these specific features of the ritual process. As Pacian, Ambrose, and others testified, the crucial significance of this stage of the ritual of baptism was that it produced a 'new man', one whose purity reproduced the original (sinless) state of Adam and Eve before the fall. Through their entry into the death and resurrection of Christ, the newly baptized had come to 'walk in the newness of life', thereby reversing the sentence of death that had fallen upon humanity after the first sin. Entry into the waters of baptism and the threefold immersion provided nothing less than participation in the resurrection of Jesus and access to the kingdom of heaven. Viewed in the light of the transformation obtained through baptismal regeneration, distinctions of merit based on degrees of ascetic practice paled into insignificance, according to Jovinian. Initiation into the Christian life—that is, baptism into the death and resurrection of Christ—was the essential principle of Christian identity and the fundamental criterion of salvation. No act of ascetic renunciation, Jovinian insisted, could achieve what had been bestowed through the death and resurrection of Jesus Christ.

iii. Phase Three: Post-Baptismal Incorporation

As the newly baptized emerged from the waters, their new status was affirmed in several ways. First they were greeted by the bishop and anointed once again. At Milan the bishop spoke these words: 'God, the Father Almighty, who regenerated you by water and the Spirit and forgave you your sins, will himself anoint you into everlasting life.'[101] Echoing the words of 1 Peter 2: 9, which identified the Church as 'a chosen race, a royal priesthood, a holy nation', Ambrose explained that the purpose of this anointing was to signify the new, priestly identity of the baptized: 'for we all are anointed into the kingdom of God and into the priesthood by means of spiritual grace.' The newly baptized were then dressed in white garments, a symbol of their state of purity. They were now ready to join the rest of the Christian congregation for the first time at the table of the Lord's Supper.[102]

---

[100] *Sacr.* 2.6.19 (SC 25bis, 84), 3.1.3 (SC 25bis, 90–2).

[101] *Sacr.* 2.7.24 (SC 25bis, 88).

[102] In *Sacr.* 3.1.4–7 (SC 25bis, 92–6) Ambrose described an additional rite of foot washing that was observed at Milan, but not at Rome. The significance of this rite, according to Ambrose, was that it offered additional protection against the power of evil.

Since early Christian baptisteries were usually separate from the main church building, the neophytes formally processed from the baptistery into the church proper, perhaps chanting the words of Psalm 22.[103] As Edward Yarnold has observed, 'the solemn entry of the baptized, clothed in their white robes, and dispelling the darkness with the light of their baptismal candles, must have been a spectacular moment.'[104] Upon entering the church the newly baptized were allowed to exchange the kiss of peace with their fellow Christians for the first time, a sign not only of their newly acquired purity but also of their full membership in the Christian community. For Ambrose the kiss symbolized the bridal relationship that subsisted between Christ and the Church, 'for a kiss is a pledge of nuptials and the privilege of wedlock.'[105]

The final stage in the long and arduous ritual of baptism was the entry of the newly baptized into full communion with the rest of the Christian congregation through reception of the eucharistic bread and wine. Ambrose described the event with an emphasis on the intoxicating joy that now belonged to those who could share in the Church's bountiful banquet:

The cleansed people, rich in these insignia, hasten to the altar of Christ, saying: 'And I shall go unto the altar of God who gives joy to my youth' (cf. Ps. 42: 4). For the people, having put aside the defilements of ancient error, renewed in the youth of an eagle, hasten to approach that heavenly banquet. They come, therefore, and, seeing the sacred altar arranged, exclaim saying: 'You have prepared a table in my sight'. David introduces these people as speaking when he says: 'The Lord feeds me and I shall lack nothing; in a place of good feeding he has placed me; he led me beside the water of refreshment'. And below: 'For though I should walk in the midst of the shadow of death, I shall fear no evil, for you are with me. Your rod and your staff have comforted me. You prepare a table in my sight, against those who trouble me. You have anointed my head with oil, and your cup that inebriates me is wonderful' (cf. Ps 22: 105).[106]

Images of comfort, refreshment, and joy surrounded the newly baptized Christian. After weeks of separation, scrutiny, and other forms of ritual 'liminality', the catechumens had completed their transformation into full members of the Christian community.

The predominant effect of this final stage of the initiation process would no doubt have been a profound sense of unity between the newly baptized

---

[103] *Sacr.* 5.3.13 (SC 25bis, 124–6); cf. Finn, *From Death to Rebirth*, 229.
[104] Edward Yarnold, *The Awe-Inspiring Rites of Initiation: The Origins of the RCIA*, 2nd edn. (Collegeville, Minn.: The Liturgical Press, 1994), 38–9.
[105] *Ep. extra collectionem* 1.18 (CSEL 82.3, 155); trans. Mary Melchior Beyenka, *Saint Ambrose: Letters* (FC 26; New York: Fathers of the Church, Inc., 1954), 392.
[106] *Myst.* 8.43 (SC 25bis, 178–80); trans. Roy J. Deferrari, *Saint Ambrose: Theological and Dogmatic Works* (FC 44; Washington, DC: The Catholic University of America Press, 1963), 20–1 (altered).

Christians and the other members of the Church. As Zeno of Verona observed, those who had been baptized, 'though differing in race, age, sex, and state of life' (*genere, aetate, sexu, condicione diversi*), were joined together as one: 'This regeneration, this resurrection, this eternal life, our mother has given to us all. She incorporates us into one body after assembling us from every race and from every nation.'[107] We should not underestimate this sense of unity, the *unum corpus*, to which Zeno referred. Drawing upon anthropological theory, Thomas Finn has suggested that the early Christian ritual of baptism was an essential factor in the creation of the sense of community that enabled the ancient church to survive, especially in the dark moments of persecution: 'In the baptismal rebirth, in the communal kiss and embrace, and in the meal, the community was itself reborn and its family ties renewed. The rites by which new members were incorporated at once increased and regenerated the body of the faithful.'[108] As I have emphasized throughout this chapter, Jovinian's arguments against the exaltation of celibacy and fasting were grounded in an experience of baptism that most Christians in the late fourth century would have known intimately. His emphasis on the power of baptism to free a person from sin, his stress on the equality of all the baptized, and his insistence on the unity of the one Church—all of these aspects of Jovinian's theology could be found ritually enacted in the contemporary practice of baptism. There is no doubt that Jovinian's initial success at Rome owed much to the resonance between his preaching and the baptismal practice of the Church.

---

[107] Zeno of Verona, *Tract.* 1.55, *Ad neophytes* (CCSL 22, 130), cited as 'Invitation 4' in Finn, *Early Christian Baptism* 56–7.

[108] Finn, 'Ritual Process and the Survival of Early Christianity: A Study of the Apostolic Tradition of Hippolytus', *Journal of Ritual Studies*, 3 (1989), 69–89.

2

Jovinian and Christian Rome

My review thus far of Jovinian's teaching and its grounding in the baptismal tradition of the Church has focused necessarily on the theological dimensions of his work. In later chapters, as I examine further the anti-heretical aspects of his thought, the theological character of his resistance to the ascetic ideal will become even more pronounced. But debates about marriage and celibacy were not simply matters of theology; they also involved issues of social status and identity. Marriage in antiquity was a distinctly public institution, and the sort of claims advanced by both Jovinian and his opponents would have had decidedly public and political implications. My aim here is to place Jovinian within the social context of late fourth-century Rome and to understand his arguments within the complex dynamics found there.

1. CHRISTIANITY, ASCETICISM, AND CULTURE

Robert A. Markus has provided an excellent starting point for this inquiry. As he observed in *The End of Ancient Christianity*, the later decades of the fourth century were a time of profound change and turmoil in the Roman empire. Tensions between pagans and Christians were running high. The 380s and 390s witnessed the first major efforts by the emperors Gratian and Theodosius to suppress traditional religious practice. These years also saw significant efforts by pagan senators at Rome to reassert their former religious rituals and prerogatives. At the same time, the spread of asceticism and monasticism in the West made the issue of conversion especially acute, since they presented an ideal of Christian conduct that required (at least in theory) radical cultural renunciation. The struggles between pagan and Christian, as well as the intra-Christian debates about asceticism, were symptomatic, as Markus put it, of a 'crisis of identity' in the late Roman world: 'In one way or another the debates of these decades all revolved about the question: What is it to be a Christian?'[1]

---

[1] Robert A. Markus, *End of Ancient Christianity*, 19. The literature on the religious crises at Rome in the late fourth century is vast. For a good introduction, see John Matthews, *Western*

The Jovinianist controversy, as Markus intimated, must be located within that 'crisis of identity' of the late fourth century. As we saw in Chapter 1, Jovinian had articulated a vision of Christian identity that emphasized continuity between the demands of Christian living and traditional social and familial values. In his writings Jovinian had made explicit appeal to the high regard in which marriage was held in 'secular literature', and he even had argued that marriage and procreation were matters of civic responsibility. Such a vision of harmony between Christianity and culture would have been especially attractive to members of the traditional aristocracy at Rome, that is, to those who were most affected by the imperial pressure to convert and by the ascetic demands for renunciation. Jovinian's arguments, as I will argue here, were part of a wider cultural and religious debate over the implications of Christian asceticism in late antiquity, one that affected both pagans and Christians alike at Rome, especially within the aristocracy.

In order to establish this point, I will begin by surveying some of the criticisms of asceticism and monasticism that appear in fourth-century sources. Such criticisms can be read as an index of the degree to which Christians had achieved significant 'assimilation and accommodation' to traditional Greco-Roman culture.[2] Although Jovinian himself did not oppose the practice of celibacy or monasticism—after all, he remained a celibate monk—his arguments would have found a receptive hearing among those who, for whatever reason, opposed the monastic movement. In the first part of this chapter, then, I will explore the social and cultural context of this wider resistance to asceticism and place Jovinian's views in relation to those of his Western contemporaries.[3]

But any discussion of the late antique debates over marriage and celibacy must take into account not only the resistance to asceticism that is evident in the sources, but also the ways in which ascetic piety itself was assimilated to and accommodated within the prevailing culture. In other words, we must

---

Aristocracies and Imperial Court. A.D. 364–425 (Oxford: Clarendon Press, 1975); Charles W. Hedrick, Jr., *History and Silence: Purge and Rehabilitation of Memory in Late Antiquity* (Austin, Texas: University of Texas Press, 2000). An extensive collection of primary sources in translation has been edited by Brian Croke and Jill Harries, *Religious Conflict in Fourth Century Rome* (Sydney: Sydney University Press, 1982).

[2] I borrow the expression from Michele Salzman, *On Roman Time: The Codex Calendar of 354 and the Rhythms of Urban Life in Late Antiquity* (Berkeley: University of California Press, 1990), *passim*.

[3] Several excellent surveys of opposition to asceticism have been published. See L. Gougaud, 'Les critiques formulées contre les premiers moines d'occident', *Revue Mabillon*, 24 (1934), 145–63; G. D. Gordini, 'L'opposizione al monachesimo a Roma'; and, by far the best, J. Fontaine, 'L'aristocratie occidentale devant le monachisme au IVème et Vème siècles', *Revista di storia e letteratura religiosa*, 15 (1979), 28–53.

attempt to explain why some cultured, aristocratic Christians found asceticism appealing and why others of the same class and background found it revolting. In the second part of this chapter, therefore, I will examine more closely the manner in which ascetic piety was gradually embraced by some elite Christians in late fourth-century Rome. Asceticism, I will suggest, was adopted, but mainly on terms acceptable to the interests of the Christian aristocratic culture. The hierarchy that was present in much ascetic discourse proved to be useful in aristocratic competition for social status. Such a development helps to explain why Jovinian's views initially found a receptive audience at Rome, as well as why the views of his opponents eventually prevailed.

i. 'A vile and disgraceful profession'

Late in the autumn of 417, a distinguished Roman nobleman, Rutilius Claudius Namatianus, set sail from the Roman port of Ostia towards the coast of Gaul. A Gallo-Roman by birth, Rutilius had attained the prestigious posts of *magister officiorum* (412) and *praefectus urbis Romae* (414). Once freed of these duties, Rutilius decided to return to his homeland, probably to inspect some property devastated by the now-chronic Gothic invasions.[4] On the fifth day at sea, as the distant peaks of Corsica began to appear, Rutilius, to his dismay, came upon the island of Caparia. It was, he said, 'an ill-kept isle full of men who shun the light': 'Their own name for themselves is a Greek one, "monachoi", because they wish to dwell alone with none to see. They fear Fortune's boons, as they dread her outrages: would anyone, to escape misery, live of his own choice in misery? What silly fanaticism of a distorted brain is it to be unable to endure even blessings because of your terror of ills?' Rutilius proceeded to describe the Christian monks as prisoners who suffered self-imposed penalties for their sins. They are victims of *melancholia*, men whose hearts are 'swollen with black bile', like Bellerophon, a character in Homer who suffers from loathing of the human race.[5]

---

[4] Pierre de Labriolle, 'Rutilius Claudius Namatianus et les moines', *REL* 6 (1928), 30–41; for the date, see Alan Cameron, 'Rutilius Namatianus, St. Augustine, and the Date of the *De reditu*', *JRS* 57 (1967), 31–9.

[5] *De reditu suo* 440–52; trans. J. Wight Duff and Arnold M. Duff, *Minor Latin Poets* (LCL; Cambridge, Mass: Harvard University Press, 1968), 802–4. The allusion is to the *Iliad* 6.202. The Christian poet Ausonius had previously used Bellerophon as an ancient prototype of the deranged Christian hermit. See *ep.* 29.70 ff., and Yves-Marie Duval, 'Bellérophon et les ascètes chrétiens: "Melancholia" ou "otium"?' *Caesarodunum*, 2 (1968), 183–90; H. Brandenburg, 'Bellerophon christianus?' *RQ* 63 (1968), 49–86.

Nor was this Rutilius' only outburst against the Christian monks. Several lines later in his account of the next day's voyage through the straits between Corsica and Pisa, he recalled the recent ascetic withdrawal of a young Roman nobleman to a 'living death' upon the island of Gorgona. Rejecting noble birth, wealth, and advantageous marriage, the young man had 'made his way, a superstitious exile, to a dishonorable hiding-place': 'Fancying, poor wretch, that the divine can be nurtured in unwashen filth, he was himself to his own body a crueler tyrant than the offended deities. Surely, I ask, this sect is no less powerful than the drugs of Circe? In her days men's bodies were transformed, now it is their minds.'[6] These are the words of a pagan critic of the Christian monastic life. They echo complaints that were uttered by numerous other pagans around the end of the fourth century.[7] Monks are 'superstitious', unwashed and unlettered, guilty of misanthropy and suffering from insanity. The similarity between Rutilius' attack on the Christian monks and traditional pagan criticism of Christianity would suggest, perhaps, that hostility to Christianity in general, and not merely to the monastic life, may lie behind Rutilius' polemic.[8]

It would be a mistake, however, to see Rutilius' complaints solely as pagan propaganda against Christianity, for there is ample evidence that many Christians felt the same way about their ascetic co-religionists. Reasons for Christian resistance to asceticism were many and varied. In some cases, there was concern about the disruptive impact of ascetic renunciation on social and economic stability. Imperial legislation in the late fourth century indicates that men sometimes sought to avoid curial duties by fleeing to the countryside and pretending to be monks. In the year 370, for example, an edict of the emperors Valentinian I and Valens decreed that such persons should be apprehended and forced to perform their public services, or else face the dissolution of their property.[9] Monks sometimes interfered in civic affairs by interrupting trials and even attempted to rescue condemned prisoners.[10] Imperial decrees

---

[6] *De reditu suo*, 517–26; trans. Duff and Duff, *Minor Latin Poets*, slightly altered.

[7] See, for example, the emperor Julian, *ep.* 89b; Libanius, *or.* 2.32, *or.* 30.8–10, *or.* 62.9–10; Eunapius of Sardis, *Vitae sophistarum* 472.

[8] So believes François Paschoud, *Roma Aeterna: Études sur le patriotisme romain dans l'occident latin à l'époque des grandes invasions* (Rome, 1967), 161; Labriolle, 'Rutilius', 39; and Cameron, 'Rutilius', who argues that Rutilius' poem was a response to Augustine's *City of God*.

[9] *C.Th.* 12.1.63, dated 1 January 370. The problem of curial flight, however, was widespread and not limited to monks. See T. Kopecek, 'Curial Displacements and Flights in Later Fourth Century Cappadocia', *Historia*, 23 (1974), 319–42.

[10] *C.Th.* 9.40.16. A notable example of monastic intervention occurred at Antioch in 387 after the famous 'Riot of the Statues'. See my discussion in 'Preaching and Propaganda in Fourth Century Antioch: John Chrysostom's *Homilies on the Statues*', in David G. Hunter (ed.), *Preaching in the Patristic Age: Studies in Honor of Walter J. Burghardt, S.J.* (New York: Paulist Press, 1989), 119–38, and the literature cited there.

also were issued to prevent monks from receiving legacies from wealthy widows, although clerics at Rome were as guilty of this offence as the monks.[11] By the year 390 these problems had become so acute that the emperors Valentinian II, Theodosius, and Arcadius attempted to ban monks altogether from entering towns or cities. Although this decree was repealed two years later, its initial appearance reflects imperial concern about the civic disruption caused by monks.[12]

But imperial officials were not the only ones who were wary of persons who identified themselves or were identified as 'monks'. Tensions between monks and the clergy had existed from the very beginning of the monastic life. Because they ostensibly (and sometimes ostentatiously) adhered to a stricter way of life, monks were often viewed as rivals to the resident clergy. Conversely, monastic sources often indicate that clergy were widely regarded as morally inferior to monks. For example, the *First Greek Life* of Pachomius, an early leader of communal monasticism in Egypt, recounted that among the Pachomian communities no one was allowed to hold clerical office:[13]

[Pachomius] had deliberated on the subject and often told them that it was good not to ask for rank and honor, especially in a community, for fear this should be an occasion for strife, envy, jealousy, and then schisms to arise in a large community of monks. He told them, 'In the same way as a spark of fire, however small at the beginning, if cast into a threshing-floor and not quickly extinguished, destroys the year's labor, so clerical dignity is the beginning of a temptation to love of power.'

This early monastic source suggests that in some monastic milieux bishops, presbyters, and deacons were viewed as too closely allied with struggles for status and influence in the Church. Clerical life was presented as a 'temptation' to be resisted by those in search of holiness.

Similar concerns are evident in the correspondence of Bishop Athanasius, an early proponent of monastic life in Egypt and the West. In a letter written

---

[11] *C.Th.* 16.2.20, addressed to Pope Damasus by emperors Valentinian, Valens, and Gratian, 30 July 370. The decree was directed against the behaviour of 'ecclesiastics, ex-ecclesiastics, and those men who wish to be called by the name of "Continents"' (*ecclesiastici aut ex ecclesiastici vel qui continentium se volunt nomine nuncupari*); trans. Clyde Pharr, *The Theodosian Code and Novels and the Sirmondian Constitutions* (Princeton: Princeton University Press, 1952), 443. Text in T. Mommsen (ed.), *Theodosiani libri XVI cum constitutionibus Sirmondianis* (Berlin, 1905), i.2, 841.

[12] *C.Th.* 16.3.1, September 2, 390; rescinded on 17 April 392: *C.Th.* 16.3.2. Popular hostility to monks in these years is also reflected in John Chrysostom's *Adversus oppugnatores vitae monasticae*, where he complains that Christians boast about beating and abusing monks. See *Oppugn.* 1.2.

[13] *Vita prima graeca* 27; text in F. Halkin (ed.), *Sancti Pachomii vitae graecae* (Subsidia Hagiographica 19; Brussels: Société Bollandistes, 1932), 17; trans. Armand Veilleux, *Pachomian Koinonia*, i, *The Life of Saint Pachomius and his Disciples* (Cistercian Studies, 45; Kalamazoo, Mich.: Cistercian Publications, 1980), 314.

in 354 to a monk Dracontius, who was reluctant to accept appointment as bishop of Hermapolis Parva, Athanasius had to address the issue of monastic resistance to clerical office. He noted that one sometimes finds bishops who live in a manner that rivals the monks in ascetic rigour, but it is clear that his monastic addressee regarded this as the exception, not the rule.[14] In his *Letter to Dracontius* Athanasius was hard pressed to reassure Dracontius that his spiritual condition would not become 'worse' ($\chi\epsilon\acute{\iota}\rho\omega\nu$), should he become a bishop, and he attempted to undermine the monastic perception that 'the bishop's office is an occasion for sin.'[15] In his *Life of Antony* Athanasius attempted to counteract these monastic reservations about the clergy by emphasizing his hero's respect for clerical authority: '[Antony] was not ashamed to bow his head before bishops and priests; and if ever a deacon came to him for help, he conversed with him on what was helpful; but when it came to prayers, he would ask him to lead, not being ashamed to learn himself.'[16] Athanasius' description of Antony's deference to the clergy was certainly meant to be a corrective to the sense of superiority evidenced by some monks.

As enthusiasm for ascetic renunciation spread from East to West, the same tensions between the clergy and monks became manifest. In the case of Jerome, we have an instance of a Christian ascetic who positively delighted in drawing contrasts between the mediocre life of the average clergyman and the spiritual heights achieved by the monk. In 376, prior to his own ordination to the presbyterate, Jerome composed Letter 14 to Heliodorus, a childhood friend. Heliodorus had once considered joining Jerome in the Syrian desert, but had decided instead to pursue the life of a clergyman in his native Italy and to undertake his familial responsibilities. For Jerome, the desire of Heliodorus to abandon the monastic life and return to his family was nothing short of a temptation to 'kill Christ'.[17] Jerome vividly described the pressure placed on Heliodorus by family members: his mother, father, nurse, widowed sister, nephew, and even household slaves importuned him to

---

[14] *Ep. Drac.* 7–8 (PG 25, 530–2), and the discussion in David Brakke, *Athanasius and the Politics of Asceticism* (OECS; Oxford: Clarendon Press, 1995), 99–110. In his history of Syrian monks Theodoret of Cyrrhus mentioned several who refused to be ordained or to exercise the functions of the priesthood. See *H. rel.* 3.11, 13.4, 15.4, and 19.2.

[15] *Ep. Drac.* 1, 8–9 (PG 25, 524, 532), cited in Brakke, *Athanasius*, 103. As Brakke has observed, 'Some monastic teachers did indeed believe that ordination and ecclesiastical office could be the opportunity for sin, particularly for pride.'

[16] *Vit. Ant.* 67.1–2 (SC 400, 310); trans. Robert T. Meyer, *St. Athanasius: The Life of Antony* (ACW 10; Westminster, Md.: The Newman Press, 1950), 76–7.

[17] *Ep.* 14.2.3 (CSEL 54, 46). On the evolution of Jerome's attitude towards the clergy, see Philip Rousseau, *Ascetics, Authority and the Church in the Age of Jerome and Cassian* (Oxford: Oxford University Press, 1978), 125–32.

remain in his ancestral home.[18] In response to Heliodorus' argument that scripture teaches we must obey our parents, Jerome responded that 'whoever loves parents more than Christ loses his own soul.'[19] All of the appeals of Heliodorus to his familial responsibilities were dismissed by Jerome as a desire for comfort and luxury.

Towards the end of Letter 14 to Heliodorus, Jerome turned to the issue of service in the clergy, which had become Heliodorus' choice of vocation. Although Jerome protested that he had nothing unfavourable to say about the clergy—after all, they succeed to the status of the apostles, partake of Christ's body with holy lips, and hold the keys of the kingdom of heaven— nonetheless it is evident that Jerome wished to lower the status of the clergy in comparison with the monastic life:

> Not all bishops are bishops. You observe Peter, but consider Judas also. You regard Stephen, but note Nicholas also, whom the Lord in His Apocalypse hates.... Ecclesiastical rank does not make a Christian. Cornelius the centurion, while still a pagan, is filled with the gift of the Holy Ghost. Daniel, a young boy, judges the elders. Amos, while plucking blackberries, is suddenly a prophet. David, a shepherd, is chosen king. Jesus loves most the least of His disciples.[20]

Although Jerome later was to admit that Letter 14 was a work of his youth and full of rhetorical conceits, we know that it remained popular with friends of his at Rome: several decades later, the widow Fabiola had committed it to memory.[21]

In Chapter 6 we shall have occasion to examine in greater detail Jerome's contentious relations with the Roman clergy. Indeed, Jerome's famous Letter 22 to Eustochium, composed at Rome in 384, contains some of the bitterest denunciations of clerical conduct in all of ancient Christian literature. This letter, along with Jerome's haughty behaviour at Rome, was no doubt partly responsible for his expulsion from the city of Rome in 385 and for his ongoing conflicts with members of the Western clergy. Moreover, as I will argue below, Jovinian's success at Rome derived partly from clergy who were suspicious of claims of ascetic superiority. Here it is enough to note that such conflicts were frequent in the later decades of the fourth century. As forms of ascetic behaviour, such as celibacy, poverty, and fasting, increasingly became sources of spiritual authority, it was inevitable that the clergy, who were not always

---

[18] *Ep.* 14.3.1–3. [19] *Ep.* 14.3.4 (CSEL 54, 48).
[20] *Ep.* 14.9.1 (CSEL 54, 57–8); trans. Charles Christopher Mierow, *The Letters of St. Jerome* (ACW 33; New York: Newman Press, 1963), 67.
[21] *Ep.* 77.9 (CSEL 55, 46). See *ep.* 52.1 (CSEL 54, 414) for Jerome's *retractatio* of *ep.* 14.

celibate, poor, or abstemious, would see in the ascetic movement a threat to their own authority.[22]

But there were additional sources of resistance to monasticism and asceticism. If the apparent virtues of monks were perceived as threatening, their alleged vices were no less problematic. In the year 386, early in his reign as bishop of Rome, Pope Siricius composed a letter to the Spanish bishop Himerius of Tarragona in response to certain disciplinary issues that Himerius had raised with Siricius' predecessor, Pope Damasus. Siricius had been informed that there were male and female ascetics who had become involved in illicit sexual relationships:

> Furthermore, you state that there are monks and nuns who have cast aside their resolution to be holy and are sunk so deep in licentiousness that after first meeting stealthily under cover of the monasteries in illicit and sacrilegious passion, they have then on a sudden through despair of conscience begotten children freely in these illicit relations, a thing condemned both by civil law and by the rules of the Church.[23]

Siricius commanded that the lapsed monks and nuns be expelled from their monasteries and sent to prison (*retrusae in suis ergastulis*) for their offences. Throughout the fourth century, canonical literature frequently treated the question of ascetics who violated their professed commitments.

The clergy, however, were not the only Christians to express concern about the dangers of monastic life. We catch a fascinating glimpse of the problem of hostility to monasticism in a late fourth-century apologetic treatise, the *Conversations of Zaccheus and Apollonius* (*Consultationes Zacchaei et Apollonii*).[24] Composed by an anonymous author as a dialogue between a fictitious pagan philosopher Apollonius and his Christian friend Zacchaeus, this apology recounts a three-day discussion in the course of which Apollonius underwent conversion and baptism into Christianity. On the third day of their encounter (book 3), the two men began to discuss the question how to live a morally upright life, and Zacchaeus expounded on the two ways of

---

[22] An interesting contrast to Jerome can be found in John Chrysostom. Having tried to lead a monastic life in the hills near Antioch, John returned to the city and the life of the clergy. In several places he argues for the value of clerical service to the Church. See *Compunct.* 1.6 (PG 47, 403–4); 2.2–3 (PG 47, 413–14); *Sac.* 6.5 (SC 272, 321–3); discussion in J. M. Leroux, 'Monachisme et communauté chrétienne d'après saint Jean Chrysostome', in *Théologie de la vie monastique* (Paris: Aubier, 1961), 143–90; id., 'Saint Jean Chrysostome et le monachisme', in Charles Kannengiesser (ed.), *Jean Chrysostome et Augustin* (Paris: Beauchesne, 1975), 125–44.

[23] Siricius, *ep.* 1.6.7 (PL 13, 1137–8); trans. James T. Shotwell and Louise Ropes Loomis, *The See of Peter* (New York: Columbia University Press, 1927; reprint New York: Octagon Books, 1965), 702.

[24] M. A. Claussen has argued persuasively that the *Consultationes* were composed around the year 394: 'Pagan Rebellion and Christian Apologetics in Fourth-Century Rome: The *Consultationes Zacchaei et Apollonii*', *JEH* 46 (1995), 589–614, esp. 600–10.

Christian life: that of 'average' Christians (*mediocres*), who marry and produce children, possess wealth, and enjoy food and drink; and that of the 'most distinguished' Christians (*clarissimi*), who renounce wealth, status, and marriage. Although Zacchaeus affirmed that the practice of the ascetic life gained a greater reward in heaven, he reassured his companion that 'honourable marriages do not displease God, nor does the modest love of the solemn marriage bed when used for the procreation of children'.[25]

After accepting the explanation of Zacchaeus regarding the diverse ways of Christian life and after expressing his own incipient enthusiasm for the 'higher way', Apollonius asked his interlocutor to address the following questions regarding the monastic life:

> Now explain to me: what is that gathering or faction of monks (*monachorum congregatio vel secta*), and why are they despised, even by our own people? Certainly, if they are engaged in honourable pursuits and are not violating the unity of the faith, they ought to be imitated, rather than avoided. As I see it, it is a crime and a sin in the eyes of God to hate good people and not to avoid wicked people.[26]

In response to Apollonius' query, Zacchaeus replied that the problem lay not with the monastic life itself, for 'the profession is irreproachable and holy'. The trouble is that 'under the cover of this way of life, some people commit deeds worthy of hate' (3.3.5). Zacchaeus proceeded to specify what kinds of acts had led many Christians to hold monks in contempt. He said that some monks used their way of life as a pretext to gain access to women in order to deprive them of their wealth or chastity (3.3.6).[27] Others began their monastic life with integrity, but gradually lost their resolve and returned to a more relaxed way of life. When they did so, they started to criticize the stricter way of life and to praise the more common way in order to justify themselves (3.3.7).[28] But most practitioners of the monastic life, the author of the *Consultationes* insisted, were faithful to their resolve and guilty of neither of

---

[25] *Zacch.* 3.1.13 (SC 402, 168). Claussen, 'Pagan Rebellion', 603–6, has demonstrated that the *Consultationes* were written at least partly as an attempt to mediate in the conflict between Jovinian and Jerome. Cf. Feiertag (SC 401, 28), who has observed, 'l'anonyme corrige les excès de ceux qui dénigrent le mariage: pour sa part, il en réaffirme la bonté, et surtout enseigne l'existence d'une *castitas* particulière dans le mariage contrairement au *Contre Jovinien*.' Feiertag, however, places the author of the *Consultationes* in the entourage of Sulpicius Severus sometime after Alaric's sack of Rome in 410.

[26] *Zacch.* 3.3.1–2 (SC 402, 178).

[27] Jerome, *ep.* 22.28.1–2 (CSEL 54, 185) stated a similar criticism of monks; cf. Claussen, 'Pagan Rebellion', 594.

[28] As Claussen, 'Pagan Rebellion', 594, has observed, the description of the second group of monks sounds much like Ambrose's account of Sarmatio and Barbatianus, two followers of Jovinian whom Ambrose attacked in *ep. extra collectionem* 14.7.

these defects. The entire 'order' of monks, therefore, should not be rejected because of the misdeeds of a few (3.3.8).

The presence of this apology for monasticism in the midst of the more general apologetic arguments of the *Conversations of Zacchaeus and Apollonius* indicates that by the late fourth century the monastic life had become something of a stumbling block, both to prospective pagan converts to Christianity and to many Christians. As a defender of monasticism, the author of the *Consultationes* tried to put the best face on the situation. He provided two possible explanations of Christian resistance to asceticism, both of which acknowledged that there were problems with the movement. Although the author of the *Consultationes* wished to vindicate the monastic life, the very need for a defence indicates that opposition to monasticism was widespread, not least among the Christians themselves.

Other texts indicate that it was not so much lapsed monks and failed ascetics who caused scandal, but rather the way in which ascetic renunciation contradicted the established values of the aristocratic elite in late antique culture. In the passage from Rutilius Namatianus cited above, it was the rejection of noble birth, wealth, and advantageous marriage—the central values of aristocratic culture—that so outraged the pagan poet. Similar objections are found in Christian sources. In the year 395, for example, when Paulinus of Nola, a man of senatorial rank and a wealthy landowner from Bordeaux, embarked on an ascetic life with his wife Therasia, the response of their Christian peers may have been much the same as that of Rutilius. Ambrose of Milan described the response he anticipated to their renunciation: 'What will our leading citizens say when they hear this? It is unthinkable that a man of such family, such background, such genius, gifted with such eloquence, should retire from the Senate and that the succession of so noble a family should be broken.'[29] From Paulinus' own letters we know that his renunciation initially received a tepid response, especially from the clergy at Rome. A few years later Jerome could assume that the senator Pammachius would be subjected to ridicule for laying aside the dignified insignia of his rank and appearing in public in monastic garb.[30]

Early in his episcopate, Ambrose also was subjected to criticism for encouraging young women to undertake a life of consecrated virginity. The opposition emerged from within his own congregation at Milan, apparently from the more well-to-do citizens. In his treatise *Concerning Virginity*, composed in 378, Ambrose illustrated some of the common Christian objections

[29] Ambrose, *ep.* 27[58].3 (CSEL 82.1, 181); trans. Beyenka, 144.
[30] See Paulinus, *ep.* 5.12–14 (CSEL 29, 32–4), with the observations of Dennis Trout, *Paulinus of Nola: Life, Letters, and Poems* (Berkeley: University of California Press, 1999), 113–15; and Jerome, *ep.* 66.6 (CSEL 54, 654).

to the ascetic life, especially when it was adopted by marriageable young women. Some people regarded it as 'shameful' (*indignum*) that a woman should renounce marriage; others considered the practice too 'novel' (*novum*) or 'useless' (*inutile*).[31] The complaints presented by Ambrose reflect the concerns of upper-class Christians, who saw the adoption of celibacy as a threat to the continued vitality of civic life. As Ambrose put it: 'I have heard a number of people say that the world is perishing, that the human race is shrinking, that marriage is in decline.... They say that it has become more difficult for young men to contract marriages.'[32] The objections to asceticism reported by Ambrose indicate that some members of his congregation shared the same concerns as the pagan critics of the monastic life.

Ambrose tried to deflect these complaints by arguing that virginity did, indeed, have social value. Populations are largest in those places where virginity thrives, he claimed. Alexandria, Africa, and 'all the East' have large communities of virgins and a thriving population. Moreover, Ambrose contended, 'the practice of the entire world shows that virginity should not be considered "useless", especially since it was through a virgin that salvation came to bring life to the Roman world.'[33] One suspects that Ambrose's arguments would have fallen largely on deaf ears, for the theological character of his response would have failed to meet the essentially civic nature of his opponents' complaints. Many Christians in Ambrose's congregation remained committed to the traditional understanding of marriage and procreation as civic duties, inextricably linked to the welfare of the community.[34] The adoption of celibacy and other forms of ascetic renunciation appeared to such Christians to be a threat to the foundations of civilized society.

The letters of Jerome further illustrate how the profession of the ascetic or monastic life at times provoked outrage among the elite citizens of Rome, Christian as well as pagan. In his eulogy for Marcella, who was one of the first noble women at Rome to embrace the ascetic life around the year 360, Jerome recalled that 'back then no noble woman had undertaken the monastic

---

[31] *Virgin.* 26–8; text in Franco Gori (ed.), *Verginità e Vedovanza* ii (SAEMO 14.2; Milan: Biblioteca Ambrosiana/Rome: Città Nuova Editrice, 1989), 30–2.

[32] *Virgin.* 35 and 38 (Gori 2, 36 and 38). See the discussion in McLynn, *Ambrose of Milan*, 61–2: 'Much in Ambrose's message, and especially in the style in which it was conveyed was new to northern Italy. Female asceticism was not foreign to the region, but the prevailing pattern was for domestic, ancillary arrangements.... Ambrose's innovation was to parade the commitment of the daughters of his well-to-do parishioners in public.'

[33] *Virgin.* 36 (Gori 2, 38).

[34] Ambrose's critics may have been responding to an actual population decrease in the later years of the fourth century. See Charles Pietri, 'Le mariage chrétien à Rome', in Jean Delumeau (ed.), *Histoire vécue du peuple chrétien* (Paris: Privat, 1979), 105–31, esp. 107–8; and A. H. M. Jones, *The Later Roman Empire 284–602: A Social Economic and Administrative Survey* (Norman, OK: University of Oklahoma Press, 1964), ii. 1040–5.

profession (*propositum monachorum*) or dared to adopt the name, which at the time was considered so vile and disgraceful on account of the novelty of the thing'.[35] Christian converts to the ascetic life, especially among the aristocracy, were sometimes regarded as 'insane' because they had chosen to renounce the wealth and comforts of their station. According to Jerome, a 'friend' once informed the widow Paula that many people considered her to be 'mad' (*insana*) because of her excessive piety; perhaps, the friend suggested, 'she ought to have her head examined' (*cerebrum illius... confovendum*).[36] A Christian who openly practised asceticism, Jerome tells us, was likely to be called a 'Greek' or an 'imposter' (ὁ Γραικός, ὁ ἐπιθέτης) for repudiating the established values of Roman aristocratic society.[37]

In at least one instance the excessive austerities of the monastic life appear to have proven fatal to a young woman of the aristocracy. In the autumn of 384 Jerome composed a letter to Paula, consoling her on the death of her daughter Blesilla, who died most likely as a result of the ascetic regimen she had adopted under the tutelage of Jerome. In this letter Jerome claimed that the untimely death of the young widow had nearly provoked a violent reaction against monks at Rome. Such was the outrage expressed by Christians at Rome: 'Is not this what we have often said? She weeps for her daughter killed by fasting. She wanted her to marry again so that she might have grandchildren. How long must we refrain from driving these detestable monks out of the city? Why do we not stone them or throw them into the river?'[38]

Within a year Jerome was, in fact, driven from the city of Rome. Writing on board ship at Ostia, while waiting to depart, Jerome described again (with more than a hint of self-pity) the widespread Christian hostility to the ascetic life. Noting that rumours had circulated regarding his friendship with Paula and other ascetic women, Jerome complained that he had been undermined by Christian opposition to ascetic renunciation: 'If it were Gentiles or Jews who attacked their mode of life, they would at least have the consolation of failing to please only those whom Christ himself failed to please. But now, alas, it is those who bear the name "Christian" who neglect the care of their own households and disregard the beam in their own eyes, while looking for a mote in the eyes of their neighbours.'[39]

---

[35] *Ep.* 127.5 (CSEL 56, 149).
[36] Jerome, *ep.* 108.19 (CSEL 55, 333). Cf. *ep.* 23.3 (CSEL 54, 213), where Lea's life is described as *amentia*.
[37] *Ep.* 54.5 (CSEL 54, 470); cf. *ep.* 38.5 (CSEL 54, 293): 'inpostor et Graecus est.'
[38] *Ep.* 39.6 (CSEL 54, 306).   [39] *Ep.* 45.4 (CSEL 54, 326).

The highly rhetorical character of Jerome's complaints about Christian opposition to asceticism should make us cautious. We may be dealing here with a literary *topos*.[40] By stressing the opposition engendered by asceticism, Jerome could portray his female heroines in the guise of early Christian martyrs; conversely, their Christian opponents could be represented as essentially like pagan persecutors in their conduct. Nevertheless, the numerous and varied complaints against the monastic life that we have cited thus far, especially those that reflect *Christian* criticism of monasticism, indicate that there must have been some social reality behind Jerome's rhetoric. Many Christians, especially among the aristocracy, would have held the same prejudices against asceticism that non-Christians did. Ascetic renunciation would have appeared to be a 'novelty', a rejection of the material benefits of civilized society, and a repudiation of traditional loyalties to family, class, and culture.

In the next section of this chapter, I will explore further the social context out of which these criticisms emerged. The resistance to asceticism and monasticism that we find reflected in the writings of Jerome, Ambrose, and their contemporaries was so acute because by the 380s there already existed at Rome a well-established aristocratic Christianity. By the end of the fourth century, Christian aristocrats at Rome had already developed a synthesis of traditional pagan and Christian values that included respect for marriage and family. The presence of this alternative vision of Christian identity provided a context in which there would have been many Christians who were receptive to the perspectives of Jovinian and hostile to those of Jerome.

ii. 'A Christian aristocratic culture'

Recent research on pagans and Christians in the late Roman aristocracy has documented how quickly some senatorial families switched their allegiance from paganism to Christianity at the accession of the emperor Constantine and his sons.[41] It is true that the majority of the senatorial families probably

---

[40] For this argument see Hagith Sivan, 'On Hymens and Holiness in Late Antiquity: Opposition to Aristocratic Female Asceticism at Rome', *JAC* 36 (1993), 81–93.

[41] Typical of this perspective are D. M. Novak, 'Constantine and the Senate: An Early Phase of the Christianization of the Roman Aristocracy', *Ancient Society*, 10 (1979), 271–310; and T. D. Barnes, 'Christians and Pagans in the Reign of Constantius', in A. Dihle (ed.), *L'Église et l'empire au IVe siècle* (Entretiens sur l'antiquité classique, 34; Geneva: Vandoeuvres, 1989), 302–37. The foundational study is that of Peter Brown, 'Aspects of the Christianization of the Roman Aristocracy', in his *Religion and Society in the Age of Saint Augustine* (London: Faber and Faber, 1972), 161–82. On all of these questions, see now Michele Salzman, *The Making of a Christian Aristocracy: Social and Religious Change in the Western Roman Empire* (Cambridge, Mass.: Harvard University Press, 2002). Salzman, however, doubts that the impact of imperial initiative was as influential in the conversion of the aristocracy as Barnes and others have claimed.

remained pagan until the end of the fourth century. Moreover, Roman senators also were at the centre of significant resistance to Christianization in the last two decades of the fourth century, although the question of the extent of this so-called 'pagan revival' of the 390s has been much disputed.[42] Nevertheless, it is indisputable that Christianity had produced significant converts among the senatorial families from the earliest years of the fourth century. Therefore, it is no exaggeration to say that already during the reigns of Constantine and his sons a 'Christian aristocratic culture' had begun to develop.[43]

Evidence of the Christianization of the Roman aristocracy in the early fourth century is available from a variety of sources. Members of distinguished senatorial families, such as the *Anicii* and the *Petronii*, had become Christian as early as the reign of Constantine. Some female members of these families converted even earlier.[44] Although pagans were by no means excluded from high office under Constantine and his sons, there was a decided preference for Christian appointees in some offices, such as that of consul and praetorian prefect. Even the prestigious office of prefect of the city of Rome was bestowed by Constantine upon Christians, although pagans continued to dominate the office for several more decades.[45]

The cumulative effect of aristocratic Christian conversion and the promotion of Christians to high office was the creation of a new Christian aristocracy. Already by the middle of the fourth century we find Christian aristocrats at Rome who are virtually indistinguishable from their pagan contemporaries in devotion to public life and traditional civic values. The famous sarcophagus of Junius Bassus will help to illustrate this point. Bassus died in 359, while

---

[42] Stressing the persistence of pagans, especially in the senatorial aristocracy, is A. H. M. Jones, 'The Social Background of the Struggle between Paganism and Christianity', in A. Momigliano (ed.), *The Conflict between Paganism and Christianity in the Fourth Century* (Oxford: Clarendon Press, 1963), 17–37; R. MacMullen, *Christianizing the Roman Empire. A.D. 100–400* (New Haven and London: Yale University Press, 1984).

[43] I have taken the phrase, 'a Christian aristocratic culture', from Novak, 'Constantine and the Senate', 306. For an argument similar to the one I have developed here, see John R. Curran, *Pagan City and Christian Capital: Rome in the Fourth Century* (Oxford: Clarendon Press, 2000), 260–320.

[44] Novak, 'Constantine and the Senate', 299; J. W. Drijvers, 'Virginity and Asceticism in Late Roman Elites', in J. Bolk and P. Mason (eds.), *Sexual Asymmetry: Studies in Ancient Society* (Amsterdam: J. C. Gieben, 1987), 241–2. Evidence for pre-Constantinian senators is assembled in W. Eck, 'Das Eindringen des Christentums in den Senatorenstand bis zu Konstantin d. Gr.', *Chiron*, 1 (1971), 381–406.

[45] The percentage of Christian to pagan office holders in the years 317–361 is calculated by Barnes, 'Christians and Pagans', 315–21; for the urban prefecture, see A. Chastagnol, *La Préfecture urbaine à Rome sous le Bas-empire* (Paris: Presses Universitaires de France, 1960), 454. Salzman concludes that pagan officeholders remained in the majority until the early 390s: *Making of a Christian Aristocracy*, 77–80, 116–24.

holding the office of prefect of the city of Rome; he had been baptized, probably on his deathbed. His father, however, also named Junius Bassus, was almost certainly a Christian. The elder Bassus held the office of consul under Constantine and had built a basilica on the Esquiline hill out of his own personal fortune.[46]

The younger Bassus commissioned for himself a sarcophagus that was 'as sophisticated and classical in design as that of any of his pagan fellow-aristocrats'.[47] The sarcophagus is a stellar example of the fourth-century Christian tendency to take traditional 'pagan' symbols and fuse them into a new Christian synthesis.[48] For example, representations of the triumphal entry and enthronement of Christ, which occupy the two central panels of the sarcophagus, are sculpted according to traditional Roman models. Scenes that in another context would be considered 'pagan'—the *klinê* meal and the harvesting of wine, wheat, olives, and other fruits—are relegated to the lid and side panels, and thus are subordinated to the biblical scenes which dominate the facade. As Elizabeth Struthers Malbon has observed,

The traditional scenes and verse inscription of the lid portray a man proud to be a Roman; the biblical scenes and the Christian inscription of the façade suggest a man secure in his Christian faith; the end scenes, with the 'pagan' models and their Christian allusions, point to a man not of two competing worlds—'pagan' and Christian—but of one world, a Christianized Roman world, in which all things have their time and place—including Junius Bassus.[49]

Another notable example of the emergence of a new Christian aristocracy is the career of the Roman aristocrat Sextus Claudius Petronius Probus, whom John Matthews has described as 'the most spectacularly successful of all Christian politicians of the age'.[50] Probably a third-generation Christian, Probus held numerous public offices during the second half of the fourth century, including four praetorian prefectures. According to Ammianus Marcellinus, whenever Probus was out of office he was like a fish out of

---

[46] *PLRE* 1, 154–5.

[47] Richard Krautheimer, *Rome: Profile of a City, 312–1308* (Princeton, NJ: Princeton University Press, 1980), 39.

[48] For this point and much of this paragraph, I am indebted to Elizabeth Struthers Malbon, *The Iconography of the Sarcophagus of Junius Bassus* (Princeton, NJ: Princeton University Press, 1990), 136–53.

[49] Malbon, *Iconography*, 149; cf. Curran, *Pagan City*, 268, who notes that Bassus' funeral was a highly public affair: 'grief was widespread and a huge crowd of citizens, from senators to the city's *matres*, turned out to pay their respects.' As Curran has observed, 292–3, both the Bassus sarcophagus and the Probus inscription were placed in St. Peter's basilica, thus attesting to their strong identification with the Christian community at Rome.

[50] Matthews, *Western Aristocracies*, 195. An excellent introduction to Probus can be found in D. M. Novak, '*Anicianae domus culmen, nobilitatis culmen*', *Klio*, 62 (1980), 473–93.

water (27.11). After marrying into the distinguished *Anicii* family, Probus and his wife, Anicia Faltonia Proba, produced a daughter and four sons, two of whom served as consuls together in 395.[51] In addition to these secular honours, as Dennis Trout has recently observed, 'the couple's Christianity was a public affair: Probus patronized the Milanese ecclesiastical career of Ambrose, while Proba eventually became a correspondent of both Augustine and John Chrysostom'.[52]

The career of Probus illustrates well the emergence of a Christian governing class that was at home with both its religious convictions and its continued commitment to traditional civic and public life. Ammianus, who was hostile to Probus, states that he was known 'for the distinction of his family, his influence, and his great wealth, throughout the whole Roman world, in almost all parts of which he possessed estates here and there, whether justly or unjustly is not a question for my humble judgement'.[53] On a more positive note, an inscription carved by some of Probus' Italian clients portrayed him as the epitome of civic virtue: 'chief of the nobility, light of letters and eloquence, model of authority, master of foresight and management, fountain of philanthropy, advocate of moderation, chief priest of devotion'.[54]

But Probus was also a Christian, and the epitaph from his own mausoleum, composed around the year 390, suggests that he possessed an equally serious (if rhetorically exaggerated) Christian piety:

> Previously you rejoiced in the honor of the royal table, in the emperor's ear and the friendship of royalty. Now, closer to Christ after attaining the abode of the saints, you enjoy a new light. Christ is present as your light.... While you were alive and the breath of life governed these limbs of yours, you were foremost and second to none of the senators in virtue. Now, renewed you have eternal rest and you wear gleaming white garments darkened by no sin, and are a new dweller in unaccustomed mansions.[55]

As John Matthews has noted, 'the epitaph almost persuades us that Probus has simply received yet another promotion in his political career'.[56] But it was

---

[51] *PLRE* 1, 736–40; Croke and Harries, *Religious Conflict*, 115–17. The sons, Anicius Hermogenianus Olybrius and Anicius Probinus, received a panegyric from Claudian. See Alan Cameron, *Claudian: Poetry and Propaganda at the Court of Honorius* (Oxford: Clarendon Press, 1970), 30–6.

[52] 'The Verse Epitaph(s) of Petronius Probus: Competitive Commemoration in Late-Fourth-Century Rome', *New England Classical Journal*, 28 (2001), 160. I am grateful to Professor Trout for making this essay available to me.

[53] *Res gestae* 27.11.1; trans. John C. Rolfe (LCL; Cambridge, Mass.: Harvard University Press, 1950) iii.73–5. Ammianus despised Probus, whom he accused of ruinous greed, ambition, and cruelty. See also *Res gestae* 30.5.4–10. Jerome, *Chron. ad 372*, issued a similar critique of Probus.

[54] *CIL* 6.1751; trans. Croke and Harries, *Religious Conflict*, 115–16.

[55] *CIL* 6.1756; trans. Croke and Harries, *Religious Conflict*, 117.

[56] Matthews, *Western Aristocracies*, 195.

precisely Probus' easy passage from the earthly to the heavenly kingdom that epitomized the new Christian aristocratic culture that had taken shape by the end of the fourth century.

It may even be the case, as Dennis Trout has recently argued, that Probus' epitaph was formulated specifically to articulate an 'alliance of tradition and innovation' at a time when relations between (and within) the pagan and Christian communities at Rome were particularly fractious. Half of the Probus epitaph focused on his secular honours; the other half emphasized the transition to heavenly rewards as a result of his Christian baptism. According to Trout, the two-part epitaph of Probus was both a response to contemporary pagan *elogia* (that attributed similar divine honours to pagan office holders) and a rebuff to ascetically minded Christians, 'who were challenging the very bases of Probus's claims to rank and status'.[57] Probus' epitaph, which may have been composed under the supervision of his wife, Anicia Faltonia Proba, was, in Trout's words, a 'final act of aristocratic self-assertion', in which Probus and his wife vigorously defended the traditional triad of elite goods—wealth, marriage, and *honores*—against the encroachment of Christian asceticism.[58]

The Romanized Christian culture (or Christianized Roman culture) of men such as Petronius Probus and Junius Bassus appears to have been well-established by the middle of the fourth century. Pagans and Christians, at least among the aristocracy, received a common rhetorical education, nourished similar ambitions for their children, and sometimes even shared a common burial ground. A stunning visual example of the latter is evident in the catacomb on the Via Latina, discovered in the 1950s. This catacomb, containing the tombs of several large noble families, includes an elaborate series of paintings dated to the years 320–350. Frescoes depicting pagan heroes in one room are juxtaposed with those of Christian heroes in another. Adam and Eve, Jonah and Daniel, Susanna and Jesus, among others, take their place next to Tellus and Medusa, Alcestis and Hercules.[59] Once thought to be an example of 'frank syncretism', it now seems more likely that the Via Latina catacomb contains the tombs of pagans and Christians from the same family. Family members had their own cubicula decorated according to their particular religious beliefs. The coexistence of pagan and Christian images side by side in this necropolis suggests that pagans and Christians at Rome lived

---

[57] Trout, 'Verse Epitaph(s)', 160.   [58] Trout, 'Verse Epitaph(s)', 176.
[59] Described and interpreted by A. Ferrua, *The Unknown Catacomb: A Unique Discovery of Early Christian Art*, trans. Iain Inglis (Florence: Nardini, 1990), 59–152.

together more or less amicably in the mid-fourth century, at least among the upper classes.⁶⁰

The Codex Calendar of 354 is yet further evidence of the coexistence and mutual accommodation of pagans and Christians that facilitated the formation of a Christian aristocratic culture. This remarkable document, illustrated by the Christian calligrapher Furius Dionysius Filocalus (later epigrapher to Pope Damasus), was a gift to a wealthy Christian aristocrat named Valentinus. The calendar contained lists of Roman emperors, consuls, urban prefects, and the traditional pagan holidays; it also included a list of the bishops of Rome, together with the dates of their deaths, as well as the earliest known cycle of Christian martyr feasts. As Michele Salzman has observed, the interweaving of pagan and Christian sections within the Codex Calendar suggests that its compiler was quite confident in the compatibility between Christian and Roman traditions: 'Christianity appears to be neither alien nor repugnant to the cultural forms and institutions of Rome; on the contrary, it seems strikingly familiar and respectable, a quality that would only facilitate its acceptance by conservative aristocratic Romans.'⁶¹

The emergence of a cultivated Christian aristocracy at Rome in the fourth century meant that there would have been many Christians who were as deeply committed to literary culture, civic life, and the traditional Roman family as any of their non-Christian contemporaries. Perhaps the clearest literary illustration of this synthesis of aristocratic and Christian values is the famous Virgilian cento, *De laudibus Christi*, sometimes ascribed to Faltonia Betitia Proba. This curious document is a poem on the creation of the world and the life of Jesus, consisting entirely of lines plucked from Vergil's *Aeneid*. An oddity by modern standards, Proba's cento illustrates the efforts of one late Roman *matrona* to express the tenets of her faith, while at the same time reverently preserving the traditional forms of Latin literature.⁶²

Unfortunately, there is no consensus in current scholarly literature regarding the precise identity of the centonist Proba. Faltonia Betitia Proba, to

---

⁶⁰ Peter Brown, 'Aspects of the Christianization of the Roman Aristocracy', 179; Ferrua, *Unknown Catacomb*, 158–9. For recent discussion, see Beverly Berg, 'Alcestis and Hercules in the Catacomb of the Via Latina', *VC* 48 (1994), 219–34; Mark Johnson, Pagan-Christian Burial Practices of the Fourth Century: Shared Tombs?' *JECS* 5 (1997), 37–59; and H. Gregory Snyder, 'Pictures in Dialogue: A Viewer-Centered Approach to the Hypogeum on Via Dino Compagni', *JECS* 13 (2005), 349–86.

⁶¹ Salzman, *On Roman Time*, 58.

⁶² R. A. Markus, 'Paganism, Christianity and the Latin Classics in the Fourth Century', in J. W. Binns (ed.), *Latin Literature of the Fourth Century* (London and Boston: Routledge and Kegan Paul, 1974), 3. The text is edited with an English translation and extensive commentary by Elizabeth A. Clark and Diana F. Hatch, *The Golden Bough. The Oaken Cross: The Virgilian Cento of Faltonia Betitia Proba* (AAR Texts and Translations, 5; Chico, CA: Scholars Press, 1981).

whom the work was traditionally ascribed, was a member of the prominent *Petronii* family, an aunt of the Sextus Petronius Probus mentioned above. If she was the author, she would have composed the cento sometime between 353 and her death around the year 370.[63] Danuta Shanzer, however, has argued that Anicia Faltonia Proba, wife of Sextus Petronius Probus, was the author of the cento. In her estimation, *De laudibus Christi* should be dated around the years 388–390.[64] Yet another possibility is that the earlier Proba was the primary author, but that a later editor (almost certainly Anicia Faltonia Proba) expanded the poem and added a dedication to the emperor Arcadius in 395.[65]

Whichever Proba authored or edited the cento, the work provides a glimpse into the world of aristocratic Christian piety and reveals something of the culture of 'assimilation and accommodation' that was widespread in Rome by the late fourth century. The Christian poetess retold the biblical stories from the perspective of a Roman matron who was decidedly devoted to traditional domestic and social values. Indeed, as Elizabeth Clark and Diane Hatch have noted, in contrast to the ascetic piety that had already begun to influence some Western aristocrats in the 360s, 'there is not a single verse in the 694 lines of Proba's cento which as much as hints that she believed asceticism to be the superior mode of Christian life'. On the contrary, filial piety, maternal devotion, and marital harmony are the themes that dominate Proba's discourse.[66]

For example, in her treatment of the early chapters of Genesis, Proba described the formation of Eve from Adam's side in terms that fused the Christian narrative of creation with imagery drawn from the Roman ritual of marriage:

> The Almighty Sire laid the ribs and entrails bare.
> One of these ribs he plucked apart from

---

[63] For a defence of Faltonia Betitia Proba as the author of *De laudibus Christi*, see John Matthews, 'The Poetess Proba and Fourth-Century Rome: Questions of Interpretation', in Michel Christol, et al. (eds.), *Institutions, société et vie politique dans l'empire romain au IVe siècle ap. J.-C.* (Paris: École Française de Rome, 1992), 277–304.

[64] Danuta Shanzer, 'The Anonymous *Carmen contra paganos* and the Date and Identity of the Centonist Proba', *REAug* 32 (1986), 232–48; and 'The Date and Identity of the Centonist Proba', *RechAug* 27 (1994), 75–96. The latter essay responds to the critique of Matthews, cited in the previous note.

[65] For this theory, see Hagith Sivan, 'The Cento of Proba and Aristocratic Conversion in the Fourth Century', *VC* 47 (1993), 140–57.

[66] Clark and Hatch, *The Golden Bough*, 111. For this last point and much of the following discussion, I am indebted to this fine study. See also Anne Jensen, 'Faltonia Betitia Proba—eine Kirchenlehrerin der Spätantike', in H. Pissarek-Hudelist and L. Schottroff (eds.), *Mit allen Sinnen glauben: feministische Theologie unterwegs* (Gütersloh: Gütersloher Verlag-Haus Mohn, 1991), 84–94.

> The well-knit joints of youthful Adam's side,
> And suddenly arose a wondrous gift—
> Imposing proof—and shone in brilliant light:
> Woman, a virgin she, unparalleled
> In figure and in comely breasts, now ready
> For a husband, ready now for wedlock.
> For him, a boundless quaking breaks his sleep;
> He calls his bones and limbs his wedded wife.
> Dazed by the Will divine he took and clasped
> Her hand in his, folded his arms around her.[67]

Proba has portrayed Adam taking Eve's hand in the familiar Roman marriage ritual known as the *dextrarum iunctio*, the joining of the right hands. This gesture, which represented the moment at which the bride passed from the authority of her father to that of her husband, was a traditional Roman symbol of *concordia* or the harmony of an ideal marriage. In Proba's poem this traditional symbol was retextualized within the biblical narrative of the divine origins of creation, thus implicitly providing divine sanction for the Roman institution of marriage.[68]

Later in the poem Proba also retold some of the Gospel stories about Jesus. In her rendering, Jesus did not command the rich young man to abandon all his possessions and to follow his lord. Rather, he was enjoined 'to despise riches... and to know what virtue is', to extend his hand to the unfortunate and not to desert a brother. Above all, the rich young man was exhorted to 'let his chaste household preserve its sense of modesty': *casta pudicitiam servet domus*.[69] It is significant that for Proba, the terms 'chastity' (*castitas*) and 'modesty' (*pudicitia*) did not bear the rigorous overtones that they carried in Christian ascetical literature. Rather, these were the normal descriptors of traditional marital virtues, often represented on Roman funeral monuments and in literary sources.[70] In general, as John Curran has observed, 'Proba's cento reflects the deep desire for social stability founded upon the virtues of

---

[67] *Laud. Chr.* 128–35; trans. Clark and Hatch, *The Golden Bough*, 29.

[68] G. Williams, 'Some Aspects of Roman Marriage Ceremonies and Ideals', *JRS* 48 (1958), 16–29; L. Reekmans, 'La *dextrarum iunctio* dans l'iconographie romaine et paléochrétienne', *Bulletin de l'Institut historique belge de Rome*, 31 (1958), 23–95. An aristocratic couple might receive a wedding gift inscribed with the *dextrarum iunctio*, such as a gold glass bowl, ring, or marriage belt. See E. H. Kantorowicz, 'On the Golden Marriage Belt and the Marriage Rings of the Dumbarton Oaks Collection', *DOP* 14 (1960), 1–16. A gold glass bowl with the *dextrarum iunctio* and the Christian blessing, 'Vivatis in deo', can be found in the collection of the Metropolitan Museum of Art, New York. See K. Weitzmann (ed.), *Age of Spirituality: Late Antique and Early Christian Art* (New York: Metropolitan Museum, 1979), 282–3.

[69] *Laud. Chr.* 522–6.

[70] See S. Treggiari, *Roman Marriage: Iusti Coniuges from the Time of Cicero to the Time of Ulpian* (Oxford: Clarendon Press, 1991), 232–6.

respect for parents and kin, the sanctity of the home and marital chastity.'[71] Proba's cento has incorporated these traditional virtues into a piety that is at once explicitly Christian and traditionally Roman.

The extent of Proba's commitment to this synthesis of Christian and Roman values can be gauged by the concluding lines of the poem in which she exhorted her unnamed husband to remain faithful to the rites of his new religion:

> ... hunc ipse teneto,
> o dulcis coniunx, et si pietate meremur,
> hac casti maneant in religione nepotes.
>
> This observance do you keep, O husband sweet,
> And if we do win merit through our piety,
> Then pure in heart may our children's children keep the Faith.[72]

This parting prayer of Proba (whichever Proba she was) was not to remain unanswered. The children of both the elder and the younger Proba continued to serve the city as consuls, prefects, and senators. Most importantly, they remained *in religione*, thereby facilitating the transition from pagan to Christian within the late Roman aristocracy.[73]

The poetry of Proba helps to shed light on the social world in which Jovinian issued his criticism of ascetic elitism. Although Proba had articulated the values of an elite aristocratic culture, her traditional piety regarding marriage and family may have been more typical of the average Christian at Rome than was the ascetic enthusiasm of Jerome.[74] Moreover, since Anicia Faltonia Proba was almost certainly responsible for the edition of the cento presented to emperor Arcadius in 395 (even if she was not its author), the cento of Proba can be read as an aristocratic Christian rebuff of ascetic piety at Rome in the immediate aftermath of Jovinian's condemnation at Rome. Jerome himself may have suggested as much around the year 395 in a letter to Paulinus of Nola, when he referred to several rival interpreters of scripture, among whom was the unnamed author of the cento. In this letter Jerome

---

[71] Curran, *Pagan City*, 284.

[72] *Laud. Chr.* 692–4; trans. Clark and Hatch, 95.

[73] The elder Proba's husband was Clodius Celsinus Adelphius (*PLRE* 1, 192–3), who served as urban prefect in 351. Their sons were Q. Clodius Hermogenianus Olybrius and Faltonius Probus Alypius. Olybrius (*PLRE* 1, 640–2) served as proconsul of Africa (361), urban prefect (369–370), and consul (379). His daughter was the younger Proba, Anicia Faltonia Proba, who was married to Sextus Petronius Probus. Alypius (*PLRE* 1, 49) was urban prefect in 391. Two sons of Anicia Faltonia Proba and Sextus Petronius Probus (Anicius Hermogenianus Olybrius and Anicius Probinus) served as joint consuls in 395.

[74] Cf. the comments of Salzman, *Making of a Christian Aristocracy*, 163, who suggests that Proba illustrates 'the typical woman's response to Christianity in the fourth century'.

characterized Proba as 'a chattering old hag' (*garrula anus*).[75] Jerome's antagonism reveals the extent to which the perspectives of Proba and her cento represented a challenge to his own ascetic vision at Rome.

In the light of these anti-ascetic tendencies within the Christian aristocracy at Rome, there are good reasons to regard Jovinian's views on marriage and celibacy as directed especially towards Christian aristocrats at Rome, and perhaps toward potential aristocratic converts to Christianity as well. We know that Jovinian's original writings had circulated among upper-class Christians at Rome. Pope Siricius indicated in his letter of condemnation that Jovinian's works had been brought to his attention by 'the most faithful Christians, men of the highest lineage (*viris genere optimis*), distinguished for religion'.[76] As we saw above, one of these Roman aristocrats was probably the senator Pammachius, who later conveyed to Jerome his criticisms of the *Adversus Jovinianum*. Moreover, a number of Jovinian's arguments seem designed to appeal to aristocratic values. His use of secular literature, for example, and his reference to the patriotic motivation for marriage both cohere with the concerns expressed by late Roman aristocrats, both pagan and Christian.[77]

But perhaps the most revealing evidence of Jovinian's aristocratic appeal and support can be found in the closing lines of *Adversus Jovinianum*, where Jerome employed all the devices of rhetorical exaggeration to satirize Jovinian's success among the cultured Christian aristocrats of Rome. Jerome spoke of Jovinian's 'many disciples' (*multos discipulos*) and likened them to the crowd that shouted 'Crucify him, crucify him' at Jesus' trial. Jovinian had assembled a following of many pigs, Jerome asserted, fattening them to provide pork for hell![78] In the course of this rhetoric of abuse, Jerome suggested that many of Jovinian's supporters came from the elite members of the city's Christian community: 'You have in your army many underlings, you have dandies and foot-soldiers in your garrison: the fat, the neatly dressed, the elegant, the noisy orators who defend you with tooth and claw. The nobles make way for you in the street, the wealthy plant kisses on your head—for if you had not come, drunkards and gluttons would not have entered paradise!'[79]

Although Jerome's description of Jovinian's supporters is full of rhetorical excess, it is likely to contain a kernel of truth. Jerome knew well the social

---

[75] *Ep.* 53.7 (CSEL 54, 453). Although Jerome did not mention Proba by name in this letter, he did cite several passages from *De laudibus Christi*.
[76] *Ep.* 7.5 (CSEL 82.3, 300).
[77] See *Jov.* 1.4 and 41 (secular literature), 1.36 (marriage and civic patriotism).
[78] *Jov.* 2.36 (PL 23, 349).   [79] *Jov.* 2.37 (PL 23, 351).

circles in which Jovinian moved and to which he addressed his message of moderation. Jovinian's preaching certainly would have found a receptive audience among those aristocratic Christians, whose commitment to Christianity entailed their continuing loyalty to the values of their class and culture. Such Christians, as we have seen, were numerous in late fourth-century Rome. While Jerome accused them of moral decadence, his very vehemence underscored their prominence in the city and their claim to represent an alternative Christian tradition.

It may even be possible to specify more precisely the environment in which Jovinian propagated his teachings. Harry O. Maier has explored how aristocratic households at Rome were a prime context in which ideas circulated that were likely to be disturbing to ecclesiastical authorities.[80] Maier pointed to Jovinian and his supporters, along with Montanists and Manichaeans, as those who thrived in such 'private space':

> Behind Jerome's exaggerated depiction of his opponent as the 'Epicurus of Christianity' who promotes sexual intercourse and surrounds himself with bare-breasted Amazons one may discern a domestic network of patrons and supporters not so different from his own. As Jerome when in Rome, Jovinian visits the homes of well-to-do men and women and has won over a series of households through which he promotes his ideas.... The severe measures against Jovinian and his supporters and the energy devoted to their suppression points to the vitality of non-sanctioned ideas and movements when promoted in private space.[81]

As Maier has noted, Jovinian appears to have thrived in the very same environment in which Jerome himself (and later Pelagius) operated. The households of aristocratic men and women offered 'a competitive salon culture', in which rival views of Christianity would have been aired and disseminated.[82] Jerome's account of Jovinian's popularity among the aristocratic elite of Rome, therefore, appears to have been more than a polemical slur; it also reflected the reality of the social environment that Jerome himself knew so well.

Jovinian's activity among the households of wealthy, aristocratic Christians at Rome helps to explain not only his initial success, but also the opposition aroused by his teaching, especially from some members of the Roman clergy and from ascetic teachers such as Jerome and Ambrose. The Christian

---

[80] Maier, 'The Topography of Heresy and Dissent in Late-Fourth-Century Rome', *Historia*, 44 (1995), 232–49. See now his 'Heresy, Households, and the Disciplining of Diversity', in Virginia Burrus (ed.), *A People's History of Christianity*, ii. *Late Ancient Christianity* (Minneapolis, Minn.: Fortress Press, 2005), 213–33.

[81] Maier, 'Topography of Heresy', 241.

[82] Salzman, *Making of a Christian Aristocracy*, 138, citing K. Hopkins, 'Elite Mobility in the Roman Empire', *Past and Present* 32 (1965), 12–26.

aristocracy at Rome was becoming a powerful force, especially in the 380s and 390s. Both clergy and lay ascetics competed for the attention and financial resources of the elite citizens of Rome, especially its women.[83] Jerome's own hostility towards both the Roman clergy and his fellow ascetics, expressed vividly in his Letter 22 to Eustochium, reveals the depth of this conflict. The ascetic debates of the late fourth century, therefore, involved not only a conflict between 'ascetic' and 'anti-ascetic' parties, but also competition for the loyalties and patronage of the new Christian aristocracy. While Jovinian appears to have garnered some support within that environment, his ultimate condemnation suggests that ascetic piety (and the hierarchy fostered by ascetic elitism) eventually proved more attractive to the leadership of the Christian community than Jovinian's brand of egalitarianism.

2. ARISTOCRATIC CHRISTIANS AND ASCETIC PIETY

If, as I have argued thus far in this chapter, opposition to asceticism was widespread in the late fourth century, and if Jovinian's preaching attracted considerable support from Christians at Rome, especially among the aristocracy, we are left with some significant questions. What accounts for the attraction to ascetic renunciation that is found among some members of the Roman aristocracy, especially women? And why did the initial support that Jovinian received not shield him from ecclesiastical condemnation and, finally, exile? These two questions are interrelated, and an answer to the first will provide at least a partial solution to the second. While many Roman Christians initially greeted asceticism with criticism, the ascetic ideal gradually gained acceptance, but only on terms that were favourable to the elite culture. This development, I will argue, was to prove fatal to the cause of Jovinian.

i. Asceticism and Aristocratic Culture

One of the most striking features of the ascetic literature of the late fourth century—most notably the letters of Jerome—is the prominence therein of wealthy, aristocratic women who were drawn to the life of permanent chastity

---

[83] The reign of Damasus was widely regarded as a highpoint of such activity. See Ammianus Marcellinus, *Res gestae* 27.3.14; *C.Th.* 16.2.20, cited above in n. 11; and Jerome, *Adv. Jo. Hier.* 8 (PL 23, 377), who reported the comment of the distinguished pagan Praetextatus: 'Make me bishop of Rome, and I'll become a Christian at once!'

or celibacy, either as widows or virgins. Indeed, Jerome's very fixation on the issue of female asceticism, as well as his own dependence on the patronage of ascetic women, has led many scholars to overestimate the actual impact of asceticism on aristocratic women of the fourth century.[84] Because of the evidence of Jerome, we know much more about a handful of aristocratic female ascetics than we do about the vast majority of Christians, male or female, who remained committed to a more conventional way of life.

Moreover, the studies of Kate Cooper have now reminded us that Jerome's emphasis on the ascetic virtues of his feminine clientele relied upon a well-established literary *topos*. Jerome's adoption of the 'rhetoric of womanly influence', as Cooper has shown, may tell us more about Jerome's own struggles for authority with other men than about the actual behaviour of ascetic women.[85] Not every representation of a woman in the ancient sources gives us access to the presence or experience of 'real' women.

In the final chapters of this book I will explore further the nature of these intra-Christian conflicts over authority, particularly the rivalries between Jerome and other leaders of the Western Church. Here I wish to examine some of the social dynamics that may have lain behind Jerome's rhetoric about the ascetic conduct of aristocratic Roman women (and men). We must begin by stressing, once again, the problematic character of our most extensive primary source, the letters of Jerome. Jill Harries has articulated precisely the issue at hand:

As a literary source for the activities and attitudes of his lady patrons and friends, he is both informative and dangerous. Although ostensibly addressed to individuals, Jerome's letters were designed for a wider readership and exploited to the full accepted conventions of rhetoric and literary artifice.... Like all propagandists, he enhanced aspects of his saintly protégées most favorable to his message, while playing down or discarding facts which showed them to be more mindful of traditional obligations than he would care to admit. It is therefore the more significant that, behind the fervent affirmations of renunciation, we can still detect the tenacious presence of property and its transmission along conventional lines.[86]

---

[84] A salutary discussion of this problem can be found in Salzman, *Making of a Christian Aristocracy*, 167–70.

[85] e.g. 'Insinuations of Womanly Influence: An Aspect of the Christianization of the Roman Aristocracy', *JRS* 82 (1992), 150–64; and *The Virgin and the Bride*, 68–115. See also Elizabeth A. Clark, 'The Lady Vanishes: Dilemmas of a Feminist Historian after the "Linguistic Turn"', *CH* 67 (1998), 1–31.

[86] '"Treasure in Heaven": Property and Inheritance Among Senators of Late Rome', in Elizabeth M. Craik (ed.), *Marriage and Property* (Aberdeen: Aberdeen University Press, 1984), 55–6.

Harries refers to the fact that Jerome often obscures the ways in which aristocratic Christians in the late fourth century, even after adopting an ascetic life, remained deeply involved in the structures of aristocratic life and committed to the values of their inherited culture.

On the issue of property, for example, Harries has shown that some of the women whom Jerome extolled for their ascetic renunciation actually distributed their property in a manner that reveals their abiding concern for traditional values, such as preservation of the family fortune. According to Jerome, the widow Paula had lavished all her wealth upon the poor, even depriving her family of their inheritance: 'In what terms shall I speak of her distinguished and noble and formerly most wealthy house, whose riches have been almost entirely distributed to the poor?... She robbed her own children, and when her relatives objected, she declared that to leave them the mercy of Christ was a better inheritance.'[87] Elsewhere, however, we learn that Paula had actually transferred much of her property to her children before leaving Rome.[88] Indeed, Paula's children may have already possessed most of her deceased husband's estate, since the Roman law of intestacy favoured the claim of children over that of the wife. As a result, as Harries has noted, in matters of property 'Paula had more regard for convention than even sympathetic (but biased) observers would allow'.[89]

A similar strategy of conventional, aristocratic 'renunciation' was adopted by the widow Marcella, another of Jerome's coterie of aristocratic women. When Marcella was widowed at a young age, her own widowed mother, Albina, attempted to procure for her daughter a second marriage with the elderly senator Naeratius Cerealis. When Marcella refused, Albina respected her wishes, and the two continued to live together as widows. Albina, however, arranged for her own property to be transferred to her brother's family. Albina does not seem to have been vigorously opposed to Marcella's choice of widowed celibacy; it was the vocation that Albina had adopted for herself. But since Albina had no direct descendants, she insisted that the family property be transmitted along conventional lines. Again, as Harries has demonstrated, Albina 'was following the principles of intestate succession by which the agnates, in this case her brother's children, would be the next heirs, in default of heirs by direct descent'.[90] As the examples of both Paula and Marcella show, the practice of ascetic divestment of property could be accomplished in conformity with the aristocratic interests of family and class. Such accommodations

---

[87] Jerome, *ep.* 108.5 (CSEL 55, 310).
[88] Jerome, *ep.* 108.6 (CSEL 55, 312): 'fateor, nulla sic amauit filios, quibus, antequam proficisceretur, cuncta largita est exheredans se in terra, ut hereditatem inueniret in caelo.'
[89] Harries, '"Treasure in Heaven"', 61.
[90] Harries, '"Treasure in Heaven"', 62.

made it possible for ascetic piety to be adopted by individuals with a minimum of economic disruption to the aristocracy as a whole.

In some instances, it may have been in the family's economic interest to allow an unmarried daughter to undertake a vow of celibacy. As long as there were other children, especially sons, available to continue the family line and to transmit familial property, adoption of celibacy could serve as a 'family strategy' for managing an excess of children. As Antti Arjava has noted, 'If there were too many children, it was expensive to raise and marry them all. A clever *paterfamilias* or a widowed mother might try to direct them into the lap of the church, to save the cost of a dowry, for example.'[91] In one place Jerome complained that Christian parents dedicated their daughters to virginity only when they were deformed, crippled, or otherwise unsuitable for advantageous marriages. He cited the example of a wealthy presbyter who left his virgin daughters a mere pittance, while he supplied his other children with 'ample provisions for self-indulgence and pleasure'.[92] While Jerome found this decision morally reprehensible, his fellow Christians no doubt would have seen it as simple fiscal responsibility.

Ascetic renunciation may have been attractive to some Roman aristocrats for reasons other than pure economics. The example of Asella, the sister of Marcella, is instructive in this regard. According to Jerome, Asella was dedicated to God before birth and was consecrated to virginity at ten years of age.[93] Since Asella's decision could not have been her own, we must assume that it was taken with the interests of her parents in mind. Albina, the mother of Asella and Marcella, was a member of the distinguished family of the *Ceionii Rufii*. Although the stemma of her family is uncertain, Albina may have been the daughter of Ceionius Rufius Albinus, who was consul in 335 and urban prefect in 335–337. If so, her brother would have been Ceionius Rufius Volusianus Lampadius, urban prefect in 365.[94] Most of the male members of the *Ceionii* were pagans and remained so well into the fifth century, although they intermarried freely with Christians. The toleration shown by the male *Ceionii* towards the Christian (and even the ascetic) inclinations of their women may have been more than an act of broadminded ecumenism. As Hagith Sivan has observed, their acceptance of Christian asceticism would have conveyed a clear political message, not simply a religious one:

---

[91] *Women and Law in Late Antiquity* (Oxford: Clarendon Press, 1996), 174. As Arjava observed, Ambrose even offered the saving of the cost of a dowry as an argument for a daughter's consecration; see Ambrose, *Virg.* 1.32.

[92] *Ep.* 130.6 (CSEL 56, 182). [93] Jerome, *ep.* 24.2.

[94] PLRE 1, 1138 (stemma 13); A. Chastagnol, 'Le sénateur Volusien et la conversion d'une famille de l'aristocratie romain au Bas-Empire', *Revue des études anciennes*, 58 (1956), 241–53.

A display, even through their women, of commitment to Christianity, was therefore likely to be perceived as an advantage rather than a nuisance. Any demonstration of loyalty to the faith of the emperor, such as the consecration of a daughter to perpetual virginity, could have added a useful edge to senatorial competition for offices solely dispensed by the ruler. To be blunt, Asella's destined fate might have been an act calculated to show that the family had some affinity with Christianity.[95]

By transferring the bulk of her estate to her brother, Albina had ensured that the family fortune would remain intact and continue to serve the interests of her class. Moreover, the family was now able to profit from the increasing spiritual status of the consecrated virgin. Aristocratic elites had long been accustomed to using marriage alliances for political ends; it was only a small step to make a similar use of spiritual alliances.

There were other ways in which the aristocratic ascetics of late fourth-century Rome demonstrated their continued adherence to the values and lifestyles of their class. Adoption of celibacy and rejection of marriage (or remarriage) did not necessarily entail a complete break with their former aristocratic habits. Wealthy ascetics often retained their servants and continued to make use of their extensive properties. Distinctions of status and class remained, even after the adoption of celibacy. For example, the monastery founded by Paula in Bethlehem had working and eating quarters for the noble women that were separate from those of lower-class women; according to Jerome, women of different social status joined together only at the liturgy.[96] Bishop Palladius of Helenopolis, the author of the *Lausiac History*, a popular collection of ascetic biographies, considered it noteworthy that the famous Melania the Younger did some daily work alongside of her slave women. Although Melania and her mother Albina practised what Palladius called the 'ascetic life' (ἡ ἄσκησις), they continued to divide their time between multiple estates and kept a household of 'fifteen eunuchs and sixty maidens, both freewomen and slaves'.[97]

This is not to say, of course, that asceticism involved no significant changes in lifestyle. To reject marriage and procreation was a profound symbol of refusal to participate in one of the central features of 'earthly' life. But the point is that such renunciations often produced not only 'heavenly' rewards, but 'earthly' ones as well, and these rewards stood in fundamental continuity with the expectations of traditional aristocratic privilege. For example, asceticism (at least for a wealthy aristocrat) rarely entailed the complete and

---

[95] Sivan, 'On Hymens and Holiness', 83.

[96] Jerome, *ep*. 108. 20 (CSEL 55, 335): 'ut in opere et cibo separatae psalmodiis et orationibus iungerentur.'

[97] Palladius, *H. Laus.* 61.6; text in Dom Cuthbert Butler (ed.), *The Lausiac History of Palladius*, ii (TaS 6; Cambridge: Cambridge University Press, 1904), 157.

Jovinian and Christian Rome

immediate divestment of property. Rather, such 'renunciation' usually took the form of a redirection of resources towards new acts of patronage. The building of churches, endowment of monasteries, and acts of generosity to the poor replaced earlier modes of civic beneficence, but older attitudes and motivations persisted.[98] Describing the massive building projects undertaken at Nola, Fundi, and elsewhere by Paulinus of Nola after his ascetic 'withdrawal', Dennis Trout has characterized the simultaneous elements of novelty and continuity involved:

The scale and magnificence of these buildings entailed the commitment of significant funds.... On the one hand, riches bestowed on Christ through the medium of his saints, like those used by Pammachius to succor the poor, were cleansed of their debilitating taint. Church building thus emerged as another mode of the appropriate use of wealth motivated by a complex sense of *caritas*, but it was one that, like Paulinus' conception of almsgiving, kept the benefactor very much at the center of attention.[99]

More than one commentator (ancient and modern) has observed that Paulinus' stature in the world may have risen as a result of his transition from aristocratic senator to ascetic patron of St. Felix at Nola. Even Paulinus himself had marvelled: 'Did I have anything when I was called senator to match what I have here and now when I am called impoverished?'[100]

For aristocratic women the gains to be derived from ascetic renunciation may have been even greater than for men.[101] Christian asceticism provided an honourable alternative to life within the confines of marriage and the patriarchal household. Although ascetic women were still expected to conduct themselves with proper domestic virtues, the scope of their activities seems to have broadened significantly. An ascetic woman with sufficient resources could travel more freely than a married woman and could engage in friendships with ascetic men on terms that approached equality. Moreover, greater

---

[98] C. Pietri, 'Evergétisme et richesses ecclésiastiques dans l'Italie du IVe à la fin du Ve s.: l'exemple romaine', *Ktema*, 3 (1978), 317–37.

[99] Trout, *Paulinus of Nola*, 153–4; cf. B. Ramsey, 'Almsgiving in the Latin Church: The Late Fourth and Early Fifth Centuries', *TS* 43 (1982), 226–59.

[100] Paulinus, *Carm.* 21.458–9 (CSEL 30, 173); cited in Salzman, *Making of a Christian Aristocracy*, 203.

[101] An extensive body of literature on female asceticism now exists. A good orientation can be found in Gillian Clark, 'Women and Asceticism in Late Antiquity: The Refusal of Status and Gender', in R. Valantassis and V. Wimbush (eds.), *Asceticism* (New York: Oxford University Press, 1995), 33–48. The essays of Elizabeth A. Clark remain essential. See 'Ascetic Renunciation and Feminine Advancement: A Paradox of Late Ancient Asceticism', and 'Authority and Humility: A Conflict of Values in Fourth-Century Female Monasticism', in her *Ascetic Piety and Women's Faith: Essays on Late Ancient Christianity* (Lewiston/Queenston: The Edwin Mellen Press, 1986), 175–208, and 209–28.

freedom to pursue education seems to have been one outcome, at least for some aristocratic women. Paula and her daughter Eustochium both learned Hebrew under the tutelage of Jerome. Melania the Elder used her ascetic leisure to develop a formidable knowledge of Greek Christian literature. According to Palladius, Melania the Elder 'turned night into day going through every writing of the ancient commentators—three million lines of Origen and two and a half million lines of Gregory, Stephen, Pierius, Basil, and other worthy men'. Moreover, Palladius claimed, Melania did not pursue her research in a cursory way, 'but she worked on them, dredging through each work seven or eight times'.[102]

Overall, it appears that there were numerous 'earthly' benefits to be derived from a commitment to celibacy, especially for wealthy, aristocratic women. As Elizabeth Clark once noted, such aristocratic ascetics

> appear to have enjoyed the best of both worlds: their ascetic profession gave them certain freedoms similar to those granted men, while their money and aristocratic connections permitted an assertiveness surprising to note among the meek who will inherit the earth. The earth was theirs before their ascetic renunciations, and they appear to have sacrificed less of it than we might have expected in their adoption of asceticism.[103]

Given the manner in which traditional Roman aristocrats, especially women, could adopt asceticism with a minimum of disruption to their way of life, it is not entirely surprising that asceticism gradually came to be seen as an alternative path to status and honour, one that could rival even traditional aristocratic modes of influence.

ii. Asceticism and the *Gens Anicia*

Perhaps the clearest example of this adoption of ascetic practice and its co-option as a mode of aristocratic competition can be found in the careers of prominent women of the Anician family, several of whom we have already encountered in this chapter. Anicia Faltonia Proba, widow of Sextus Petronius Probus and likely editor of the Virgilian cento *De laudibus Christi*, survived the death of her husband (*c.*390) and lived well into the fifth century. Her own stature as a prominent aristocratic *materfamilias* was commemorated by her sons, Anicius Hermogenianus Olybrius and Anicius Probinus, who served as

---

[102] Jerome, *ep.* 108.15 (on Paula and Eustochium); Palladius, *H. Laus.* 55.3 (on Melania; ed. Butler 2, 149); trans. Robert T. Meyer, *Palladius: The Lausiac History* (ACW 34; Westminster, Md.: The Newman Press, 1965), 136–7.

[103] Clark 'Ascetic Renunciation and Feminine Advancement', 190.

consuls together in 395. She was described in an inscription as *consulis uxori, consulis filiae, consulum matri* ('wife of a consul, daughter of a consul, mother of consuls').[104] After Alaric's sack of the city in 410, Proba fled to Africa along with her daughter-in-law Anicia Juliana and her granddaughter Demetrias.

Like other late Roman Christians, Anicia Faltonia Proba seems to have made a seamless transition from the role of aristocratic *matrona* to that of ascetic *patrona*. Settled in Carthage by 412, Proba was the recipient of a treatise on prayer by Augustine, addressed to 'a devoted handmaid of God' (*religiosae famulae dei*).[105] Her daughter-in-law Juliana received Augustine's treatise *The Good of Widowhood* (*De bono viduitatis*) shortly thereafter. A letter of Pope Caelestinus to Emperor Theodosius II, dated 15 March 432, recorded her many donations to the clergy, the poor, and monasteries.[106]

Despite their own commitment to a life of celibacy, when the time came for Demetrias to be married, the widows Proba and Juliana initially expected that she would follow in their footsteps and undertake an advantageous marriage. When Demetrias declined and chose to take the veil as a consecrated virgin from the hands of Bishop Aurelius of Carthage in 414, neither Proba nor Juliana objected to her decision. But Demetrias' mother and grandmother orchestrated the event to redound to the fame and glory of the Anician *gens*. Throughout the empire learned Christian men were recruited to advise (and to praise) the aristocratic young virgin. From Palestine Jerome and Pelagius both responded to the call. Pope Innocent and Augustine, addressing themselves to Juliana and Proba, also sent their congratulations.[107] As Augustine noted, word of Demetrias' virginal consecration had spread throughout the world with astonishing speed. Announcements of the event were accompanied by gifts to prominent churchmen.[108] Several decades later the anonymous author of the *Epistula ad Demetriadem de vera humilitate* recalled that the consecration of Demetrias had provoked 'many men who were then prominent figures in the church' (*multi qui tunc in ecclesia praeeminebant*) to convey their congratulations and exhortations to the young virgin.[109]

The transition from the Virgilian cento *De laudibus Christi* to the virginal consecration of Demetrias helps to illustrate the manner in which ascetic

---

[104] Dessau, *ILS* 1269; cited in *PLRE* 1, 732.
[105] Augustine, *ep.* 130.1 (CSEL 44, 40); cf. *Vid.* 24 (CSEL 41, 334–5), where Augustine urged Anicia Juliana to seek out the advice of her mother-in-law, Proba, for guidance in the ascetic life.
[106] *PLRE* 1, 733.
[107] Jerome, *ep.* 130; Pelagius, *Dem.*; Augustine, *ep.* 150; Innocent, *ep.* 15.
[108] Augustine, *ep.* 150 (CSEL 44, 380), gratefully acknowledged receipt of a *velationis apophoretum* from Proba and Juliana. Cf. Jerome, *ep.* 130.6 (CSEL 56, 181).
[109] *Ep. ad Demetriadem* 1; ed. and trans. by M.K. Krabbe, *Epistula ad Demetriadem De Vera Humilitate* (Washington, DC: The Catholic University of America Press, 1965), 140–1. The work is sometimes attributed to Prosper of Aquitaine.

renunciation was accepted (and transformed) within the most prominent Christian family among the Roman aristocracy. Despite their commitment to the life of celibate widows, Proba and Juliana remained, in the words of Jerome, 'distinguished women with the authority to command, the faith to seek, and the perseverance to extract' whatever they wished.[110] Through the mediation of her mother and grandmother, Demetrias acquired not only the attention of the most distinguished churchmen of the age, but also the substantial dowry that would have accompanied her marriage.[111] Jerome knew better than to suggest that Demetrias should reject her inheritance; he simply advised that she should exercise care in choosing the eunuchs and slaves that would constitute her future retinue. After all, he wrote, it was the way of the *Anicii* both to have riches and to despise them.[112] Although Jerome urged Demetrias to spend her fortune on the poor, the sick, and the homeless (rather than on elaborate churches with marbled walls and altars covered with gold and gems), it appears that his appeal fell on deaf ears. Upon returning to Rome, Demetrias constructed a church dedicated to St. Stephen at her estate on the Via Latina. When she died, her passing was commemorated by no less a personage than Pope Leo the Great.[113]

It is likely that Proba, Juliana, and Demetrias were aware that the adoption of celibacy was likely to enhance the glory and fame of the Anician family as much as any advantageous marriage. They certainly sought to publicize her consecration as widely as possible. And if not, Jerome and others were there to remind them. As Jerome wrote in his Letter to Demetrias, 'you have gained more as a virgin than you gave up. As the bride of a man, you would have come to the attention of one province; as a virgin of Christ, you are known to the whole world.'[114] This is one point on which contemporary scholars agree with the rhetoric of Jerome. Describing the effects of Demetrias' virginal consecration, Hagith Sivan has observed that the fortunes of the family stood to gain more by this public declaration of faith than by a traditional marriage: 'With a single act of pious devotion, [Demetrias] revived its image as the leading Christian family of the western empire.'[115]

In sum, the Christian aristocrats of Rome proved to be remarkably adept at adopting aspects of ascetic piety and utilizing these as strategies of aristocratic competition. It was precisely such adaptations that facilitated the conversion

---

[110] Jerome, *ep.* 130.1 (CSEL 56, 175).   [111] Jerome, *ep.* 130.7 (CSEL 56, 182).
[112] *Ep.* 130.13 (on choice of servants); 14 (on riches).
[113] *Lib. pont.* 47 (Duchesne 1, 238); *ILCV* 8988, cited in *PLRE* 2, 352. The remains of Demetrias' church have been excavated. See the discussion in Hugo Brandenburg, *Ancient Churches of Rome from the Fourth to the Seventh Century: The Dawn of Christian Architecture in the West*, trans. Andreas Kropp (Turnhout: Brepols, 2005), 235.
[114] Jerome, *ep.* 130.6 (CSEL 56, 182).   [115] Cf. Sivan, 'Hymens and Holiness', 85.

of the Roman aristocracy in the last two decades of the fourth century and early years of the fifth century, as Michele Salzman has recently shown.[116] Key features of ascetic practice, such as celibacy, could be adopted without entailing any fundamental disruption of the traditional aristocratic way of life. In some cases, asceticism provided a broader array of opportunities to display acts of munificence and new forms of civic pride. In other cases, as we have seen, the selective practice of celibacy allowed greater flexibility in inheritance strategies.

Perhaps the most attractive feature of ascetic renunciation, from the point of view of the social elite, is that it provided a ready made 'Christian alternative language of power and society', to borrow a phrase from Kate Cooper.[117] That is, the notion that celibacy was superior to marriage was easily absorbed into the traditional aristocratic quest for honour and glory. Ascetic teachers and clergy eagerly colluded in this rhetorical enterprise, promising young virgins, such as Demetrias, that their nobility in this world was merely a prelude to the greater, transcendent nobility that they would achieve through spiritual marriage. It was a message that late Roman aristocrats were eager to assimilate.

In such an environment, the ultimate failure of Jovinian's message of baptismal equality was, perhaps, inevitable. Although some features of his resistance to ascetic elitism, especially his defence of the goodness of marriage, would have been attractive to some members of the Roman aristocracy, Jovinian's 'old-fashioned denial of hierarchy', as Peter Brown has put it, must have appeared to be simply irrelevant, perhaps even dangerous: 'Jovinian denied the central tenet of the late Roman sense of hierarchy—that certain holy individuals could stand between heaven and earth, representing, on earth, the majesty of the invisible world.... It threatened to undo all that the revolution of late antiquity had achieved for the Christian church. Hierarchy, and not community, had become the order of the day.'[118]

As we shall see in the final chapters of this book, there were numerous interests at stake in the differentiation and distribution of heavenly rewards according to ascetic merit. But while bishops, priests, and ascetic teachers differed in the emphasis they placed on asceticism, they all agreed that a hierarchy could be established on the basis of degrees of sexual renunciation. As I have argued here, despite initial signs of resistance, some elite citizens of Christian Rome increasingly found such a hierarchy amenable to their interests.

---

[116] Salzman, 'Competing Claims to "Nobilitas" in the Western Empire of the Fourth and Fifth Centuries', *JECS* 9 (2001), 359–85; and *Making of a Christian Aristocracy*, 200–19.
[117] Cooper, *Virgin and the Bride*, 58.
[118] Brown, *Body and Society*, 360–1.

Part II

Jovinian, Heresy, and Asceticism

3

Asceticism, Heresy, and Early Christian Tradition

One of the central contentions of this book is that Jovinian's resistance to ascetic elitism was motivated by anti-heretical concerns. As we saw in Chapter 1, Jovinian's assertion of the equality of all baptized Christians was supplemented by accusations of heresy directed against those who believed that celibacy or fasting merited for the Christian a higher reward in heaven. My aim in this chapter is to provide a further context for interpreting Jovinian's accusations of heresy by examining discussion of asceticism and heresy in previous Christian tradition. I will review evidence from the first three centuries, highlighting the moments when Christian thinkers voiced resistance to ascetic piety and thus provided a precedent for Jovinian's polemics. A number of sources, including both the Pastoral Epistles and the writings of Clement of Alexandria, offer examples of resistance to ascetic thinking that parallel in many ways the views of Jovinian. Much of the Christian discussion of marriage in the second century was devoted to the refutation of encratism and other forms of ascetic 'heresy'. When viewed in the light of this earlier Christian tradition, Jovinian's defence of the equality of marriage and celibacy appears to be fully compatible with Christian 'orthodoxy'.

1. TRADITIONS IN TENSION

i. Jesus and Paul

From its very inception early Christian tradition was fractured on the question of marriage and sexuality. Indeed, Jesus himself may have been partly responsible for this ambivalence. Numerous sayings preserved in the synoptic gospels suggest that Jesus believed commitment to the kingdom of God might entail profound divisions within families: 'Whoever comes to me and does not hate father and mother, wife and children, brothers and sister, yes, and even life itself cannot be my disciple' (Luke 14: 26).[1] In a similar vein all three synoptic gospels report an incident in which Jesus, after being asked about the status of marriage at the resurrection, replied that 'when the dead rise, they will neither marry nor be given in marriage, but they will be like angels in heaven' (Mark 12: 25; cf. Matt 22: 30, Luke 20: 34–6). Read in the light of Jesus' acknowledgement that 'there are eunuchs who have made themselves eunuchs for the sake of the kingdom of heaven' (Matt 19: 12), sayings such as these indicate that entry into God's kingdom might entail the renunciation of marriage, sex, and family life.[2]

There is, however, another tendency in the biblical evidence that stands in some tension with this emphasis on renunciation, namely the tradition of Jesus' prohibition of divorce, which is preserved in all three synoptic gospels and in the writings of Paul. In Mark's version, when asked whether divorce should be permitted, as in Mosaic Law, Jesus replied:

> It was because of your hardness of heart that Moses wrote you this law. But at the beginning of creation God 'made them male and female' (Gen 1: 27). 'For this reason a man will leave his father and mother and be united to his wife, and the two will become one flesh' (Gen 2: 24). So they are no longer two, but one flesh. Therefore, what God has joined together, let no one separate (Mark 10: 5–9 NRSV).[3]

Jesus' prohibition of divorce, which many scholars regard as an authentic feature of his teaching, provided a counterbalance to the more radically antimarital and anti-familial traditions cited above, although it too reflects a thoroughly eschatological point of view. Like the Jewish sectarians at Qumran, who also forbade divorce by invoking the Genesis texts, Jesus seems to have regarded the permanence of marriage as a restoration of the original unity of creation to become fully evident at the end of time.[4]

A similar ambivalence towards marriage and family can be found in the teaching of the apostle Paul. In his famous discussion of marriage in

---

[1] There are parallels in Matt 10: 37–8, 19: 29, Mark 10: 29, and *Gospel of Thomas*, logion 55 and logion 101. According to J. A. Fitzmyer, the word 'hate' is original. See *The Gospel According to Luke* (AB 28A; Garden City, NY: Doubleday, 1985), 1060–2.

[2] See e.g. the interpretation of Jesus' preaching as 'eschatological asceticism' in Dale Allison, *Jesus of Nazareth: Millenarian Prophet* (Minneapolis, Minn.: Fortress Press, 1998), 172–216. Allison argues that both Jesus and Paul may have been closer to later Christian 'Encratites' than most scholars have been willing to acknowledge.

[3] Parallels in Matt 5: 31–2, 19: 1–12, Luke 16: 18, 1 Cor 7: 10–11.

[4] *Damascus Document* 4. Further discussion in E. P. Sanders, *Jesus and Judaism* (Philadelphia: Fortress Press, 1985), 257–9; David Dungan, *The Sayings of Jesus in the Churches of Paul* (Philadelphia: Fortress Press, 1971), 115–20; J. R. Mueller, 'The Temple Scroll and the Gospel Divorce Texts', *Revue de Qumran*, 10 (1979–81), 247–56. Cf. Abel Issakson, *Marriage and Ministry in the New Temple* (Lund: Gleerup, 1965), 147, who stresses the 'priestly eschatology' behind Jesus' rejection of divorce.

1 Corinthians 7 Paul wrote in response to a set of questions from the predominantly Gentile Christian community at Corinth. Certain teachers had been propagating the view that 'it is good for a man not to touch a woman' (7: 1), apparently advocating the desirability (perhaps even the necessity) of sexual renunciation.[5] Paul's response is a model of equivocation, whose ambivalence still leads readers today to dramatically different interpretations of his views on marriage and celibacy.[6]

On the one hand, Paul rejected any suggestion that celibacy should be required of all Christians. He insisted that married couples should remain married and that they should continue to engage in sexual relations in order to avoid the danger of illicit sexual activity (7: 2–5). Citing the teaching of Jesus, Paul also forbade divorce between Christians (7: 10–11) and even encouraged Christians to remain married to non-Christians (7: 12–16). On the other hand, Paul expressed his clear preference that the unmarried should remain unmarried (7: 7–8, 25–7), although he acknowledged that it was no sin to marry (7: 28, 36). In general, Paul portrayed marriage as a source of anxieties and distractions that were best forgone in expectation of the imminent end of this age (7: 29–35).

Most telling of all, like Jesus before him, Paul made no mention of procreation, which was considered the primary purpose of marriage by Jews and Gentiles alike. For Paul, the only reason for a Christian to marry was because he or she might fall victim to sexual temptation: 'But if they are not practicing self-control ($\epsilon i \ \delta \grave{\epsilon} \ o\mathring{v}\kappa \ \grave{\epsilon}\gamma\kappa\rho\alpha\tau\epsilon\acute{v}o\nu\tau\alpha\iota$), they should marry. For it is better to marry than to be aflame with passion' (7: 9). It is fair to say that in 1 Corinthians 7 Paul failed to provide a truly positive rationale for Christian marriage. Ultimately he presented marriage as merely a defence against illicit desire. 'By this essentially negative, even alarmist strategy', Peter Brown has observed, 'Paul left a fatal legacy to future ages.'[7]

The teachings of Jesus and Paul provided a rather inauspicious beginning for early Christian reflection on marriage and sexuality. Indeed, they seem to have inspired contradictory tendencies in early Christian piety. On the one

---

[5] The precise background of the Corinthian ascetics has been much discussed. For a recent review and proposal, see Judith M. Gundry-Volf, 'Controlling the Bodies: A Theological Profile of The Corinthian Sexual Ascetics (1 Cor 7)', in R. Bieringer (ed.), *The Corinthian Correspondence* (Leuven: Peeters, 1996), 519–41, who argues that the ascetics are 'pneumatics' who 'seek to facilitate divine inspiration and communication with God through sexual asceticism' (540).

[6] See e.g. the contrasting perspectives of two recent studies: Will Deming, *Paul on Marriage and Celibacy: The Hellenistic Background of 1 Corinthians 7* (Cambridge: Cambridge University Press, 1995); and Daniel Boyarin, *A Radical Jew: Paul and the Politics of Identity* (Berkeley: University of California Press, 1994), 158–79. The former denies any real 'ascetic' content in Paul's teaching; the latter sees Paul as a 'proto-Encratite'.

[7] Brown, *Body and Society*, 55.

hand, the eschatological sayings of Jesus and Paul's ambivalent responses to the Christians at Corinth laid the foundation of a tradition that gave pride of place to celibacy and other forms of renunciation, what is sometimes called 'the tradition of *enkrateia*'.[8] On the other hand, the explicit acceptance of marriage by Jesus and Paul made it possible for another tradition to develop, one that stressed the possibility of authentic Christian life in the context of marriage, family, and household.[9] It is the latter tradition that is of primary interest here, for it provided the precedent for Jovinian's resistance to the ascetic ideal.

ii. Resistance to the Ascetic Ideal

It is striking how quickly the eschatological and ascetical tendencies of Jesus and Paul were forgotten (or ignored) by a significant portion of Christians in subsequent decades. Numerous Christian writings from the late first to the early second centuries—particularly the deutero-Pauline and Pastoral Epistles—offered a decidedly non-ascetic (and, occasionally, even anti-ascetic) interpretation of the apostle's teaching. The acceptance of these writings into the New Testament canon by the end of the second century attests to the persistence of a moderate tradition of Christian discourse on sex and marriage that sought to modify or even supplant the eschatological asceticism of Jesus and Paul.

We have, for example, numerous instances of 'household codes' in the later New Testament epistles and other early Christian documents.[10] These tables, which are derived from ancient treatises on economics and politics, list the reciprocal duties of the members of a Greco-Roman household, thus providing an idealized account of how a Christian household should be managed.[11]

---

[8] The studies of Giulia Sfameni Gasparro are crucial. See her *Enkrateia e antropologia: Le motivazioni protologiche della continenza e della verginità nel cristianesimo dei primi secoli e nello gnosticismo* (Rome: Institutum Patristicum Augustinianum, 1984); *eadem*, 'Asceticism and Anthropology: *Enkrateia* and "Double Creation" in Early Christianity', in Vincent L. Wimbush and Richard Valantasis (eds.), *Asceticism* (New York and Oxford: Oxford University Press, 1995), 127–46; also the valuable collection of essays in U. Bianchi (ed.), *La tradizione dell'enkrateia: Motivazioni ontologiche e protologiche* (Rome: Edizioni dell'Ateneo, 1985).

[9] There may be a sociological explanation for this bifurcation in the first generations of Christianity. From its inception Christianity required both itinerant preachers committed to a life of physical renunciation, as well as married householders who provided them with material support. Such a view of Christian origins has been advanced especially by Gerd Theissen, *Social Reality and the Early Christians*, trans. M. Kohl (Minneapolis, Minn.: Fortress Press, 1992).

[10] Col 3: 18—4: 1; 1 Pet 2: 11—3: 12; Eph 5: 21-33; 1 Tim 2: 8-15, 6: 1-10; Titus 2: 1-10; *1 Clem.* 3, 21.6-8; Ignatius, *Pol.* 4.1—5.3; Polycarp, *Phil.* 4.1-3.

[11] On the origins of the household codes, see Elisabeth Schüssler Fiorenza, *In Memory of Her: A Feminist Theological Reconstruction of Christian Origins* (New York: Crossroad, 1983), 254–70.

The Letter to the Colossians, for example, offered one of the earliest examples of these household codes:

Wives, be subject to your husbands, as is fitting in the Lord. Husbands, love your wives and never treat them harshly. Children, obey your parents in everything, for this is your acceptable duty in the Lord. Fathers, do not provoke your children, or they may lose heart. Slaves, obey your earthly masters in everything, not only while being watched and in order to please them, but wholeheartedly, fearing the Lord.... Masters, treat your slaves justly and fairly, for you know that you also have a Master in heaven (Col 3: 18–4: 1 NRSV).

The presence of these household codes in Colossians and elsewhere indicates that marital and familial relationships had grown in importance by the later decades of the first century. This development was related, no doubt, to the decline in eschatological fervour in many quarters that must have followed the delay of the end-times. It probably also reflects the increasing prominence of Christian householders in the leadership of the church, as well as the decreasing influence of itinerant apostles and teachers.[12]

These guides for early Christian ethics give no indication that celibacy was regarded as a 'higher' or 'better' way of life than marriage. In fact, the household code of Ephesians 5 actually portrays the reciprocal love between husband and wife as modelled on the love between Christ and the Church: 'Husbands, love your wives, just as Christ loved the church and gave himself up for her.... In the same way, husbands should love their wives as they do their own bodies. He who loves his wife loves himself. For no one ever hates his own body, but he nourishes and tenderly cares for it, just as Christ does for the church, because we are members of his body' (Eph 5:25, 28–30 NRSV). These verses of the Letter to the Ephesians may even have an anti-ascetic slant, for the mutual love of husband and wife is presented as natural and as necessary as the intake of food. In contrast to the ascetic renunciation of sexual union, Ephesians takes the very love of the flesh (and fleshly love) as an appropriate analogy for the love of Christ and the Church.[13]

By the late first and early second centuries we already encounter evidence of considerable tension between those Christians who advocated celibacy and those who favoured marriage and traditional family life. These conflicts sometimes touched the sensitive nerve of clerical authority. For example, *1 Clement*, a letter to the church at Corinth traditionally ascribed to the Roman presbyter Clement (c.96), portrayed the Corinthian community as

---

[12] *Didache* 11–15 illustrates this process in action.

[13] For a helpful commentary on these verses, see J. Paul Sampley, *'And the Two Shall Become One Flesh': A Study of Traditions in Ephesians 5:21–33* (Cambridge: Cambridge University Press, 1971).

wracked by schism over the issue of leadership. Clement's letter indicated that the 'rebellious' party claimed to have special spiritual gifts and 'knowledge', much as some Corinthian Christians had claimed in the days of the apostle Paul. But Clement also suggested that some of the dissidents were celibates, who had appealed to their ascetic virtue as grounds for spiritual authority. Clement abruptly rejected such claims: 'Let the one who is pure in the flesh (ὁ ἁγνὸς ἐν τῇ σαρκὶ) not act arrogantly, knowing that another has provided him with his self-restraint (ἐγκράτειαν).'[14]

Ignatius of Antioch, a bishop from Antioch in Syria writing in the early second century, also came into contact with celibate Christians whose ascetic virtue (he believed) caused disruption in the Christian community. Like Clement, Ignatius strongly opposed placing excessive value on ascetic renunciation. Writing to Bishop Polycarp of Smyrna sometime between the years 110 and 117, Ignatius cautioned: 'If anyone is able to remain continent to the honour of the Lord's flesh, let him remain (so) without boasting; if he boasts, he is lost; and if it is known beyond the bishop, he is destroyed.'[15] Both Clement and Ignatius appear to believe that the formation of an ascetic elite posed a potential danger to Christian community. As Giulia Sfameni Gasparro has noted, these two Christian leaders, both of whom were intensely concerned with maintaining order in the Church and the authority of the ecclesiastical hierarchy, 'did not fail to understand the discriminatory impact that chastity would have had on the community, if viewed as a mark of distinction of a privileged, charismatic minority'.[16]

Perhaps the most striking instance of an anti-ascetic position in early Christian literature can be found in the three New Testament letters known collectively as the 'Pastoral Epistles': the First and Second Letters to Timothy and the Letter to Titus. These documents have had a particularly controversial history in modern scholarship. Nearly all scholars accept that the letters were not written by Paul himself or even by a close associate. But there is widespread disagreement about their provenance and date of composition.

---

[14] *1 Clem.* 38.2; trans. Bart D. Ehrman, *The Apostolic Fathers*, i (LCL 24; Cambridge, Mass.: Harvard University Press, 2003), 103. Cf. *1 Clem.* 6.3, where the author complains that 'jealousy estranged wives from their husbands and nullified what was spoken by our father Adam: "This now is bone from my bones and flesh from my flesh"'; trans. Ehrman, *The Apostolic Fathers*, i (LCL 24, 47). According to James S. Jeffers, Clement's understanding of church leadership was shaped by the Roman ideology of the family with its emphasis on the absolute authority of the *paterfamilias*. See *Conflict at Rome: Social Order and Hierarchy in Early Christianity* (Minneapolis, Minn.: Fortress Press, 1991), 121–44.

[15] Ignatius, *Pol.* 5.2; trans. W. R. Schoedel, *Ignatius of Antioch: A Commentary on the Letters of Ignatius of Antioch* (Philadelphia: Fortress Press, 1985), 272.

[16] Sfameni Gasparro, 'Asceticism and Anthropology', 131. Cf. Schoedel, *Ignatius*, 272: 'The emergence of a polarized ascetic elite poses a challenge to [Ignatius'] conception of the Christian community.'

Plausible estimates have ranged from 80 to 120, with a few scholars positing even later dates. Hans von Campenhausen argued that there were close verbal similarities between the Pastoral Epistles and the *Letter to the Philippians* composed by Bishop Polycarp of Smyrna sometime after the death of Ignatius of Antioch (c.110).[17] Furthermore, the development of church order and theology in the Pastorals seems to reflect conditions in Asia Minor in the opening decades of the second century. For these reasons a date of composition around the year 120 is highly probable and will be adopted here.

Another disputed question regarding the Pastorals has been the identity of the so-called 'false teachers' whose views are attacked throughout the letters. It is not even clear whether one group of opponents or several different groups are implied. The author has provided only a few, imprecise details about them: they are Jewish Christians, who are engaged in discussions of law, including 'myths and endless genealogies' (1 Tim 1: 4, 7; cf. 1 Tim 4: 7, 2 Tim 2: 14–116, Titus 1: 10–11, 3: 9). They claim that the resurrection has already taken place (2 Tim 2: 17–18). They forbid marriage and demand abstinence from certain foods (1 Tim 4: 1–5). This 'false teaching' has caused dissension within households, especially among women (1 Tim 1: 10, 2 Tim 3: 6).[18] Noting the similarity between these teachings and views later espoused by Christian 'Gnostics', many scholars have suggested that the Pastoral Epistles were written to combat an early form of 'Jewish Christian Gnosticism' or even Marcionism.[19]

There are many problems with such a proposal, not least of which is that the very coherence of the label 'Gnosticism' is increasingly under fire.[20] Moreover, there is no evidence that the 'false teachers' denied that the true God created the world or that Jesus was truly human, positions associated

---

[17] 'Polykarp von Smyrna und die Pastoralbriefe', in his *Aus der Frühzeit des Christentums* (Tübingen: J.C.B. Mohr, 1963), 197–252. Campenhausen concluded that Polycarp was the author of the Pastorals, but his conclusion has not been widely accepted. Recently, however, several scholars have drawn attention to the strength of his arguments. See Gerd Lüdemann, *Heretics: The Other Side of Early Christianity*, trans. J. Bowden (London: SCM Press, 1996), 140–1; Helmut Koester, *Introduction to the New Testament*, ii. *History and Literature of Early Christianity*, 2nd edn. (New York and Berlin: W. de Gruyter, 2000), 307–8.

[18] Robert J. Karris, 'The Background and Significance of the Polemic of the Pastoral Epistles', *JBL* 92 (1973), 549–64.

[19] Jouette M. Bassler, *1 Timothy. 2 Timothy. Titus* (Nashville: Abingdon Press, 1996), 27–8. Cf. M. Dibelius and H. Conzelmann, *The Pastoral Epistles: A Commentary on the Pastoral Epistles* (Philadelphia: Fortress Press, 1972), 3: 'The little that can be known definitely about the opponents points not to the great Gnostic systems, but rather to a kind of Judaizing Gnosticism (with speculation and observance of the Law) as is to be found elsewhere (Col and Ign.)'. Both Lüdemann and Koester, who are inclined to date the Pastorals after 120, appear to favour the view that the Pastorals were composed to oppose Marcion.

[20] See the persuasive arguments of Michael Allen Williams, *Rethinking 'Gnosticism': An Argument for Dismantling a Dubious Category* (Princeton, NJ: Princeton University Press, 1996).

with the teaching of Marcion and of 'Gnostics' such as Valentinus and Ptolemy. On the contrary, the most plausible theory has been proposed by Dennis MacDonald, who has argued that the teachers attacked in the Pastorals were circulating the sort of stories later found in the apocryphal *Acts of Paul and Thecla*. These stories portray Paul preaching that participation in the resurrection requires celibacy and that women (e.g. Thecla) should abandon their husbands, families, and households to become apostles for Christ. In short, the ideal of Christian discipleship proclaimed by the *Acts of Paul and Thecla* was the precise opposite of everything cherished by the author of the Pastoral Epistles.[21]

Whatever the precise character of the 'false teaching', the Pastoral Epistles offer a clear alternative to the ascetic Christianity of their opponents. Rather than upsetting families and subverting households (Titus 1: 11; 2 Tim 3: 6), the Pastorals present the household itself as the model of good order in the Church, 'the household of God' (1 Tim 3: 15). We see this emphasis, for example, in the prescribed qualifications for the office of 'overseer' or 'bishop' ($\dot{\epsilon}\pi\acute{\iota}\sigma\kappa o\pi o s$). The ideal bishop is portrayed as a married man, but one who is married 'to one wife' (1 Tim 3: 2). In addition to the virtues of temperance, hospitality, and good sense, the prospective bishop must demonstrate his suitability for church office by his behaviour as head of a household: 'He must manage his own household well, keeping his children submissive and respectful in every way—for if someone does not know how to manage his own household, how can he take care of God's church?' (1 Tim 3: 4–5; cf. Titus 1: 7–8).[22] In contrast to the itinerant, charismatic, and celibate apostles of the apocryphal acts, the Pastoral Epistles present a thoroughly 'domesticated' portrait of church leadership.[23]

---

[21] *The Legend and the Apostle: The Battle for Paul in Story and Canon* (Philadelphia: Westminster Press, 1983). His thesis has recently been endorsed by Stephen J. Davis, *The Cult of Saint Thecla: A Tradition of Women's Piety in Late Antiquity* (OECS; Oxford: Clarendon Press, 2001), 8–18. If MacDonald is correct, the theology underlying the opponents' claims about asceticism and the resurrection would more closely reflect the views of later Christian 'Encratites', evident in the writings of Tatian, Julius Cassian, and the *Acts of Thomas*, rather than Gnosticism or Marcionism.

[22] It is unclear whether the description of the ideal bishop as 'a man of one wife' (1Tim 3: 2, Titus 1: 6) was intended simply to place a limit on the number of times a bishop might be married, or whether it also prescribed that the bishop *must* be married. For the latter interpretation, see MacDonald, *Legend and the Apostle*, 72.

[23] David C. Verner, *The Household of God: The Social World of the Pastoral Epistles* (SBL Dissertation Series, 71; Chico, CA: Scholars Press, 1983). Dibelius and Conzelmann, *Pastoral Epistles*, 50–4, have shown that the author of the Pastoral Epistles employed stereotypical lists of publicly recognized virtues to characterize church leaders. See also Elaine Pagels, 'Adam and Eve, Christ and the Church: A Survey of Second-Century Controversies Concerning Marriage', in A. H. B. Logan and A. J. M. Wedderburn (eds), *The New Testament and Gnosis: Essays in Honor of R. Mcl. Wilson* (Edinburgh: T & T Clark, 1983), 149: 'All [the deutero-Pauline letters]

Another way in which the author of the Pastoral Epistles opposed ascetic practice was by encouraging women (especially younger women) to 'marry, bear children, and manage their households, so as to give the adversary no occasion to revile us' (1 Tim 5: 14). Again, in contrast to the apocryphal Acts whose heroines (e.g. Thecla) reject marriage and family life, the Pastorals present childbearing as the privileged path of salvation for women, who are burdened with the guilt of the first sin: 'For Adam was formed first, then Eve; and Adam was not deceived, but the woman was deceived and became a transgressor. Yet she will be saved through childbearing, provided they continue in faith and love and holiness, with modesty' (1 Tim 2: 13–15). If, as most scholars believe, the 'false teachers' preached an ascetic message that entailed in some way the liberation of women, the author of the Pastoral Epistles leaves no doubt about where he stands on the matter. Women are to 'learn in silence with full submission' (1 Tim 2: 11); they are not to teach or to have authority over men (1 Tim 2: 12). Older women are to teach the younger women 'to love their husbands, to love their children ... to be good managers of the household' (Titus 2: 4–5). The Pastoral Epistles present marriage and the submission of women within the patriarchal household as the proper antidote to the liberation offered in the ascetic preaching of their opponents.

The most explicit discussion in the Pastorals on the issue of asceticism is the following passage that was cited by Jovinian:

Now the Spirit expressly says that in later times some will renounce the faith by paying attention to deceitful spirits and teachings of demons, through the hypocrisy of liars whose consciences are seared with a hot iron. They forbid marriage and demand abstinence from foods, which God created to be received with thanksgiving by those who believe and know the truth. For everything created by God is good, and nothing is to be rejected, provided it is received with thanksgiving, for it is sanctified by God's word and by prayer (1 Tim 4: 1–5 NRSV).

Here the author of the Pastorals makes it clear that the compulsory celibacy and abstinence preached by the 'false teachers' was problematic not simply because it threatened to undermine the order of the household and church leadership. Rather, a theological reason is given for resisting their asceticism. Rejection of marriage and food is seen as a rejection of creation. The Pastoral Epistles insist that both eating and sex are activities that are capable of being 'sanctified' ($ἁγιάζεται$) when they are acknowledged with thanksgiving as God-given realities. To deny the value of creation by compelling acts of renunciation, the author argues, is to ally oneself with demons and other errant spirits.

challenge radically ascetic interpretations of Paul, presenting instead an anti-ascetic version of his teaching that is far more consonant with Jewish teaching.' Pagels, however, does not consider that the ascetics themselves may be Jewish Christian teachers.

The Pastoral Epistles provided a foundation on which developed a Christian tradition that favoured the emerging clerical hierarchy and conformity to the established values of Greco-Roman society. They also proved to be extremely useful documents in the struggle between 'orthodox' and 'heretical' parties that increasingly consumed the attention of Christian leaders in the second century. Writing about 180 Bishop Irenaeus of Lyons was the first to show knowledge of the Pastorals and to quote them as letters of Paul. Indeed, the full title of his *magnum opus* against heresies, 'The Unmasking and Refutation of the Gnosis Falsely So-Called', derived directly from 1 Timothy 6: 20, and the work began with a quotation from 1 Timothy 1: 4.[24] Early in the third century, Hippolytus and Clement of Alexandria also cited the Pastorals in their polemics against the Encratites, and Tertullian did so against the Gnostics.[25] It appears that the very inclusion of the Pastoral Epistles within the catholic corpus of scripture by the end of the second century (e.g. the Muratorian Canon) was an effort by late second-century leaders to provide a 'correct' interpretation of Paul's letters, that is, one that favoured marriage and rejected compulsory asceticism.[26]

Despite the harsh polemic against compulsory asceticism evident in the Pastoral Epistles, the conflict between moderate and radically ascetic factions persisted throughout the second century. Eusebius of Caesarea, for example, reported that Bishop Dionysius of Corinth had discussed the question of marriage and celibacy at great length in his letters to various churches (c.170). In one letter to Bishop Pinytos of Cnossos on Crete, Dionysius urged his fellow bishop 'not to place the heavy burden of celibacy on the brethren as a requirement, but to remember that most people were weak creatures'. According to Eusebius, Bishop Pinytus was not impressed with the moderation of his episcopal colleague. Pinytus replied that he admired Dionysius, but he urged him to 'provide more solid food in the future'. Eusebius states that Pinytus requested of Dionysius 'a further letter, this time a more advanced one, so that they may not be kept all their lives on a diet of milky words and treated like babes till they grow old without knowing it'.[27]

---

[24] As noted by Gerd Lüdemann, *Heretics*, 135 and 201; also W. Schenk, 'Die Briefe an Timotheus I und II und an Titus (Pastoralbriefe) in der neueren Forschung (1945–1985)', *ANRW* ii.25.4 (1987), 3405–6.

[25] Hippolytus, *Haer.* 8.20.1–3 (PTS 25, 339); Clement, *Strom.* 3, *passim*; Tertullian, *Praescr.* 33.6–8 (CCSL 1, 214).

[26] As argued by Lüdemann, *Heretics*, 135–42. If Lüdemann is correct, such a development would have been consistent with the original intention of the author of the Pastorals who also wished to provide the 'correct' interpretation of Paul.

[27] Eusebius, *Hist. eccl.* 4.23.7–8 (SC 31, 204); trans. G. A. Williamson, *Eusebius: The History of the Church from Christ to Constantine* (Minneapolis, Minn.: Augsburg Publishing House, 1975), 184, slightly altered.

The correspondence between Dionysius of Corinth and Pinytus of Cnossos suggests, at the very least, that the perspectives of the Pastoral Epistles did not achieve immediate success among all Christians in the second century. Since Eusebius praised the 'orthodoxy' and learning of Bishop Pinytus, it appears that in the mid-second century it was not yet 'unorthodox' for a Christian bishop to attempt to require celibacy of his congregation, despite the gentle effort at dissuasion from his senior colleague. Giulia Sfameni Gasparro is surely correct when she states that around the year 170 'extremely different, at times conflicting, positions on the issue of sexual conduct coexisted and struggled for primacy within the church'.[28] The popularity of a variety of apocryphal Gospels and Acts throughout the second and third centuries (and beyond) attests to the persistence of the ascetic impulse in early Christianity.

By the end of the second century these deep tensions within Christianity led some bishops and Christian teachers to adopt a more aggressive discursive strategy to deal with those who attempted to enforce sexual renunciation on all Christians, namely the composition of anti-heretical treatises. As we shall see in the next section of this chapter, this new heresiological genre gave expression to notions of 'heresy' and 'orthodoxy' that now included the 'Encratite' heresy. The resultant discourse on marriage and celibacy marked the delimitation of new and sharper boundaries within the Christian communities of the second and third centuries.

2. ASCETIC HERESY AND THE FORMATION OF ORTHODOXY

The development of an 'orthodoxy' and 'heresy' of asceticism, to which I have just referred, was the result of at least two trends in second-century thought, both of which were foreshadowed in the teaching of the Pastoral Epistles. On the one hand, the spread of Christianity within the Greco-Roman world and the sporadic threat of Roman persecution led to the rise of early Christian apologetics. The Greek and Latin apologists of the second and early third centuries developed arguments in favour of Christianity that frequently stressed the high standards of conjugal morality practised by Christians. On the other hand, the increased prominence of radically ascetic groups, such as the followers of Marcion and Tatian, led to the formation of an anti-heretical tradition that built explicitly on the foundations laid by the Pastoral Epistles.

---

[28] 'Asceticism and Anthropology', 127.

Both of these currents contributed distinctive elements to the development of early Christian thought, and both must be examined further.

i. The Apologetic Argument

The earliest direct evidence of an official Roman view of Christianity dates from the opening decade of the second century. The relevant documents—the famous letter of Pliny to the emperor Trajan and the descriptions of Nero's persecution by Tacitus and Suetonius—all agree in classifying Christianity as 'superstition'. The term *superstitio* implied contempt for the social and religious traditions of Rome, and Tacitus further specified that Christians were guilty of 'hatred of the human race'. What lay behind the charge was primarily the Christian refusal to worship the gods of the state and to offer divine honours (*supplicatio*) to the Roman emperor, but there were social and familial dimensions as well. To accept new gods and to reject the old meant repudiating the *mos maiorum*, one's ancestral customs. In practice, to become a Christian often meant rejecting the religious authority of the head of the household, especially if the *paterfamilias* did not join his wife, children, or slaves in adopting the new religion.[29]

When Christian apologists began to respond to Roman criticism, they often focused on the charge of 'superstition' or 'impiety' and argued that Christianity fostered an authentic (and in many ways superior) brand of 'piety'. This apologetic strategy nearly always entailed an appeal to the strict marital practices of Christians. To a certain extent, the stress on marital morality was a response to the rumours of sexual immorality that circulated about Christians in the second century. But the Christian apologists went beyond a merely defensive posture and argued that Christian beliefs and the teaching of scripture provided Christians with moral guidance that enabled them to lead exemplary lives, particularly in the marital arena.

For example, Aristides of Athens, who addressed the earliest extant apology to the emperor Hadrian early in the second century, argued that God had provided Christians with strict precepts of marital morality that they observed in faith and in expectation of rewards and punishments in the world to come. As a result, Christians 'do not commit adultery or fornication', they 'honour

---

[29] This point is well developed by J. Kevin Coyle, 'Empire and Eschaton', *Église et Théologie*, 12 (1981), 36–41. On 'superstition' see L. F. Janssen, '"Superstitio" and the Persecution of Christians', *VC* 33 (1979), 131–59; Robert L. Wilken, *The Christians as the Romans Saw Them* (New Haven and London: Yale University Press, 1984), 48–67; and now Dale B. Martin, *Inventing Superstition: From the Hippocratics to the Christians* (Cambridge, Mass.: Harvard University Press, 2004).

father and mother', and they 'abstain from all illicit intercourse and from all uncleanness'.[30] Another early apologist, the anonymous author of the *Epistle to Diognetus*, expressed similar sentiments: '[Christians] marry like everyone else and have children, but they do not expose them once they are born. They share their meals but not their sexual partners.'[31] For these authors the probity of Christian marriage was a sign of the superiority of the Christian religion.

The appeal to the high moral stature of marriage among Christians became a recurrent theme in early Christian apologetics. Justin Martyr and Athenagoras of Athens both repeated the argument, adding that Christians marry only for the sake of procreation and that they strongly disapprove of divorce and remarriage.[32] Athenagoras even forbade remarriage after the death of a spouse, characterizing it as merely 'respectable adultery' ($εὐπρεπής ἐστι μοιχεία$): 'For he who detaches himself from his previous wife, even if she has died, is a covert adulterer. He thwarts the hand of God (because in the beginning God formed one man and one woman), and he destroys the communion of flesh with flesh in the unity characteristic of the intercourse of the sexes.'[33] Although not all Christians in the second century disapproved of remarriage after the death of a spouse as strenuously as did Athenagoras, there was a widespread consensus (promoted by the Christian apologists) that the Christian ethic was distinguished either by strict monogamy within marriage or else by total celibacy.[34]

Perhaps the most positive presentation of Christian marriage by an apologist was that of Bishop Theophilus of Antioch, who wrote in the latter part of the second century (*c*.180). In his apology *To Autolycus*, Theophilus spoke of marriage in terms that bordered on the language of romantic love. Describing the creation of Eve out of Adam's side, for example, Theophilus noted that

---

[30] Aristides, *Apol.* 15. I have translated from the Greek fragments edited by J. Armitage Robinson, *The Apology of Aristides on Behalf of the Christians* (TaS 1; Cambridge: Cambridge University Press, 1893; Reprint Nendeln/Liechtenstein: Kraus Reprint Limited, 1967), 111. The full text is extant only in Syriac translation.

[31] *Diogn.* 5.6–7; trans. Ehrman, *The Apostolic Fathers*, ii (LCL 25, 141).

[32] Justin, *1 Apol.* 15, 29; Athenagoras, *Leg.* 33.4–6.

[33] *Leg.* 33.6; trans. W. R. Schoedel, *Athenagoras: Legatio and De Resurrectione* (OECT; Oxford: Clarendon Press, 1972), 81.

[34] Minucius Felix, *Oct.* 31.5 (CSEL 2, 45), is typical: 'it is our pleasure to abide by the bond of a single marriage; in our desires for begetting children, we know one woman or none at all'; trans. G. W. Clarke, *The Octavius of Marcus Minucius Felix* (ACW 39; New York, NY and Paramus, NJ: Newman Press, 1974), 110. Cf. Tertullian, *Apol.* 9.19–20 (CCSL 1, 105); Theophilus, *Autol.* 3.13. The issue of remarriage was much discussed in the second and third centuries. See Hermas, *Mand.* 4.32.4, who concludes that remarriage is permitted, but that the person who remains a widow merits 'greater honour and glory with the Lord'. Clement of Alexandria, *Strom.* 3.1.4 and 3.12.82, expresses a similar view.

'God made woman by taking her from his side so that man's love for her might be greater':

> Adam said to Eve, 'This is now bone from my bones and flesh from my flesh,' and in addition he prophesied, saying, 'For this reason a man will leave his father and mother and will cleave to his wife, and the two shall be one flesh' (Gen 2: 23–24). This is actually fulfilled among us. For what man who marries lawfully does not disregard his mother and father and his whole family and all his relatives, while he cleaves to his own wife and unites with her, loving her more than them? For this reason husbands have often suffered even death for the sake of their wives.[35]

Unlike the earlier Greek apologists, Theophilus stressed the goodness of marriage and conjugal union more than the rigours of marital morality. The reason for this may be that Theophilus was already doing battle with some of the radical ascetic theologies that had arisen in the second century, most notably that of Marcion. His works profoundly influenced the next generation of Christian thinkers, among them the anti-heretical writers Irenaeus and Tertullian.[36]

The writings of the second-century apologists contributed significantly to the formation of a Christian discourse that fostered the acceptance of marriage and family life. Like the author of the Pastoral Epistles, the apologists sought to reassure outsiders that Christianity was not hostile to the values and social structures of the Greco-Roman world. Although they frequently contrasted Christian virtue with the supposed immorality of pagans, the arguments of the apologists presupposed that outsiders would recognize and admire the Christian practices of strict monogamy and sexual restraint. As Judith Evans Grubbs has observed, 'in addition to trying to refute pagan charges of immorality, Christians were also presenting those aspects of Christian social life which they felt would be most understandable and attractive to pagans.'[37] While the Christian appreciation of celibacy and strong disapproval of divorce were genuine novelties in the ancient world, the apologetic image of the Christian couple devoted to strict monogamy and procreation was

---

[35] Theophilus, *Autol.* 2.28; trans. R. M. Grant, *Theophilus of Antioch: Ad Autolycum* (OECT; Oxford: Clarendon Press, 1970), 71–3.

[36] According to Eusebius, *Hist. eccl.* 4.24 (SC 31, 206–7), Theophilus wrote a (now lost) treatise against Marcion, as well as one against Hermogenes. On the influence of Theophilus, see R. M. Grant, 'The Textual Tradition of Theophilus of Antioch', *VC* 6 (1952), 146–59; and Alain Le Boulluec, *La notion d'hérésie dans la littérature grecque (IIe–IIIe siècles)* (Paris: Études Augustiniennes, 1985), 210–15.

[37] Evans Grubbs, *Law and Family in Late Antiquity*, 71. As Evans Grubbs has noted, 64–5, during the late republic and early empire there emerged in the Roman world 'a newly emphasized ideology of the union of husband and wife as a permanent relationship of mutual respect and affection in which the wife was expected to be obedient and totally faithful to her husband, and in return was entitled to a position of dignity in her husband's eyes and in society'.

calculated to appeal to pagan sentiments that were already deeply sympathetic to the notion of conjugal virtue.

ii. Irenaeus, Tatian, and the Making of 'Encratism'

At the same time as the apologists were building a bridge between Christianity and Greco-Roman culture, another battle was being waged on a different front. In the second century the tensions we have glimpsed in Paul and the Pastorals erupted into open conflict and produced permanent divisions within the Christian community. Teachers such as Valentinus and Basilides, Cerdon and Marcion, Tatian and Julius Cassian, among others, produced versions of Christian theology and morality that differed in varying degrees from those of 'catholic' teachers. By the end of the second century Bishop Irenaeus of Lyons wrote his massive treatise *Against Heresies* in an effort to define the boundaries between authentic Christian teaching ('orthodoxy') and its opposite ('heresy'). Although this second-century conflict is sometimes referred to as the 'Gnostic crisis', on the issue of marriage and celibacy the debate actually had little to do with what might be called 'Gnosticism'. The discussion of Irenaeus, in fact, indicates that the link between the 'Encratites' and the 'Gnostics' was tenuous (and tendentious) at best.

The first book of *Against Heresies* was devoted to the views of those normally characterized as 'Gnostics': Valentinus, Ptolemy, Marcus, Saturninus, Basilides, and the like. But towards the end of the book, Irenaeus began to discuss the principle that 'heretical sects' tend to produce offshoots from one another. In this context he presented the following paragraph on the 'so-called Encratites' and their leader Tatian:

To cite an example, the so-called Encratites, who sprang from Saturninus and Marcion, preached abstinence from marriage and so made void God's pristine creation, and indirectly reprove him who made male and female for generating the human race. They also introduced abstinence from what is called by them animal food, being thus ungrateful to the God who made all things. They deny salvation to the first-formed man. This was but recently fabricated by them.

After thus introducing the 'Encratites', Irenaeus then proceeded to imagine a single source for their heretical opinions:

A certain Tatian was the first to introduce this blasphemy. He had been a follower of Justin and, as long as he was with him, he did not express such a view. However, after Justin's martyrdom, he apostatized from the Church and as a teacher he was conceited and elated and puffed up as if he were superior to the rest. It was then that he composed his own standard of teaching. He related a myth about invisible Aeons similar to those of Valentinus. Like Marcion and Saturninus, he declared that marriage was corruption and fornication. The denial of salvation to Adam was his own invention.[38]

As several scholars have observed, Irenaeus' entry on the Encratites is less than fair-minded. He has assembled under the single label of 'Encratite' the perspectives of several teachers whose views differed significantly from each other; some of them, as the Pastoral Epistles indicate, must have predated Tatian. Moreover, by connecting the 'Encratites' to the opinions of Valentinus, Saturninus and Marcion, Irenaeus was attempting to place them within a line of 'Gnostic' succession that is more a heresiological fiction than fact.[39]

For example, all of the extant sources of Tatian's theology indicate that he differed significantly from Marcion and the so-called 'Gnostics'.[40] As Clement of Alexandria noted, Valentinus and his followers tended to be positively disposed towards marriage and (possibly) towards sexual union, at least between fellow Valentinians. Others, such as Basilides and his son Isidore, preferred celibacy but tolerated marriage on the basis of Paul's advice in 1 Corinthians 7, a position that differed in no way from that of Tertullian or Jerome.[41] Marcion certainly rejected marriage, but he did so because he believed that an inferior Creator-God had produced the world, not the beneficent and transcendent Father of Jesus. For Marcion, to engage in sex and to procreate children was to perpetuate a corrupt creation and to fulfil the mandate of the Creator-God, 'Increase and multiply'.[42]

Tatian, by contrast, explicitly rejected the Marcionite doctrine of creation by a lesser God.[43] In his *Oration to the Greeks*, a work which, in some respects,

---

[38] *Haer.* 1.28.1 (SC 264, 354–6); trans. Dominic J. Unger, with further revisions by John J. Dillon, *St. Irenaeus of Lyons: Against the Heresies*, i (ACW 55; New York, NY and Mahwah, NJ: The Newman Press, 1992), 93. The Greek of this passage is preserved in Eusebius, *Hist. eccl.* 4.29.2–3 (SC 31, 213). Cf. Irenaeus, *Haer.* 3.23.8 (SC 211, 466), where he claimed that Tatian had become 'the connecting point of all the heretics' (*connexio... omnium haereticorum*).

[39] See the comments of Le Boulluec, *La notion d'hérésie*, 173; Sfameni Gasparro, *Enkrateia e antropologia*, 23–31; and G. Quispel, 'The Study of Encratism', in U. Bianchi (ed.), *La tradizione dell'enkrateia*, 73–4. All are dependent upon the detailed analysis of Franco Bolgiani, 'La tradizione eresiologica sull'encratismo, i. La notizie di Ireneo', *Atti dell'Accademia delle scienze di Torino*, 91 (1956–7), 343–419.

[40] As Michael Williams has demonstrated, *Rethinking 'Gnosticism'*, 139–62, there never was a consistent 'Gnostic' view on asceticism. R. M. Grant, however, believes that there is much 'Valentinian' influence on Tatian's *Oratio ad graecos*: 'The Heresy of Tatian', *JTS*, n.s. 5 (1954), 62–8; 'Tatian (or. 30) and the Gnostics', *JTS*, n.s. 15 (1964), 65–9.

[41] Clement, *Strom.* 3.1.1–2; Irenaeus, *Haer.* 1.6.4 (SC 264, 98–100), implied such ambivalence on the part of Valentinians as well.

[42] Tertullian, *Marc.* 1.29.1–9 (CCSL 1, 472–4); Clement, *Strom.* 3.3.12; 3.4.25.

[43] Tatian himself may even have authored an anti-Marcionite discussion of problematic biblical texts. Eusebius, *Hist. eccl.* 5.28.4 (SC 41, 75), speaks of Tatian writing against heretics, and in *Hist. eccl.* 5.13.8 (SC 41, 44) he mentions an anti-Marcionite book by Tatian's disciple

does evince heterodox tendencies,[44] Tatian portrayed the creation of human beings as the work of the divine Word who was present 'in the beginning' with the Father.[45] Created as an 'image of immortality' and originally destined to share in God's own eternal life (*or.* 7.1), the first human beings consisted of a harmonious union of body (σῶμα), soul (ψυχή), and spirit (πνεῦμα). Had they remained united with the divine Spirit, they would have lived forever. But through the exercise of free will, they rejected union with the Spirit of God. As a result their souls lost the power to escape death and suffered mortality along with the body: 'If the soul lives alone it inclines downwards towards matter and dies with the flesh, but if it gains union with the divine Spirit it is not unaided, but mounts to the realms above where the Spirit leads it; for the Spirit's home is above, but the soul's birth is below.'[46] Contrary to the insinuations of Irenaeus, Tatian began from an impeccably 'orthodox' starting point: the unity of body, soul, and spirit as the creation of a good God.[47]

While Tatian was neither a Gnostic nor a follower of Marcion, the inferences he drew from his theology of the fall did lead him to 'encratite' conclusions. Having lost their primal union with the divine Spirit and having suffered the penalty of death, human beings came under the dominion of demons and started to live like animals (*or.* 15.3). Lust for power, wealth, glory, and sex have afflicted humanity after the fall (*or.* 11.1). But all is not lost. People still retain their freedom and a trace of the divine Spirit within them. Echoing Paul (Col 2: 20, Rom 6: 10), Tatian asserted that people still have the potential to 'die to the world' and to 'live to God':

'Die to the world' by rejecting its madness; 'live to God' by comprehending him and rejecting the old birth (τὴν παλαιὰν γένεσιν). We were not born to die, but die

Rhodon, which was based on Tatian's work. See L. W. Barnard, 'The Heresy of Tatian—Once Again', *JEH* 19 (1968), 3–4, and Le Boulluec, *La notion d'hérésie*, 209–10.

[44] Demonstrated decisively by R. M. Grant, 'The Heresy of Tatian', although Grant follows Irenaeus too closely in stressing the affinities with Valentinianism. See now Emily J. Hunt, *Christianity in the Second Century: The Case of Tatian* (London and New York: Routledge, 2003), 20–36.

[45] *Or.* 5.1, cf. John 1: 1. I cite Tatian from the edition of Molly Whittaker, *Tatian: Oratio ad Graecos and Fragments* (OECT; Oxford: Clarendon Press, 1982). The date of Tatian's oration cannot be determined with any certainty. R. M. Grant, 'The Date of Tatian's Oration', *HTR* 46 (1953), 99–101, argued that it could be located precisely to the years 177/178, but his arguments have not found universal acceptance. See the criticisms of G. W. Clarke, 'The Date of the Oration of Tatian', *HTR* 60 (1967), 123–36, and L. W. Barnard, 'The Heresy of Tatian', 1–3.

[46] *Or.* 13.1–2; trans. Whittaker, 27, slightly altered.

[47] As Tatian observed in *or.* 19.2, 'the structure of the world is good, but conduct in it is bad'; trans. Whittaker, 39. Brown, *Body and Society*, 90–102, provides a valuable overview of Tatian and the encratite worldview. See also Martin Elze, *Tatian und seine Theologie* (Göttingen: Vandenhoek and Ruprecht, 1960), 83–100; and Kathy L. Gaca, *The Making of Fornication: Eros, Ethics, and Political Reform in Greek Philosophy and Early Christianity* (Berkeley: University of California Press, 2003), 221–46.

through our own fault. Free will has destroyed us; born free, we have become slaves; we have been put up for sale because of sin. God has done nothing bad, it was we who exhibited wickedness; but we who exhibited it are still capable of rejecting it.[48]

The aim of the Christian life, as Tatian envisioned it, was to restore the lost union with the Holy Spirit: 'we ought now to search for what we once had and have lost, and link the soul to the Holy Spirit and busy ourselves with the union ordained by God.'[49] If a person was willing to reject the 'constitution that makes for death', Tatian believed, it was possible to re-establish the ancient connection with God's Spirit and to regain immortality.

In his *Oration to the Greeks* Tatian did not explicitly address the question of sexual relations within marriage. This may have been due to the apologetic character of that work. But there is little doubt about the eventual evolution of his thought. In his treatise, *On Perfection According to the Saviour*, which was known and cited by Clement of Alexandria, Tatian made it clear that he regarded all sexual union, whether within or outside marriage, as 'fornication'. For example, when the apostle Paul urged sexual continence for the sake of prayer (1 Cor 7: 5), Tatian argued, he demonstrated that sexual union was an obstacle to union with God's Spirit. And when Paul distinguished between the 'old man' and the 'new man', Tatian insisted, he intended to draw a sharp boundary between the sexual activity permitted in the Old Testament and the sexual abstinence prescribed in the New Testament.[50] Although he was neither a Gnostic nor a follower of Marcion, Tatian certainly did reject all Christian involvement in sex or marriage.

The teaching of Tatian gave definitive expression to a 'tradition of *enkrateia*' that would continue to exert a powerful influence on early Christian thought. The centrepiece of this 'encratite' theology was the notion that sexuality was not a feature of the original creation by God, but rather a result of the original sin or fall of Adam and Eve. Sexual restraint or continence ($\dot{\varepsilon}\gamma\kappa\rho\dot{\alpha}\tau\varepsilon\iota\alpha$) thus had a 'protological' motivation; it was an attempt to return to the pre-lapsarian state of humanity: before sin, before death, and before sex.[51] Celibacy and salvation go hand in hand in the encratite vision, as the

---

[48] *Or.* 11.2; trans. Whittaker, 23.   [49] *Or.* 15.1; trans. Whittaker, 31.

[50] Clement, *Strom.* 3.12.81–2, 89 (Stählin-Früchtel 2, 232–4, 237); cf. Irenaeus, *Haer.* 1.28.1 (SC 264, 354–6). In *Haer.* 3.23.8 (SC 211, 466–8) Irenaeus states that Tatian also used 1 Cor 15: 22 ('For as all die in Adam ...') to demonstrate that Adam could not be saved. Tatian's ascetical inclinations also appeared in his *Diatesseron*, which included numerous ascetically oriented readings. See William L. Peterson, 'Tatian's Diatesseron', in H. Koester, *Ancient Christian Gospels: Their History and Development* (Philadelphia: Trinity Press International, 1990), 403–30; Quispel, 'Study of Encratism', 55.

[51] Well summarized in U. Bianchi, 'La tradition de l'*enkrateia*: motivations ontologiques et protologiques', in Bianchi (ed.), *La tradizione dell'enkrateia*, 293–315.

ascetic Christian attempts to acquire once more the pristine purity of paradise. Quite distinct from Valentinianism or Marcionism, insofar as it allowed for a single God and an originally good creation, the encratism of Tatian eventually found expression in the Thomas literature of Syrian Christianity.[52] And as we shall see below, it will reappear, though with some significant modifications, in more 'orthodox' currents of early Christian thought.

Despite the long afterlife of Tatian's encratism, the condemnation by Irenaeus in *Against Heresies* was a decisive moment in the development of early Christian discourse on 'orthodoxy' and 'heresy'. The toleration shown towards a Pinytus of Cnossos was a thing of the past, at least within the mainstream Christian churches. From this point forward, the notion of 'heresy' was to include the encratite rejection of sexual intercourse and marriage, and subsequent heresiologists did not fail to echo Irenaeus and to inscribe Tatian and his followers within a 'Gnostic' succession of teachers.[53] Irenaeus, however, did not attempt to refute the encratite conclusions of Tatian in any detail. For Irenaeus, Tatian's alleged association with Marcion and Valentinus was enough to justify his condemnation. It was left to another anti-heretical writer, Clement of Alexandria, to develop more fully the 'orthodox' refutation of Tatian and 'the so-called Encratites'. In the course of doing so, Clement produced the most extensive and articulate defence of marriage in the first three centuries of Christian literature. He also provided a powerful precedent for Jovinian's polemics against radical asceticism.

iii. Clement of Alexandria

In the writings of Clement of Alexandria both the apologetic and the anti-heretical traditions of the second century reached a definitive culmination. Like the previous Greek apologists, Clement tried to demonstrate the compatibility between Christianity and the highest ideals of Greco-Roman culture. Because he believed that the divine Logos who became incarnate in Jesus Christ had also inspired (however imperfectly) the ancient Greek philosophers, Clement saw Christianity as the true fulfilment of the Hellenic tradition. Clement could certainly be hostile to particular teachings of

---

[52] G. Quispel, 'L'Evangile selon Thomas et les origins de l'ascèse chrétienne', in his *Gnostic Studies*, ii (Leiden: Nederlands Historisch-Archaeologisch Instituut te Istanbul, 1975), 98–112. The links between Tatian and Syriac texts such as the *Acts of Thomas* and *Odes of Solomon* have been demonstrated by E. Hunt, *Christianity in the Second Century*, 155–66. See also my discussion in 'Acts of Thomas: Scene One', in R. Valantassis (ed.), *Religions of Late Antiquity in Practice* (Princeton, NJ: Princeton University Press, 2000), 207–9.

[53] Epiphanius, *Haer.* 46–7; Filastrius, *Haer.* 48, 72; Augustine, *Haer.* 25. By contrast, Hippolytus, *Haer.* 8.20.1–3 (PTS 25, 339), who preferred to give a philosophical pedigree to heretics, claimed that the 'Encratites' were influenced by the Cynics.

individual philosophers; for example, he blamed Plato and Pythagoras for holding excessively negative views of the body and, therefore, for leading Christian heretics to reject marriage. In many respects, however, Clement's teaching on marriage closely followed the pattern set by Greco-Roman moralists, such as Plutarch and Musonius Rufus, who saw marriage as fully compatible with the life of philosophical virtue.[54]

Like many of his Christian and non-Christian contemporaries, Clement displayed a deep circumspection and caution regarding sexual activity. Like the Stoic philosopher Musonius Rufus, Clement argued that sexual relations should take place only within marriage and only for the purpose of procreation. He also shared the view of certain medical writers, such as Galen, who held that sexual activity, at least among males, could drain the body of its vital energy or *pneuma*.[55] But Clement could also speak of marriage in terms that echoed the contemporary philosophical ideal of marriage as a chaste and harmonious partnership. And echoing verbatim the teaching of Musonius, Clement could envision marriage as necessary for the well-being of the city and the world at large: 'For when people do not marry and produce children they contribute to the scarcity of human beings and destroy both the cities and the world that is composed of them.'[56]

This essentially positive attitude prevailed in Clement's discussion of marriage in the third book of his *Stromata* ('Miscellanies'). Although he dealt briefly with Marcion and with Christians such as Carpocrates, who allegedly advocated sexual licentiousness, the bulk of Clement's discussion was aimed at Tatian, Julius Cassian, and those whose thinking could be broadly characterized as 'encratite'.[57] The reason for this is plain. Unlike Marcion, Christians

---

[54] *Strom.* 3.3.12–13, 16–20. In 3.3.21 Clement claims that Marcion's pessimistic evaluation of marriage derived from the influence of philosophy. For Clement's evaluation of philosophy in general, see *Strom.* 1.12.80 and 7.3.20 (SC 428, 84–8). On the Middle Platonic background of Clement's own thought, see S. Lilla, *Clement of Alexandria: A Study in Christian Platonism and Gnosticism* (Oxford: Clarendon Press, 1971), and Annawies Van den Hoek, *Clement of Alexandria and his Use of Philo in the Stromateis* (Leiden: Brill, 1988).

[55] *Paed.* 2.10.94 (SC 108, 180–2). On the second-century medical view, see A. Rouselle, *Porneia: On Desire and the Body in Antiquity* (Oxford: Blackwell, 1988), 5–23; Brown, *Body and Society*, 18–20.

[56] *Strom.* 2.23.141 (Stählin-Früchtel 2, 191). The parallels with Musonius were established by P. Wendland, *Quaestiones Musonianae: De Musonio Stoico Clementis Alexandrini aliorumque auctore* (Berlin, 1886); discussed in J. Behr, *Asceticism and Anthropology in Irenaeus and Clement* (OECS; Oxford: Clarendon Press, 2000), 162–3.

[57] *Strom.* 3.3.12–4.39 (Marcion); 3.2.5–11, 3.5.40–4 (Carpocrates). When referring to specific groups mentioned by the heresiologists (whether real or imagined), I shall use the upper-case 'Encratites'. When referring to views that follow the general outlines of Tatian's theology, I shall use the lower-case 'encratite' or 'encratism'. Later in this chapter I shall have occasion to distinguish between encratite views that were 'radical' (i.e. that rejected sex and marriage altogether) and those that were 'moderate' (i.e. that elevated celibacy over marriage, but did not reject marriage altogether).

influenced by encratism adhered to the orthodox belief in one supreme God and the original goodness of creation. Because they shared this common ground, a more extensive theological conversation was possible between orthodox and encratite Christians. Moreover, as noted above, ascetics such as Tatian based their repudiation of sex and marriage on an alternative reading of the same scriptures that the orthodox possessed. Much of Clement's response, therefore, consisted of presenting a rival, non-ascetic interpretation of various encratite proof-texts.

The starting point of Clement's defence of marriage was the doctrine of the goodness of creation. The basic error of all the heretics, Clement argued, was 'hatred of what God has created'.[58] To reject marriage and procreation is simply to 'blaspheme under a pious cloak both the creation and the holy Creator, the almighty only God'.[59] In contrast to the encratite heretic who disparages creation, Clement presented the ideal ('Gnostic') Christian as one who has learned 'to love the creation of the God and Creator of all things'.[60] He regards the world and all that is in it as sanctified by God, who in the beginning declared all things good. Into this vision of a good creation Clement integrated the work of marriage and procreation, which he describes as 'cooperation with the work of creation'.[61]

When Clement came to discuss the encratite use of the bible, he gave a central place to the teaching of Jesus and Paul. For example, in response to Tatian's drawing of contrasts between the characteristics of the 'old' and the 'new' dispensations, Clement cited the gospel text that presented Jesus' prohibition of divorce, along with its citations from the book of Genesis. Since Jesus came 'not to destroy the law, but to fulfill it', Clement observed, it must be possible to make use of marriage in a self-restrained manner and not to divide what God has joined. By prohibiting divorce, Clement insisted, Jesus showed his clear support for marriage.[62] Moreover, by citing the two passages from Genesis, Clement argued, Jesus had demonstrated that the Old

---

[58] *Strom.* 3.5.40 (Stählin-Früchtel 2, 214). I cite Clement's *Stromata* 3 from the translation of Henry Chadwick in John Ernest Leonard Oulton and Henry Chadwick (eds.), *Alexandrian Christianity* (LCC 2; Philadelphia: Westminster Press, 1954). Clement's teaching on marriage has been thoroughly studied by Jean-Paul Broudéhoux, *Mariage et famille chez Clément d'Alexandrie* (Paris: Beauchesne, 1970). See also M. Mees, 'Clemens von Alexandrien über Ehe und Familie', *Aug* 17 (1977), 113–31; Gaca, *Making of Fornication*, 247–72.

[59] *Strom.* 3.6.45 (Stählin-Früchtel 2, 216).

[60] *Strom.* 3.10.69 (Stählin-Früchtel 2, 227); trans. Chadwick, 72.

[61] *Strom.* 3.9.66 (Stählin-Früchtel 2, 226). Cf. *Paed.* 2.10.83 (SC 108, 164): 'In this way the human person becomes the image of God, by cooperating in the creation of another human being.'

[62] *Strom.* 3.6.45 (Stählin-Früchtel 2, 217).

and the New Testaments, the Law and the Gospel, could not stand in any fundamental contradiction:

> How then can marriage be a state only intended for ancient times and an invention of the law, and marriage on Christian principles of a different nature, if we hold that the Old and the New Testaments proclaim the same God? 'For what God has joined together no man may ever put asunder' for any good reason; if the Father commanded this, so much the more also will the Son keep it. If the author of the law and the gospel is the same, he never contradicts himself.[63]

Tatian and his encratite followers had based their ascetic renunciation on the belief that Jesus Christ had instituted a new dispensation of salvation that required repudiating a creation that had become irrevocably steeped in error and corruption. Against them Clement insisted that there is a profound continuity between the old and the new dispensations and that Jesus himself had illustrated this with his teaching on divorce.

Clement made a similar use of the writings of Paul, both the authentic Paul of the First Letter to the Corinthians and the pseudo-Paul of the Pastoral Epistles and the Letter to the Ephesians. This is especially evident when Clement discussed Tatian's treatise *On Perfection According to the Saviour*. As we have seen, Tatian made prominent use of 1 Corinthians 7: 5, where Paul advised the Christian couple not to abstain from sex, 'except perhaps by agreement for a set time, to devote yourselves to prayer, and then come together again, so that Satan may not tempt you because of your lack of self-control'. Clement quoted Tatian's interpretation of the text as follows:

> While agreement to be continent makes prayer possible, intercourse of corruption destroys it. By the very disparaging way in which [the apostle Paul] allows it, he forbids it. For although he allowed them to come together again because of Satan and the temptation to incontinence, he indicated that the man who takes advantage of this permission will be serving two masters, God if there is 'agreement', but, if there is no such agreement, incontinence, fornication, and the devil.[64]

As Tatian read the text of Paul, the 'temptation' of Satan was not the desire for sex outside marriage, but the desire for sex even within marriage. All marital intercourse, in Tatian's view, involved incontinence, fornication, and enslavement to the devil.

In his response to Tatian's encratite reading of Paul, Clement argued that the apostle had conceded to the Christian couple only that they should adopt a temporary period of celibacy; he had not meant to denigrate sex or marriage. Paul's point, Clement observed, was that excessive abstinence

---

[63] *Strom.* 3.12.83 (Stählin-Früchtel 2, 234); trans. Chadwick, 79.
[64] *Strom.* 3.12.81 (Stählin-Früchtel 2, 232); trans. Chadwick, 77–8.

might lead to fornication, not, as Tatian would have it, that marital intercourse was itself fornication. Moreover, like Jesus, Paul also affirmed the continuity between the old and new dispensations when he stated, 'the law is holy and the commandment holy, righteous, and good' (Rom 7: 12). If the law is holy, Clement concluded, then marriage is also holy. That is why the apostle in Ephesians 5: 31–2 could cite the Old Testament law (Gen 2: 24) and refer the marital imagery of Genesis to the 'mystery' of the union between Christ and the Church.[65]

Clement further developed his rehabilitation of the apostle Paul by turning to the view of marriage expressed in the Pastoral Epistles. Because of their anti-ascetical tendencies, the Pastorals were particularly suited to Clement's anti-encratite agenda. In several places Clement noted that the author of the Pastorals had expressed his preference that candidates for the office of bishop and deacon should be married men who had demonstrated their suitability by the orderly management of a household.[66] Clement also observed that in 1 Timothy 5: 14–15 the apostle had advised younger widows to 'marry, bear children, and manage their households', so as to avoid the temptation of Satan.[67] Moreover, in 1 Timothy 2: 15 'Paul' had explicitly stated that the married person would be 'saved by child-bearing'.[68] As a result, Clement concluded, marriage itself could not be the temptation of Satan nor the 'fornication' that Tatian claimed it was.

Above all, Clement appealed to the apostle's prediction in 1 Timothy 4: 1–5 that there would arise 'hypocritical sophists' who would 'forbid marriage and demand abstinence from foods which God created to be eaten with thanksgiving by believers who know the truth'. Such a prediction, Clement argued, decisively demonstrated that 'it is wrong to forbid marriage and indeed eating meat or drinking wine.' Like Jovinian, Clement denied that there was any intrinsic merit to either eating or not eating: 'But both he who eats with thanksgiving and he who does not eat, who also offers thanksgiving and has a continent enjoyment, should live in accordance with reason.'[69] In short, Clement insisted:

All the epistles of the apostle teach self-control and continence and contain numerous instructions about marriage, begetting children, and domestic life. But they nowhere rule out self-controlled marriage. Rather they preserve the harmony of the law and the gospel and approve both the man who with thanks to God enters upon marriage with

---

[65] *Strom.* 3.12.84 (Stählin-Früchtel 2, 234).
[66] *Strom.* 3.12.79 (Stählin-Früchtel 2, 231–2); 3.18.108 (Stählin-Früchtel 2, 246).
[67] *Strom.* 3.12.89 (Stählin-Früchtel 2, 237).
[68] *Strom.* 3.12.90 (Stählin-Früchtel 2, 237).
[69] *Strom.* 3.12.85 (Stählin-Früchtel 2, 235); trans. Chadwick, 80.

sobriety and the man who in accordance with the Lord's will lives as a celibate, even as each individual is called, making his choice without blemish and in perfection.[70]

Reading the authentic Paul in the light of the Pastoral Epistles, Clement refuted the encratite interpretation by pointing to the domestic, familial, and marital virtues stressed in these letters. For Clement, as for Jovinian, the 'Paul' of the Pastorals was the hermeneutical key to the Paul of 1 Corinthians 7.[71]

But Clement's opposition to encratite theology concerned more than rival interpretations of biblical texts. Behind the strictly exegetical dispute lay a deeper theological question: What was the nature of the 'original sin' of Adam and Eve? As we have seen, Tatian's encratism derived from his conviction that the sin of the first human beings had led directly to the practice of sexual intercourse. For Tatian the loss of primal unity between the human soul and the divine Spirit had entailed human mortality and the subsequent necessity of sexual reproduction. Other advocates of encratism envisioned an even more pessimistic scenario. For example, Julius Cassian, a second-century writer whom Clement also attacked in Book Three of the *Stromata*, had argued that human beings were originally constituted as spiritual creatures. The soul itself, originally divine, fell into the 'birth and corruption of this world' after it had conceived 'lust' ($\epsilon\pi\iota\vartheta\upsilon\mu\iota\alpha$).[72] Hence Julius interpreted the 'coats of skins' of Genesis 3: 21 as the bodies that Adam and Eve put on after being driven from paradise.[73] Moreover, Clement observed, Julius held that it was the serpent that had persuaded Adam and Eve to imitate irrational animals by engaging in sexual intercourse.[74]

In response to the encratite link between sex, human birth, and original sin, Clement developed several arguments. First, he maintained that the doctrine of the Incarnation refuted the encratite assumption that physical birth was unequivocally evil: 'If birth is something evil, let the blasphemers say that the Lord who shared in birth was born in evil, and that the virgin gave birth to him in evil. Woe to these wicked fellows! They blaspheme against the will of

---

[70] *Strom.* 3.12.86 (Stählin-Früchtel 2, 235); trans. Chadwick, 80.

[71] Clement's exegetical strategy is precisely the reverse of that employed by Jerome and other ascetic teachers. As Elizabeth Clark has observed, Jerome deployed the Paul of 1 Corinthians 7 to 'answer back' the 'Paul' of the Pastoral Epistles and other late New Testament books. See her discussion in *Reading Renunciation: Asceticism and Scripture in Early Christianity* (Princeton, NJ: Princeton University Press, 1999), 355–70.

[72] *Strom.* 3.13.93 (Stählin-Früchtel 2, 239).

[73] *Strom.* 3.14.95 (Stählin-Früchtel 2, 239–40). According to Clement, Julius Cassian even denied that human sexual organs were created by the one true God (*Strom.* 3.13.91). Julius' interpretation of the 'coats of skins' (Gen 3: 21) was to have a long history in Christianity, especially in the Origenist tradition. See Pier Franco Beatrice, 'Le tuniche di pelle: Antiche letture di Gen. 3, 21', in U. Bianchi (ed.), *La tradizione dell'Encrateia*, 433–82 (471–7 on Julius Cassian and the encratite interpretation).

[74] *Strom.* 3.17.102 (Stählin-Früchtel 2, 243).

God and the mystery of creation in speaking evil of birth.'[75] It was no accident, Clement suggested, that heretics such as Marcion and Julius Cassian taught that Jesus had never undergone a truly human birth. The encratite attempt to denigrate human conception and birth, Clement argued, inevitably led to a docetic christology since it alienated bodily reality from the events of salvation. By contrast, an 'orthodox' understanding of creation and salvation, he insisted, must involve the body in both spheres of divine action: 'Without the body how could the divine plan for us in the Church achieve its end? Surely the Lord himself, the head of the Church, came in the flesh, though without form and beauty (Is 53: 2) to teach us to look upon the formless and incorporeal nature of the divine Cause.'[76] For Clement the very 'fleshliness' of the Incarnation implied the essential goodness of fleshly realities such as human birth.

In addition to this emphasis on the Incarnation, Clement also attacked the encratite notion that sex was somehow connected with the transmission of original sin. According to Clement, some encratite teachers (he seems to have Julius Cassian in mind) had cited a number of biblical passages, among them Job 14: 4 ('No one is pure from defilement, not even if his life last one day') and Psalm 51: 5 ('In sin I was born and in unrighteousness my mother conceived me'). Such texts were invoked to support the encratite view that birth was an evil, 'not only for the body, but also for the soul'.[77] Clement responded by arguing that the newborn child could not be guilty of sin in any way: 'Let them tell us how the newly born child could commit fornication, or how that which has done nothing has fallen under the curse of Adam.' As for the birth of the psalmist, Clement observed that even if he was conceived in sin, 'yet he was not himself in sin, nor is he himself sin.'[78] Although Clement was willing to entertain the idea that the 'original sin' of Adam and Eve might have involved a premature indulgence in sexual relations, he insisted that sex itself—and indeed the human body and the entire material world—was part of the original creation that God had blessed and declared 'very good'.[79]

Clement's profound appreciation of marriage and family life eventually led him to conclude that in a certain way the married man could be regarded as

---

[75] *Strom.* 3.17.102 (Stählin-Früchtel 2, 243); trans. Chadwick, 88.
[76] *Strom.* 3.17.103 (Stählin-Früchtel 2, 243–4); trans. Chadwick, 89.
[77] *Strom.* 3.16.100 (Stählin-Früchtel 2, 242).
[78] *Strom.* 3.16.100 (Stählin-Früchtel 2, 242); trans. Chadwick, 87.
[79] *Strom.* 3.17.103 (Stählin-Früchtel 2, 243–4). For Clement's suggestion that the first sin might have involved sexual relations by a 'youthful' Adam and Eve, see *Strom.* 3.14.94 and 3.17.103. The idea that Adam and Eve might have originally sinned because of their immaturity was widespread in the second century. It is found in both Irenaeus and Theophilus. See A. Orbe, 'El pecado original y el matrimonio en la teología del s. II', *Greg* 45 (1964), 449–500, esp. 468–81. The idea was discussed and rejected by Augustine, *Gen. litt.* 11.41.57.

superior to the celibate. In the seventh book of the *Stromata*, in the midst of a discussion of the conduct of the true 'Gnostic' (that is, the ideal Christian), Clement argued that the highest virtue is not necessarily shown in the choice of a celibate life:

> Hence with him eating and drinking and marrying are not the main objects of life, though they are its necessary conditions. I speak of marriage sanctioned by reason and in accordance with right: for being made perfect he has the apostles as his patterns.[80] And true manhood is shown not in the choice of a celibate life; on the contrary, the prize in the contest of men is won by him who has trained himself by the discharge of the duties of husband and father and by the supervision of a household, regardless of pleasure and pain—by him, I say, who in the midst of his solicitude for his family shows himself inseparable from the love of God and rises superior to every temptation which assails him through children and wife and servants and possessions.[81]

In contrast to the married man, the celibate who has no family is 'in most respects untried'. While the celibate has the advantage of being able to attend to his own salvation and is freer of temptation, Clement writes, the married householder is superior in his actual conduct of life (ἐν τῇ κατὰ τὸν βίον οἰκονομίᾳ) because he preserves a 'faint image of the true Providence'.

Clement's argument on behalf of the 'superiority' of the married man over the celibate should not be misunderstood. There is no evidence that Clement wished to denigrate celibacy or to invert the ascetic hierarchy in favour of marriage. Elsewhere in the *Stromata*, for example, he spoke of marriage and celibacy as equally valid Christian vocations:

> Whether a man becomes a celibate or whether he joins himself in marriage with a woman for the sake of children, his purpose ought to be to remain unyielding to what is inferior.... Both celibacy and marriage have their own different forms of service and ministry to the Lord; I have in mind the caring for one's wife and children. For it seems that the particular characteristic of the married state is that it gives the man who desires a perfect marriage an opportunity to take responsibility for everything in the home which he shares with his wife. The apostle says that one should appoint bishops who by their oversight over their own house have learned to be in charge of the whole church. Let each man therefore fulfil his ministry by the work in which he was called, that he may be free in Christ and receive the proper reward of his ministry.[82]

Both marriage and celibacy, Clement insisted, provide distinctive forms of service (λειτουργία) and ministry (διακονία) for the Lord. Clement's aim was not to depreciate celibacy, but to emphasize the value of marriage in a world

---

[80] Like Jovinian, Clement had previously argued that most of the apostles were married men, including Peter, Philip, and even Paul. See *Strom.* 3.6.52–3.
[81] *Strom.* 7.12.70; trans. Chadwick, 138.
[82] *Strom.* 3.12.79 (Stählin-Früchtel 2, 231–2); trans. Chadwick, 76–7.

of increasing enthusiasm for the ascetic ideal. One might even say that Clement sought to articulate once more the vision of the Pastoral Epistles and to defend the role of the Christian householder and the Christian household within the 'household of God'.

Through the efforts of church leaders such as Irenaeus and Clement, a new boundary had emerged within Christianity by the beginning of the third century. Christian 'orthodoxy' now entailed the acceptance of marriage and the repudiation of radical encratism. To reject marriage had become 'heresy', and, as noted above, the 'Encratites' now entered the growing lists of deviant groups compiled by early Christian heresiologists. If the writings of Irenaeus and Clement accurately reflect the orthodox consensus in the early third century, it appears that the voices of moderation had achieved a tentative victory over radical encratism. Especially in the work of Clement of Alexandria, we see a defence of marriage that deliberately balanced the competing claims of ascetic and non-ascetic Christians. While neither celibacy nor marriage was considered an intrinsically higher form of Christianity, Clement argued, both ways of life provided opportunities for virtue and obedience to the divine Logos.

The orthodox 'victory' over encratism, however, was to be short-lived. Although the churches of the third century were constituted by a 'silent majority' of Christians who married, raised children, and remained committed to the social values of the Christian household, a new rigorism soon emerged in the churches of the third and fourth centuries. As Peter Brown has observed:

> In the upper echelons of the Church, Clement's voice was soon drowned. The copious works written by the bishops and clergy of the third and fourth centuries pass for the history of late antique Christianity. It is they that now line the shelves of our libraries. These writings tacitly abandoned Clement's mission. A younger generation of leaders were simply not interested in rethinking the issue of the sanctification of the married, as Clement plainly felt himself obliged to do. Their slogan was 'virginity'.[83]

As we shall see in the next section of this chapter, third-century thinkers, such as Tertullian, Cyprian, and Origen, while avoiding the extremes of radical encratism, developed approaches to marriage and sexuality that echoed in significant ways the perspectives of Tatian and his followers. Through their mediation, prominent themes from earlier encratite theology entered into the mainstream of Western Christian theology, particularly into the writings of Jerome and Ambrose. Central to this new discourse was the notion that celibacy is superior to marriage.

---

[83] Brown, *Body and Society*, 138.

3. THE LEGACY OF THE THIRD CENTURY

Although Irenaeus and Clement could be said to have articulated the 'orthodox' response to radical encratism—that is, to have rejected celibacy as a requirement for membership of the Christian community—this did not mean the end of encratite Christianity. On the contrary, when Tatian abandoned the church in Rome (c.170), he 'merged back without remark into a Syrian Christianity that may always have been as radical as himself'.[84] Throughout the third and fourth centuries, Syria continued to be a source of ascetic radicalism that inspired many in the West to emulation. For example, a document such as the *Acts of Thomas*, written in Syria early in the third century, perpetuated the encratite vision of Tatian in a popular narrative form that was to appeal to ascetics of many stripes, from the Manichees of fourth-century Rome and Carthage to the Priscillianists of Spain. Translated immediately from Syriac into Greek, and subsequently into Latin and other late antique languages, the *Acts of Thomas* (together with texts such as the *Acts of Paul and Thecla* and the *Acts of John*) ensured that radical encratism would remain a potent force well into the end of antiquity.[85]

The Syrian radicalism evident in the apocryphal Acts soon produced Latin fruit. In the early third century at Carthage an unknown author composed a sermon, *The Hundredfold, Sixtyfold, and Thirtyfold Reward* (*De centesima, sexagesima, tricesima*), which offered a distinctively encratite reading of the parables of Jesus, especially the Parable of the Sower (Matt 13: 3–9).[86] For the author of this sermon, the 'hundredfold' reward was reserved for martyrs, the 'sixtyfold' for virginal ascetics (who are styled 'combatants' (*agonistae*)), and the 'thirtyfold' for married persons who had renounced sex upon receiving baptism. Those who remained sexually active appear to have been

---

[84] Brown, *Body and Society*, 87.

[85] On the encratite theology of the *Acts of Thomas*, see Yves Tissot, 'L'Encratisme des Actes de Thomas', *ANRW* II.25.6 (1988): 4415–30; H. J. W. Drijvers, 'The Acts of Thomas', in Edgar Hennecke and Wilhelm Schneemelcher (eds.), *New Testament Apocrypha*, ii. *Writings relating to the Apostles, Apocalypses, and Related Subjects*, 2nd edn., trans. R. McL. Wilson (Louisville, Ky: Westminster/John Knox Press, 1992), 322–39. On their use by Manichees, see Jean-Daniel Kaestli, 'L'Utilisation des Actes apocryphes des apôtres dans le manichéisme', in M. Krause (ed.), *Gnosis and Gnosticism* (Leiden: Brill, 1977), 107–16; and Peter Nagel, 'Die apokryphen Apostelakten des 2. und 3. Jahrhunderts in der manichäischen Literatur', in Karl-Wolfgang Tröger (ed.), *Gnosis und Neues Testament* (Gütersloh, 1973), 148–82.

[86] First edited by Richard Reitzenstein, 'Eine frühchristliche Schrift von den dreierlei Früchten des christlichen Lebens', *ZNW* 15 (1914), 60–90; reprinted in PLS 1, 53–67. The text has been newly edited with an English translation by Philip Sellew, *The Hundredfold Reward: Martyrdom and Sexual Renunciation in Christian North Africa* (WGRW; Atlanta: SBL/Leiden: Brill, forthcoming).

Asceticism, Heresy, and Tradition

excluded from reward altogether. Addressing married persons the author urged them to take seriously their baptismal commitment and to embrace total celibacy:

> At first the Lord did lay down the precept of procreation, to be sure, but then he modeled celibacy. Since you have been reborn through the Holy Spirit, why do you not understand that you have been transformed for celibacy?... If you have been reborn through the life-giving bath from unrighteous work, why not also from lust? Remember that desire for increase is the Devil's first deception![87]

Like his Syrian forebears, the author of *The Hundredfold Reward* envisioned baptism as the occasion to repudiate all aspects of one's former birth, especially sexual activity. Laced with biblical readings that echoed the *Diatesseron* of Tatian, the *Acts of Paul and Thecla*, and the *Gospel of Thomas*, the Latin sermon *The Hundredfold Reward* influenced the thought and language of later orthodox Christians, such as Cyprian of Carthage, even when they did not follow all of its radical encratite prescriptions.[88]

But radical encratism was not the only challenge to the view of marriage promoted by Clement of Alexandria. In the third century we encounter several Christian thinkers who did not require celibacy of all the baptized, but who did relegate married persons to a lower status within the Christian community. Tertullian, Cyprian, and Origen produced bodies of work that definitively shaped Western Christian thought on marriage and sexuality. Indeed, the elevation of celibacy over marriage was articulated by these writers with a trenchancy that forever changed the character of Christian discourse. Tertullian, Cyprian, and Origen cannot be classified as 'radical' encratites, since each of them allowed Christians to marry. Nevertheless all three exhibit tendencies that could be classified as 'moderate encratism'. By 'moderate encratism' I refer to a theological position that reproduces key features of Tatian's theology, but without fully condemning marriage.[89] Through the writings of Tertullian, Cyprian, and Origen, a variety of encratite themes entered into the mainstream of Western ascetical theology and influenced the contemporaries of Jovinian, most notably Ambrose and Jerome.

---

[87] *Cent.* 35 and 38 (PLS 1, 63–4); trans. Sellew, slightly altered.

[88] For Cyprian's use of *De centesima*, see Jean Daniélou, *A History of Early Christian Doctrine Before the Council of Nicaea*, iii. *The Origins of Latin Christianity*, trans. David Smith and John Austin Baker (Philadelphia: Westminster Press, 1977), 63–92; Quispel, 'Study of Encratism', 64–5.

[89] I have borrowed the concept and language of 'moderate encratism' from Sfameni Gasparro, 'Asceticism and Anthropology', 130–1.

i. Tertullian

At first glance Tertullian seems an unlikely champion of the celibate life. He was a married man, and in his writings against Marcion he had vigorously defended marriage and procreation against Marcionite attack.[90] Like Clement, Tertullian based much of his response to Marcion on the interpretation of Paul. For example, he observed that Marcion had included Paul's Letter to the Ephesians in his canon of scripture. Since Ephesians 5: 31 contains the citation from Genesis 2: 24, which Paul used to characterize the Church as the body and bride of Christ, Tertullian argued, Paul must have intended to approve of marriage and procreation.[91]

Moreover, when not writing with the aim of enforcing an ascetic ethos, for example, in his treatise *On the Soul* (*De anima*), Tertullian could even describe the intimacies of sex without any sense of revulsion or disgust: 'Nature should be an object of reverence, not of embarrassment. It is lust (*libido*), not the natural condition, that has defiled sexual relations. It is the excess, not the normal state, that is impure, for the normal state has been blessed by God: *Increase and multiply*.'[92] Contrary to the usual encratite doctrine, in *De anima* Tertullian portrayed sexual relations as the natural means of propagating the human race that had been decreed by God at the beginning of creation.[93]

In other contexts, however, Tertullian's approach to marriage was not so optimistic. Over the course of his literary career, Tertullian authored several treatises dealing with the topic of second marriage among Christians. It is well known that his opinions on the issue gradually grew more rigorous over time. In his earliest writing, the letter *To His Wife* (*c*.204), Tertullian strongly discouraged the practice of remarriage, although he did not absolutely forbid it. By the time of his latest writing on the subject, *On Monogamy* (after 213), Tertullian had become implacably hostile to second marriages and even condemned his fellow Christians as 'Sensualists' (*psychici*) for tolerating the practice.[94] Remarriage, however, was not the only issue for Tertullian in these

---

[90] *Marc.* 1.29.6–7 (CCSL 1, 474).

[91] *Marc.* 5.18.9 (CCSL 1, 719).

[92] *An.* 27.4; trans. by J.H. Waszink, *Quinti Septimi Florentis Tertulliani De anima* (Amsterdam: J. M. Meulenhoff, 1947), 38.

[93] See *An.* 27.9, where Tertullian described the creation of body and soul at conception as a transmission of the original unity of 'clay' and 'breath' that was formed by God in paradise: 'Therefore from the one man [Adam] comes this whole abundance of souls, as nature evidently observes the decree of God, *Increase and multiply*'; trans. Waszink, 39.

[94] I have followed the chronology of Tertullian's works given in R. Braun, *'Deus Christianorum': Recherches sur le vocabulaire doctrinal de Tertullien* (Paris: 1962), 567–77. There is a detailed analysis of the three works on remarriage, especially from the point of view of their dependence on the rhetorical tradition, in Jean-Claude Fredouille, *Tertullien et la conversion de la culture antique* (Paris: Études Augustiniennes, 1972), 89–142.

treatises, for his hostility to sex is apparent, even when he discusses first marriages.

The main factor that shaped Tertullian's evaluation of Christian marriage was a sharply eschatological outlook that grew ever more extreme as he embraced the 'New Prophecy'. Also known as 'Montanism', this movement of prophetic apocalypticism had emerged out of Phrygia in the late second century. The prophets Montanus, Priscilla, and Maximilla had proclaimed the dawning of a new age, in which increased ascetical rigour, including prolonged fasting and abstention from sex, was deemed necessary in order to facilitate reception of the Holy Spirit and exercise of the gift of prophecy.[95] Citing the prophetess Priscilla in his *Exhortation to Chastity*, Tertullian found an apt vehicle to express this view: 'For continence effects harmony of soul, and the pure see visions and, bowing down, hear voices speaking clearly words salutary and secret.'[96] Under the influence of the New Prophecy, Tertullian came to regard all marriages, even perpetually monogamous ones, as merely a grudging concession to human weakness and, therefore, as greatly inferior to celibacy.

Like Tatian and encratite thinkers before him, Tertullian supported this rigorism with an interpretation of Paul's First Letter to the Corinthians that stretched to the breaking point Paul's already tenuous regard for marriage. In *To His Wife* Tertullian had suggested that Paul allowed Christians to marry only because of the danger of fornication. When Paul said, 'It is better to marry than to burn' (1 Cor 7: 9), Tertullian insisted, he clearly indicated that marriage was merely a lesser evil than fornication. Such 'goods', Tertullian explained, really were in a sense forbidden.[97] Later, in his *Exhortation to Chastity*, a treatise written around the year 208, Tertullian took an even harsher stance. Since God, through the apostle Paul, had stated his preference for celibacy, failure to follow God's preferential will actually is a kind of sin: 'When you do what God merely wills and despise what God preferentially wills, your choice is more offensive than meritorious. You are, in part, guilty of sin; and in part, even though you do not sin, you do fail to merit. And is not one's very unwillingness to merit itself a sin?'[98]

---

[95] Eusebius, *Hist. eccl.* 5.18.3 (SC 41, 56), quotes a second-century source that accuses Montanus of dissolving marriages and charges that Priscilla and Maximilla had abandoned their husbands. Cf. Christine Trevett, *Montanism: Gender, Authority and the New Prophecy* (Cambridge: Cambridge University Press, 1996), 109–14; Brown, *Body and Society*, 76–82.

[96] *Exh. cast.* 10.5 (SC 319, 106); trans. William P. Le Saint, *Tertullian: Treatises on Marriage and Remarriage* (ACW 13; New York, NY and Ramsey, NJ: Newman Press, 1951), 59.

[97] *Ux.* 1.3.5 (SC 273, 100).

[98] *Exh. cast.* 3.4–5 (SC 319, 78); trans. Le Saint, *Marriage and Remarriage*, 46 (slightly altered).

According to Tertullian's later reading, Paul did not merely teach that marriage is a lesser evil than fornication. Like Tatian, he argued that marriage actually is a sin, that is, a kind of 'fornication' (*stuprum*). Although the main object of Tertullian's attack was the practice of remarriage, he applied this negative judgement even to monogamous first marriages: 'Yes, and with good reason, since this, too, in the shameful act which constitutes its essence, is the same as fornication.'[99] As one scholar has noted, Tertullian's interpretation of Paul in his works on remarriage was so extreme that it resembled that of Marcion, the very 'heretic' whom Tertullian had opposed so vigorously elsewhere.[100] Tertullian, of course, was no Marcionite; he granted that the true God had created the world. Nor was he a radical encratite in the manner of Tatian, for he held that human sexuality was part of the original created order. Nevertheless, Tertullian's starkly eschatological outlook led him to denigrate sex, marriage, and procreation in a manner that resembled traditional encratite theology.[101]

Another parallel between Tertullian and the encratite tradition is that Tertullian, like Tatian, argued that a radical divide lay between the morality of the Old Testament and that of the New. Although he acknowledged that God had originally established marriage for the propagation of the human race, Tertullian held that with the coming of Christ the command to 'increase and multiply' had been abrogated by Paul's warning that 'the time is short; from now on let even those who have wives be as though they had none.'[102] In these last days the only reasons for marrying even once are disreputable ones: sexual desire, a wish for comfort and security, or the desire to live on in one's children.[103] While some Christians might argue that procreation is a civic duty, Tertullian complained, children are in reality troublesome burdens that distract their parents from preparing for martyrdom and the approach of the kingdom of God.[104] Although Tertullian did not completely reject first marriages, thereby remaining technically 'orthodox' on this question, his emphasis on the profound gulf between the old dispensation and the new reiterated the traditional encratite contrast between the Old Law and the New.

---

[99] *Exh. cast.* 9.4 (SC 319, 100): 'Nec immerito, quia et ipsae ex eo constant quod est stuprum.'

[100] For the suggestion that Marcion's exegesis influenced that of Tertullian, see R. Braun, 'Tertullien et l'exégèse de I Cor 7', in J. Fontaine and C. Kannengiesser (eds.), *Epektasis: Mélanges patristiques offerts au Cardinal Jean Daniélou* (Paris: Beauchesne, 1972), 21–8. There are also many parallels between Tertullian's reading of Paul and the encratite exegesis of Tatian and Julius Cassian; see Sfameni Gasparro, *Enkrateia e antropologia*, 174–84.

[101] Cf. *Virg.* 10.4 (SC 424, 162), where Tertullian referred to a married couple's decision to renounce the 'common insult' (*contumeliam communem*) of marriage.

[102] *Exh. cast.* 6.1–3 (SC 319, 88–90).

[103] *Ux.* 1.4.2 (SC 273, 102).

[104] *Ux.* 1.5.1–2 (SC 273, 106–8); *Exh. cast.* 12.1–5 (SC 319, 108–12).

Asceticism, Heresy, and Tradition 119

Tertullian's hostility to sex and marriage is evident in writings beyond those on remarriage. For example, his treatise *On Purity* (*De pudicitia*) was written late in his career under the full influence of the New Prophecy. This work discusses and opposes the 'Sensualist' (i.e. catholic) policy of granting ecclesiastical penance for the sin of adultery. In it Tertullian portrayed the contrast between the sexual standards of the old dispensation and those of the new dispensation in terms as harsh as those of Tatian or any encratite thinker:

Let us grant, if the Sensualists wish it, that in the ancient days every kind of impurity was allowed. Let us grant that before Christ the flesh was wanton, even that it was lost before it was sought out by its Lord. It was not yet worthy of the grace of salvation; it was not yet ready for the obligation of sanctity. It was still reckoned as being *in Adam*, sinful, quickly lusting for what seemed to it beautiful, preoccupied with things base, repressing prurience with fig leaves. The poison of lust and infecting filth were everywhere within it, and well were they able to cling to it, since as yet there were no waters which themselves had cleansed it.[105]

Tertullian has articulated a theme dear to the encratite tradition: the waters of Christian baptism ought to mark the complete removal of the old 'Adam' with its sensual lusts and the adoption of perfect purity in imitation of the chaste flesh of Christ. Tertullian continued with specific allusions to the connection between the virginal conception of Jesus and the cleansing waters of baptism:

But when the Word of God descended into flesh which not even marriage had unsealed, and when the Word was made flesh which not even marriage was ever to unseal, flesh which approached the tree of suffering, not of incontinence, and tasted there the bitter, not the sweet, flesh which belonged to heaven, not to hell and which was girt with flowers of sanctity and not with leaves of lust, flesh which imparted its own purity to the waters—from this time on, all flesh which is in Christ loses its old, residual stains. Now it is something different. Now it emerges new, not from the slime of sperm, not from the filth of concupiscence (*non ex seminis limo, non ex concupiscentiae fimo*), but from pure water and the Holy Spirit.[106]

Although Tertullian's main concern in this treatise was the issue of post-baptismal penance, his perspective on marriage clearly echoed traditional encratite themes. He contrasted the first birth—characterized by the 'slime of sperm' and the 'filth of concupiscence'—with the 'pure water' of Christian baptism sanctified by the virginal conception of Christ. The implications are clear: sexual desire and activity (derived from the first birth) reflect the fallen

---

[105] *Pud.* 6.14–15 (SC 394, 172); trans. William P. Le Saint, *Tertullian: Treatises on Penance: On Penitence and On Purity* (ACW 28; New York: Newman Press, 1959), 67.
[106] *Pud.* 6.16 (SC 394, 172–4); trans. Le Saint, *Treatises on Penance*, 67–8.

Adam; sexual purity (derived from baptismal rebirth) is the mark of the virginal Christ.

Tertullian's influence on subsequent generations of Western Christians was immense. Despite his alliance with the New Prophecy and his bitter attacks on moderate North African Christians, Tertullian was often read and imitated by later Latin authors. Cyprian, bishop of Carthage in the middle of the third century, is said to have read Tertullian daily. According to Jerome, Cyprian would say to his secretary, 'Give me the master,' meaning the works of Tertullian.[107] Cyprian's own treatise, *On the Dress of Virgins* (*De habitu virginum*) borrowed extensively from Tertullian's writings on marriage, chastity, and women. About the same time, Novatian, a rigorist Roman presbyter and rival to Bishop Cornelius of Rome, composed a treatise *On the Good of Chastity* (*De bono pudicitiae*), which also depended heavily on a number of Tertullian's writings.

But, most of all, it was Jerome, the great proponent of sexual asceticism in fourth-century Western Christianity, who provided a vigorous afterlife for Tertullian's ascetical writings. The appearance of Tertullian verbatim, and usually unacknowledged, in the pages of Jerome's writings on celibacy, most notably in his polemic *Against Jovinian*, ensured that later generations of Christians, for better or for worse, would be exposed to the moderate encratism of Tertullian.[108] It was just such an audience, as we shall see, to which Jovinian directed his appeal for a more moderate, and indeed traditional, form of Christian piety.

ii. Cyprian of Carthage

There was yet another North African writer who exercised a demonstrable influence on the ascetical treatises of the late fourth century, Bishop Cyprian of Carthage (*c.*248–258). Cyprian was the author of the earliest treatise dedicated to Christian virgins, that is, to women who had committed themselves to a life of perpetual celibacy. *The Dress of Virgins* (*De habitu virginum*) is of special interest here because it was widely read in the days of Jovinian. Jerome, for example, recommended the book as spiritual reading in his

---

[107] *Vir. ill.* 53 (PL 23, 698).
[108] On Jerome's reading of Tertullian, see Pierre Petitmengin, 'Saint Jérôme et Tertullien', in Yves-Marie Duval (ed.), *Jérôme entre l'occident et l'orient* (Paris: Études Augustiniennes, 1988), 43–59, and the literature cited there; also C. Micaeli, 'L'influsso di Tertulliano su Girolamo: le opere sul matrimonio et le seconde nozze', *Aug* 19 (1979), 415–29; Patrick Laurence, *Jérôme et le nouveau modèle feminin* (Paris: Études Augustiniennes, 1997), 205–24. Jerome's reliance on Tertullian in the *Adversus Jovinianum* has now been amply documented by Duval, *L'affaire Jovinien*, 112–205.

famous Letter 22 to the virgin Eustochium (384), and he frequently had recourse to Cyprian in his own writings on celibacy.[109] Ambrose, likewise, borrowed verbatim from Cyprian's treatise in his own writings on virginity.[110] Moreover, *The Dress of Virgins* reflected the influence of both the moderate encratism of Tertullian and the radical encratism of *The Hundredfold Reward*. As a result, the treatise provides an excellent illustration of the manner in which encratite themes entered the Western theological tradition and, from there, passed into the ascetical literature of the late fourth century.

Following Tertullian and the encratite tradition before him, Cyprian emphasized the connection between the sin of Adam and Eve and the realities of sex and marriage. The virgin, he observed, has escaped the sentence decreed for Eve in Genesis 3: 16 ('I will greatly increase your pangs in childbearing; in pain you shall bring forth children, yet your desire shall be for your husband, and he shall rule over you'). In place of a human husband the virgin had Christ as her husband, head, and master. Moreover, Cyprian cited a favourite encratite proof-text: 'Those who belong to this age marry and are given in marriage; but those who are considered worthy of a place in that age and in the resurrection from the dead neither marry nor are given in marriage. Indeed they cannot die anymore, because they are like angels and are children of God' (Luke 20: 34–6). According to Cyprian, this statement of Jesus showed that the Christian virgin already participated in the life of the resurrection: 'The glory of the resurrection you already have in this world; you pass through the world without the pollution of the world; while you remain chaste and virgins, you are equal to the angels of God.'[111]

Another theme that Cyprian borrowed from Tertullian and the encratite tradition was a drawing of sharp contrasts between the marital standards of the Old Testament and those of the New Testament:

The first pronouncement gave the command to increase and multiply; the second counseled continence. While yet the world was uncultivated and empty, we, begetting large numbers in our fecundity, propagated ourselves and increased for the extension of the human race. Now, when the earth is filled and the world is peopled, those who

[109] See Jerome, *ep.* 22.22.3 (CSEL 54, 175), and the discussion of Simone Deléani, 'Présence de Cyprien dans les oeuvres de Jérôme sur la virginité', in Duval (ed.), *Jérôme entre l'occident et l'orient*, 61–82.

[110] For the influence of Cyprian on Ambrose, the best starting point is the essays of Yves-Marie Duval, 'Sur une page de saint Cyprien chez saint Ambroise: *Hexameron* 6,8,47 et *De habitu virginum* 15–17', *REAug* 16 (1970), 25–34; 'L'originalité du *De virginibus* dans le mouvement ascétique occidental: Ambroise, Cyprien, Athanase', in Yves-Marie Duval (ed.), *Ambroise de Milan: XVIe Centenaire de son election épiscopale* (Paris: Études Augustiniennes, 1974), 9–66, esp. 21–9; 'L'influence des écrivains africains du IIIe siècle sur les écrivains chrétiens de l'Italie du nord dans la seconde moitié du IVe siècle', *Antichità Altoadriatiche* 5 (1974), 191–225, esp. 213–17.

[111] *Hab. virg.* 22 (CSEL 3, 203); trans. Angela Elizabeth Keenan, *Saint Cyprian: Treatises* (FC 36; New York: Fathers of the Church, 1958), 50.

can take continence, living in the manner of eunuchs, make themselves eunuchs for the kingdom.[112]

Cyprian emphasized, of course, that celibacy for the sake of the kingdom was not mandatory. Unlike the radical encratites, he acknowledged that 'the Lord does not command this, but rather encourages it.' Nevertheless, the association of marriage with the 'old' and celibacy with the 'new' became the grounds for Cyprian's contention that virgins would receive 'better dwelling-places' (*habitacula... meliora*) and the 'reward of a greater grace' (*maioris gratiae praemium*) in heaven.

Cyprian enunciated this theme with particular clarity in a passage that is directly dependent on the treatise *The Hundredfold Reward*. As we saw above, the author of this radical encratite homily had discerned a threefold hierarchy in the Parable of the Sower: the hundredfold reward belonged to the martyrs, the sixtyfold to virgins (both male and female), and the thirtyfold to married persons who were committed to sexual renunciation. Cyprian adopted the threefold levels of reward, although he discretely modified the radical encratite hierarchy by omitting any reference to the category of the 'thirtyfold'. For Cyprian, as for the encratite author, the virgins follow the Christian martyrs and possess, respectively, the hundredfold and sixtyfold rewards:

Avoid wide and broad roads. In them are deadly allurements and death-bringing pleasures; in them the devil flatters that he may deceive, smiles that he may harm, entices that he may kill. The first fruit, that of a hundredfold, belongs to martyrs; the second, sixtyfold, is yours. Just as with the martyrs there is no thought of the flesh and of the world, and no slight and trivial and dainty struggle, so also in you, whose reward is second in the order of grace, let the power of endurance be next to theirs.[113]

Although Cyprian willingly acknowledged that all baptized Christians 'are cleansed from the impurities of the old contagion by a second birth', he insisted that 'the greater sanctity and the reality (*veritas*) of the second birth' belonged to virgins 'who no longer have desires of the flesh and of the body'.[114] Cyprian did not deny the possibility of salvation to married Christians and thus avoided the extreme of radical encratism. However, by stressing the close connection between baptismal regeneration and celibacy, he showed that a moderate encratism characterized his thought on marriage and celibacy.

---

[112] *Hab. virg.* 23 (CSEL 3, 203); trans. Keenan, 51.
[113] See *Hab. virg.* 21 (CSEL 3, 202); trans. Keenan, 49. Irenaeus, *Haer.* 5.36.2 (SC 153, 456–8), had applied the same biblical passage to the various 'dwelling-places' and 'many mansions' in the kingdom of God. He did not, however, specify who belonged where. See Antonio Quacquarelli, *Il triplice frutto della vita cristiana: 100, 60 e 30* (Rome: Coletti Editore, 1953), 22–3.
[114] *Hab. virg.* 23 (CSEL 3, 204).

iii. Origen of Alexandria

There is yet another third-century thinker whose views must be examined here: Origen of Alexandria. Although he wrote in Greek, Origen's influence on the fourth-century Latin contemporaries of Jovinian was as deep as that of Tertullian and Cyprian. Indeed, in the decade after Jovinian's condemnation, both the Eastern and the Western churches were sharply divided over the question of Origen's legacy.[115] Ambrose had borrowed verbatim from several writings of Origen, and, as we shall see in Chapter 5, he drew key elements of his Christology and Mariology from Origen. Jerome, likewise, was strongly influenced by the ascetical perspectives of Origen. Not only did he translate several of Origen's exegetical writings into Latin during his sojourn in Rome in the early 380s, but he also was influenced by Origen's theological writings at this time, including *On First Principles*.[116] Although neither Ambrose nor Jerome adopted the whole of Origen's theological system, both of them perpetuated certain aspects of his ascetical outlook. Moreover, like Tertullian and Cyprian, Origen presented an approach to Christian asceticism that reproduced key features of the earlier encratite worldview.

Perhaps the most striking parallel between Origen and the encratite tradition lies in Origen's theory of the 'double-creation' articulated in his treatise *On First Principles* (*De principiis*). For Origen the first two chapters of Genesis did not describe the fully physical creation of the world and the first human beings, but rather a spiritual world in which rational creatures with ethereal bodies lived in rapt contemplation of the triune God. Only because of a fall, that is, by turning away from this life of contemplation, did the various rational creatures take on the forms of existence that we know today.[117] According to the depth and character of their fall, rational creatures received different kinds of bodies: angels, demons, and other celestial beings were all originally rational creatures who now inhabit bodies created by God according to their merits in the pre-existence.[118] One group of rational creatures was given gross, material bodies; these are the souls of human beings.[119] They have been clothed in 'garments of skins', as narrated in Genesis 3: 21. For these

---

[115] See, most recently, Elizabeth A. Clark, *The Origenist Controversy: The Cultural Construction of an Early Christian Debate* (Princeton, NJ: Princeton University Press, 1992).

[116] Jerome's reliance on Origen—including his doctrine of the pre-existence of souls—has been decisively demonstrated by Y.-M. Duval, 'Traces de lecture de *Peri Archôn* d'Origène avant le depart de Rome de Jérôme en 385', in Duval (ed.), *Jérôme entre l'occident et l'orient*, 139–51.

[117] *Princ.* 1.4.1 (SC 252, 166–8). See the discussion in Henri Crouzel, *Origen: The Life and Thought of the First Great Theologian*, trans. A. S. Worrall (San Francisco: Harper and Row, 1989), 205–18; Brown, *Body and Society*, 160–77.

[118] *Princ.* 1.5.1–3 (SC 252, 174–82).

[119] *Princ.* 1.8.4 (SC 252, 228–32).

creatures God created the physical world in order to provide an occasion for their chastisement and rehabilitation. While this world has been made to accommodate the diverse kinds of fallen spirits, it is still an ordered cosmos administered by the providence of a benevolent God.[120]

Origen's theory of the pre-existence and fall of the rational spirits shaped his understanding of human nature and sexuality in significant ways. On the one hand, like some radical encratites, such as Julius Cassian, Origen could not accept that the human body—and hence the act of sexual reproduction—was part of God's original plan of creation. Because the body and sexuality belonged to the second creation, they were, to a significant degree, seen as 'un-natural' and invariably associated with the primal fall. On the other hand, Origen held that the true God had created the body and the entire material world as part of the economy of salvation. Therefore, he was not entirely hostile to sexual activity. Indeed, in one place Origen could even speak of procreation as something 'holy'.[121]

On the whole, however, Origen tended to view the physical world, the body, and sexuality as profoundly ambiguous, even dangerous. Since the destiny of rational creatures was to return to their original state of contemplation and to recover their original spiritual existence, ultimately, for Origen, the body could be little more than the locus of perpetual temptation. Like the rest of the material world, the body was meant to be transcended; that is, the very existence of the body provided an opportunity for the created spirits to turn away from the physical world and return to their original state of spiritual contemplation. Because sexuality continually threatens to divert the attention of the rational creatures away from the spiritual world and towards the material, Origen believed, it could not serve the salvific purposes of God.[122]

Origen's deep ambivalence about sex and marriage is especially apparent in his treatment of 1 Corinthians 7, the litmus test of all early Christian discussion on these issues. Origen certainly accepted the Apostle Paul's concession of marriage to those who could not control their sexual desires (1 Cor 7: 9).[123] In his *Commentary on 1 Corinthians*, for example, Origen warned of the danger that could arise when one spouse tried to practice celibacy without the consent of the other. Such a practice, Origen observed, violated the balanced teaching presented by the apostle: '[Paul] did not exaggerate the teaching on celibacy and suppress marriage, nor did he prefer marriage and

---

[120] *Princ.* 2.1.1–4 (SC 252, 234–44).

[121] *Fr. 35 in 1 Cor.*; ed. Claude Jenkins, 'Origen on I Corinthians', *JTS* 9 (1908), 505: 'παιδοποιίας ἁγίας'.

[122] For much of my account of Origen's discussion of marriage, I have relied on the excellent survey by Henri Crouzel, *Virginité et mariage selon Origène* (Paris: Desclée de Brouwer, 1963).

[123] *Fr. 29 in 1 Cor.* (Jenkins, 370).

suppress celibacy.'[124] Citing 1 Corinthians 13: 5 ('Love does not insist on its own way'), Origen stressed that charity required married people to abstain from sex only by agreement in order to be free for prayer. The unilateral adoption of celibacy was forbidden: 'For it is preferable that two should be saved through the works of marriage than that one should fall from hope in Christ because of the glory of the other. Indeed, how can a man who is responsible for the death of his wife be saved? For a man's holiness is not pure when the discipline ("to be free for prayer before God") is imposed on both of them without the agreement of his wife.'[125]

Like his Alexandrian predecessor Clement, Origen also strongly resisted the radical demand for sexual renunciation, particularly that of Marcion. Origen explicitly attacked the Marcionite insistence on celibacy because it rested on a rejection of creation and a refusal to cooperate with the will of the Creator-God.[126] In several places Origen cited 1 Timothy 4: 1–3 to condemn those who forbade marriage and demanded abstinence from foods that God had created. Such persons, he says, are 'wiser than is fitting in respect to chastity'.[127] Moreover, Origen took the apostle Paul at his word when he stated that marriage, like celibacy, was a 'gift' (*charisma*). Citing 1 Corinthians 7: 7 ('I wish that all were as I myself am. But each has a particular gift from God, one having one kind and another a different kind'), Origen affirmed that marriage and procreation had been ordained by the providence of God. Therefore, Jesus' prohibition of divorce, like the apostle's injunctions in 1 Timothy 4: 1–3 and Ephesians 5, was intended to subvert the heretical demand for celibacy.[128]

But that is not the whole story. Elsewhere in his writings, especially in his discussion of 1 Corinthians 7, Origen often emphasized the more negative dimensions of Paul's teaching. Paul's recommendation that married couples should abstain from sex temporarily for the sake of prayer suggested to Origen that there was a fundamental incompatibility between sexual activity and union with God. In his treatise *On Prayer*, for example, Origen stated his opinion that people should not pray in a place where sexual relations take place. He reasoned thus: 'For if it is impossible to have leisure for prayer as we should unless someone dedicates himself to this "by agreement for a season"

---

[124] Fr. 33 in 1 Cor. (Jenkins, 500); cited in Crouzel, *Virginité*, 164.
[125] Fr. 33 in 1 Cor. (Jenkins, 501); cited in Crouzel, *Virginité*, 165.
[126] Fr. 37 in 1 Cor. (Jenkins, 507).
[127] Comm. Rom. 9.2.9 (VL 34, 723); trans. Thomas P. Scheck, *Origen: Commentary on the Epistle to the Romans. Books 6–10* (FC 104; Washington, DC: The Catholic University of America Press, 2002), 201. Cf. Princ. 2.7.3 (SC 252, 330–2).
[128] Comm. Matt. 14.16 (GCS 10, 324); cited in Crouzel, *Virginité*, 132. On marriage as a 'charism', see Origen, Fr. 34 in 1 Cor. (Jenkins, 501–3), and the discussion in Crouzel, *Virginité*, 142–3.

(1 Cor 7: 5), then perhaps the same consideration should apply, if possible, to the place.'[129] Although in the same treatise Origen acknowledged that the 'mysteries of marriage' could be conducted 'with holiness, deliberately, and without passion', he still argued that sexual relations were fundamentally incompatible with prayer.[130]

One source of Origen's view in this matter was certainly the Old Testament traditions regarding ritual purification. Given his usual preference for a spiritual reading of scripture, it is ironic that Origen tended to preserve the literal sense of these ritual prescriptions when it came to sex.[131] For example, Origen explicitly appealed to the ancient purity regulations in order to justify his teaching on the necessity of sexual abstinence before prayer and reception of the Eucharist:

> You should know that the prayer of a man and woman who live in purity is not the same as the prayer of those who engage in sexual relations. . . . Even Moses purified the people and said, 'For three days do not go near a woman' (Ex 19: 15), so that after this period of purification they might be able to hear God. And in the Book of Kings, when the priest wished to offer the holy bread to David, who was fleeing from the deceit of Saul, what did the priest ask? 'Have the young men kept away from women?' (1 Sam 21: 4). And he was speaking not of strange women, but of their own wives. Therefore, in order for someone to receive the 'bread of the Presence', he had to be pure from women. And so, in order to receive the breads that are greater than the 'bread of the Presence'—those breads over which the names of God, Christ, and the Holy Spirit are invoked—should not a person be even more pure, so that he might receive those breads truly for salvation and not for condemnation?[132]

Like Tatian and Tertullian before him, Origen interpreted Paul to be an advocate of sexual renunciation. The apostle's *suggestion* in 1 Corinthians 7: 5 that temporary sexual abstinence should be allowed for prayer was taken as a *demand* for temporary abstinence in order to make prayer possible.[133]

Origen is an excellent example of the moderate encratite perspective that became increasingly prominent in third-century ascetical discourse. Although he did not embrace the full extremes of radical encratism, his reflections on the body and sexuality reflect the encratite dichotomies that we have seen in Tatian and elsewhere: physical union opposed to spiritual union, the Old Law opposed to the New Law, the body destined for death opposed to the body resurrected to life. As he wrote in his *Commentary on 1 Corinthians*:

---

[129] *Or.* 31.4 (PG 11, 553); trans. Rowan A. Greer, *Origen* (CWS; New York: Paulist Press, 1979), 166.
[130] *Or.* 2.2 (PG 11, 420); trans. Greer, 83.
[131] Cf. Brown, *Body and Society*, 352.
[132] Fr. 34 in 1 Cor. (Jenkins, 501–2); cited in Crouzel, Virginité, 55.
[133] This theme later became prominent in the writings of Jerome. See the discussion in Clark, *Reading Renunciation*, 277–82; Duval, *L'affaire Jovinien*, 120–1.

Do not think that the body is meant for sexual intercourse, just because 'the stomach is meant for food and food for the stomach' (cf. 1 Cor 6: 13). If you want to know the chief reason for the existence of the body, take note: It is meant to be a temple for the Lord, and the soul is meant to be holy and blameless, to serve as a handmaid to the Holy Spirit and to become a priest to the Holy Spirit that is within you. For Adam had a body in paradise, and yet it was not in paradise that 'Adam knew his wife Eve' (Gen 4: 1), but when he had been expelled after the disobedience.

At this point Origen interjected that he did not intend to forbid marriage. Citing 1 Corinthians 7:9 he acknowledged that Paul had taught: 'If a man is not living chastely, he should marry. For it is better to marry than to burn.' But the apostle granted such a concession, Origen argued, 'not as a guiding principle, but on account of weakness. The guiding principle (τὸ γὰρ προηγούμενον) is to be pure, to be chaste, and to "be free for prayer" (1 Cor 7: 5). For if a person has already been awakened with Christ and has come "to share in the likeness of his resurrection" and "in the newness of life" (Rom 6: 4), the body should belong to no one but the Lord.'[134]

Even though Origen was willing to accept the presence of married Christians in the Church, it is clear that his deepest instinct was to view them as second-class citizens. Unlike celibate Christians, married persons were considered 'slaves' to their conjugal obligations.[135] Unlike the virgin who was 'free' through her chastity, the married woman had fallen under the obligation of Genesis 3: 16 ('In pain you shall bring forth children, yet your desire shall be for your husband and he shall rule over you').[136] As Origen observed, 'every marriage takes place in darkness, which is why [scripture says] "not in debauchery and licentiousness" (Rom 13: 13). But the marriage of Christ, when he takes to himself the Church, occurs in the light.' The five wise virgins in the gospel parable, who attended the wedding with their lamps filled with oil, symbolize the luminous nobility of that spiritual wedding. Whereas union in the flesh produces merely 'one body', as the apostle said, union with the Lord produces 'one spirit': 'And what can be nobler than the soul which unites with the Spirit and becomes one with it and no longer is a soul, but becomes that which the Spirit is?'[137] There appears to be little in Origen's statement that Tatian could not have affirmed.

Tertullian, Cyprian, and Origen, each in his own way, articulated an ascetic vision that reflected significant features of the ancient encratite tradition.

---

[134] *Fr. 29 in 1 Cor.* (Jenkins, 370–1).
[135] *Comm. Rom.* 1.2 (VL 16, 49).   [136] *Fr. 39 in 1 Cor.* (Jenkins, 510).
[137] 1 Cor 6: 16–17, paraphrased in *Fr. 39 in 1 Cor.* (Jenkins, 510). It is significant that Origen has drawn from Paul's discussion of fornication with prostitutes in 1 Cor 6 in order to characterize the nature of marital union. This argument is typical of that used by encratites, both radical and moderate.

While accepting marriage as permissible, these writers approached the topic of celibacy and marriage from within the basic encratite framework that associated sexuality with sin and linked salvation with sexual purity. As a result, they inevitably supported a hierarchy that relegated married Christians to the lowest rung of salvation. Human ('carnal') marriage invariably took second place to the divine–human ('spiritual') marriage of celibacy. In the fourth century, this moderate encratite theology supported a hierarchy of 'states of life' that gradually supplanted the vision articulated by the Pastoral Epistles and Clement of Alexandria. As a result, both in the East and West Christian writers increasingly articulated the notion that celibacy and other forms of ascetic renunciation created a better and higher class of Christians.

In this chapter I have argued that early Christian discourse on sex and marriage was extraordinarily diverse in the first three centuries. From its ambivalent origins in the teachings of Jesus and Paul, there emerged contrasting traditions: some emphasized the complete rejection of sexual activity (radical encratism); others allowed marriage and sexual union and yet strongly devalued both (moderate encratism); still others stressed the original goodness and enduring value of marriage and procreation. This last stream of tradition, evident especially in the Pastoral Epistles and in the writings of Irenaeus and Clement of Alexandria, defined radical encratism as 'heresy' and insisted on the acceptance of sex and marriage as intrinsic to God's work of creation and redemption. Such, it appears, was the state of Christian 'orthodoxy' by the early years of the third century.

Jovinian's affinities with the tradition articulated by Clement and the Pastorals are strikingly clear. Like Clement and other early heresiologists, Jovinian frequently invoked the Pastoral Epistles (especially 1 Tim 4: 1–5) to cast the accusation of 'heresy' against the proponents of the ascetic hierarchy.[138] Both Clement and Jovinian appealed to the respect for marriage, family, and household evident in the Pastorals and noted that the apostles had chosen married men to be bishops, elders, and deacons in the Church. Clement's emphasis on the equality of celibacy and marriage as forms of Christian ministry also was echoed in the teaching of Jovinian. Both writers cited Jesus' prohibition of divorce, along with the marital imagery of Ephesians 5, to stress the continuity between marriage in the Old Testament and in the New, and both appealed to the presence of married men among the apostles and teachers of the primitive church. Moreover, both Clement and Jovinian appear to have had similar apologetic interests, insofar as they both tried to show that Christians could embrace the traditional structures of Greco-Roman society, especially marriage, and that marriage was a civic responsibility.

[138] *Jov.* 1.5, 34; 2.5.

These parallels between the anti-encratite arguments of Clement of Alexandria and those found in the extant fragments of Jovinian do not necessarily mean that Jovinian had access to the writings of Clement of Alexandria or that he was directly dependent on Clement's arguments.[139] As I will argue in the next chapter, the anti-encratite tradition continued in the fourth century and was developed even further in the anti-heretical writings of men such as Epiphanius of Salamis, Filastrius of Brescia, and Ambrosiaster. Jovinian's warning about the danger of radical encratism, as we shall see, reflected the concerns of many of his contemporaries, even those with sympathies to the ascetic or monastic life. My aim in this chapter has not been to trace the 'sources' of Jovinian's teaching, but rather to demonstrate the extent to which the patterns of his argumentation had a precedent in earlier Christian tradition. The arguments that Jovinian marshalled to oppose the formation of an ascetic elite were parallel to those issued by Clement against the radical encratites and by the Pastoral Epistles against the 'false teachers'. Moreover, Jovinian attempted to apply the label of 'heretic' to his ascetic opponents, as did his proto-orthodox predecessors. In this sense, Jovinian continued an 'orthodox' strand within early Christian tradition.

But, as we have seen, that was not the whole story. As the third century progressed, a new generation of Christian thinkers arose with views that echoed, albeit in a more moderate form, the encratite tradition of Tatian. Although Tertullian, Cyprian, and Origen each allowed Christians to marry, they also developed theologies of the body and sexuality that resolutely located married Christians at the bottom of an ascetic hierarchy. In the fourth century this discourse of hierarchy was to attain virtually the status of Christian doctrine, particularly in the writings of men such as Jerome and Ambrose. Jovinian's own condemnation for promoting a 'new heresy', as Pope Siricius put it, marked the definitive emergence of this 'new orthodoxy'.

---

[139] Such dependence, of course, was not impossible. Clement's writings did circulate in the late fourth century. Jerome, for example, knew several writings of Clement, including *Stromata* 3. See Pierre Courcelle, *Late Latin Writers and their Greek Sources*, trans. Harry E. Wedeck (Cambridge: Harvard University Press, 1969), 61, 79, 99, 125.

4

Jovinian, Heresy, and Fourth-Century Asceticism

Jovinian's protest against the exaltation of asceticism, as we saw in the previous chapter, had potent precedents in the previous Christian tradition, especially among those writers engaged in polemics against radical encratism. But concerns about the connections between heresy and asceticism did not end with the pre-Constantinian church. On the contrary, in the fourth century as ascetic piety increased in popularity with the spread of new forms of monastic life, the issue of heresy became even more acute. In this chapter I will investigate more closely the immediate context surrounding Jovinian's accusations of heresy. The charge of 'Manichaeism', which Jovinian directed against his opponents, while technically inaccurate, is an example of a type of polemic that was increasingly common in his day. Jovinian's charges reflect heightened concern about asceticism and heresy that can be documented in a variety of sources from legal texts to the anti-heretical handbooks of his day.

I will proceed in three steps. In the first half of this chapter, I will argue that there was a noticeable increase in heresy accusations in the later years of the fourth century, and many of these were directed against forms of ascetic theory or practice. We find polemics against several ascetic teachers who espoused varieties of encratism: Hieracas in Egypt, Eustathius in Armenia, and Priscillian in Spain were notable instances. In the case of Priscillian, the label of 'Manichaean' emerged as a polemical device of extraordinary potency. The spread of actual Manichaean Christianity in the fourth century further intensified these anxieties. Moreover, the Manichees were sometimes confused with other radical ascetic groups in imperial legislation, and this confusion was further compounded by fourth-century heresiologists. As a result, by the end of the fourth century the term 'Manichaean' had become a label for virtually any type of ascetic who was perceived as troublesome or deviant, or who represented a challenge to clerical authority.

After thus establishing the persistence of accusations of both Manichaeism and radical encratism (and their mutual confusion) in the later fourth century, I will turn to the writings of two anti-heretical authors, whose works were influential in Western Christianity in the age of Jovinian. Epiphanius of Salamis and Filastrius of Brescia both composed handbooks of heresy that focused attention on the problems of radical encratism and Manichaeism. Not only did these writers tend to blur the boundaries between these two 'heresies', but they introduced further confusion into the mix: the teachings of Origen and the Montanists now became linked to those of Tatian and Mani. The writings of Epiphanius and Filastrius indicate how accusations of heresy continued to animate the theological climate of the late fourth century, especially on issues pertaining to the body and sexuality. Their anti-encratite polemics, therefore, will shed further light on the environment in which Jovinian issued his critique of ascetic piety.

Finally, in the concluding section of this chapter, I will examine one further anti-heretical author, whose work is relevant to the world of Jovinian. Sometime in the early 380s an anonymous Roman presbyter, now called the 'Ambrosiaster', composed a little treatise titled 'On the Sin of Adam and Eve'. This document, like the heresiological writings of Epiphanius and Filastrius, reveals the concerns of a fourth-century Christian leader about the links between ascetic piety and encratite theology. The writings of Ambrosiaster, like those of his anti-heretical predecessors, show that questions about the origins of the body, sex, and original sin were hotly contested in the West at the end of the fourth century and provided the occasion for accusations of heresy against ascetic teachers. The case of Ambrosiaster, moreover, is of particular interest here because Ambrosiaster, like Jovinian, was an opponent of Jerome. When viewed in the light of these contemporary reactions against asceticism, it appears that Jovinian shared much in common with other fourth-century polemicists and was closer to the mainstream of Christian opinion than his opponents would have allowed.

1. 'ENCRATITES', MONKS, AND 'MANICHEES'

i. Hieracas and Eustathius

There is no doubt that accusations of heresy accompanied early Christian monasticism from its very inception. Even the most avid proponents of the ascetic life were willing to accuse fellow ascetics of 'heresy' when their visions of ascetic practice differed. In Egypt, for example, Bishop Athanasius of Alexandria, author of the famous *Life of Antony*, attacked a learned monastic teacher named Hieracas, who allegedly propounded a version of asceticism that strongly resembled the teaching of Tatian. According to Athanasius, who refuted Hieracas in his *First Letter to Virgins*, Hieracas held that 'marriage is evil inasmuch as virginity is good.'[1] Like Tatian, Hieracas appears to have based his renunciation of marriage on a radical reading of the letters of Paul, especially 1 Corinthians 7, as well as on selected sayings of Jesus. Athanasius, for example, presented the following quotation from Hieracas: 'I have read the epistle that Paul wrote to the Corinthians, in which he wrote about virginity, but about married people (he wrote), 'The time is short,' and then, 'Let those who have wives live like those who have none'(1 Cor 7: 29).[2]

Like Tatian and earlier radical encratites, Hieracas regarded marriage in the time of the Old Testament as acceptable, but argued that Christ came to institute a new discipline of celibacy that was incumbent on all Christians. As Athanasius put it, Hieracas 'says that this institution [marriage] was given to humanity at first, but now it has been taken away and forbidden'.[3] Bishop Epiphanius of Salamis, who provided an extensive entry on the 'Hieracites' immediately following the Manichees in his *Panarion*, offered a similar account of the views of Hieracas:

He says that marriage is allowed in the Old Testament, but that after Christ's coming marriage is no longer acceptable, and cannot inherit the kingdom of heaven. For what did the Word come to do, he asks, that was new? What new message did the Only-Begotten come to give, and set us straight? If it was about the fear of God, the Law had this. If it was about marriage, the scriptures had proclaimed it. If it was about envy, covetousness and iniquity, all this is in the Old Testament. But Christ came to make only this correction—to preach continence ($\frac{2}{3}\gamma\kappa\rho\acute{\alpha}\tau\epsilon\iota\alpha$) in the world, and choose purity and continence for his own; and without continence no one can be saved.[4]

Although the ascetical teachings of Hieracas were later to become associated with Manichaeism, it is clear that Hieracas had much more in common with the ancient encratite tradition. Like Tatian, Hieracas appears to have based his call to ascetic renunciation on a radical interpretation of the sayings of Jesus and Paul. By all accounts, then, the ascetical theology of Hieracas

---

[1] *Ep. virg.* 24; trans. in David Brakke, *Athanasius and the Politics of Asceticism* (OECS; Oxford: Clarendon Press, 1995), 282. On Hieracas, see James E. Goehring, 'Hieracas of Leontopolis: The Making of a Desert Ascetic', in his *Ascetics, Society, and the Desert: Studies in Early Egyptian Monasticism* (Harrisburg, PA: Trinity Press International, 1999), 110–33.

[2] *Ep. virg.* 27; trans. Brakke, 282–3. Epiphanius, *Haer.* 67.2.2–6 (Holl-Dummer 3, 134), also attested the centrality of 1 Corinthians 7 in the encratite theology of Hieracas. Against Hieracas, Athanasius responded that Paul had merely recommended temporary abstinence for the sake of prayer (cf. 1 Cor 7: 5), not perpetual sexual continence.

[3] *Ep. virg.* 26; trans. Brakke, 282.

[4] Epiphanius, *Haer.* 67.1.8–9 (Holl-Dummer 3, 133–4); trans. in Frank Williams, *The Panarion of Epiphanius of Salamis* (NHMS 36; Leiden: Brill, 1994), 309, slightly altered.

represented a continuation of Tatian's radical encratism in fourth-century monastic garb.[5]

Considerations of theology, however, may not have been the sole factor in the condemnation of Hieracas by Athanasius. As David Brakke has suggested, Athanasius and Hieracas also differed in their conceptions of the social forms that the ascetic life should take: 'While Athanasius was developing an ascetic programme that placed virgins in households and communities connected to local churches, Hieracas was promulgating an alternative vision of the Christian Church that placed virgins in communities with ascetic men, disconnected from married Christians.'[6] Brakke refers to the fact that Hieracas and his followers may have had 'separatist tendencies' that manifested themselves in separate liturgies and new male–female relations. According to Epiphanius, 'no one can worship with them without being a virgin, a monk, continent or a widow'.[7] Moreover, Epiphanius also accused the Hieracites of fostering the practice of 'surreptitious wives' ($συνεισάκτους$ $γυναῖκας$), that is, ascetic women who lived with ascetic men in a spiritual partnership.[8] From the point of view of Athanasius, these social dynamics may have been as problematic as the theological deviations of Hieracas.

A similar form of radical encratism may have inspired the ascetical practices adopted in the middle of the fourth century by Bishop Eustathius of Sebaste in Armenia. According to a number of sources, Eustathius promoted an ascetic movement that involved the repudiation of marriage and other forms of conventional social life. The canons of the synod of Gangra in Paphlagonia, which condemned the activities of Eustathius and his followers around the year 340, state that the monastic bishop had forbidden married women to sleep with their husbands (can. 1 and can. 14), encouraged slaves to abandon their masters (can. 2), and prohibited the eating of meat (can. 3).[9] Eustathius also is said to have discouraged people from attending liturgies performed by married priests and from praying in the homes of married

---

[5] Susanna Elm has suggested that the radicalism of Hieracas may have been a 'strand of asceticism prevalent in all of Egypt' throughout the fourth century. See her *'Virgins of God': The Making of Asceticism in Late Antiquity* (Oxford: Clarendon Press, 1994), 339–42, quotation at 341. Later Byzantine Christians associated Hieracas with the Manicheans: S. Lieu, 'An Early Byzantine Formula for the Renunciation of Manichaeism: the *Capita VII Contra Manichaeos* of (Zacharias of Mitylene)', *JAC* 26 (1983), 152–218.

[6] Brakke, *Athanasius*, 48.

[7] *Haer.* 67.2.9 (Holl-Dummer 3, 135); trans. Williams, 310.

[8] *Haer.* 67.8.3 (Holl-Dummer 3, 140); and the comments of Brakke, *Athanasius*, 48.

[9] The date of the Council of Gangra is disputed. See the recent discussion in Andrea Sterk, *Renouncing the World Yet Leading the Church: The Monk–Bishop in Late Antiquity* (Cambridge, Mass. and London: Harvard University Press, 2004), 27–35. A good overview of the life and work of Eustathius is given in Charles A. Frazee, 'Anatolian Asceticism in the Fourth Century: Eustathios of Sebastea and Basil of Caesarea', *Catholic Historical Review*, 66 (1980), 16–33.

people (can. 4). Male followers of Eustathius adopted a distinctive garment, the περιβόλαιον (can. 12); female followers dressed like men and cut their hair short (can. 13 and can. 17). The 'Eustathians' also observed fasts on the Lord's Day (can. 18), while neglecting the common fasts of the church (can. 19).[10]

Unfortunately, none of the extant sources mentions the precise theological grounds on which Eustathius and his followers based their asceticism, nor do we have any evidence of attempts to refute the theological positions of the 'Eustathians'. This silence may suggest that it was the social disruption caused by the Eustathian movement that was the primary source of conflict between Eustathius and his fellow bishops, rather than any precise theological or doctrinal heresy. As Susanna Elm has observed, 'Judging from the canons issued at Gangra, Eustathius' followers, men and women, were condemned because they had severed all ties with their natural families, questioned the legitimacy of the clergy, and disregarded distinctions considered fundamental by society, such as that between slaves and their masters.'[11] Similarly, Andrea Sterk has recently proposed that Eustathius (or his followers) created conflict because they did not withdraw to deserted places, 'but sought to pursue their ascetic vocation *within* the world and in the church. Their presence as a kind of countercultural community within the urban milieu would naturally stand as a challenge to the status quo'.[12]

Whatever the doctrinal source, if any, of his asceticism, the condemnation of Eustathius and his followers at Gangra indicates how easy it was for ascetic Christians in the fourth century to attract ecclesiastical censure, especially when their conduct threatened the established order of church and society. While the bishops at Gangra did not impugn asceticism per se, they did reject the 'Eustathians' for 'exalting themselves over those who lead a simpler life' and for 'introducing novel ideas that are not found in the Scriptures or in the writings approved by the church'.[13] Ascetic enthusiasm, therefore, was sometimes regarded with suspicion, even when there was no clear doctrinal heresy at issue. At Gangra ascetic elitism was rejected as radical encratism.

---

[10] According to Sozomen, *Hist. eccl.* 3.14 (PG 67, 1080), many people defended Bishop Eustathius and claimed that the excesses attributed to him were really the actions of his followers.

[11] Elm, 'Virgins of God', 110–11.

[12] Sterk, *Renouncing the World*, 30. Sterk and other scholars have questioned the accuracy of the portrait of Eustathius presented at Gangra and suggested that his followers may have exaggerated the ascetical tendencies of the bishop.

[13] 'Canons from the Council of Gangra', trans. O. Larry Yarbrough in Vincent L. Wimbush (ed.), *Ascetic Behavior in Greco-Roman Antiquity: A Sourcebook* (Minneapolis, Minn.: Fortress Press, 1990), 454. Accounts of Eustathius' asceticism and condemnation can be found in Socrates, *Hist. eccl.* 2.43 (PG 67, 352–4) and Sozomen, *Hist. eccl.* 3.14 (PG 67, 1080–2), 4.24 (PG 67, 1192).

ii. Priscillian of Avila

The case of Priscillian of Avila provides yet another example of an ascetical teacher whose views provoked frequent accusations of heresy in the later years of the fourth century. Priscillian is of special interest here because his condemnation and execution at Trier occurred around the year 386 and thus takes us close in time and place to Jovinian. Prior to his execution Priscillian had visited Rome and Milan in a fruitless effort to gain the support of Pope Damasus and Ambrose. After Priscillian's death Pope Siricius received a letter from the usurping emperor Magnus Maximus regarding the execution, and Ambrose and Jerome both commented on the case.[14] Unlike Hieracas and Eustathius, Priscillian has left several writings which make it possible to determine the character of his teachings, as well as the nature of the charges that had been made against him.[15] Moreover, since Priscillian was accused of Manichaeism, he provides a clear example of the way in which the label of 'Manichaean' could easily become attached to Christians with encratite leanings, whether moderate or radical.

In 380 a group of twelve bishops had met at Saragossa in Spain to discuss various problems associated with the ascetic life. Priscillian himself, who was not yet a bishop, was neither present at the council nor mentioned in its canons. The bishops assembled at Saragossa, however, were concerned about problems they attributed to asceticism. For example, they forbade women to meet with unrelated men (*viri alieni*) for the purpose of teaching (can. 1); they prohibited women from taking the veil of consecrated virginity prior to reaching forty years of age (can. 8); and they pronounced excommunication on any clergyman who sought to leave his office ('on the presumption of luxury and vanity') in order to undertake the monastic life (can. 6).[16] Other canons from Saragossa forbade fasting on Sundays and required church attendance during Lent and the weeks around Christmas (can. 2 and 4); further prohibited actions during the latter season included walking barefoot

---

[14] The letter of Maximus is *ep.* 40 in the *Collectio Avellana* (CSEL 35, 90–1); see also Jerome, *Vir. ill.* 121 (PL 23, 750); Ambrose, *ep.* 30 (Maur. 24) to Valentinian II (CSEL 82.1, 207–15); and the discussion of A. R. Birley, 'Magnus Maximus and the Persecution of Heresy', *BJRL* 66 (1982–3), 13–43.

[15] The Würzburg Tractates were discovered in 1885 and published by Georg Schepss in CSEL 18 (1889); reprinted in PLS 2, 1413–83. The case for Priscillian's authorship has been persuasively argued by Henry Chadwick, *Priscillian of Avila: The Occult and the Charismatic in the Early Church* (Oxford: Clarendon Press, 1976), 62–9. The *Canons on the Pauline Epistles* (CSEL 18, 110–47; PLS 2, 1391–412) is another writing of Priscillianist provenance, although it has been emended by a bishop Peregrinus to conform more closely to orthodox beliefs. See Chadwick, *Priscillian*, 58–62.

[16] The text of the canons of the Council of Saragossa is found in José Vives (ed.), *Concilios Visigóticos et Hispano-Romanos* (Barcelona and Madrid: Consejo Superior de Investigaciones Cientificas Instituto Enrique Flórez, 1963), 16–18.

and withdrawing to private estates or mountains (can. 4). The council also stated that Christians should not take the title of 'teacher' without ecclesiastical permission (can. 7).

On the surface the canons issued by the bishops at Saragossa appear to have been more concerned with church discipline than with theological doctrine. Like the earlier decrees of the Council of Gangra, the Saragossan canons seem designed mostly to redirect ascetic piety towards the institutional church and to reaffirm control by the clerical hierarchy.[17] The ascetical activities of women, in particular, were severely curtailed, and any forms of lay piety that were not directly under clerical supervision were strongly discouraged. As in the case of Hieracas and Eustathius, the social disruption and challenge to clerical authority that resulted from ascetic practice seem to have set the stage for the eventual accusations of heresy.

Soon after the council, opposition to Priscillian escalated when he was installed as bishop of Avila in the spring of 381 by several episcopal supporters. In response, some of the bishops who were present at Saragossa, most notably Hydatius of Merida and Ithacius of Ossonuba, opposed Priscillian's appointment and managed to secure a decree from the emperor Gratian condemning 'pseudo-bishops and Manichaeans'.[18] Faced with deposition, Priscillian travelled to Rome, then to Milan, to appeal the decision before Damasus and Ambrose. Priscillian's *Tractatus 2*, addressed to Damasus, contained his profession of faith and response to the accusations against him.

The second tractate presented Priscillian's answers to the following charges: 1) denying hope of salvation to married Christians; 2) holding Patripassianist doctrines of the divine monarchy; 3) holding a docetic notion of the Incarnation; 4) studying heretical apocrypha; 5) adhering to Manichaeism and practicing magic; and 6) teaching wicked morals and indecency.[19] The most consequential of all these accusations was to be the charge of 'Manichaeism'. When Priscillian later appealed his deposition before the emperor Maximus, he was convicted of sorcery and condemned to death along with several companions. When Maximus later wrote to explain his behaviour to Pope Siricius, he claimed that the 'Manichaeans' had convicted themselves by their own confession.[20]

---

[17] For this interpretation of Saragossa, see Virginia Burrus, 'Ascesis, Authority, and Text: *The Acts of the Council of Saragossa*', *Semeia*, 58 (1992), 95–108; eadem, *The Making of a Heretic: Gender, Authority, and the Priscillianist Controversy* (Berkeley: University of California Press, 1995), 25–46.

[18] Priscillian, *Tract.* 2 (CSEL 18, 40); cf. Sulpicius Severus, *Chron.* 2.46 (SC 441, 332), who characterized Priscillian and his companions simply as the 'heresy of the Gnostics'.

[19] Summarized in Chadwick, *Priscillian*, 35. Chadwick believes it was likely that such charges had already surfaced at Saragossa, although they do not appear in the conciliar canons.

[20] *Ep.* 40.4 (CSEL 35, 91). The 'confession', of course, was extracted under judicial torture.

Modern scholars of the Priscillianist controversy are united in their opinion that Priscillian was no Manichee.[21] Yet all agree that several features of Priscillian's teaching lent credibility to the charge of Manichaeism, at least as that charge was popularly understood.[22] Close scrutiny of extant Priscillianist texts suggests that his views fell somewhere between the poles of moderate and radical encratism. On the one hand, Priscillian explicitly disavowed the radical encratite view that married Christians could not be saved. On the other hand, he clearly regarded married life as inherently sinful. In his letter to Damasus, for example, Priscillian acknowledged that 'pardon' (*venia*) was possible for Christians who did not renounce family and possessions; after all, there were 'many dwelling-places in the Father's house' (John 14: 2). As Priscillian pointed out, even the apostle Paul had confessed that he fell short of perfection (cf. Rom 7: 18), that concessions were allowed to the weak (cf. 1 Cor 7: 6), and that he had no command for virgins (cf. 1 Cor 7: 25).[23] Like Tertullian before him, Priscillian regarded marriage as in some sense sinful, though he seems to have stopped just short of espousing a thoroughgoing radical encratism.

But most of the Priscillianist writings present the Christian life as a battle between the spirit and the flesh and strongly endorse the encratite ideal. In one of the Priscillianist *Canons on the Pauline Epistles*, for example, we find the following exhortation: 'The bodies of the saints ought to be temples of God or the Holy Spirit and members of Christ. Therefore, they should always be living and pleasing sacrifices, and they should abstain from every work of the flesh and from whispering and vain speech and from other sins. And so they should remain as virgins, according to the apostle's advice.'[24] Although Priscillian was willing to allow that 'pardon' (*venia*) was available to married Christians, the conduct of the 'saints' was to be different: 'The saints should crucify their flesh with its vices and desires, boasting in the cross of Christ, through which they have died to the world and its works.'[25]

---

[21] Chadwick, *Priscillian*, 96–9; Burrus, *Making of a Heretic*, 69–76; and Samuel N. C. Lieu, *Manichaeism in the Later Roman Empire and Medieval China: A Historical Survey* (Manchester: Manchester University Press, 1985), 114–16.

[22] Cf. Chadwick, *Priscillian*, 99, who notes that parallels between the views of Priscillian and those of the Manichees 'show how genuinely vulnerable he is to orthodox anxieties about his position'.

[23] *Tract.* 2 (CSEL 18, 36). Among the Priscillianist *Canons on the Pauline Epistles*, we find the affirmation that '[Paul] orders those without self-control to marry, and women ought to be saved through bearing children.' See *Can.* 57, alluding to 1 Cor 7: 9 and 1 Tim 2: 15 (CSEL 18, 134).

[24] *Can.* 33 (CSEL 18, 124).

[25] *Can.* 34 (CSEL 18, 124). The *Canons on the Pauline Epistles* contain similar endorsements of voluntary poverty and fasting. See *Can.* 35–7.

Priscillian's emphasis on the necessity of celibacy for the acquisition of sanctity appears to stem from his deep-seated sense of the corruption that has befallen humanity since the original sin of Adam and Eve. Unlike most radical encratites, Priscillian affirmed that God had created human beings and intended them to reproduce physically. He explicitly stated that God had 'embodied' (*corporasset*) the divine image and likeness in human flesh, with the intention that 'flesh should be born from flesh' (*caro nasceretur ex carne*).[26] Originally, however, human beings were supposed to possess a 'purified flesh' (*castificata caro*), that is, a body capable of overcoming the nature of its earthly material; they were not supposed to be 'deceived by the will of concupiscence'. But all that changed as a result of the primal sin. Now, in the words of the *Wisdom of Solomon*, 'the body that is corrupted makes the soul heavy, and the earthly habitation drags down the mind that thinks many things'.[27] As Henry Chadwick has observed, Priscillian did not view bodily appetites as a diabolical creation; he did emphasize, however, that they are now exploited by the wiles of the devil: 'and a particular cause of corruption is sexual desire'.[28]

Priscillian's sense of the corruption introduced into human nature by sin was matched by an equally strong emphasis on the power of the devil over the created order. This, along with Priscillian's asceticism, was one of the features of his teaching that lent plausibility to the accusation of 'Manichaeism'.[29] In a sermon on Psalm 1, for example, Priscillian offered the following reflection on the opening verses of the psalm ('Happy the man who does not walk in the counsel of the wicked, or stand on the path of sinners, or sit in the seat of pestilence'):

> Understanding the eloquence of the prophetic word, you should strive to be such as God the Father made you, you should be what the hand of God originally established. For the image and likeness of God, which you are, does not seek the enticements and allurements of corruption; and all the counsel of the wicked and ways of sinners and seats of pestilence [are] the cunning of the corrupt flesh and the workshop of the polluted body, as scripture says: 'The body that is corrupted makes the soul heavy, and the earthly habitation drags down the mind that thinks many things' (Wis 9: 15).

Proceeding to describe the works produced in the 'workshop of the polluted body' (*polluti corporis officina*), Priscillian emphasized the impact of the devil's activity in the 'corrupt flesh' of fallen humanity:

[26] *Tract.* 5 (CSEL 18, 65).
[27] *Tract.* 5 (CSEL 18, 63), citing Wis 9: 15, a favourite text of Priscillian. See the detailed discussion of Priscillian's use of this passage in Burrus, *Making of a Heretic*, 71–6.
[28] Chadwick, *Priscillian*, 71, alluding to *Tract.* 10 (CSEL 18, 101): 'si credentibus nobis nato per virginem Christo et ea, quae corruptelae causa exstitit, concupiscentiae carnalis natura vincatur.'
[29] Burrus, *Making of a Heretic*, 49.

For this is the calculation of lust, the blow of anger, the incurable promise, the weapons of the serpent, the craftiness of the enemy, the fawning of the stranger, the subjugation of us, and the corruption of himself. In this way the hostile conqueror sows his stratagems, and the devil (*zabolus*) stealthily lays his traps that secretly (*per occulta*) deceive, while he strikes to terrify or flatters to deceive!'[30]

Proof of the persistent danger of satanic influence operating through the evil impulses in the flesh, Priscillian argued, was the testimony of the apostle Paul himself: 'I see another law in my members at war with the law of my mind and leading me captive in the law of sin' (Rom 7: 23), and in another place, 'I know that in me, that is, in my flesh, no good dwells; for with my mind I serve the law of God, but with my flesh the law of sin' (Rom 7:18, 25). While Priscillian certainly believed that salvation was possible through rebirth and incorporation into Christ, such a rebirth was considered an act of 'mercy', not 'nature'; it required repudiation of the vices associated with carnal birth.[31]

Another feature of Priscillian's teaching that raised suspicions of 'Manichaean' tendencies was his interest in apocryphal literature. Priscillian had defended his reading of the apocrypha in several of his tractates, especially in his letter to Damasus and, at greater length, in *Tractatus 3, Liber de fide et de apocryphis*. It is not difficult to discern what lies behind Priscillian's enthusiasm for these writings. As Henry Chadwick has observed: 'The apocryphal Gospels and Acts, particularly the Acts, found their way to Priscillian's heart because with one voice they proclaimed the specific content of the message of Jesus to consist in the call to give up sexual intercourse. The mission of Thomas or John or Paul or Peter or Andrew was none other than a zealous advocacy of the encratite ideal of virginity.'[32]

Writings such as the *Acts of Thomas*, the *Acts of John*, and the *Acts of Paul and Thecla*, as we noted above, were an important vehicle that carried radical encratite theology into the West during the fourth century. Moreover, it was well known that the Manichees also held these documents in the highest regard.[33] Although in many respects Priscillian's ascetical theology was no more

---

[30] *Tract.* 7 (CSEL 18, 83–4).

[31] Cf. *Tract.* 7 (CSEL 18, 83): 'Omnes enim *corpus Christi sumus et membra* ex parte; nam quod renascimur in salutem, misericordiae est, non naturae, ut, si nativitate carnis adstricti et mundialis mali vitiis obligati peccatorum viam et consilia non evasimus inpiorum vel *baptizati in Christo Christum induentes*, ita perennis vitae sequamur heredem, ut nec cui renuntiativimus inveniamur participes nec cui credimus infideles.'

[32] Chadwick, *Priscillian*, 77; and now Andrew S. Jacobs, 'The Disorder of Books: Priscillian's Canonical Defense of Apocrypha', *HTR* 93 (2000), 135–59.

[33] According to Augustine, *Faust.* 22.79 (CSEL 25.1, 681–2) and 30.4 (CSEL 25.1, 751–2), Faustus the Manichee appealed to the Acts of Peter, Paul, Thomas, Andrew, and John in order to support his teaching on virginity. See also Filastrius, *Haer.* 88, on the Manichaean use of the apocryphal Acts.

radical than that of many other fourth-century Christians, his single-minded stress on the opposition between 'flesh' and 'spirit', his insistence on celibacy for the saints, and his enthusiasm for the Christian apocrypha encouraged his opponents to use (and misuse) the charge of 'Manichaean' in their efforts to suppress him.

The label was to be remarkably durable. I refer not only to Priscillian's execution for sorcery (a charge often associated with Manichaeism), but also to the way in which subsequent anti-heretical writers were to remember and to record Priscillian's activity. For example, the north Italian bishop, Filastrius of Brescia, who composed his 'Book of Various Heresies' (*Diversarum hereseon liber*) sometime in the later 380s, could write as if there were virtually no difference between Priscillian and the Manichees. In his entry on the Manichees, he noted that the sect was still active in his day: 'Both in Spain and in the Five Provinces they are said to lie hidden and each day to capture many with their deceit.'[34] Later in the book Filastrius alluded to a group of ascetics who were clearly the supporters of Priscillian; he associated them with the teaching of the Manichees: 'There are others in Gaul and Spain and Aquitania who practice a kind of abstinence and pursue the most pernicious association of the Gnostics and Manichaeans. And they do not hesitate to preach the same things: they persuade married couples to separate and urge abstinence from meat.'[35] Several decades later Augustine could comment that the Priscillianists 'babble blasphemies not much different from those of the Manichees'.[36] The responses of these fourth-century heresiologists to Priscillian indicate that anyone perceived to be preaching the tenets of radical encratism was liable to be labelled a 'Manichaean'.

The examples of Hieracas, Eustathius, and Priscillian illustrate the continued popularity of the encratite tradition, in both its moderate and radical forms, within fourth-century asceticism and monasticism. Conversely, the ecclesiastical condemnations of these ascetical teachers show that some church leaders were deeply suspicious of ascetic piety when it challenged clerical authority or threatened the established social order, especially on the role of women. It was certainly no accident that Hieracas, Eustathius, and Priscillian each seemed to have fostered unconventional activities, especially for female ascetics. Moreover, even though Priscillian seems not to have been a thoroughgoing 'radical' encratite, his ascetical theology still attracted the

---

[34] Filastrius, *Haer*. 61.5 (CSEL 38, 32).

[35] Ibid., 84.1 (CSEL 38, 45).

[36] *Ep*. 166.7 (CSEL 44, 556), dated 415. In 427 Augustine could write that Priscillianists 'follow a mixture of teachings, especially those of the Gnostics and Manichees'; see *Haer*. 70 (CCSL 46, 333); also the treatise, *De natura boni* 47 (CSEL 25.2, 886–7), where Augustine confused Priscillian and his followers with the Manichees.

charge of 'Manichaeism'. In the case of Priscillian, this accusation served both as shorthand for his encratite theology and as a cipher for activities that were perceived by his fellow bishops as subversive of good ecclesiastical order.

The accusations of 'Manichaeism' which dogged Priscillian and his followers help to shed light on the accusations which Jovinian directed against his opponents. In his critique of ascetic piety Jovinian used the label of 'Manichaean' with the same sort of polemical intent (and imprecision) as did the episcopal persecutors of Priscillian. As we shall see below, fourth-century heresiologists, such as Epiphanius and Filastrius, also employed the same strategy in their criticisms of Encratites, Montanists, and the followers of Origen. But such accusations would never have been so potent, had there not been actual Manichaeans in the Roman Empire, whose persistent presence was a source of alarm to both ecclesiastical and imperial officials. Moreover, the evidence of both imperial legislation and Christian theological polemic indicates that the boundaries between 'Manichaeans' and 'Encratites' were increasingly (and, perhaps, intentionally) blurred in the later fourth century. In such a context, Jovinian's accusations acquired some plausibility, despite their essential inaccuracy.

iii. The Persistence of Manichaeism

The spread of Manichaeism in the fourth century further intensified the concerns of some Christians regarding the link between asceticism and heresy. Founded by the Persian visionary Mani, the Manichaean religion was always aggressive in proselytizing, and Manichaean missionaries had reached Egypt before the end of the third century, probably before the death of Mani himself in 276.[37] Egyptian polemicists, both pagan and Christian, wrote refutations of Manichaeism as early as the first part of the fourth century.[38] The doctrinal grounds and motivations of Manichaean asceticism differed dramatically from that of orthodox Christians, and even from that of the ancient 'Encratites', such as Tatian. Nevertheless, the ascetical practices of the Manichees—especially the celibacy and abstinence from meat and wine required of the Manichaean 'Elect'—were identical to those adopted by many 'orthodox'

---

[37] P. Brown, 'The Diffusion of Manichaeism in the Roman Empire', in his *Religion and Society in the Age of Saint Augustine* (London: Faber and Faber, 1972), 94–118; Lieu, *Manichaeism*, 63–78; G. Stroumsa, 'The Manichaean Challenge to Egyptian Christianity', in B. Pearson and J. Goehring (eds.), *The Roots of Egyptian Christianity* (Philadelphia: Fortress Press, 1986), 307–19.

[38] S. Lieu, 'Some Themes in Later Roman Anti-Manichaean Polemics: I–II', *BJRL* 68 (1986), 434–72; 69 (1986), 235–75; G. Stroumsa, 'Aspects of Anti-Manichaean Polemics in Late Antiquity and Under Early Islam', *HTR* 81 (1988), 37–58.

monks.[39] Hence we see early monastic enthusiasts, such as Athanasius, attempting to distance orthodox Christian monasticism from Manichaean asceticism.[40]

Moreover, Manichaeism spread into the West at the same time as did knowledge of Egyptian monasticism. As a result, the presence of Manichees contributed greatly to the atmosphere of hostility and suspicion which Western ascetics sometimes encountered. For example, there is considerable evidence that Manichaeism was especially strong in Western Christianity, particularly at Rome, in the later decades of the fourth century. Imperial legislation against the Manichees had appeared as early as the reign of the emperor Diocletian, several years before he initiated his persecution of Christians.[41] Diocletian ordered Manichaean leaders to be burned to death along with their scriptures. In 313 Constantine's Edict of Toleration, however, had granted religious freedom to all religious groups within the Roman Empire, and Manichees appear to have benefited from this general amnesty for several decades. Only in the later fourth century did Manichaeism once again become the object of imperial hostility. After Diocletian, the first evidence of anti-Manichaean legislation is an edict of the emperors Valentinian I and Valens, issued at Trier in 372, that ordered the confiscation of any dwellings dedicated to the use of the Manichaeans.[42]

During the 380s and 390s legislation against the Manichees increased in frequency and severity, especially under the emperor Theodosius. In 381 Gratian, Valentinian II, and Theodosius deprived Manichees of the right to bequeath or receive any inheritance and banned Manichaean assemblies.[43] Significantly, this decree claimed that some Manichees attempted to defend themselves by taking the names of other ascetic groups: 'Encratites', 'Apotactites', 'Hydroparastatae', and 'Saccophori'. In the following year the penalties against the Manichees were repeated and extended to the 'Encratites', 'Saccophori', and 'Hydroparastatae'.[44] This decree of 382 also granted permission for informers

---

[39] Some scholars have suggested that Manichaean asceticism may have directly influenced the rise of organized monasticism in Egypt. See F. Wisse, 'Gnosticism and Early Monasticism in Egypt', in B. Aland (ed.), *Gnosis: Festschrift für Hans Jonas*. (Göttingen: Vandenhoeck & Ruprecht, 1978), 431–40; G. Stroumsa, 'Monachisme et Marranisme chez les Manichéens d'Egypte', *Numen* 2 (1982): 184–201; *id.*, 'Manichaean Challenge', 308–9. The work of Jason Beduhn, however, has raised serious questions about this connection; see 'The Battle for the Body in Manichaean Asceticism', in Valantasis and Wimbush (eds.), *Asceticism*, 513–19.

[40] e.g. *Vit. Ant.* 68 (SC 400, 314), where Athanasius described the hermit Antony as an opponent of the Manichees.

[41] Diocletian's edict of 297 is cited in the *Lex dei sive Mosaicarum et Romanarum legum collatio*, 15.3.4, probably to be ascribed to Ambrosiaster. See also Ambrosiaster, *Comm. in Tim. secundam* 3: 7 (CSEL 81.3, 312).

[42] *C.Th.* 16.5.3.   [43] *C.Th.* 16.5.7.

[44] *C.Th.* 16.5.9. The 'Hydroparastatae' were distinguished by their use of water instead of wine at the eucharist. The 'Saccophori' were, literally, 'sack-wearers'. Both had been condemned

(*delatores*) to present accusations against the Manichees, a practice that was normally strongly discouraged.[45] In the year 383 yet another edict forbade assemblies and decreed exile for 'all persons whatsoever who are tossed about by the false doctrines of diverse heresies, namely the Eunomians, the Arians, the Macedonians, the Pneumatomachi, the Manichaeans, the Encratites, the Apotactites, the Saccophori, and the Hydroparastatae'.[46] Heresies associated with ascetic thought and practice now ranked with those that dealt with Trinitarian doctrine.

If the 380s marked a turning point in imperial attitudes towards the Manichaeans (and towards other groups of radical 'Encratites'), by the end of the decade legislation against the Manichees had adopted an even more hostile tone. In 389 an edict of Theodosius, Valentinian II, and Arcadius suggested that previous legislation had failed to discourage the spread of Manichaeism: 'If any persons whatever should disturb the world under the name of Manichaeans, they shall indeed be expelled from the whole world, but especially from this City [Rome], under the threat of judgment.'[47] By the later 390s, special regulations were introduced authorizing the active persecution of Manichees and of those who provided them with asylum.[48]

The anti-Manichaean legislation of the 380s and 390s shows that Manichaeism was increasingly regarded as a public nuisance in the later fourth century; it also indicates that opponents of Manichaeism tended to blur the boundaries between the Manichees and other radical ascetic groups. This confusion arose partly because there was little to distinguish the Manichees from other radical ascetics, at least in terms of external behaviour. Moreover, both the Manichees and the other types of radical Encratites were perceived as threatening to the established social order. As Per Beskow has argued:

The ascetic underground movements were regarded by the Roman authorities as socially harmful, not because they were ascetic, which might in itself be acceptable, but because they tended to upset law and order by questioning the laws of marriage, property, and social behavior in general. They were not satisfied with withdrawing from society but also wanted to transmit their values to society as a whole.[49]

along with Encratites in the canonical letters of Basil of Caesarea, *ep.* 188.1 (Courtonne 2, 122–3) and *ep.* 199.47 (Courtonne 2, 163), composed in 374–375. The imperial decree of 381 seemed to confuse the Manichees with the other groups; the decree of 382 recognized a distinction but condemned them all.

[45] A *delator* was ordinarily subject to capital punishment. See *C.Th.* 10.10.1–3.
[46] *C.Th.* 16.5.11; trans. Pharr, *Theodosian Code*, 452.
[47] *C.Th.* 16.5.18; trans. Pharr, *Theodosian Code*, 453–4.
[48] *C.Th.* 16.5.35, issued by Arcadius and Honorius, 17 May 399.
[49] Per Beskow, 'The Theodosian Laws against Manichaeism', in P. Bryder (ed.), *Manichaean Studies: Proceedings of the First International Conference on Manichaeism* (Lund: Plus Ultra, 1988), 11.

The assimilation of the Manichees to other groups in the legal texts proved useful in another way. As Caroline Humphress has recently observed, the prohibition of the 'Encratites' and other ascetical groups was accomplished by incorporating them under the umbrella of the earlier anti-Manichaean legislation. Just as the Manichaeans were originally persecuted under laws pertaining to 'magicians' (*malefici*) and 'astrologers' (*mathematici*), so, by further extension, all radical ascetics came to be regarded as crypto-Manichaeans from the standpoint of imperial legislation.[50]

Ecclesiastical attempts to root out Manichaeism also show the persistence of the sect in the Western Church. According to the *Liber pontificalis*, Pope Miltiades (310–314) was the first to discover Manichaeans in the city of Rome.[51] Seventy years later, in the time of Pope Siricius (384–399), they remained an active presence. The *Liber pontificalis* describes Siricius' efforts against the Manichees:

> He discovered Manichaeans in the city and sent them into exile, and decreed that they should not share communion with the faithful, since it would be wrong to abuse the Lord's holy body with a defiled mouth; he decreed that any convert from the Manichaeans who returned to the church should on no account be given communion but should be removed to a monastery and held in subjection throughout his life, so that tortured by fasting and prayer and tested by every trial till the final day of his death, through the church's mercy the *viaticum* should be given them.[52]

Attempts to suppress the Manichees continued under subsequent popes. Siricius' successor, Pope Anastasius, was so concerned about the presence of Manichees in the church at Rome that he refused to ordain any cleric from abroad unless he presented a certificate signed by five bishops.[53] Throughout the fifth century, the Roman pontiffs, especially Pope Leo I, were active in their efforts to remove Manicheans from the clergy and laity.[54]

The writings of Augustine also provide evidence of the presence and popularity of Manichaeism in Rome in the years immediately prior to Jovinian's activity there. As a Manichaean Auditor for nine years, Augustine knew firsthand the extent of the Manichaean community at Rome. When Augustine arrived in Rome in 384 to establish his school of rhetoric, he encountered a large number of Manichees there and found lodging with a

---

[50] 'Roman Law, Forensic Argument and the Formation of Christian Orthodoxy (III–VI Centuries)', in Elm, Rebillard, and Romano (eds.), *Orthodoxy, Christianity, History* (Rome: École Française de Rome, 2000), 125–47, esp. 137–8.

[51] *Lib. pont.* 33 (Duchesne 1, 168).

[52] *Lib. pont.* 40 (Duchesne 1, 216); trans. Raymond Davis, *The Book of Pontiffs* (Translated Texts for Historians; Liverpool University Press, 1989), 30.

[53] *Lib. pont.* 41 (Duchesne 1, 218).

[54] Lieu, *Manichaeism*, 164–8.

fellow Manichaean Auditor.[55] According to Augustine's account in the *Confessions*, his enthusiasm for Manichaeism had already begun to wane by the time he arrived in Rome; nevertheless he remained attached to the community there:

> I did not neglect to tell my host that he should not put the excessive trust, which I perceived him to have, in the fabulous matters of which Manichee books are full. But I was in more intimate friendship with them than with others who were not in that heresy. I did not defend it with the zest that at one time I had. Nevertheless my close association with them (the number of them secretly living in Rome was large) made me reluctant to look elsewhere.[56]

Several years later, when the opportunity arose for an appointment to a chair of rhetoric in Milan, Augustine applied for the position 'through the mediation of those intoxicated with Manichee follies'.[57] Since the appointment was the responsibility of the urban prefect, the distinguished pagan Q. Aurelius Symmachus, Augustine's accession to the chair shows that the Manichaean sect 'still enjoyed the support of the rich and the powerful in the capital despite the anti-Manichaean legislations'.[58]

Much of the attraction exercised by Manichaean missionaries derived from their commitment to asceticism, especially the celibacy and abstinence from meat and wine required of the Elect. In the *Confessions*, for example, Augustine noted that his friend Alypius was especially drawn to the Manichees by their displays of sexual continence.[59] In his earliest polemical writings against the Manichees, begun at Rome in 387 and later completed in North Africa, Augustine claimed that the Manichees enticed the unwary into the sect by finding fault with the scriptures and by 'feigning chaste lives and extraordinary continence'.[60] Augustine's two books, *De moribus ecclesiae catholicae* and *De moribus Manichaeorum*, were composed with the precise aim of distinguishing the Manichaean practice of asceticism from the (externally identical) practice of asceticism by orthodox Christians. As Samuel Lieu has observed, at a time when organized monasticism was beginning to become established in the West, Manichaeans 'had few rivals in their claim to be true Christians through their ostentatious acts of self-denial'.[61]

---

[55] *Conf.* 5.10.18. In *Conf.* 5.8.14 Augustine indicated that he had gone to Rome at the invitation of Manichaean friends there. Augustine's host at Rome may have been Constantius, the Manichaean Auditor mentioned elsewhere. See *Faust.* 5.5 (CSEL 25.1, 277–8) and *Man.* 20.74 (CSEL 90, 154–6).

[56] *Conf.* 5.10.19 (BA 13, 498); trans. H. Chadwick, *Saint Augustine: Confessions* (Oxford and New York: Oxford University Press, 1991), 84–5.

[57] *Conf.* 5.13.23 (BA 13, 506); trans. Chadwick, 87.   [58] Lieu, *Manichaeism*, 137.

[59] *Conf.* 6.7.12.   [60] *Mor. eccl.* 1.2 (CSEL 90, 4–5).

[61] Lieu, *Manichaeism*, 146–7.

Because of the similarity between the ascetic practices of the Manichaeans and those of other Christians, it was not long before the term 'Manichaean' had become a label for any unpopular or disreputable type of ascetic. At the same time as the imperial legislation was incorporating 'Encratites' and other radical ascetics under the umbrella of 'Manichaeism', Jerome observed in his Letter 22 to Eustochium, composed at Rome in 384, that whenever lax Christians saw a woman who was sad or pale from fasting, 'they call her a poor wretch, a nun (*monacha*), and a Manichean: and with reason, for according to their belief fasting is heresy'.[62] Such comments, of course, did not stop Jerome from making his own criticisms of Manichaean asceticism.[63] Apologists for asceticism, such as Jerome, stressed the difference between 'orthodox' and 'heretical' forms of asceticism in an effort to deflect the accusation of 'Manichaeism' that Western ascetics frequently encountered.

2. ASCETICISM AND FOURTH-CENTURY HERESIOLOGY

But imperial decrees were not the sole cause of popular confusion between the Manicheans and other ascetic Christians. As Samuel Lieu has noted, the treatment of Manichaeism by fourth-century heresiologists also tended to encourage the use of 'Manichaean' as a malevolent label: 'These anti-Manichaean works which were also highly popular, tended to simplify Manichaean doctrines and create the impression that the main tenets of the sect were dualism, asceticism and astrology. Soon orthodox-minded churchmen began to detect "Manichaean" traits among the more ascetical members of the Christian church.'[64] This tendency to label all radical ascetics as 'Manichaeans', which resulted in fatal consequences for the Spanish bishop Priscillian, helps to explain Jovinian's use of the term in his effort to discredit ascetic elitism.

i. Epiphanius and Filastrius

The observations of Samuel Lieu just cited suggest that another indicator of heightened concern regarding asceticism and heresy can be found in the writings of the fourth-century heresiologists, Epiphanius of Salamis and Filastrius of Brescia. Although Epiphanius and Filastrius were both bishops who were deeply sympathetic to the monastic life, they also strongly opposed

---

[62] *Ep.* 22.13.3 (CSEL 54, 161); trans. Mierow, 145. [63] *Ep.* 22.38.7.
[64] Lieu, *Manichaeism*, 87.

ideas or practices that led to what they would consider 'heresy'. Epiphanius and Filastrius were quite innovative in their use of the term 'heresy' and liberal in its application to new ideas. Their concerns extended not only to the teachings of the Manichees, but also to the views of other groups and teachers with ascetical leanings, including Encratites, Montanists, and the followers of Origen. Moreover, both Epiphanius and Filastrius used the label of 'Manichaean'—sometimes openly, sometimes by insinuation—to describe these diverse instances of moderate and radical encratism. The writings of these heresiologists, therefore, will illustrate how malleable the label of 'Manichaean' had become in the polemical discourse of the late fourth century.

There are further reasons for considering Epiphanius and Filastrius to be relevant to the world of Jovinian. Both men were present and active in Italy during the 380s. Epiphanius had come to Rome in 382, in the company of Jerome, to attend a council that dealt with a schism at Antioch and with the heresy of Apollinarius. His *Panarion* ('Medicine-Chest') against heresies had been written several years earlier (c.376–378). Filastrius, who knew and used the handbook of Epiphanius, composed his own *Diversarum hereseon liber* sometime between 380 and 390. Like the *Panarion*, the handbook of Filastrius circulated widely in the West. The work was later consulted by Augustine for his own *De haeresibus* (c.427) and by Gregory the Great.[65] The writings of both Epiphanius and Filastrius, therefore, although partisan, enable us to glimpse some of the ideas about heresy and asceticism that were circulating in Italy in the years immediately prior to Jovinian's activity there.

Epiphanius has not inspired much enthusiasm among church historians. He was, as J. Rebecca Lyman has put it, 'a bishop of narrow, but energetic, theological views'.[66] Or, as Frances Young has stated, 'few would claim that Epiphanius was an original thinker or an attractive personality'.[67] Filastrius has fared even less well. Augustine, who knew the writings of both men, judged Epiphanius to be 'by far the more eminent scholar... who spoke with greater learning than Filastrius'.[68] To some extent, the problem is the nature of heresiology itself; it is a severe and cantankerous genre that has been largely 'an embarrassment to modern scholars'.[69] The polemical character of the

---

[65] Judith McClure, 'Handbooks Against Heresy in the West, from the Late Fourth to the Late Sixth Centuries', *JTS*, n.s. 30 (1979), 186–97.

[66] 'Ascetics and Bishops: Epiphanius on Orthodoxy', in Elm, Rebillard, and Romano (eds.), *Orthodoxy, Christianity, Heresy*, 151.

[67] *From Nicaea to Chalcedon* (London: SCM Press, 1983), 133; cited in Averil Cameron, 'How to Read Heresiology', *JMEMS* 33 (2003), 488, n. 30.

[68] *Ep.* 222.2 (CSEL 57, 447): 'Epiphanius longe Philastrio doctior eminuerit.'

[69] Cameron, 'How to Read Heresiology', 472. Cameron, 474, proposes an alternative approach to the genre. Historians, she argues, should view heresiologies as 'performative or functional texts', rather than as sources of information.

handbooks of heresy presents obvious problems to historians attempting to reconstruct the original thought of the heretics. But despite their limitations as documentary sources, the writings of the heresiologists enable us to gauge the ideological concerns of the authors themselves and of their contemporaries. In other words, the handbooks of both Epiphanius and Filastrius have much to teach us about the ways in which certain ascetical ideas were being perceived and labelled as 'heresy' in the late fourth century.

One of the most striking features of the heresiological writings of both Epiphanius and Filastrius is the manner in which the number and variety of 'heresies' have wildly proliferated since the days of Irenaeus. Epiphanius' *Panarion* delineated no less than eighty individual heresies, dating back well before the time of Christ. The number was based on Song of Songs 6: 8–9, 'There are sixty queens and eighty concubines, and maidens without number. My dove, my perfect one, is the only one.' For Epiphanius, the 'perfect one' was the Bride of Christ, the holy and virginal Church; the eighty concubines were the various sects or 'heresies': 'They have not been entire strangers to the covenant and inheritance, but have no stated dowry and are not receptacles of the Holy Spirit, but have only an illicit union with the Word.... they cannot have the honor, title, security, marriage portion, wedding gifts, dowered status and legitimacy of the free wife.'[70] Not to be outdone, Filastrius included 156 'heresies' in his collection: 28 from before the time of Christ and 128 from the Christian era. Filastrius also divided his collection into two lists: heresies 1–92 covered individual heresiarchs and their followers; heresies 93–156 treated particular theological or exegetical opinions with which Filastrius disagreed.[71] The very proliferation of 'heresies' in the writings of Epiphanius and Filastrius is an index of the degree to which the boundaries of 'orthodoxy' were being increasingly contested (and constricted) in the later decades of the fourth century.

Epiphanius is best known for his zealous defence of the Nicene Creed and for his role in instigating the late fourth-century opposition to Origen. While these issues may have constituted the core of his concerns in the *Panarion*,[72] he also devoted considerable attention to refuting a variety of sects that held views consistent with radical encratism. For example, following the genealogical strategy inherited from previous heresiologists, Epiphanius drew lines connecting contemporary 'Encratites' with their predecessors, Tatian and the 'Tatianists'. Although in one place Epiphanius had described Tatian and his followers

---

[70] *Fid.* 6.1, 4 (Holl-Dummer 3, 501–2); trans. Williams 2, 643.

[71] Many of these, as Augustine observed, were not heresies at all, and so he eliminated them from his own collection. See Augustine, *Haer.* 80 (CCSL 46, 336).

[72] Cf. Jon F. Dechow, *Dogma and Mysticism in Early Christianity* (PMS 13; Macon, GA: Mercer University Press, 1988), 13.

as extinct,[73] he proceeded to recount the existence of 'Encratites' who were dependent on the ancient heresiarch and yet still thriving in his own day:

> Certain persons whom we call Encratites are Tatian's successors. They were led astray and deceived by Tatian in person, but have ideas different from his and have devoted themselves to worse foolishness in their own turn. Even today their numbers are increasing in Pisidia and the land called Scorched Phrygia.... There are also Encratites in Asia, Isauria, Pamphylia, Cilicia and Galatia. And by now this sect has also been planted in Rome to a certain extent, and at Antioch in Syria, though not everywhere.[74]

Epiphanius' effort to characterize contemporary 'Encratites' as the continuation of the tradition of Tatian is typical of the heresiologist's strategy that we have seen in Irenaeus: Epiphanius was trying 'to produce a *traditio haereticorum*, the perfect antithesis of the *traditio legis*'.[75] According to Epiphanius, the chief link between the ancient 'Tatianists' and the contemporary 'Encratites' was the fact that both groups considered marriage to be the work of the devil and rejected the eating of meat and drinking of wine.[76]

In addition to constructing these connections between Tatian and the 'Encratites' of his own day, Epiphanius discussed a number of other heretical groups whose views were reminiscent of the errors of Tatian. We have already seen Epiphanius' opposition to the ascetical teachings of the monastic leader Hiercas. But Epiphanius included in his handbook a considerable number of other contemporary sects who espoused ascetical views. For example, Epiphanius characterized the 'Phrygians or Montanists' as a continuation of the Encratite heresy. Citing 1 Timothy 4: 1–3 (one of the classic anti-encratite proof-texts favoured by Jovinian), Epiphanius portrayed the Montanists as falling under the same prophetic condemnation as the Manichees and Encratites: 'Most of these sects forbid marriage and prescribe abstinence from foods, though they do not enjoin these things for discipline's sake or for greater virtue with its rewards and crowns, but because they regard these creatures of the Lord as abominations.'[77] Although Epiphanius knew that the Montanists did not forbid all marriages, he nonetheless attempted to portray them as akin to both the Encratites and the Manichees.

---

[73] *Haer.* 46.2.4 (Holl-Dummer 2, 206); trans. Williams 1, 349: 'Indeed, I believe that [Tatian] has been snuffed out and come to an end already, and his school as well.'
[74] *Haer.* 47.1.1–3 (Holl-Dummer 2, 215); trans. Williams 2, 3.
[75] Cameron, 'How to Read Heresiology', 477.
[76] *Haer.* 47.1.6–7 (Holl-Dummer 2, 216). Aline Pourkier, *L'hérésiologie chez Épiphane de Salamine* (Paris: Beauchesne, 1992), 343–61, has observed that Epiphanius' account of Tatian was coloured by his knowledge of the practices of later Encratites (e.g. on the use of water rather than wine in the eucharist).
[77] *Haer.* 48.8.8 (Holl-Dummer 2, 230); trans. Williams 2, 14.

In the course of the *Panarion* Epiphanius treated a wide variety of sects, many of which had some extreme ascetic component to their teaching: the 'Adamians', who gathered for worship naked and regarded the church as paradise and themselves as Adam and Eve;[78] the 'Valesians', who enforced celibacy by compulsory castration;[79] the 'Cathari' or 'Purists', who forbade second marriages;[80] the 'Apostolics' (also known as 'Apotactites'), natives of Phrygia, Cilicia, and Pamphylia, whom Epiphanius portrayed as 'an offshoot of the doctrines of Tatian, the Encratites, the Tatianists, and the Purists';[81] and the 'Origenists', a sect in which members of both sexes allegedly cohabited and practiced masturbation in order to appear celibate to outsiders.[82] Last, but certainly not least, Epiphanius devoted the lengthiest entry in the entire *Panarion* to a discussion of the doctrines of the Manichaeans.[83] It is evident from even this cursory listing of 'ascetical' heresies that Epiphanius had a special interest in the varieties of ascetic practice that were proliferating in the fourth century and an even greater interest in labelling the apparent excesses as heretical.

Like Epiphanius, who was a source for his own 'Book of Various Heresies', Filastrius also devoted special attention to heresies that advocated radical encratism. But Filastrius did not simply reproduce the heresiological catalogue of Epiphanius. In his handbook Filastrius had an eye for heresies of distinctively Western origin, and he attempted to apply the label of 'heresy' to ideas and groups that were circulating in his own environment.[84] Filastrius' approach to heresiology also tended to be more simple-minded than that of Epiphanius. Rather than construct the elaborate genealogies favoured by his predecessors, Filastrius was content simply to apply the classic labels of 'Gnostic' and 'Manichaean' to groups that favoured ascetic renunciation. We have already noted, for example, Filastrius' interest in Priscillian and his followers in Spain and Gaul and his willingness to characterize them as 'Gnostics' and 'Manichaeans'.[85] In the second part of his handbook, in

---

[78] *Haer.* 52.   [79] *Haer.* 58.

[80] *Haer.* 59. Epiphanius had in mind the followers of Novatian, the third-century Roman presbyter. As he did with the Montanists, Epiphanius tended to blur the distinction between groups that forbade second marriages and those that forbade all marriages.

[81] *Haer.* 61.1.2 (Holl-Dummer 2, 380); trans. Williams 2, 114.

[82] *Haer.* 63.1.4-8 (Holl-Dummer 2, 399). According to Epiphanius, this sect had its beginning in Rome and North Africa. They are distinct from the followers of Origen of Alexandria, whom Epiphanius treated in *Haer.* 64.

[83] *Haer.* 66.

[84] See Mark Humphries, *Communities of the Blessed: Social Environment and Religious Change in Northern Italy, AD 200–400* (OECS; Oxford: Oxford University Press, 1999), 133: 'Filastrius' book is not a diluted Latin version of its Greek predecessors; rather, it is a catalogue of heresies produced in an undeniably western context.' Humphries, 133–5, provides several examples of Filastrius' Western, and specifically North Italian, perspectives on heresy.

[85] *Haer.* 61.5; 84.1.

which he attacked individual ideas apart from the teachers who espoused them, Filastrius attributed a number of different ideas to groups that he labelled 'Gnostic' and 'Manichaean'. As a result, the very imprecision of his use of labels such as 'Manichaean' and 'Gnostic' enabled Filastrius to connect a wider array of groups and ideas to these archetypal heresies.

The heresiological handbooks of Epiphanius and Filastrius pointed to several specific ideas that tended to raise suspicions of 'heresy', especially when combined with ascetical activities, such as celibacy and renunciation of meat and wine. For example, both Epiphanius and Filastrius argued that the reading of apocryphal literature, especially the apocryphal Acts of the Apostles, was a typical heretical practice. Epiphanius attacked the 'Severians', the 'Encratites', and the 'Apotactics' (also known as 'Apostolics') for their interest in the apocrypha.[86] The *Acts of Thomas* and the *Acts of Andrew*, Epiphanius observed, were held in high regard by the latter two groups. Similarly, Filastrius attributed interest in the apocryphal scriptures to 'the Manichees, Gnostics, Nicolaitians, Valentinians, and many others'.[87] He explicitly mentioned the *Acts of Andrews*, the *Acts of John*, the *Acts of Peter*, and the *Acts of Paul* as the objects of heretical scrutiny. Since elsewhere Filastrius characterized Priscillian and his followers as 'Gnostics' and 'Manichaeans', it is likely that he had in mind the use of apocrypha by ascetical teachers such as Priscillian, and not only their use by actual Manichaeans.

Another view that both Epiphanius and Filastrius presented as characteristic of a heretical asceticism was the belief that all sexual activity was of demonic origin. This view could manifest itself in very radical forms, such as the belief that the body was created by rebellious angels or archons. Epiphanius noted that the second-century teacher Satornilus (also known as Saturninus) and the 'Severians' both adhered to this doctrine.[88] The 'Encratites' likewise, according to Epiphanius, believed that the power of the devil was manifested in the created world, especially in sexual activity and the eating of meat: 'Encratites too say that there are certain sovereign authorities ($ἀρχαί$), and that the power of the devil is ranged against God's creatures because the devil is not subject to God; he has power of his own and acts in his own right, and not as though he had fallen into perversity. For they do not agree with the church, but differ from its declaration of the truth.'

---

[86] Epiphanius, *Haer.* 45.4.1 (Severians), 47.1.5 (Encratites), 61.1.5 (Apostolics). Epiphanius, *Haer.* 67.3.4, also criticized Hieracas for using the *Ascension of Isaiah*.

[87] *Haer.* 88.3 (CSEL 38, 48). Filastrius allowed that apocryphal scriptures might be read 'for the sake of morals by the perfect, but they should not be read by everyone'.

[88] *Haer.* 23.1.3 (Satornilus on creation by rebellious angels); 23.2.5 (Satornilus on marriage and procreation as works of Satan); 45.2.1 (Severus teaches that woman is the work of Satan and those who have marital intercourse are doing Satan's work).

As a result of this teaching and because of their reliance on apocryphal literature, Epiphanius remarked, the Encratites 'declare that marriage is plainly the work of the devil. And they regard meat as an abomination—though they do not prohibit it for the sake of continence or as a pious practice but from fear and for appearance' sake, and in order not to be condemned for eating flesh.'[89] One of the central tenets of radical encratism, as portrayed by Epiphanius, was the belief that the devil retained a strong role in human affairs and exercised his power when human beings consumed meat or engaged in sexual relations.

Like Epiphanius, Filastrius also noted that radical ascetics tended to ascribe the physical creation to the work of the devil. As he did in the case of the reading of the apocrypha, Filastrius attributed this view generically to 'Manichees, Gnostics, Nicolaitians, and others'. For example, in a brief discussion of the creation story in Genesis, Filastrius observed that the aforementioned heretics believed that a good God created the soul, but that an evil one created the body.[90] In his entry on the Manichees (which, again, may also have the Priscillianists in view), Filastrius also included this view as one of the primary Manichaean tenets: 'They claim that there are two gods, one good and one evil, declaring that there is a struggle between god and god. And they believe that the human soul takes its origin properly from God, but that the body has been made by the devil.'[91] Such beliefs, Filastrius noted, have led the Manichees to deny the resurrection, to worship demons and cosmic elements, and to invoke the names of pagan gods and goddesses.

In addition to attacking these extreme forms of encratism, which attributed the formation of the human body to the devil, both Epiphanius and Filastrius also addressed the more subtle or moderate encratism of those who characterized marital intercourse as tainted in some way by sin. Unlike Clement of Alexandria and Jovinian, who insisted on the equality of marriage and celibacy, Epiphanius and Filastrius believed that celibacy was an intrinsically 'higher' vocation for Christians. They recognized, however, that the preference for asceticism often rested on dubious theological foundations, that is, on assumptions about the created order that they labelled as 'Gnostic', 'Encratite', or 'Manichaean'.[92] In their heresiological discussions, therefore,

---

[89] *Haer.* 47.1.4 (Holl-Dummer 2, 215–16); tr. Williams 2, 4, slightly altered. As Williams, 3, n. 5, observes, several of the apocryphal Acts represented the devil as 'a powerful, dangerous being'.

[90] *Haer.* 115.2 (CSEL 38, 79).

[91] *Haer.* 61.2–3 (CSEL 38, 32). Filastrius attributed nearly identical views to one Patricius in the following entry on the 'Patricians' (*Patriciani*). See *Haer.* 62.1–2 (CSEL 38, 32–3), and the speculations of Augustine regarding the identity of the little-known Patricius in *Leg.* 2.2.3 (CCSL 49, 90) and 2.12.40–1 (CCSL 49, 130). Ambrosiaster spoke of the *Patriciani*, along with Marcion and the Manichees, as the target of the prophecy of 1 Tim 4: 1–5 (CSEL 81.3, 272).

[92] As Filastrius put it in his entry on the Priscillianists, they encourage abstinence because they believe that certain foods have not been made by God, but by the devil: *Haer.* 84.6 (CSEL 38, 46).

Epiphanius and Filastrius tried to articulate a positive rationale for human sexual activity, despite their own preferences for celibacy, and stressed the original goodness of the body and sexuality as part of God's creation.

Many of the arguments on behalf of the goodness of sexuality presented by Epiphanius and Filastrius were reminiscent of those offered by Clement of Alexandria and previous anti-heretical writers. For example, Epiphanius frequently noted that the book of Genesis strongly endorsed marriage and procreation (Gen 1: 28, 2: 24) and that both Jesus (Mt 19: 4–6) and Paul (Eph 5: 31–2) had affirmed the truth of these passages in their own discussions of marriage.[93] Epiphanius also cited the Letter to the Hebrews 13: 4 ('Let marriage be held in honour by all, and let the marriage bed be kept undefiled') and the Pastoral Epistles on numerous occasions to underscore the same point.[94] The *Panarion* also included an interpretation of 1 Corinthians 7 in which Epiphanius attempted to counter the traditional encratite reading of that text.[95] All of these biblical passages, as we have seen, were included in the anti-heretical dossier of proof-texts assembled in the writings of Jovinian.

In his effort to defend sexual activity as a God-given, created reality, Epiphanius could even speak in surprisingly laudatory terms about the nature of sexual desire. Contrary to classic encratite teaching, which saw sexual desire as either a cause or a consequence of the first sin, Epiphanius emphasized that these desires were instilled by God as part of the natural, created order:

The entire body is mixed with the desires that God has rightly implanted in it. I mean the desires that God has given, not for a wrong purpose but for a good use and as urgent necessity prescribes. (I am speaking of men's desire for sleep, drink, clothing, and all the other desires that come to us at their own pleasure and God's.) Thus I can prove that not even sexual desire is wrong. It has been solemnly given for procreation and the glory of the maker of all, as seeds were given to the soil for an outpouring of an abundance of the good produce which God has created, I mean greenery and fruit-trees. So seeds were given to man, for the fulfillment of the commandment, 'Increase, and multiply and fill the earth.'[96]

Although Epiphanius was a strong proponent of the monastic life and although he held that a life of virginity or celibacy merited for the Christian a greater reward in heaven, his own anti-heretical interests led him to stress

---

[93] See the citations of these texts in *Haer.* 23.5.6–7 (against Satornilus); 47.2.1–2 (against Encratites); 61.1.8 (against Apostolics); 64.31.1–4 (against Origen, citing Methodius); 66.56.2–7 (against Manichaeans).

[94] Citations or allusions to Heb 13: 4 occur at *Haer.* 23.5.7 (against Satornilus); 47.2.2 (against Encratites); 61.3.5 (against Apostolics); 67.2.2 and 67.6.4 (against Hieracites). Citations from the Pastoral Epistles occur frequently throughout the *Panarion*.

[95] See *Haer.* 61.5–6.7 (against Apostolics).

[96] *Haer.* 45.3.2–3 (Holl-Dummer 2, 201); trans. Williams 1, 347, slightly altered.

the goodness of human sexuality and its original place in the order of God's creation.

Filastrius' handbook of heresies was much shorter than that of Epiphanius, and his responses to the ascetical theologies of his opponents tended to be much briefer. In one place, however, Filastrius did make an extended reply to a classic encratite proof-text: Psalm 51(50): 5, which reads, 'In iniquity I was conceived, and in sin my mother gave birth to me.' According to Clement of Alexandria, this verse from the psalm had been used by Encratites to condemn human conception and childbirth,[97] and Filastrius was responding to a similar use of the text in his own day. According to Filastrius, 'some heretics think that the words of the prophet David mean that the legitimate right of marriage (*ius nuptiarum legitimum*) is "iniquity" and "sin".'[98] After citing both Gen 1: 28 and Heb 13: 4 to counter the encratite interpretation of the psalm, Filastrius observed that many of the saints in the Old and New Testaments had been 'sanctified in the womb', according to the scriptures.[99] Therefore, human conception and birth could not be considered evil in themselves. When the psalmist spoke of being conceived 'in iniquity' and born 'in sin', Filastrius argued, he was referring not to the natural process of generation, but to the transgression of Adam and Eve, which had led to their expulsion from paradise.[100] David was not teaching that his own conception and birth had occurred 'in iniquity' or 'in sin', Filastrius insisted. He simply meant that Adam and Eve had produced their first children after their transgression of God's commandment and that all human beings are descended from them.

At this point in his response, Filastrius reflected briefly on the nature of the 'iniquity' inherited from Adam and Eve and its relevance to human sexuality:

For this reason, after their violation of the commandment, [God] said: 'In pain you will give birth to children' (Gen 3: 16), because from those prior parents of transgression we have the common and general iniquity of the flesh that comes down into all from the first inheritance. As the apostle says: 'Just as through one man death entered into all men' (Rom 5:12). For this right of marriage (*ius coniugii*), which has been promulgated by God, is praised every day and customarily blessed.[101]

---

[97] Clement, *Strom.* 3.16.100 (Stählin-Früchtel 2, 242). Clement's answer to the encratite interpretation was that the psalmist was saying in a prophetic manner that Eve was his mother, because she was 'mother of all the living' (Gen 3: 20). Even if the prophet was conceived in sin, Clement argued, 'yet he was not himself in sin, nor is he himself sin'; trans. Chadwick, 87.

[98] Filastrius, *Haer.* 120.1 (CSEL 38, 84).

[99] Filastrius, *Haer.* 120.2 (CSEL 38, 84). He has in mind passages such as Jer 1: 5, Judg 13: 5, and Luke 1: 15.

[100] *Haer.* 120.3 (CSEL 38, 84).

[101] *Haer.* 120.6–7 (CSEL 38, 85). Filastrius' reference to the fact that marriage is 'customarily blessed' (*benedicitur consuete*) is most likely a reference to the practice of a nuptial blessing pronounced by a bishop or presbyter at marriages between Christians. The practice was

Heresy and Fourth-Century Asceticism   155

For Filastrius, the 'common and general iniquity of the flesh' was the penalty of death, which comes to all through the sin of the first parents. This is clearly distinct from the marital activity which produces human progeny. In opposition to the encratite tradition, which linked sex and procreation to the primal sin, Filastrius insisted that the penalty inherited from Adam and Eve was the death of the body; it did not affect the original goodness of sex or procreation.

There is one final issue in the polemics of Epiphanius and Filastrius that deserves attention here. The two men also criticized teachings associated with the name of Origen of Alexandria. As we saw in the previous chapter, Origen's notion of the pre-existence of rational spirits and their embodiment as a result of a primal sin was similar, in several respects, to the encratite views of Julius Cassian. Both Origen and Julius Cassian regarded the body and sexuality as inherently post-lapsarian realities, although Origen did acknowledge that the true God had made the body. In the heresiology of Epiphanius and Filastrius, however, the speculation of Origen regarding the pre-existence of the human soul prior to embodiment was firmly rejected as 'heresy'. The crucial error in the Origenist doctrine, according to Epiphanius, was its denial of the original goodness of the body and its place in the original creation.

In his *Panarion*, as well as in an earlier writing, the *Ancoratus* of 374, Epiphanius had criticized several ideas of Origen, including his subordinationist Christology and his allegorical exegesis of scripture. But the major focus of Epiphanius' attack was Origen's teaching on the origin and ultimate destiny of the human body.[102] From the perspective of Epiphanius, both Origen's teaching on the pre-existence of human souls prior to their embodiment and his spiritualized view of the resurrected body were ideas to be rejected as heresy. Epiphanius' objection to Origen's teaching on the body was twofold. First, Origen's notion of the pre-existence and fall of the soul implied for Epiphanius an excessively pessimistic view of bodily existence; it was, he argued, too redolent of the ancient Greek philosophical idea of the body as a 'prison' of the soul:

[Origen] says that the human soul is pre-existent, and that souls are angels and celestial powers, but have sinned and been shut up in this body as a punishment. They are sent down by God as a punishment to submit to a first judgment here. And so the body is called a 'frame' ($\delta\acute{\epsilon}\mu\alpha s$), says Origen, because the soul has been 'bound' ($\delta\acute{\epsilon}\delta\epsilon\sigma\vartheta\alpha\iota$) in the body—but he is picturing the ancient Greek fabrication. And he tells

---

becoming increasingly popular in the West in the later fourth century. See the references to Ambrosiaster and the nuptial blessing in the next section of this chapter.

[102] For a thorough account of the polemics of Epiphanius against Origen, both in the *Ancoratus* and the *Panarion*, as well as in the later Origenist debate, see Clark, *Origenist Controversy*, 86–104.

other stories about this as well. He says that we speak of a 'soul' (ψυχή) because it 'cooled off' (ἐψύχθαι) in coming down.[103]

Like Clement of Alexandria, who claimed that the heretic Marcion had derived his pessimistic view of human birth from Greek philosophers, such as Plato and Pythagoras, Epiphanius suggested that Origen's view of the pre-existence and fall of the soul echoed ancient Greek pessimism about the body.[104]

In addition to suggesting this negative philosophical pedigree of Origen's teaching, Epiphanius also argued that the notion of an originally spiritual creation contradicted the literal meaning of the Genesis text, which contained the command to 'increase and multiply' (Gen 1: 28) and prescribed that Adam and Eve should become 'one flesh' (Gen 2: 24). Quoting from an earlier attack on Origen's teaching composed in the late third century by Methodius of Olympus, the *Aglaophon: On the Resurrection*, Epiphanius used Methodius to demonstrate that human bodies had been created by God long before the fall of humanity:

The first man himself acknowledged that he had bones and flesh before the tunics were made, when he saw the woman brought to him and cried, 'This is now bone of my bone and flesh of my flesh. She shall be called, "woman", for she was taken out of the man. For this reason a man shall leave his father and mother and be joined to his wife, and the two shall be one flesh' (Gen 2: 23–24). Now, I have no intention of putting up with certain chatterboxes who do violence to the scripture without a blush, suggest that they were 'intelligible bones' and 'intelligible flesh', and turn things topsy-turvy with allegories in one passage after another, as the excuse for saying that the resurrection is not a resurrection of flesh. Christ confirms the fact that the scripture should be taken as written, when he answers the Pharisees' question about the divorce of a wife with 'Have you not read that in the beginning the creator made them male and female, and said, For this reason a man shall leave his father and mother', and so forth? How can 'Be fruitful and fill the earth' (Gen 1: 28) be taken merely of souls?[105]

Influenced by both Irenaeus and Clement of Alexandria, Methodius had been critical of those Christians who embraced the ascetic life out of contempt for the physical world.[106] Although Methodius himself was a strong proponent

---

[103] *Haer.* 64.4.5–6 (Holl-Dummer 2, 411–12); trans. Williams 2, 135, slightly altered.
[104] Clement, *Strom.* 3.3.12–24.
[105] *Haer.* 64.31.2–4 (Holl-Dummer 2, 449–50); trans. Williams 2, 159, altered.
[106] The influence of Irenaeus and Clement on the writings of Methodius has been amply documented by L. G. Patterson, *Methodius of Olympus: Divine Sovereignty, Human Freedom, and Life in Christ* (Washington, DC: The Catholic University of America Press, 1997). Even in his ascetical writings, such as the *Symposium*, according to Patterson, 10, Methodius took pains 'to celebrate the positive aspects of the life of chastity (ἁγνεία) within the Christian community, while at the same time discouraging notions of what we have come to call the life of "continence" (ἐγκράτεια), which assume that embodiment is the source of evil'.

of the celibate life, in the foregoing passage from the *Aglaophon*, he argued that belief in the pre-existence of human souls prior to embodiment made nonsense of the biblical warrant for marriage and procreation and undermined the truth of the scriptures. By citing Methodius in his polemic against Origen, Epiphanius signalled his assent to this position.[107]

The other feature of Origen's teaching on the body to which Epiphanius directed his attention was Origen's notion that it was a spiritual body which was to partake of the resurrected life, not the actual flesh in which human beings now live. This aspect of Origen's teaching had also been attacked in the late third century by Methodius, although, as several modern scholars have pointed out, Methodius seems to have misunderstood and distorted Origen's views on the resurrection.[108] The question of the accuracy of Methodius' presentation of Origen need not detain us here. What is significant for our argument is the fact that Epiphanius (again following Methodius) rejected the overly spiritualized view of the resurrection that he attributed to Origen. In this instance, however, it was not the implications of Origen's teaching for marriage, but rather its implications for asceticism that troubled Epiphanius.

In his response to Origen's teaching on resurrection, Epiphanius presented a number of arguments for a bodily resurrection, some derived from Methodius and some of them his own. The centrepiece of Epiphanius' argument was the notion that body and soul operate as a unity: because both soul and body participate in the ascetic struggle, it is fitting that both should share in the reward of resurrected life: 'For if the body does not rise, the soul will have no inheritance either. The partnership of the body and the soul is one and the same, and they have one work. But faithful men exhaust themselves in body and soul in their hope of the inheritance after resurrection—and you [Origen] say there will be none!'[109]

Since body and soul work together, they share responsibility for human action and will share the future judgment as well.[110] Epiphanius' emphasis on

---

[107] *Haer.* 64.31.1–6 (citing the argument from Methodius) and 64.65.10–11 (Epiphanius' own response to Origen). In his later letter to Bishop John of Jerusalem (c.394), Epiphanius placed even greater emphasis on the goodness of procreation in his argument against Origen; see Jerome, *ep.* 51.4 (CSEL 54, 401–2). Clark, *Origenist Controversy*, 96–9, has suggested that Epiphanius' later emphasis on the goodness of procreation reflects the influence of Jerome's debate with Jovinian.

[108] H. Crouzel, 'Les critiques adressées par Méthode et ses contemporains à la doctrine origénienne du corps ressuscité', *Greg* 53 (1972), 679–716; J. Dechow, 'Origen and Corporeality: The Case of Methodius' *On the Resurrection*', in Robert J. Daly (ed.), *Origeniana Quinta* (Louvain: Peeters Press, 1992), 509–18; L. G. Patterson, 'Who Are the Opponents in Methodius' *De resurrectione?*', *StPatr* 19 (1989), 121–9. See now the comprehensive account of the question in Patterson, *Methodius of Olympus*, 141–99.

[109] *Haer.* 64.63.9 (Holl-Dummer 2, 502); trans. Williams 2, 189.

[110] *Haer.* 64.70.17.

the continuity between the nature of the body in this life and its character after the resurrection was motivated especially by his concern that the bodily labours of ascetic Christians should receive their due reward: 'But if the body is the soul's partner in its disciplines, purity, fasting and other virtues, "God is not so unrighteous" (Heb 6: 10) as to deprive the laborer of the fruit of his labor, and award no recompense to the body which has labored with the soul.'[111] Bodily reality, as Epiphanius saw it, was essential both to the act of creation and to salvation. Even Christ's coming in the flesh was meant to confirm this teaching in opposition to the views of Origen, the Manichaeans, and the Marcionites.[112] Origen's theory of the pre-existence of souls and their future restoration to a spiritual state, according to Epiphanius, violated these fundamental principles of Christian orthodoxy.

Epiphanius' attack on Origen, which was echoed at several places in the *Diversarum haereseon liber* of Filastrius,[113] shows several points of contact with his polemics against the various forms of encratism that we have seen in the *Panarion*. Although he was a strong proponent of the monastic life and believed in the value of ascetic practices, Epiphanius was deeply suspicious of an asceticism that rested on what he considered to be faulty theological principles. He repudiated both the moderate encratism of Origen and the Montanists, as well as the radical encratism of Tatian and his so-called 'successors'. What seems to have linked all of these varieties of ascetic heresy in the mind of Epiphanius was their depreciation of the created world and consequent failure to acknowledge the original goodness of marriage and sexuality. Epiphanius' willingness to liken Origen's teaching to that of the Manichees and Marcionites suggests that he regarded even a moderate encratite theology as a serious departure from orthodoxy.

The polemics of Epiphanius and Filastrius shed valuable light on the context in which Jovinian issued his critique of ascetic elitism. Like his predecessors in the heresiological tradition, Jovinian believed that certain emphases in ascetic piety led inexorably to heresy. Excessive pessimism regarding the body and doubts about the original goodness of sex and marriage were features of fourth-century ascetical theology that both Jovinian and the other heresiologists sought to correct. Like Filastrius and Epiphanius, Jovinian attacked even moderate encratism with the accusation of 'Manichaeism'

---

[111] *Haer.* 64.71.8 (Holl-Dummer 2, 519); trans. Williams 2, 204, slightly altered.
[112] *Haer.* 64.71.14.
[113] Although Filastrius did not mention Origen by name, several of the positions he labelled as 'heresy' were reminiscent of Origen's ideas and appear to have derived from Epiphanius' collection. See *Haer.* 99 (against the idea of the fall of 'mind' (*intellectus*) and its transformation into 'soul' (*anima*)); 117 (against the idea that the 'tunics of skins' of Gen 3: 21 were bodies given to Adam and Eve after the fall); 124 (against the idea that certain wicked souls pass into the bodies of beasts).

and attempted to connect contemporary enthusiasm for asceticism with the errors of Tatian and the Encratites. It is, perhaps, not too much to suggest that a continuous, anti-encratite tradition—leading from Irenaeus and Clement, through Methodius of Olympus, and continuing into the writings of Epiphanius and Filastrius—eventually found expression in the *commentarioli* of Jovinian. As the handbooks of Epiphanius and Filastrius show, resistance to encratism (both moderate and radical) remained a prominent feature of fourth-century heresiological discourse, and Jovinian's views largely cohered with this tradition.

ii. Ambrosiaster

There is one further writer whose views on asceticism and heresy must be examined before this chapter comes to a close. In the early 380s, at the same time as the anti-heretical writings of Epiphanius and Filastrius had begun to circulate in the West, an anonymous Roman presbyter, now called the 'Ambrosiaster' ('Pseudo-Ambrose'), issued a series of *Questions on the Old and New Testaments* (*Quaestiones veteris et novi testamenti*). Among these *Quaestiones* was an extensive discussion of the opening chapters of Genesis, titled 'On the Sin of Adam and Eve' (Q. 127, *De peccato Adae et Evae*). In this treatise Ambrosiaster engaged in a vigorous defence of marriage and procreation against ascetic enthusiasm. Like the anti-heretical treatises of Epiphanius and Filastrius, the writings of Ambrosiaster show that concern about asceticism and heresy remained strong in the West, especially among the clergy. In the case of Ambrosiaster, moreover, we have evidence to suggest that he also had in mind the ascetical teachings of Jerome, and not simply those of radical encratites.[114]

Ambrosiaster is one of the more mysterious writers in the early church. In addition to the *Quaestiones*, he composed the earliest extant commentary on all of the Pauline epistles (exclusive of the Letter to the Hebrews). Both of these works may have originally been issued anonymously, for they were quickly attributed to other authors. The Pauline commentary was cited as the work of 'Hilary' by Augustine in *Contra duas epistulas Pelagianorum* around the year 420.[115] Later, however, the work was attributed to Ambrose of Milan, and thus it was known throughout the Middle Ages. In the early sixteenth century Erasmus finally discerned the false attribution to Ambrose.

---

[114] Some of the arguments presented here first appeared in my article, '*On the Sin of Adam and Eve*: A Little-known Defense of Marriage and Childbearing by Ambrosiaster', *HTR* 82 (1989), 283–99.

[115] *C. du. ep. Pel.* 4.4.7 (CSEL 60, 528).

Similarly, the *Quaestiones* were long thought to be the work of Augustine, but in 1905 Alexander Souter definitively proved that the author of the Pauline commentary also wrote the *Quaestiones*.[116] In addition to these two major works, a number of fragments of other writings have been attributed to Ambrosiaster at one time or another.[117]

The precise identity of the Ambrosiaster has continued to elude modern scholars, despite many attempts to solve the mystery.[118] But despite uncertainty about his name, we can discern several important facts about him. First, it is clear that Ambrosiaster was writing at Rome sometime during the episcopate of Damasus. In his Commentary on 1 Timothy 3: 15, he referred to the church at Rome 'whose rector at present is Damasus'.[119] In Q. 115, *De fato*, Ambrosiaster spoke of his own place of residence as 'here in the city of Rome'.[120] It also is virtually certain that Ambrosiaster served as a presbyter in the church at Rome. Although Souter argued that Ambrosiaster was a layman, he admitted that his arguments were not conclusive.[121] In favour of the view that Ambrosiaster was a cleric is his extensive knowledge of ecclesiastical customs, especially those pertaining to church office and liturgy. In his Commentary on 1 Corinthians 14: 14, for example, he spoke of Christians at Rome singing hymns in Greek, 'delighted by the sounds of the words, but unaware of what they are saying'.[122] He had much to say about the roles of bishop, presbyters, and deacons, particularly within the church at Rome. Ambrosiaster's Q. 101, 'On the Boasting of the Roman Deacons', for example, is best understood as the protest of a Roman presbyter against the efforts of a deacon to claim equality with presbyters and bishops.[123] Ambrosiaster also frequently alluded to disciplinary practices, such as the requirement of sexual continence for the higher clergy and temporary sexual abstinence for married

---

[116] *A Study of Ambrosiaster* (TaS 7.4; Cambridge: Cambridge University Press, 1905).

[117] On the fragments, see C. Martini, *Ambrosiaster: De auctore, operibus, theologia* (Rome: Pontificium Athenaeum Antonianum, 1944), 16–17, 65–73.

[118] See the most recent effort of Othmar Heggelbacher, 'Beziehungen zwischen Ambrosiaster und Maximus von Turin?' *FZPhTh* 41 (1994), 5–44; refuted by A. Merkt, 'Wer war der Ambrosiaster? Zum Autor einer Quelle des Augustinus—Fragen auf eine neue Antwort', *Wissenschaft und Weisheit*, 59 (1996), 19–33. The current state of scholarship on Ambrosiaster is summarized in my essay, 'Fourth-Century Latin Writers: Hilary, Victorinus, Ambrosiaster, Ambrose', in Frances Young, Lewis Ayres, and Andrew Louth (eds.), *The Cambridge History of Early Christian Literature* (Cambridge: Cambridge University Press, 2004), 307–9. See also Henry Chadwick, *The Church in Ancient Society: From Galilee to Gregory the Great* (New York and Oxford: Oxford University Press, 2001), 379–81.

[119] *Comm. in 1 Tim.* 3: 15 (CSEL 81.3, 270).

[120] *Quaest.* 115.16 (CSEL 50, 323).

[121] Souter, *Study of Ambrosiaster*, 175–6.

[122] *Comm. in 1 Cor.* 14: 14 (CSEL 81.2, 153).

[123] See *Quaest.* 101.2 (CSEL 50, 194): 'Quidam, igitur, qui nomen falsi dei, duce stultitia et civitatis Romanae iactantia levitas sacerdotibus et diaconos presbiteris coequare contendit.'

couples during special church feasts.[124] Moreover, some of the *Quaestiones* appear to be sermons addressed to an audience in the second person. Q. 120, 'On Fasting', for example, began with words that identify the speaker as a 'priest' (*sacerdos*).[125] Other questions address the audience as *fratres carissimi* or *dilectissimi fratres*.[126] The sum of this evidence makes Ambrosiaster's clerical status a virtual certainty.

Finally, there are several indications that Ambrosiaster was active during Jerome's stay in Rome, that is, during the latter years of Damasus' episcopate (382–384), and that the two men may have been rivals. Correspondence between Jerome and Damasus from the year 384 addressed several questions on the Old Testament that were taken directly from Ambrosiaster's *Quaestiones*.[127] Moreover, in a letter to Marcella of 384 Jerome complained bitterly about certain 'two-legged asses' (*bipedes asellos*) who were criticizing his revisions of the Old Latin versions of the gospels in the light of Greek codices. Jerome provided several examples of the disputed readings, and H. Vogels has shown that all of them were taken from Ambrosiaster's commentary on Paul.[128] Since we know that Ambrosiaster was critical of the use of Greek codices and preferred the Old Latin versions,[129] it is likely that Ambrosiaster was meant to be one of the 'asses' mentioned in Jerome's letter to Marcella. Furthermore, given Jerome's familiarity with the writings of Ambrosiaster, it is remarkable that he made no mention of the author of the Pauline commentary or the *Quaestiones* in his catalogue of ecclesiastical writers, *De viris illustribus*, composed in 393. This silence is best explained if we assume that Jerome perceived Ambrosiaster to be not merely a critic of his revision of the gospels, but also a rival in the arena of biblical interpretation.

There may, in fact, be grounds for supposing yet a further conflict between the two men. In his study of sexual asceticism in the ancient church, Peter Brown has drawn attention to the contrast between Ambrosiaster and Jerome in their

---

[124] Both of these are mentioned in *Quaest.* 127.35 (CSEL 50, 414–15). See also *Comm. in 1 Cor.* 7: 5 (CSEL 81.2, 71–2) on temporary abstinence for married couples; *Comm. in 1 Tim.* 3: 12–13 (CSEL 81.3, 268–70) on clerical continence.

[125] *Quaest.* 120.1 (CSEL 50, 361). For Ambrosiaster, the term *sacerdos* ('priest') included both *episcopi* ('bishops') and *presbyteri* ('presbyters' or 'elders'). See *Comm. in 1 Tim.* 3: 8–10 (CSEL 81.3, 267): 'episcopi et presbyteri una ordinatio est.' Cf. *Comm. in Eph.* 4: 12 (CSEL 81.3, 100).

[126] See, e.g. *Quaest.* 100.1 (CSEL 50, 191); *Quaest.* 116.1 (CSEL 50, 349).

[127] *Ep.* 35 contains Damasus' request to Jerome for explanation; *ep.* 36 contains Jerome's response. See the discussion in H. Vogels, 'Ambrosiaster und Hieronymus', *RBen* 66 (1956), 14–19; and now Andrew Cain, 'In Ambrosiaster's Shadow: A Critical Re-evaluation of the Last Surviving Letter Exchange Between Pope Damasus and Jerome', *REAug* 51 (2005), 257–77.

[128] Jerome, *ep.* 27.3 (CSEL 54, 225), and H. Vogels, 'Ambrosiaster und Hieronymus'. Later letters of Jerome also referred to opinions of Ambrosiaster. See *ep.* 73 and *ep.* 146.

[129] See Ambrosiaster's comments on Greek codices at *Comm. in Rom.* 5: 14 (CSEL 81.1, 177–8), where he observed that Greek codices often contained divergent readings, whereas sometimes the early Latin translations preserved better readings because they were based on earlier Greek codices.

respective attitudes towards celibacy, particularly among the clergy. Brown observed that Ambrosiaster 'went out of his way to show that it was quite possible to enjoy the dignity of a celibate priesthood without sharing Jerome's undisguised contempt for once-married clergymen'.[130] Brown refers to the fact that Ambrosiaster could speak with relative equanimity about human sexual activity and yet still support the emerging practice of clerical celibacy:

> 'Ambrosiaster' adopted a less alarmist, more old-fashioned, attitude to the power of the sexual drive. He presented sexuality as amenable to self-control. The postmarital celibacy of the clergy was a practicable course. The aging process, by which the body lost its youthful heat, could be counted on to support the will. It reduced the force of sexual desire to manageable proportions in middle-aged clergymen. Even among the young, the prolonged periods of sexual abstinence imposed on married couples by the ceremonial life of the Roman Church, with its feast-days, fasts, and vigils of preparation for the Eucharist, ensured that Christian couples had little enough time for sex. They did not need to fill their heads with misplaced anxiety about the subtle and perpetual ravages of sexual feeling that so evidently obsessed Jerome.[131]

Brown's account of Ambrosiaster's enthusiasm for clerical celibacy underscores an important feature of Ambrosiaster's attitude towards asceticism, one that contrasted dramatically with that of Jerome. For Ambrosiaster, the value of celibacy lay primarily in its fulfilment of the ritual requirements of the Christian priesthood. Like Pope Siricius, whose views on priestly celibacy we shall examine in Chapter 6, Ambrosiaster endorsed celibacy mainly as a way for Christian priests to fulfil the demands of Levitical purity in the context of the new Christian rituals of baptism and eucharist. Just as the priests of the Old Testament abstained from sex temporarily to serve in the Jewish Temple, Ambrosiaster argued, so the priests of the new dispensation had to remain permanently abstinent in order to be ready each day to offer prayer, baptism, and eucharist.[132] Although Ambrosiaster did not completely ignore the phenomenon of asceticism among the laity, his primary interest lay in celibacy as a defining feature of clerical office and ritual. In this respect Ambrosiaster stood in dramatic contrast to Jerome, for whom 'priests were holy only in so far as they possessed the purity of virgins'.[133]

---

[130] Brown, *Body and Society*, 377. For a similar view, see C. Pietri, 'Le mariage chrétien à Rome', in Jean Delumeau (ed.), *Histoire vécue du peuple chrétien* (Paris: Privat, 1979), 105–31.

[131] Brown, *Body and Society*, 378.

[132] *Quaest.* 127.36 (CSEL 50, 415): 'necesse habet cotidie Christi vicem agere aut orare pro populo aut offere aut tinguere.' See also *Comm. in 1 Tim.* 3: 12–13 (CSEL 81.3, 269–70), and the discussion of these passages in Roger Gryson, *Les origines du célibat ecclésiastique du premier au septième siècle* (Gembloux: J. Duculot, 1970), 132–6.

[133] Brown, *Body and Society*, 377; cf. 378, where Brown observes that Ambrosiaster's view was 'more acceptable to the *esprit de corps* of the clergy than was Jerome's invidious exaltation of a purity better left to nuns'.

The contrast between Jerome and Ambrosiaster, however, went far beyond their respective opinions on priestly celibacy. Ambrosiaster also shared the heresiological preoccupations that we have seen in Epiphanius and Filastrius. In Q. 127, 'On the Sin of Adam and Eve', Ambrosiaster expressed deep concern about the spread of an ascetic piety that seemed to be tainted with heresy. To a certain extent, his concern was linked to the persistence of Manichaeism, which, as we have seen, was still a potent presence at Rome during the 380s. Ambrosiaster spoke of Manichees on numerous occasions, and he even cited verbatim Diocletian's edict against the Manichees issued in 297.[134] For Ambrosiaster, the Manichees were identified as exponents of a docetic Christology; that is, they were accused of denying the humanity of Christ and asserting a fictitious crucifixion.[135] He also spoke of the elaborate Manichaean cosmologies, in which the world was created by God, but the first human beings were fashioned by a demon named Saclas.[136] But Ambrosiaster was also aware of Manichaean asceticism, and at several points he argued against the Manichaean prohibition of marriage and enforced abstinence from meat.[137] In his commentary on the Pauline epistles, for example, Ambrosiaster asserted that the prophecy of 1 Timothy 4: 1–5, predicting the appearance of heretics who would attempt to impose celibacy and abstinence from certain foods, is now fulfilled 'in the Marcionites (although they have almost died out), in the Patricians, and especially in the Manichaeans'.[138]

Concern with Manichaean asceticism, however, was not Ambrosiaster's primary preoccupation in 'On the Sin of Adam and Eve'. In fact, there is reason to believe that in this work Ambrosiaster conjured up the spectres of 'Manichaeus' and 'Marcion' mainly as a way of casting suspicion of heresy upon more orthodox Christians. At one point in Q. 127 Ambrosiaster referred briefly to positions held by Marcion and the Manichaeans; he then turned, however, and directed his arguments specifically to a 'catholic' audience: 'Hear now, O Catholic, while the gospel testifies that the birth of a human being is something good.'[139] One is left with the strong impression that Ambrosiaster's main interest in Q. 127 was in deterring the influence of what

---

[134] *Comm. in 2 Tim.* 3: 6–7 (CSEL 81.3, 312).
[135] *Comm. in Gal.* 1: 1 (CSEL 81.3, 5): 'Manichaeus Christum hominem negat et non negat crucifixum.' Cf. *Comm. in 1 Cor.* 1: 2 (CSEL 81.2, 6): 'Negabant enim Christum vere crucifixum, sed tantum visum crucifixum, sicut Marcion et Manichaeus'; and *Comm. in Filip.* 1: 1 (CSEL 81.3, 130): 'Fotinus enim Christum deum negat et Manichaeus hominem.'
[136] *Quaest.* 3.1 (CSEL 50, 21); cf. *Comm. in 2 Tim.* 4: 3–4 (CSEL 81.3, 316), where Ambrosiaster referred to the 'fabulas vanitatum conpositas sub nomine doctrinae'.
[137] *Comm. in 1 Cor.* 7: 2 (CSEL 81.2, 70–1); *Quaest.* 76.1 (CSEL 50, 129).
[138] *Comm. in 1 Tim.* 4: 1–5 (CSEL 81.3, 272). On the 'Patriciani', see n. 91 above.
[139] *Quaest.* 127.19 (CSEL 50, 407); cf. *Quaest.* 127.17 (against Marcion) and *Quaest.* 127.18 (against Manichaeus).

he perceived to be deviant ascetical ideas on the mainstream of the Christian community at Rome, rather than the persistence of Marcionism or Manichaeism per se.

Furthermore, most of Ambrosiaster's arguments in Q. 127 were directed at views that strongly resembled those of Tatian and the encratite tradition, rather than Marcionism or Manichaeism.[140] For example, Ambrosiaster articulated three distinct arguments in favour of marriage and procreation, each of which addressed a specific aspect of traditional encratite theology. First, he drew attention to the positive place of human sexual relations within God's original plan of creation and the enduring validity of the blessing and command, 'Increase and multiply'. Secondly, he emphasized the continuity that still exists between the positive marital ethic of the Old Testament and that of the New. Finally he discussed the original sin of Adam and Eve and argued that neither the primal sin nor its punishment could be used to impugn sexual relations. Each of these arguments must be examined further.

The bulk of Q. 127 was devoted to the first topic, namely the implication of a doctrine of creation for an appreciation of human sexuality. Ambrosiaster began by observing that each living thing has been created with an 'innate power' (*insitam potentiam*) for the procreation of its own species, and the human race is no exception.[141] Just as the whole creation was blessed by God and commanded to 'increase and multiply' (Gen 1: 22), so God also commanded the human race to 'increase and multiply' (Gen 1: 28). Like Epiphanius, Ambrosiaster also observed that human beings propagate themselves through the same natural means as other creatures, namely through 'seeds' (*semina*). Since all created things 'increase and multiply' as a result of God's will and blessing, Ambrosiaster concluded, human sexual generation cannot be regarded as either evil or illicit.[142] Ambrosiaster even noted that the tradition of God's original blessing continued both in the Jewish synagogue and in the Christian church in the form of a nuptial blessing bestowed on married couples.[143]

After thus establishing the 'original blessing' of God as the foundation of procreation, Ambrosiaster proceeded to argue that the unified order of creation required that human beings continue to 'increase and multiply' as

---

[140] For this argument, see Sfameni Gasparro, *Enkrateia e antropologia*, 110–13.
[141] *Quaest.* 127.1 (CSEL 50, 399).
[142] *Quaest.* 127.2–3 (CSEL 50, 399–400).
[143] *Quaest.* 127.3 (CSEL 50, 400): 'cuius rei traditio et in sinagoga mansit et nunc in ecclesia celebratur, ut dei creatura sub dei benedictione iungatur, non utique per praesumptionem, quia ab ipso auctore sic data est forma.' On the liturgical setting of Ambrosiaster's work, see Thomas Fisch and David G. Hunter, 'Echoes of the Early Roman Nuptial Blessing: Ambrosiaster, *De peccato Adae et Evae*', *Ecclesia Orans*, 11 (1994), 225–44.

long as the rest of creation continues in being. Human generation will come to an end only when the creation itself comes to an end: 'For the world cannot partly continue and partly end. Either it operates as a whole, or it ceases to function as a whole. Is a body useful, if some of its members thrive, while the rest wither?'[144] Like Clement of Alexandria, Irenaeus, and other anti-heretical writers before him, Ambrosiaster suggested that those who criticize the works of God, such as human reproduction, do so because they hold wicked ideas about the Creator himself. 'For when the work causes displeasure, the Maker is criticized...Who are you to condemn what has been blessed by the God of the Law, unless you either deny that he is this God or accuse the scriptures of being false?'[145] It is clear from the initial arguments of Q. 127 that Ambrosiaster believed that sexual reproduction was part of God's original plan for the human race and that the biblical injunction to 'increase and multiply' was still in force. In this respect, Ambrosiaster's views cohered with those of Epiphanius and Filastrius, who also appealed to the Genesis story to validate the role of human procreation in God's original creation and to counter encratite theology.

The question whether sex was originally ordained by God for the human race is one of the issues on which it is possible to see a conflict between Jerome and Ambrosiaster.[146] Jerome, like many ascetic teachers of the fourth century, liked to point out that the 'increase and multiply' of Genesis 1: 28 was a commandment that was fulfilled only *after* Adam and Eve had sinned.[147] In Letter 22 to Eustochium, for example, Jerome cited Genesis 1: 28 and commented:

This command is fulfilled after Paradise, and nakedness, and the fig leaves that betoken the lasciviousness of marriage (*pruriginem nuptiarum*). Let him marry and be given in marriage who eats his bread in the sweat of his face, for whom the earth brings forth thorns and thistles, whose crops are choked with brambles. My seed produces fruit a hundredfold.... Eve was a virgin in Paradise. After the garments of skins her married life began.[148]

---

[144] *Quaest.* 127.4 (CSEL 50, 400).
[145] *Quaest.* 127.5 (CSEL 50, 400).
[146] For this suggestion, see Jeremy Cohen, '*Be Fertile and Increase, Fill the Earth and Master It*': *The Ancient and Medieval Career of a Biblical Text* (Ithaca and London: Cornell University Press, 1989), 244–5; and my article, '*On the Sin of Adam and Eve*: A Little-known Defense of Marriage and Childbearing by Ambrosiaster', *HTR* 82 (1989), 283–99.
[147] On Jerome's place in the exegetical tradition of Gen 1: 28, see Cohen, '*Be Fertile and Increase*', 235–6; and Elizabeth A. Clark, 'Heresy, Asceticism, Adam and Eve: Interpretations of Genesis 1–3 in the Later Latin Fathers', in her *Ascetic Piety and Women's Faith: Essays on Late Ancient Christianity* (Lewiston, NY: Edwin Mellen Press, 1986), 353–85.
[148] *Ep.* 22.19 (CSEL 54, 168–9); trans. Mierow, 150–1.

Virginity is the original and 'natural' state of humanity, Jerome insisted, while marriage originated only after the fall: *virginitatem esse naturae, nuptias post delictum*. As Jeremy Cohen has noted, 'The idea of sex in Eden would have horrified Jerome, as it did his contemporary John Chrysostom.'[149] Ambrosiaster, by contrast, was quite clearly unembarrassed by the possibility of prelapsarian sexuality and procreation for in Q. 127 he ascribed these directly to God's original providential will.

Ambrosiaster's second argument followed logically from the first. If the one true God originally decreed a blessing on human procreation, then the standards of the New Testament should not differ radically from those of the Old Testament in regard to sex and marriage. The central problem with the ascetic perspective, Ambrosiaster argued, was that ascetic Christians assumed that accepting the standards of the New Testament meant rejecting those of the Old:[150]

> Indeed, some people, while seemingly accepting the new, think that the old must be repudiated. But the new commandments delivered by Christ to the people do not differ from these [old ones]. Christ himself, when invited to a wedding, did not refuse to go, and not only did he illumine it with his presence, but he also provided what was lacking for joy. For as scripture says, 'Wine gladdens the heart.'

Ambrosiaster went on to quote Jesus' prohibition of divorce from Matthew's gospel (19: 4–6), where Jesus cited both Genesis 1: 27 and Genesis 2: 24 to endorse the marriage bond. Jesus purposely quoted these verses from the Hebrew scriptures, Ambrosiaster argued, in order to demonstrate that the teaching of the old law and the new law are in harmony: 'Thus he showed by a salutary precept that what God has joined should neither be prohibited nor separated.' Like Clement of Alexandria before him and Jovinian after him, Ambrosiaster also pointed out that Jesus had chosen married men (e.g. Peter) to serve as his apostles and that Paul had recommended that married men be chosen for the episcopacy (e.g. 1 Timothy 3: 2–5). Therefore, he concluded, there could be no radical disjunction between the two testaments on the question of marriage.[151] In all of these arguments Ambrosiaster closely followed the anti-heretical tradition of Clement, Epiphanius, and Filastrius.

Here, too, we see a significant contrast between the position advocated by Ambrosiaster and that maintained by Jerome. Jerome, borrowing verbatim from the Montanist writings of Tertullian, stressed the radical difference between the sexual standards of the Old Testament and those of the New. For example, in his treatise *Against Helvidius*, composed at Rome in 383,

---

[149] 'Be Fertile and Increase', 245.　[150] *Quaest.* 127.7 (CSEL 50, 401).
[151] *Quaest.* 127.33–4

Jerome replied to Helvidius' appeal to Genesis 1: 28 by maintaining that the moral standards which applied to people in the Hebrew dispensation were no longer acceptable to Christians. The command to 'increase and multiply' was now abrogated by 1 Corinthians 7: 9 ('The time is short; from now on let those who have wives live as though they had none').[152] The world is already full, Jerome argued; now is the time to reap (not to sow) the population. Similarly, in Letter 22 Jerome had noted that at the beginning of the human race it was quite appropriate that God should have promised the blessing of children. 'But as the crowd gradually increased, a reaper was sent in.'[153] In contrast to Jerome's eschatological emphasis on virginity as a vocation for the end of time, Ambrosiaster stressed that as long as creation continues in existence, there is a legitimate place for human procreation.

Ambrosiaster's discussion of creation led him quite naturally to the third of his main arguments: the nature and impact of the sin of Adam and Eve. As we have seen, Jerome and other ascetically minded Christian writers emphasized that Adam and Eve engaged in sexual relations only after the fall. In such a view, sex was highly suspect because it was regarded as in some way symptomatic of the original sin. In a form strikingly similar to the encratite theology of the second and third centuries, Jerome could hold that to engage in marital relations was to relive the fall of Adam and Eve from their pristine, sexless state in Eden. In Letter 22, for example, Jerome took full rhetorical advantage of this ascetic reading of Genesis: 'Should I not weep, should I not groan, when the serpent invites me again to the forbidden fruit, when, in having driven me from the paradise of virginity, he wishes to clothe me in skins, such as Elias cast upon the earth as he was returning to paradise? What have I to do with pleasure which is so soon at an end?'[154]

The sentence passed on Eve in Genesis 3: 16 ('In sorrow and pain you shall bring forth children; you will turn to your husband, and he will rule over you'), Jerome suggested, could be avoided by the Christian virgin. By rejecting both husband and sexual intercourse the virgin could return to the 'paradise of virginity' as it existed before the sin of Adam and Eve.

Ambrosiaster, by contrast, insisted throughout Q. 127 that there was no connection between sexual relations and the original sin. Sex was not the cause of the first sin, nor was it affected by the punishment of the sin. 'Bodily

---

[152] *Helv.* 20 (PL 23, 213), echoing Tertullian, *Exh. cast.* 6 and *Mon.* 7.

[153] *Ep.* 22.21 (CSEL 54, 172). Jerome, *Jov.* 1.16 (PL 23, 246), developed the same theme against Jovinian. See Duval, *L'affaire Jovinien*, 154–5, on Jerome's use of Tertullian at this point; also *Helv.* 21 (PL 23, 215), where Jerome's comment on the need to cut down the 'forest' produced by marriage echoed Tertullian, *Exh. cast.* 6.3, as noted in C Micaeli, 'L'influsso di Tertulliano su Girolamo', 420.

[154] *Ep.* 22.18 (CSEL 54, 167); trans. Mierow, 150–1.

desire was not the cause of Adam's sin,' Ambrosiaster argued. 'Rather, the soul, allured by the hope of deity, transgressed God's command, so that it subjugated even its body to sin and people were born under sin.'[155] The penalty suffered by the body was death, not sex or sexual desire. Although Ambrosiaster did refer to the body as having been 'stained' (*maculatum*) by sin, he nowhere suggested the presence of any disordered desire or sexual concupiscence. On the contrary, he insisted that sex and procreation were given to humanity from the very beginning of creation, not as a result of original sin. For Ambrosiaster, the regeneration afforded by Christian faith involved a reversal of Adam's disobedience, not a repudiation of sexuality; the penalty of death was replaced by the possibility of resurrection, not by the rejection of procreation.[156]

As for the condition of human sexuality after the first sin, Ambrosiaster stated that it remained the same afterwards as before; in other words, the essential goodness of sex and procreation remains unaffected by original sin. For example, after noting that the penalty imposed on Eve included that she should 'turn to' her husband (i.e. engage in sexual relations), Ambrosiaster pointed out that God would never have decreed that Eve should 'turn to' her husband if sex were something prohibited.[157] In other words, the penalty imposed on Eve involved a restoration of the original order of creation. Even in the case of Eve's subordination to her husband, Ambrosiaster insisted, the original order of creation was preserved—or, rather, restored—by the penalty: 'Because it was through the woman that the man was made subject, and because, without a doubt, he was formerly in a superior position...God's order was restored by the sentence.'[158]

Similarly, Ambrosiaster argued, the pain of labour that was included as part of Eve's penalty represented an addition to a small amount of pain that would have been present, even if Adam and Eve had not sinned:

Was it decreed otherwise than that a woman should be subject to the dominion of her husband? From this it is apparent that the woman has been recalled to her original created state, but with an addition.... To the woman is added pain in childbirth; a difficulty is imposed, but no new form of procreation is composed.... She who was to have a small amount of pain from children received an increase because of sin, because children are born in sorrow and groaning and those who are born are not produced without sadness.[159]

---

[155] *Quaest.* 127.24 (CSEL 50, 409).   [156] *Quaest.* 127.23 (CSEL 50, 408–9).
[157] *Quaest.* 127.29 (CSEL 50, 411).
[158] *Quaest.* 127.29 (CSEL 50, 411). For a discussion of Ambrosiaster's views of female subordination, see my article, 'The Paradise of Patriarchy: Ambrosiaster on Woman as (Not) God's Image', *JTS*, n.s. 43 (1992), 447–69.
[159] *Quaest.* 127.30 (CSEL 50, 412).

Unlike Jerome, who attributed sex, procreation, and female subordination to the original sin—and who, therefore, argued that all of these human realities could and should be transcended by the true, virginal Christian—Ambrosiaster argued that all of the current conditions of human sexuality were part of the original order of creation and were confirmed by God's response to the original sin.

Ambrosiaster's discussion of sex and procreation in Q. 127 has added a further dimension to our knowledge of the context in which Jovinian issued his critique of the ascetic hierarchy. Like Epiphanius and Filastrius, Ambrosiaster criticized an ascetic piety that rested on what he regarded as dubious theological grounds. He insisted that God's original command that human beings should 'increase and multiply' was still valid. Ambrosiaster also emphasized that neither Jesus nor the apostles rejected marriage, and he cited married apostles, such as Peter, as examples of the possibility of marital holiness. Furthermore, Ambrosiaster repudiated the suggestion that marriage should be regarded merely as a post-lapsarian phenomenon or that sexual relations were somehow sinful. In all of these respects, Ambrosiaster's positions stood much closer to those of Jovinian than to those of Jerome. Indeed, like Jovinian, Ambrosiaster appears to have written partly in an effort to refute the encratite theology in Jerome's ascetical writings.

My aim in this chapter has been to examine the context in which Jovinian issued his accusations of heresy—especially the charge of 'Manichaeism'—against advocates of the ascetic hierarchy. I have argued that the connection between ascetic piety and encratite theology remained a hotly contested issue in the late fourth century. Anti-heretical authors, such as Epiphanius and Filastrius, attacked the adherents of radical encratism, as well as those who advocated more moderate positions, such as Origen and the Montanists. The spread of Manichaeism in the West seems to have intensified the anxieties of orthodox Christians, and 'Manichaean' quickly became a label for any type of ascetic whose views appeared to denigrate the material creation. Against this background, Jovinian's own concern about the possibility of heretical tendencies among Western ascetic teachers appears to be neither excessive nor idiosyncratic. On the contrary, he fits within a recognizable heresiological tradition.

Furthermore, in their efforts to counter the influence of encratism, the fourth-century heresiologists we have surveyed articulated a similar pattern of argument, one that echoed the earlier views of Clement of Alexandria. At the heart of this argument was a rejection of the fundamental encratite premise that sex was a symptom of the original sin. Epiphanius, Filastrius, and Ambrosiaster each stressed the original created goodness of sex and procreation and emphasized that the demands of the Christian gospel did not require a repudiation of God's original creation or a rejection of the positive marital ethos of the Old Testament. All of these points later found a place in Jovinian's attack on the ascetic hierarchy and the moderate encratite theology that informed it.

Finally, as my discussion of Ambrosiaster has suggested, the ascetical theology espoused by Jerome in the 380s was not immune to the influence of a moderate encratism. Jerome's reliance on the writings of Origen and Tertullian left him vulnerable to the accusation of heresy, especially after Epiphanius and Filastrius had raised the alarm about both the Montanists and the Origenists.[160] Jerome's enforced departure from Rome in 385 by demand of the clergy is a matter we shall take up in a later chapter. Here it is enough to note that Jerome's ascetic enthusiasm appears to have been considerably out of the mainstream of Roman clerical opinion, at least as represented by Ambrosiaster. In such an environment Jovinian's defence of marriage certainly would have found a receptive audience, and to this Jerome himself attested.[161]

---

[160] In the next chapter we shall have occasion to note that Ambrose's enthusiasm for the perpetual virginity of Mary exposed him to similar accusations of encratite sympathies.

[161] In *ep.* 49.2 to Pammachius (CSEL 54, 352), Jerome complained that Jovinian had received support from clergy and monks at Rome.

5

Mary Ever-Virgin? Jovinian and Marian Heresy

In the previous two chapters I have argued that the anti-heretical impulses in Jovinian's teaching were consonant with a longstanding tradition of Christian discourse. On many specific points the views of Jovinian cohered with those of previous heresiologists, especially in their refutation of encratite theories of creation, sin, and sexuality. But perhaps the clearest evidence of Jovinian's anti-heretical concerns lies in his teaching on the virginity of Mary, the mother of Jesus. As we saw in Chapter 1, Jovinian had accused Ambrose of being a 'Manichaean' for teaching that Mary remained physically a virgin, even in the process of giving birth to Jesus. According to Augustine, Jovinian rejected the notion of Mary's *virginitas in partu* because it seemed to imply that Jesus did not have a true human body and that his birth was not a truly human one. Ambrose's own vigorous defence of the *virginitas in partu* in his letter against Jovinian confirms Augustine's report that Jovinian had attacked Ambrose's orthodoxy on the Marian question.[1]

In this chapter I will investigate further the context of Jovinian's opposition to the doctrine of Mary's *virginitas in partu*. While Augustine may be correct in his claim that Jovinian had accused Ambrose of docetism, I will suggest that this was only one of several reasons for Jovinian's opposition to the doctrine. The notion of *virginitas in partu* could be regarded as problematic on several grounds. Few Christians in the first three centuries are known to have embraced this teaching, and it is found primarily in several biblical apocrypha of dubious theological pedigree. Moreover, a number of early Christian writers explicitly opposed the *virginitas in partu*, most notably Tertullian and Origen. Even Jerome, who in other respects was quite supportive of Marian doctrine (e.g. her *virginitas post partum*), proved to be resistant to the new teaching. When the doctrine finally appeared in some later fourth-century writers, such as Zeno of Verona and Ambrose of Milan, it continued to bear the traces of its heterodox origins. Hence Jovinian's opposition to

---

[1] Augustine, *Jul.* 1.2.4 (PL 44, 643); *Nupt.* 2.5.15 (CSEL 42, 267); Ambrose, *ep. extra collectionem* 15 (CSEL 82.3, 302–11).

Ambrose on this point reflected his persistent concern with the heretical character of ascetic teaching. Again, I will suggest, on this point Jovinian was much closer to the mainstream of Christian tradition than previous critics have recognized.[2]

1. MARY'S VIRGINITY IN EARLY CHRISTIAN TRADITION

From the perspective of the later history of ascetical theology and Marian devotion, the doctrines regarding Mary's perpetual virginity—that is, both her *virginitas in partu* and her *virginitas post partum*—were destined to triumph. Both teachings were to become generally accepted in Catholic theology down to the end of the twentieth century.[3] From the point of view of a fourth-century observer, however, such a development would not have been self-evident. Several passages from the gospels clearly indicate an early Christian belief in the virginal conception of Jesus, but the New Testament declared nothing about the miraculous intactness of Mary's virginity during the birth process. Nor did it offer any clear testimony regarding the post-partum marital life of Mary and Joseph. Both teachings arose during the second century, and both remained disputed questions among Christians well into the fourth century. We have no evidence to suggest that Jovinian opposed the idea of Mary's perpetual virginity after the birth of Jesus, as did his near-contemporary Helvidius. His polemic focused exclusively on the question of the *virginitas in partu*, that is, on the issue of the character of Jesus' actual birth. In this chapter, therefore, my primary concern is to elucidate the background and history of the *virginitas in partu*; the question of the *virginitas post partum* will be addressed only when relevant to the former teaching.

i. From Virginal Conception to Virgin Birth

Interest in Mary and the circumstances surrounding the conception and birth of Jesus developed rather slowly in early Christianity and in several different

---

[2] Some of the arguments in this chapter previously appeared in my article, 'Helvidius, Jovinian, and the Virginity of Mary in Late Fourth-Century Rome', *JECS* 1 (1992), 47–71.

[3] The doctrine of *virginitas in partu* is still maintained in the Roman Catholic Church. See *Catechism of the Catholic Church*, 499; citing *Lumen gentium* 57. For a Catholic theologian's attempt to interpret the doctrine, see Karl Rahner, '*Virginitas in partu*: A Contribution to the Problem of the Development of Dogma and of Tradition', in his *Theological Investigations*, iv (Baltimore: Helicon Press, 1966), 134–62.

directions. Prior to the middle of the second century even the virginal conception of Jesus seems to have had little theological significance to most Christians. Among the Apostolic Fathers, for example, only Ignatius of Antioch made any extended references to the birth of Jesus or to the virginity of Mary. Whenever Ignatius mentioned the birth of Jesus from a virgin, he seems to have been most concerned with emphasizing the reality of Jesus' human birth as a polemical response to those Christians ('Docetists') who denied his humanity. In his Letter to the Christians at Smyrna, for example, Ignatius wrote that Christ 'was truly from the family of David according to the flesh, Son of God according to the will and power of God, truly born from a virgin (γεγεννημένον ἀληθῶς ἐκ παρθένου), and baptized by John that all righteousness might be fulfilled by him. In the time of Pontius Pilate and the tetrarch Herod, he was truly nailed for us in the flesh'.[4]

In another place Ignatius described the conception, birth, and death of Jesus as 'three mysteries of a cry which were accomplished in the silence of God'.[5] These mysteries, Ignatius claimed, had been kept hidden from the prince of this world but were now revealed at the end of the ages. It has sometimes been claimed that Ignatius here reflects an early belief in the idea of a hidden birth of Jesus, such as we shall see described in the *Ascension of Isaiah*. Ignatius' presentation of Jesus' birth, however, was entirely free from the docetic elements that surround the account in the *Ascension of Isaiah*. On the contrary, as William Schoedel has observed, Ignatius always insisted on the virgin birth in order to make 'a vigorous anti-docetic statement'.[6]

Around the middle of the second century, the situation began to change, and the virginal conception of Jesus began to gain some theological prominence. In the *First Apology* of Justin Martyr, for example, the virginal conception of Jesus appeared as part of Justin's apologetic argument from the fulfilment of prophecy. Justin cited the text of Isaiah 7: 14 ('A virgin will conceive and bear a son and will call him Emmanuel') to argue on behalf of the divine origins of Jesus.[7] In Justin we also see for the first time the typological parallel between Eve and Mary, a theme that was destined to exercise a great influence on subsequent Marian theology. As Justin put it:

---

[4] Ignatius, *Smyr.* 1.1–2; trans. Ehrman, *Apostolic Fathers*, i (LCL 24, 297).

[5] Ignatius, *Eph.* 19.1; trans. Ehrman, *Apostolic Fathers*, i (LCL 24, 239).

[6] William R. Schoedel, *A Commentary on the Letters of Ignatius of Antioch* (Hermeneia; Philadelphia: Fortress Press, 1985), 90. Joseph C. Plumpe, 'Some Little-Known Early Witnesses to Mary's *virginitas in partu*', TS 9 (1948), 567–77, has argued that Ignatius taught the *virginitas in partu*, but his arguments have not convinced most scholars. See Giancarlo Rocca, 'La perpetua verginità di Maria nelle lettere di s. Ignazio di Antiochia', *EphMar* 25 (1975), 397–414.

[7] 1 *Apol.* 33.1–4 and 54.8; text in André Wartelle (ed.), *Saint Justin: Apologies* (Paris: Études Augustiniennes, 1987), 143 and 175. In *Dial.* 48, Justin acknowledged that there were some Christians who did not share his view of Jesus' divine conception.

He became man by a virgin in order that the disobedience which proceeded from the serpent might receive its destruction in the same manner in which it derived its origin. For Eve, who was a virgin and undefiled, having conceived the word of the serpent, brought forth disobedience and death. But the virgin Mary received faith and joy, when the angel Gabriel announced the good tidings to her that the Spirit of the Lord would come upon her, and the power of the Most High would overshadow her.[8]

For Justin, the parallel between Eve as the origin of sin and death and Mary as the origin of goodness and life was a powerful symbol of the salvation brought to humanity through the incarnation of Christ.

By the end of the second century Irenaeus had adopted the Eve–Mary parallel as a way to express his understanding of salvation as 'recapitulation'. For Irenaeus, the saving event of the Incarnation had 'summed up' and reversed the negative events of the Fall:

For just as Eve was seduced by the word of an angel to flee from God, having rebelled against his Word, so Mary by the word of an angel received the glad tidings that she would bear God by obeying his Word. The former was seduced to disobey God, but the latter was persuaded to obey God, so that the virgin Mary might become the advocate of the virgin Eve. As the human race was subjected to death through a virgin, so was it saved by a virgin, and thus the disobedience of one virgin was precisely balanced by the obedience of another.[9]

While both Justin and Irenaeus had drawn attention to the status of Mary as a 'virgin' at the conception of Jesus, it is important to note that neither of them developed the ascetical dimensions of this teaching. Indeed, in the description of Irenaeus, it was not so much the virginity of Mary that was necessary for salvation as her obedience to the Word of God. Moreover, neither Justin nor Irenaeus affirmed the perpetual virginity of Mary either *in partu* or *post partum*.[10] For both writers the virginal conception of Jesus was the focal point of theological significance.

---

[8] Justin, *Dial.* 100.4–5; text in Miroslav Marcovich (ed.), *Iustini martyris Dialogus cum Tryphone* (PTS 47; Berlin and New York: Walter de Gruyter, 1997), 242–3. See Hilda Graef, *Mary: A History of Doctrine and Devotion* (London and New York: Sheed and Ward, 1963), 37–8; Hans von Campenhausen, *The Virgin Birth in the Theology of the Ancient Church*, trans. Frank Clarke (Studies in Historical Theology, 2; London: SCM, 1964), 20–1, 31–3; Raymond Brown, Karl P. Donfried, Joseph A. Fitzmyer, and John Reumann (eds.), *Mary in the New Testament* (Philadelphia: Fortress Press, 1978), 253–4.

[9] Irenaeus, *Haer.* 5.19.1 (SC 153, 248–50). See also *Haer.* 3.22.3–4 (SC 211, 438–44), and the discussion in Campenhausen, *Virgin Birth*, 34–41.

[10] In *Haer.* 4.33.11 (SC 100b, 830) Irenaeus referred to 'the pure One purely opening that pure womb which regenerates human beings into God, and which he himself made pure' (*purus pure puram aperiens vulvam, eam quae regenerat homines in Deum, quam ipse puram fecit*), an apparent denial of the *virginitas in partu*. But see *Demon.* 54 (SC 406, 162), where Irenaeus cited Is 66: 7: 'Before she was in labor she gave birth; before her pain came upon her she delivered a son.' In neither case did Irenaeus develop his thoughts further. See the discussion in Hugo Koch, *Virgo Eva–Virgo Maria: Neue Untersuchungen über die Lehre von der Jungfrauschaft und der Ehe Mariens in der ältesten Kirche* (Berlin and Leipzig: Walter de Gruyter, 1937), 37–46.

ii. *Virginitas in Partu* in the Christian Apocrypha

At the same time as Justin and Irenaeus were developing their teachings on the virginal conception of Jesus, other Christians had begun to take a deeper interest in the actual birth of Jesus. Several biblical apocrypha from the second century present the birth of Jesus as a miraculous event in which his mother remained free from all pain of labour and physically free of any sign of parturition (*virginitas in partu*). In several cases these imaginative reconstructions of Jesus' birth were accompanied by exotic speculations about the nature of salvation and strongly suggested a docetic view of Christ. For example, the nineteenth ode of the *Odes of Solomon*, an early second-century Syriac hymnbook, spoke of Mary's conception and birth without the pain of labour in terms that resembled certain 'Gnostic' speculations:

> The Holy Spirit opened Her bosom,
> And mixed the milk of the two breasts of the Father.
> Then She gave the mixture to the generation without their knowing,
> And those who have received (it) are in the perfection of the right hand.
> The womb of the Virgin took (it),
> And she received conception and gave birth.
> So the Virgin became a mother with great mercies.
> And she labored and bore the Son but without pain,
> Because it did not occur without purpose.
> And she did not require a midwife,
> Because He caused her to give life.
> She brought forth like a strong man with desire,
> And she bore according to the manifestation,
> And acquired with great power.
> And she loved with redemption,
> And guarded with kindness,
> And declared with grandeur. Hallelujah.[11]

The precise provenance of the *Odes of Solomon* remains unknown. In the past many scholars have regarded the hymns as 'Gnostic', although current scholarship tends to reject this label.[12] However, even those who do not see the Odes as Gnostic have admitted that their Christology tends towards docetism. For example, Ode 28 in the collection places these words on the lips of Christ:

---

[11] *Odes Sol.* 19.4–11; trans. J. H. Charlesworth, *The Odes of Solomon* (Oxford: Clarendon Press, 1973), 82–3.

[12] See J. H. Charlesworth, 'The Odes of Solomon—Not Gnostic', *CBQ* 31 (1969), 357–69; H. Chadwick, 'Some Reflections on the Character and Theology of the Odes of Solomon', in P. Granfield and J. Jungmann (eds.), *Kyriakon: Festschrift Johannes Quasten*, i (Münster: Aschendorff, 1970), 266–70.

> Those who saw me were amazed,
> Because I was persecuted.
> And they thought that I had been swallowed up,
> Because I seemed to them as one of the lost....
> But I was carrying water in my right hand,
> And their bitterness I endured by my sweetness.
> And I did not perish, because I was not their brother,
> Nor was my birth like theirs.[13]

It is difficult to escape the conclusion that the *Odes of Solomon* presents a view of Christ in which his essential dissimilarity from other human beings is emphasized. While the text affirms a genuine 'incarnation' of the Son (the 'milk' of the Father) in the Virgin, his miraculous birth distinguishes him from other human beings. In this instance, the singular character of Jesus' birth—without pain and without a midwife—appears to be closely linked to docetic assumptions about the person of Christ.

Similar remarks can be made about another second-century text that attributed a miraculous birth to Jesus. The *Ascension of Isaiah* is an apocalyptic document that describes the martyrdom of the prophet Isaiah and his ascent through the seven heavens. Like the *Odes of Solomon*, the *Ascension of Isaiah* shares many affinities with so-called 'Gnostic' writings, although its precise provenance also remains unknown.[14] In one of the revelations offered by Isaiah, we find the following account of Jesus' extraordinary birth:

And when she was betrothed, it was found that she was with child, and Joseph, the carpenter, wished to put her away. But the angel of the Spirit appeared in this world, and after that Joseph did not put Mary away, but kept her; but he did not reveal the matter to anyone. And he did not approach Mary, but kept her as a holy virgin, although she was with child. And he did not [yet] live with her for two months. And after two months, when Joseph was in his house, and his wife Mary, but both alone, it came to pass, while they were alone, that Mary straightway beheld with her eyes and saw a small child, and she was amazed. And when her amazement wore off, her womb was found as it was before she was with child. And when her husband Joseph said to her, 'What made thee amazed?' his eyes were opened and he saw the child and praised God, that the Lord had come to his portion. And a voice came to them: 'Tell this vision to no one'. And the report was noised abroad in Bethlehem. Some said, 'The virgin Mary has given birth before she was married two months', and many said, 'She has not given birth: the midwife has not gone up [to her] and we have heard no cries

---

[13] *Odes Sol.* 28.9–10, 16–17; trans. Charlesworth, 109.

[14] J. H. Charlesworth, *The Old Testament Pseudepigrapha*, ii (Garden City, NY: Doubleday, 1985), 145–51, suggests a mid-second-century date for this section of the *Ascension of Isaiah*. On its allegedly 'Gnostic' character, see Andrew K. Helmbold, 'Gnostic Elements in the "Ascension of Isaiah" ', *NTS* 18 (1972), 222–7.

of pain'. And they were all in the dark concerning him, and they all knew of him, but no one knew whence he was.[15]

In the *Ascension of Isaiah* the miraculous elements surrounding Jesus' birth were taken a step further than in the *Odes of Solomon*. Jesus' sudden appearance and birth, which takes place without Mary even being aware of it, points in the direction of a docetic Christology, although Jesus' humanity is not explicitly denied.[16] In any case, as in the *Odes of Solomon*, the focus here is less on Mary herself than on the extraordinary character of the child who is 'born' from her. Mary's painless childbirth and the absence of a midwife are elements in the narrative designed to stress the mysterious identity of the child who has suddenly and miraculously appeared.

Of all the biblical apocrypha, however, it is the *Protevangelium of James* that is by far the most significant text for its teaching on the perpetual virginity of Mary. Composed probably towards the end of the second century in Syria, the *Protevangelium* stands as the ultimate source of almost all later Marian doctrine.[17] Unlike the *Odes of Solomon* and the *Ascension of Isaiah*, the *Protevangelium* has as its primary aim to glorify the virgin Mary and to defend her perpetual virginity. But the text offers much more than simply a restatement of the canonical gospel traditions. It presents an extended narrative of Mary's entire life, from her own miraculous conception to the birth of Jesus, as a testimony to the power of virginal purity. Moreover, unlike the other apocrypha, the *Protevangelium* places a distinctively ascetic emphasis on the virginity of Mary, both prior to and in the process of birth.

The *Protevangelium* begins by describing Mary's own conception as a direct act of God's providence (1.2—4.4). She is consecrated as a virgin from the time that she is six months old. Her mother, Anna, makes her bedroom into a sanctuary and allows nothing common or unclean to enter it (4.1). At the age of three Mary is brought to the Jewish Temple to be raised by the priests (7.2). When she is twelve years old, the priests decide she must leave on account of the danger of ritual impurity from her menstrual period. She is then given in marriage to Joseph, an elderly widower who has several sons by his previous

---

[15] *Ascens. Is.* 11.2–14 (CCSA 7, 118–20); trans. R. McL. Wilson, in Hennecke and Schneemelcher (eds.), *New Testament Apocrypha* 2, 618.

[16] On the 'naive docetism' of the *Ascension of Isaiah*, see Jonathan Knight, *Disciples of the Beloved One: The Christology, Social Setting, and Theological Context of the Ascension of Isaiah* (JSPSup 18; Sheffield: Sheffield Academic Press, 1996), 89–90.

[17] For background see H. R. Smid, *Protevangelium Jacobi: A Commentary* (Apocrypha Novi Testament, 1; Assen: Van Gorcum, 1965); O. Cullman, 'Infancy Gospels', in Hennecke and Schneemelcher (eds.), *New Testament Apocrypha* 1, 370–4; Edouard Cothenet, 'Le Protévangile de Jacques: origine, genre et signification d'un premier midrash chrétien sur la Nativité de Marie', *ANRW* II.25.6 (1988), 4252–69.

marriage. The *Protevangelium* stresses, however, that theirs is not a true marriage; Mary is entrusted to Joseph only to be protected by him, and he does not live with her (9.1–2). After the virginal conception of Jesus, both Mary and Joseph are accused by the temple priests of violating their agreement of chastity (15.1–2). They are then tested according to a ritual prescribed in Numbers 5: 11–31 and are found to be guiltless. The *Protevangelium* wants it to be clearly understood that Mary and Joseph have entered into a pact of perpetual virginity and that such an agreement was now publicly known, especially by the temple priests.

When the document comes to the story of Jesus' birth, even more extraordinary elements are present. After finding a midwife to assist in the child's delivery, Joseph and the midwife approach the cave only to discover that Jesus has suddenly appeared (19.2). The midwife is present only to testify to the miraculous birth of the child. The narrative continues with the story of Salome, another midwife, who questions the evidence of Mary's *virginitas in partu*. Like the doubting Thomas, Salome declares that she must put her finger into Mary's womb, for she cannot believe that a virgin has given birth (19.3). When Salome's hand is suddenly withered and consumed by fire, she accepts the doctrine without further inspection.

The *Protevangelium* is a puzzling text. Its high Mariology stands at variance with the sort of concerns evidenced by other second-century sources such as Justin and Irenaeus. It is unique even among the apocrypha because of its intense focus on Mary's perpetual virginity. Whereas the Christological element was still dominant in the *Odes of Solomon* and the *Ascension of Isaiah*, the *Protevangelium* is entirely preoccupied with the figure of Mary and with her consecration to a life of perpetual virginity. Furthermore, the entire narrative is focused on her *sexual* purity; no other virtue of Mary is mentioned: neither her faith at the annunciation, nor her devotion to Jesus at the crucifixion. Mary's sole merit, according to the *Protoevangelium*, is her sexual purity, and the sole purpose of the narrative is to exalt and defend that purity.

These various features of the *Protevangelium of James* have led some scholars to suggest that the text emerged from the milieu of radical Syrian asceticism or encratism. For example, Edouard Cothenet has observed that the intense emphasis on Mary's sexual purity in the *Protevangelium* has much in common with the praise of chastity that is found in the various apocryphal Acts of the Apostles that emerged from Syria in the second century.[18] Moreover, the image of Mary and Joseph living in a chaste partnership corresponds precisely with the ideal of 'spiritual marriage' cherished in Syrian ascetical circles. In the *Protevangelium* the virgin Mary appears to be no different from

---

[18] E. Cothenet, 'Le Protévangile de Jacques', 4267–8.

countless other *virgines subintroductae*, that is, young virgins who lived in celibate relationships with older, male ascetics. As the high priest tells the elderly Joseph: 'Joseph, Joseph, you've been chosen by lot to take the virgin of the Lord into your care and protection.'[19]

Above all, it is the notion of the *virginitas in partu* itself that suggests an encratite origin for the *Protevangelium of James*. The most likely biblical source of the idea of *virginitas in partu* is the text of Genesis 3: 16, which includes the pain of labour as one of the penalties placed on Eve after the first sin. In the light of this text, Mary's giving birth to Jesus without pain and without any corruption of her integrity represented a reversal of the penalty of Eve's sin and a restoration of the original purity of paradise prior to sin. In classic encratite theology, such as that of Tatian, it was celibacy that enabled a Christian to recapture the pre-lapsarian purity of Eden and, simultaneously, to anticipate the resurrected life, 'where they will neither marry nor be given in marriage' (cf. Mt 22: 30). The ever-virgin Mary, as depicted in the *Protevangelium*, whose very parturition reversed the penalty imposed on Eve, would have been a powerful endorsement of the encratite ideal.

Whatever the precise origins of the *Protevangelium* are, its doctrine was a novelty and an oddity in second-century Christianity. It is the only document from this period to focus so intensively on Mary's *virginitas in partu*. Moreover, it was a work whose time had not yet come. In the third century most Christian writers either ignored the teaching or explicitly rejected it. In fact, there is only one third-century writer whose works show any sympathy for the notion of Mary's *virginitas in partu*, and that, perhaps surprisingly, is Clement of Alexandria. In a passage from the seventh book of his *Stromata* Clement alluded directly to the story of Jesus' miraculous birth and demonstrated that he was aware of the views presented in the *Protevangelium*:

But, just as most people even now believe, as it seems, that Mary ceased to be a virgin through the birth of her child, though this was not really the case—for some say that she was found by the midwife to be a virgin after her delivery—so we find it to be with the Lord's Scriptures, which bring forth the truth and yet remain virgins, hiding within them the mysteries of the truth. 'She has brought forth and has not brought forth', says the Scripture, speaking as of one who had conceived of herself and not from another.[20]

Although Clement's comment suggests some knowledge of the *Protevangelium* and some approval of its message, several points must be noted. First, Clement acknowledged that 'most people' in his day did not accept the

---

[19] *Prot. Jac.* 9.1; trans. Ronald F. Hock, *The Infancy Gospel of James and Thomas* (Santa Rosa, CA: Polebridge Press, 1995), 49.
[20] Clement, *Strom.* 7.16.93.7–94.2 (SC 428, 284–6); trans. Chadwick, 154.

virginitas in partu; that is, he claimed that to 'most people' (τοῖς πολλοῖς) it seemed that Mary gave birth as did a normal woman (λεχώ). Secondly, Clement immediately applied the notion of a virginal birth allegorically to the scriptures and paid little attention to the concept in its historical sense. At most, Clement appears disinterested in the issue of Mary's actual virginity and interested primarily in its allegorical value. As Hans von Campenhausen has observed regarding this passage, 'It is clear from the context that Clement has his eye on the *Protevangelium* tradition, but does not want to discuss further the question of its possible trustworthiness.'[21]

Clement's preference for an allegorical interpretation of the *virginitas in partu* is also evident in a passage from his *Paedagogos*, where he discussed 1 Corinthians 3: 2 ('I fed you with milk, not solid food, for you were not ready for solid food'). For Clement, Christians are children, who are fed on the milk that is Christ the Word. After a lengthy examination of the process by which milk is formed,[22] Clement observed that after the birth of Christ the breasts of women were no longer blessed (cf. Luke 11: 27–8), since the Word himself is 'spiritual nourishment' (τροφὴ ... πνευματικήν):

O mystic wonder! The Father of all is one, the Word who belongs to all is one, the Holy Spirit is one and the same for all. And one alone, too, is the virgin Mother. I like to call her the Church. She alone, although a mother, had no milk because she alone never became a wife. She is at once virgin and mother: as virgin, undefiled; as mother, full of love. Calling her children about her, she nourishes them with milk that is holy: the Infant Word.[23]

Here Clement again seems to be aware of the earlier Christian traditions that ascribed perpetual virginity to Mary. It is significant, however, that Clement presented the notion of someone who is simultaneously 'virgin' and 'mother' in a purely allegorical sense. He said nothing of Mary, the mother of Jesus. The *only* virgin mother to whom he referred was the Church, and he carefully avoided any historical reference to the actual circumstances of Jesus' birth. Once again, the comments of Campenhausen are germane: '[Clement] shows in his own way, when he mentions it, a far-reaching indifference towards the historical tradition as such; he at once makes it the subject of purely allegorical reflections.'[24]

---

[21] *Virgin Birth*, 55–6.

[22] In *Paed.* 1.6.39–41 (SC 70, 180–6) Clement explained how after childbirth the blood that once nourished the embryo is now diverted to the breasts and converted into milk.

[23] *Paed.* 1.6.42 (SC 70, 186); trans. Simon P. Wood, *Clement of Alexandria: Christ the Educator* (FC 23; New York: Fathers of the Church, 1954), 40.

[24] *Virgin Birth*, 55.

It is only in the fourth century and in writings associated with the ascetic movement that we find an interest in the *virginitas in partu* comparable to what we have seen in the *Protevangelium*. There the seeds sown by the *Protevangelium* finally bore fruit in the sermons of Zeno of Verona and the ascetical discourses of Ambrose. But that is not the whole story. This survey of the first three centuries would be incomplete without some attention to two further writers, Tertullian and Origen. Despite their own deep affinities with Christian asceticism and their own adherence to a moderate form of encratism, neither Tertullian nor Origen showed any sympathy for the idea of Mary's *virginitas in partu*, and only Origen had an interest in her *virginitas post partum*. The writings of both Origen and Tertullian, therefore, suggest that the perspectives of the *Protevangelium* were not widely shared in third-century Christianity, even among those with ascetic leanings.

iii. Early Opposition to *Virginitas in Partu*: Tertullian and Origen

In Tertullian's writings early in the third century, we find an unusually strong polemic against the idea of Mary's *virginitas in partu*. It is found in his treatise, *De carne Christi*, written in defence of the Incarnation against a variety of second-century teachers who in various ways denied the reality of Jesus' flesh. In *De carne Christi* Tertullian had several opponents in mind. He attacked Marcion, to whom he attributed the view that Jesus had no flesh at all and, therefore, that Jesus could not have been born.[25] He also mentioned Apelles, allegedly a follower of Marcion, who held that Jesus possessed an astral body but not real human flesh.[26] Finally, Tertullian included in his refutation Valentinus, to whom he ascribed the view that Jesus possessed a 'spiritual' body and underwent a type of birth, but not in the ordinary sense.[27] What all these heretics had in common, Tertullian argued, was that they regarded not only Jesus' flesh, but also the conception, pregnancy, and birth from a virgin to be τὸ δοκεῖν, that is, a mere appearance or illusion.[28]

In defence of Jesus' real humanity Tertullian argued for a genuine human birth of the saviour from the virgin Mary. He did not deny the virginal conception of Jesus; in fact, he vigorously affirmed it, drawing on the

---

[25] *Carn. Chr.* 1.2 (CCSL 2, 873). On Marcion's docetic Christology, see also Tertullian, *Marc.* 1.19 (CCSL 1, 459–60); 3.11 (CCSL 1, 521–3); 4.7 (CCSL 1, 553).
[26] *Carn. Chr.* 6.3 (CCSL 2, 883–4).
[27] *Carn. Chr.* 15.1–6 (CCSL 2, 900–2). Tertullian may have in mind the view presented by Irenaeus, who said that some heretics taught that Jesus did become incarnate, but that 'he passed through Mary just as water through a tube'. See *Haer.* 3.11.3 (SC 211, 146).
[28] *Car. Chr.* 1.4 (CCSL 2, 874).

Eve–Mary parallel he had inherited from Justin and Irenaeus.[29] But Tertullian refused to extend the virginity of Mary to encompass the physical circumstances of Jesus' birth. Tertullian's reluctance to accept the *virginitas in partu* clearly stemmed from his anti-docetic agenda. It is apparent from his responses to Marcion, Apelles, and Valentinus that Tertullian believed it was essential to affirm the fully physical character of Jesus' human birth in order to uphold the genuine corporeality of his human flesh.

Tertullian presented several arguments in *De carne Christi* to counter the docetic views of his opponents. Part of his refutation involved the claim that Christ's love for humanity was demonstrated precisely by his willingness to embrace all of the most embarrassing physical aspects of human birth:

Christ, there is no doubt of it, did care for the sort of man who was curdled in uncleannesses in the womb (*in immunditiis in utero*), who was brought forth through organs immodest (*per pudenda*), who took nourishment through organs of ridicule (*per ludibria*).... Along with man he loved also his nativity, and his flesh besides: nothing can be loved apart from that by which it is what it is. Else you must remove nativity and show me man, you must take away flesh and present to me him whom God has redeemed.[30]

Citing 1 Corinthians 1: 27 ('God chose what is foolish in the world to shame the wise'), Tertullian noted that what is 'foolish' (*stulta*) is the very notion that God would undergo the indignity of birth in a body of genuine human flesh. What could be more 'foolish', he exclaims, than the belief that God has 'wallowed through those insults of nature' (*per illas naturae contumelias volutatus sit*)? For Tertullian, the truth of the Incarnation was demonstrated in the very 'foolishness' of God becoming truly human.[31] The depth of God's love for humanity, he insisted, was evident in God's assuming even the basest physical aspects of human existence.

In one chapter of *De carne Christi* Tertullian further illustrated the genuinely physical character of Jesus' incarnation and birth by citing the physiology of breast-feeding. Commenting on Psalm 22: 9 ('You took me from the womb; my hope is from my mother's breast'), Tertullian observed that Mary would not have been able to produce milk with which to nurse Jesus unless she had actually given birth to her son in the flesh:

---

[29] *Carn Chr.* 17.5–6 (CCSL 2, 905).

[30] *Carn. Chr.* 4.3–4 (CCSL 2, 878–9); trans. Ernest Evans, *Tertullian's Treatise on the Incarnation* (London: SPCK, 1956), 15.

[31] *Carn. Chr.* 4.6 (CCSL 2, 879). In *Carn. Chr.* 5.4 (CCSL 2, 881) Tertullian uttered his famous aphorism regarding the crucifixion and resurrection of Jesus: 'The Son of God was crucified: I am not ashamed—because it is shameful (*quia pudendum est*). The Son of God died: it is immediately credible—because it is silly (*quia ineptum est*). He was buried, and rose again: it is certain—because it is impossible' (*quia impossibile*); trans. Evans, 19.

Jovinian and Marian Heresy

Moreover, since he also mentions his mother's breasts—undoubtedly implying that he sucked them—let midwives, physicians, and biologists bear witness concerning the nature of breasts, whether they are wont to flow except at the genital experience of the womb (*sine vulvae genitali passione*), from which the veins pay over into the teat that cess of the lower blood, and in the course of that transfer distil it into the more congenial material of milk. That is why, during lactation, the monthly periods cease.

For Tertullian, the Incarnation required an actual birth of Jesus from Mary with all of the physical changes in his mother's body that birth normally implies. The presence of breast milk was a sign that Mary had experienced the usual changes associated with childbirth: 'But if the Word was made flesh out of himself, and not out of what the womb contributed, how did a womb which had wrought nothing, performed nothing, experienced nothing, decant its fountain into those breasts in which it causes change only by the process of giving birth?'[32]

Finally Tertullian applied his argument on behalf of the genuinely physical birth of Jesus explicitly to the question of Mary's integrity *in partu*. Commenting on the text of Isaiah 7: 14 ('Behold a virgin shall conceive in the womb and bear a son'), Tertullian argued that Mary was 'a virgin as regards her husband, not a virgin as regards child-bearing' (*virgo quantum a viro, non virgo quantum a partu*). He explained the apparent contradiction as follows:

She who gave birth gave birth, and if as a virgin she conceived, in her child-bearing she became a wife. For she became a wife by that same law of the opened body, in which it made no difference whether the force was of the male let in or let out: the same sex performed that unsealing. This in fact is the womb by virtue of which it is written also concerning other wombs: 'Every male that opens the womb shall be called holy to the Lord' (Ex 13: 2, cited in Luke 2: 23). Who is truly holy, except that holy Son of God? Who in a strict sense has opened a womb, except him who opened this that was shut? For all other women marriage opens it. Consequently, hers was the more truly opened in that it was the more shut. Indeed she is rather to be called 'not-virgin' than 'virgin', having become a mother by a sort of leap, before she was a bride.[33]

Tertullian's position on the *virginitas in partu* of Mary is quite clear. Taken literally, the doctrine was considered incompatible with Christian belief in the Incarnation. Although he fully acknowledged that Jesus' birth was unique, insofar as he was virginally conceived, Tertullian insisted that the Incarnation required that Jesus' flesh be genuinely human and that his birth, likewise, be a normal birth from a normal human mother.

Tertullian's opposition to the *virginitas in partu* in the early third century, like that of Jovinian in the late fourth century, highlighted the problematic

[32] *Carn. Chr.* 20.6 (CCSL 2, 910); trans. Evans, 69.
[33] *Carn. Chr.* 23.3–5 (CCSL 2, 914–15); trans. Evans, 77 (slightly altered).

character of this new Marian doctrine. Its docetic overtones would have made many Christians cautious about adopting this teaching, especially because it was not stated in the New Testament and was found primarily in apocryphal scriptures. It is not entirely surprising, then, that even so avid an ascetic as Origen of Alexandria shared Tertullian's resistance to the *virginitas in partu*. Origen's case is an interesting one, because, unlike Tertullian, he was willing to speculate that perhaps Mary had remained a virgin throughout her life. Origen was the first Christian author outside the *Protevangelium* to teach explicitly that Mary might have remained perpetually a virgin after the birth of Jesus. He also was the earliest Christian on record to have argued that the virginal conception of Jesus was necessary in order for Jesus to avoid contracting the taint of sin that is derived from sexual intercourse.[34] Both ideas exercised great influence on Western theology and especially on the Marian theology of Ambrose. Hence we must take a close look at Origen's thinking before proceeding to Ambrose and literature of the fourth century.

Origen's understanding of Jesus' virginal conception was directly related to his belief in the contamination or defilement that inevitably accompanied sexual intercourse. In a homily on Leviticus 12: 2 ('Every woman who conceives and bears a male child will be unclean for seven days'), Origen argued that all human beings who are conceived through sexual intercourse are 'unclean'. Citing for support the favourite (encratite) proof-texts, Psalm 50: 7 ('In iniquity I was conceived and in sins my mother brought me forth') and Job 14: 4–5 ('No one is pure from uncleanness, not even if his life is only one day long'), Origen noted that the Church's practice of infant baptism provided firm evidence of the inherited nature of sin: 'certainly if there were nothing in infants that ought to pertain to forgiveness and indulgence, then the grace of baptism would appear superfluous.'[35] Only Jesus was exempt from the contamination that affected all human beings, Origen noted, because his conception did not occur by means of human semen. As he put it in another homily on Leviticus 21: 11:

Everyone who enters this world is said to be made with a certain contamination (*in quadam contaminatione*). This is also why Scripture says, 'No one is clean from filth, even if his life were only one day' (cf. Job 14: 4–5). Therefore, from the fact that he is placed 'in the womb' (cf. Job 3: 11) of his mother and that he takes the material of the body from the origin of paternal seed, he can himself be called 'contaminated in his father and mother' (cf. Lev 21: 11).... Therefore, every man 'was polluted in his father

---

[34] Campenhausen, *Virgin Birth*, 57–63. A fine summary of Origen's views on Mary can be found in the introduction by Henri Crouzel, 'La théologie mariale d'Origène', in Crouzel (ed.), *Origène: Homélies sur. s. Luc* (SC 87; Paris, 1962), 11–64.

[35] *Hom. in Lev.* 8.3.5 (SC 287, 20); trans. Gary Wayne Barkley, *Origen: Homilies on Leviticus 1–16* (FC 83; Washington, DC: The Catholic University of America Press, 1990), 158.

and mother', but only Jesus my Lord came pure into the world in this birth and 'was not polluted in his mother'.[36]

As in the later theology of Augustine of Hippo, Origen believed that the transmission of the 'original' sinfulness of humanity occurred by means of sexual relations.[37] Such a view required that the conception of Jesus should occur in a virginal manner, for only in this way could Jesus have been born without the 'contamination' of the flesh.[38] Origen's belief in the virginal conception of Jesus, therefore, was inseparable from his notion that all sexual relations somehow conveyed contamination to the human person.[39]

Origen's belief in Mary's *virginitas post partum* also was based in his view that sex caused contamination.[40] His most extensive discussion is found in his *Commentary on Matthew*.[41] After stating that many of Jesus' contemporaries believed him to be the son of Mary and Joseph, Origen observed that some say the brothers of Jesus were sons of Joseph by a previous marriage, basing their view on a tradition in the *Gospel According to Peter* and the *Book of James*:

> Those who say so wish to preserve the honour of Mary in virginity to the end, so that that body of hers which was appointed to minister to the Word which said 'The Holy Spirit shall come upon you, and the power of the Most High shall overshadow you' (Luke 1: 35), might not know intercourse with a man after that Holy Spirit had come upon her and the power from on high overshadowed her.[42]

---

[36] *Hom. in Lev.* 12.4.1 (SC 287, 178); trans. Barkley, 223–4. Cf. *Hom. in Lev.* 8, which discusses the problem at length.

[37] Jean Laporte has argued that Origen's teaching stands somewhere between Philo's notion of an impure birth due to impure blood and Augustine's idea of the transmission of a moral disorder. See 'From Impure Blood to Original Sin', *StPatr* 31 (1997), 438–44.

[38] For Origen the benefits of this conception also pertained to Jesus' mother, for she too managed to avoid 'contamination' by avoiding intercourse. Lev 12: 2 applied only to women who conceived by male seed and bore children, Origen argued. This did not apply to Mary: 'But concerning Mary, it is said that "a virgin" conceived and gave birth. Therefore, let women carry the burdens of the Law, but let virgins be immune from them.' See *Hom. in Lev.* 8.2.2 (SC 287, 10–14); trans. Barkley, 154.

[39] Behind Origen's insistence on the virginal conception of Jesus lies a rather pessimistic evaluation of sexual relations. For example, Origen spoke of a 'sort of defilement' that accompanied all acts of sexual intercourse, even legitimate ones in marriage: *Comm. Matt.* 17.35 (GCS 40[10], 698–9). See the extensive discussion in H. Crouzel, *Virginité et mariage selon Origène* (Paris and Bruges: Desclée de Brouwer, 1963), 49–66, on which I rely in these paragraphs.

[40] Crouzel, 'La théologie mariale', 35. Origen was the first writer to refer explicitly to the *Protevangelium*, although, as I have noted, Clement of Alexandria had alluded to the story of a midwife attesting to Mary's virginity after birth.

[41] See also *Comm. Jo.* 1.4.23 (SC 120, 70–2), where Origen stated that 'Mary had no children other than Jesus, according to those who think properly about her.' Cf. *Hom. in Lc.* 7.4 (SC 87, 158), where Origen, like the *Protevangelium*, affirmed that Jesus' siblings were children of Joseph by a previous marriage.

[42] *Comm. Matt.* 10.17 (SC 162, 216).

Origen then proceeded to offer his own opinion on this disputed question: 'I think it is in harmony with reason that Jesus was the firstfruits among men of the purity which consists in chastity, just as Mary was among women. For it would not be pious to attribute to anyone but to her the firstfruits of virginity.' Origen's comment shows that his belief in Mary's *virginitas post partum*, like his belief in the virginal conception of Jesus, was based on the notion that sexual relations were inherently defiling. Because of the special sanctity caused by the descent of the Holy Spirit and the divine Logos into the flesh of Mary, it was unseemly, in Origen's view, that Mary should afterwards sully her flesh by having marital relations with Joseph.[43]

Despite his emphasis on Mary's *virginitas ante partum* and *virginitas post partum*, however, Origen did not follow the apocrypha in upholding the *virginitas in partu*. Like Tertullian before him, Origen was anxious to maintain the genuine corporeality of Jesus' human existence against those Christians, such as Marcion and Apelles, who taught that Jesus had a purely spiritual or astral body.[44] Origen, therefore, insisted that Jesus' body had truly 'opened' the womb of Mary, which had not previously been opened by sexual intercourse. For example, in a homily on the Gospel of Luke, while commenting on the same passages of Exodus 13: 2 and Luke 2: 23 to which Tertullian had referred ('Every male that opens its mother's womb shall be designated as holy to the Lord'), Origen observed:

Males were sacred because they opened their mother's wombs. They were offered before the altar of the Lord.... In the case of every other woman, it is not the birth of an infant but intercourse with a man that opens the womb. But the womb of the Lord's mother was opened at the time when her offspring was brought forth, because before the birth of Christ a male did not even touch her womb, holy as it was and deserving of all respect.[45]

Despite his belief in Mary's *virginitas post partum*, Origen did not think that this entailed strict adherence to the notion of her *virginitas in partu*. Indeed, it appears that Origen's strong stance against docetism, as well as his belief that Jesus literally fulfilled the Jewish law contained in Exodus 13: 2 and Luke 2: 23, led him to insist that Jesus' birth had actually 'opened' Mary's womb.[46]

---

[43] Crouzel, 'La théologie mariale', 39.

[44] *Hom. in Lc.* 14.4 (SC 87, 220–2).

[45] *Hom. in Lc.* 14.7–8 (SC 87, 226); trans. Joseph T. Lienhard, S.J. *Origen: Homilies on Luke. Fragments on Luke* (FC 94; Washington, DC: The Catholic University of America Press, 1996), 60. The verse from Luke 2: 23 is derived from Ex 13: 2 and Num 8: 16.

[46] A thorough discussion of Mary's *virginitas in partu* in Origen can be found in Crouzel, 'Le théologie mariale', 40–8.

To sum up this brief survey of early Marian theology, it appears that the doctrine of Mary's *virginitas in partu* did not have extensive support in the tradition of the first three centuries. Except for the passing allusions in Clement of Alexandria, the notion of Mary's *virginitas in partu* was present only in the apocryphal writings, such as the *Odes of Solomon* and *Ascension of Isaiah*, though neither of these works was greatly preoccupied with Mary herself. The *Protevangelium of James*, by contrast, was unique in the second century for its narrative portrayal of Mary as a consecrated virgin; her physical integrity *ante partum*, *in partu*, and *post partum* was the focal point of the story. Tertullian and Origen, by contrast, who in other respects were quite sympathetic to the virginal ideal, declined to follow this path. Both emphasized the genuinely human birth of Jesus and rejected fanciful accounts of Jesus' birth that seemed to echo the docetic Christologies of Marcion and Apelles.

As we move into the later fourth century, it is important to keep in mind that the doctrine of Mary's *virginitas in partu* had remained a marginal feature in the intervening years, especially in the West. None of the significant writers of the third or early fourth centuries endorsed the idea: it is not found in Cyprian, Novatian, Arnobius, or Lactantius.[47] Even Jerome, for whom Mary's *virginitas post partum* was an important emblem of sanctity, did not adhere to the *virginitas in partu* with any explicitness. Jerome, in fact, translated Origen's *Homilies on Luke* into Latin around the year 390, thereby preserving for a Western audience Origen's resistance to the notion of an extraordinary birth of Jesus. Therefore, when Jovinian opposed this doctrine, he stood squarely within the mainstream of the Christian tradition, as it had developed by the later fourth century. The docetic associations of the teaching, its origins in the apocryphal scriptures, and its lack of support in the prior Christian tradition would have enhanced Jovinian's claim that the notion was heretical.

2. MARY'S VIRGINITY IN THE LATE FOURTH CENTURY

If attention to Mary's virginity remained a marginal preoccupation in the early church, the situation changed dramatically in the later decades of the fourth century. At that time zeal for ascetic renunciation fuelled a new enthusiasm for the doctrine of her *virginitas post partum* and, eventually, for the *virginitas in partu* as well. Both in the East and West Christian

---

[47] As Campenhausen, *Virgin Birth*, 51, observed, prior to the late fourth century a 'Mariologically indifferent attitude' was characteristic of Western Christian writers.

theologians began to appeal to Mary as a model for the life of Christian celibates, and especially for female virgins. A key figure in this development was Athanasius of Alexandria, who composed a *Letter to Virgins*, now extant only in Coptic translation.[48] Athanasius's letter circulated in the West; by 377 it was available to Ambrose, who borrowed extensively from it in his three books *De virginibus*.[49] Ambrose's treatise was instantly popular among Western ascetics. Jerome, for example, admired it and stated that Ambrose 'has expressed himself with such eloquence that he has sought out, arranged, and given expression to all that pertains to the praise of virgins'.[50]

i. Helvidius and Jerome

But not all Christians accepted this ascetic appropriation of Mary's virginity as eagerly as did Jerome and Ambrose. In the early 380s Jerome wrote a brief tract attacking one Helvidius, who denied that Mary remained a virgin after the birth of Jesus. Helvidius, Jerome tells us, had written in response to a monk named Carterius, who had written in praise of virginity using Mary as an example. It is evident from Jerome's discussion that Helvidius did not intend to denigrate Mary or the practice of virginity.[51] His aim, like that of Jovinian in the next decade, was to maintain the equal merits of celibates and married persons: 'Virgins and married women are equally glorious,' Helvidius is alleged to have argued.[52] Reflecting (and repudiating) the new ascetic emphasis on Mary as a model for virgins, Helvidius presented the mother of Jesus as the perfect model of both the virginal and the married lives.

---

[48] The text was published by Louis-Théodore Lefort, 'Saint Athanase: Sur la Virginité', *Mus* 42 (1929), 197–275; also in *Athanase: Lettres festales et pastorales en copte* (CSCO 150–1; Louvain, 1955). An English translation of the letter can be found in D. Brakke, *Athanasius and the Politics of Asceticism* (Oxford: Clarendon Press, 1995), 274–91. For an analysis of the letter, see Yves-Marie Duval, 'Le problématique de la Lettre aux vierges d'Athanase', *Mus* 88 (1975), 405–33.

[49] Y.-M. Duval, 'L'originalité du *De virginibus* dans le movement ascétique occidental: Ambroise, Cyprien, Athanase,' in Duval (ed.), *Ambroise de Milan: XVIe Centenaire de son election épiscopale* (Paris: Études Augustiniennes, 1974), 9–66, has demonstrated Ambrose's simultaneous dependence on his predecessors and his originality. Brakke, *Athanasius*, 269, speculates that Athanasius may have brought the Greek original of this letter with him when he moved from Rome to Milan in May 342.

[50] *Ep.* 22.22.3 (CSEL 54, 175); trans. Mierow, 155. Duval, 'L'originalité', 64–6, shows the influence of *De virginibus* on Jerome and Augustine.

[51] An excellent account of Helvidius' teaching can be found in G. Jouassard, 'La personnalité d'Helvidius', *Mélanges J. Saunier* (Lyons, 1944), 139–56; and Giancarlo Rocca, *L'Adversus Helvidium di san Girolamo nel contesto della letteratura ascetico-mariana del secolo IV* (New York: Peter Lang, 1998).

[52] *Helv.* 22 (PL 23, 216): 'eiusdem vis esse gloriae virgines et maritatae'.

Helvidius' polemic against the perpetual virginity of Mary is significant for several reasons. First, it shows that around the year 380 even Mary's *virginitas post partum* was not universally accepted by Christians in the West. Helvidius marshalled an impressive array of passages from the New Testament, such as the many testimonies to Jesus' 'brothers', to demonstrate that after the birth of Jesus Mary and Joseph lived a normal married life and produced other children. He also presented evidence from previous Christian writers to support this claim. According to Jerome, Helvidius cited the precedent of Tertullian and Victorinus of Pettau to add the argument from tradition to his argument from scripture.[53] None of Jerome's responses to these arguments was entirely persuasive, and he resorted to his characteristic rhetoric of abuse in order to refute Helvidius.

Helvidius' defence of the equality of marriage and celibacy is also important because it anticipated several of the arguments later developed more fully by Jovinian. For example, towards the end of his account of Helvidius' teaching, Jerome cited the following extract from Helvidius' tract:

> You say: 'Are virgins better than Abraham, Isaac, and Jacob, who had wives? Are not babies fashioned daily in wombs by the hands of God, that we should have reason to blush at the thoughts that Mary was wed after she brought forth her son? But if such a thought seems degrading to them, it remains that they do not believe that even God was born through the organs of a virgin (*per genitalia virginis*). For according to their view, it is more degrading that God was born through the lower organs of a virgin (*per virginis pudenda*), than that a virgin was married to her husband after she brought forth her son.'[54]

Like Jovinian, Helvidius appealed to the example of the Old Testament saints as evidence of the sanctity of married people and the place of marriage within the history of salvation. He also noted that procreation involved God's own participation in the ongoing work of creation, an argument that is also found among the fragments of Jovinian cited by Jerome. Most significantly, Helvidius suggested that those ascetic teachers who rejected the thought of Mary's sexual life did so because they found the very notion of God's involvement with the flesh to be unacceptable. Such Christians, Helvidius intimated, were akin to those heretics who denied the Incarnation.[55]

---

[53] *Helv.* 17 (PL 23, 211); further discussion in Rocca, *L'Adversus Helvidium*, 85–7.

[54] *Helv.* 18 (PL 23, 212); trans. John N. Hritzu, *Saint Jerome: Dogmatic and Polemical Works* (FC 53; Washington, DC: The Catholic University of American Press, 1965), 37–8.

[55] Rocca, *L'Adversus Helvidium*, 44–5, has suggested that Helvidius was motivated by the same anti-Manichaean concerns as Jovinian.

In his response to Helvidius, Jerome vigorously defended Mary's *virginitas post partum*, but he said nothing about the *virginitas in partu*. Immediately following the citation from Helvidius just quoted, Jerome responded by insisting on the reality of the physical birth of Jesus. He even echoed (without acknowledgment) Tertullian's emphasis on all the 'insults of nature' (*naturae contumelias*) which Jesus had undergone in birth:

> Add, if you like, the other insults of nature: the womb swelling for nine months, the sickness, the delivery (*partus*), the blood, the rags. Picture to yourself the infant enveloped in the usual covering of membranes; imagine the hard manger, the wailing of the child, the circumcision on the eighth day, the time of purification so that he may be proved to be unclean. We do not blush, we are not silent. The greater the humiliations he endured for me, the more I owe him.[56]

When he composed *Against Helvidius* in 383, Jerome evinced no sympathy for the notion of Mary's *virginitas in partu*. In fact, he even alluded to the story of the midwife in the *Protevangelium of James* and dismissed it as the 'mad ravings of the apocrypha' (*apocryphorum deliramenta*).[57] At this point Jerome appears to have shared all of the reservations of Tertullian regarding the idea of a supernatural birth of Jesus.

Even after Jovinian had raised the issue of Mary's *virginitas in partu* and had accused Ambrose of heresy, Jerome continued to remain cautious about adopting the teaching in any explicit way.[58] In his initial response to Jovinian in *Adversus Jovinianum* Jerome mentioned the matter of Mary's virginity only in passing, although he seemed to be aware of Jovinian's rejection of the doctrine. Citing a passage from the Song of Songs 4: 12 ('A garden enclosed is my sister, my bride; a garden enclosed, a fountain sealed'), Jerome observed: 'What is "closed" and "sealed" bears a likeness to the mother of the Lord, who was a mother and a virgin. That is why no one before or after our Savior was laid in his new tomb, which was hewn in solid rock. And yet she that was ever a virgin (*virgo perpetua*) is the mother of many virgins.'[59] If Jerome had adhered to the doctrine of *virginitas in partu*, a discussion of the Song of Songs passage would have provided the perfect opportunity for him to develop an explicit defence. But Jerome was content to offer only very general comments about Mary's perpetual virginity; indeed, his comment on Song of Songs 4: 12 asserts nothing more than a *virginitas post partum*. As Charles

---

[56] *Helv.* 18 (PL 23, 212–13), with verbal parallels to Tertullian, *Carn. Chr.* 4.

[57] *Helv.* 8 (PL 23, 201). Jerome repeated virtually the same phrase in *Matt.* 2.86 (PL 26, 88): 'deliramenta apocryphorum'.

[58] For the argument developed in the following paragraphs, I am dependent on the detailed discussion of Charles Neumann, *Virgin Mary*, 144–52.

[59] *Jov.* 1.31 (PL 23, 265).

Neumann has observed, 'there seems to be no other reason for Jerome's not taking up the challenge here than... that his own mind on the subject was not sufficiently made up at this time to make him desirous of engaging his adversary on such terrain.'[60]

Approximately one year after composing *Adversus Jovinianum* Jerome wrote his apologetic letters to Pammachius and Domnio in defence of his earlier treatise. It is clear that by the time he wrote these letters Jerome had learned of Jovinian's condemnations at Rome and Milan.[61] In one of the letters to Pammachius, Jerome dwelt at somewhat greater length on the issue of Mary's virginity and cited one of the biblical texts that had appeared in Ambrose's letter to Siricius reporting the Milanese condemnation:

Christ himself is a virgin, and the mother of our virgin is a perpetual virgin; she is both mother and virgin. For Jesus entered through the closed doors; in his tomb—a new one that had been carved into the hardest rock—no one had been placed, either previously or afterward. *A garden enclosed, a fountain sealed* (Song 4: 12).... She is the east gate in Ezekiel (cf. Ez 44: 1–3), always shut and shining and either concealing or revealing the Holy of Holies; through her the Sun of Righteousness, our High Priest after the order of Melchizedek, enters and exits. Let them respond to me how Jesus entered through the closed doors when he allowed his hands and side to be examined and showed that he had bones and flesh; thus he showed that his body was real and no phantom. Then I will explain how holy Mary is both mother and virgin: a virgin after the birth, a mother before she was wed (*virgo post partum, mater ante, quam nupta*). Therefore, as we had begun to say, Christ the virgin and the virgin Mary have established the foundations of virginity for both sexes.[62]

In his Letter to Pammachius, Jerome devoted further attention to the issue of Mary's virginity. Having learned of the condemnations of Jovinian at Rome and Milan, perhaps Jerome felt emboldened to approach the topic somewhat more directly than he had the previous year when he composed *Adversus Jovinianum*. In addition to quoting Song of Songs 4: 12 Jerome now alluded to the 'east gate' of the Temple sanctuary mentioned in Ezekiel 44: 1–3, a passage to which Ambrose had also referred in his letter to Siricius.[63] Even now, however, Jerome's approach to the *virginitas in partu* was much less direct and less explicit than that of Ambrose. Like Origen, Jerome emphasized

---

[60] Neumann, *Virgin Mary*, 147. The same conclusion is reached by G. Rocca, *L'Adversus Helvidium*, 82.

[61] As I noted in Chapter 1, Jerome seems to have been unaware of the ecclesiastical condemnations of Jovinian when he composed *Adversus Jovinianum* in spring of 393. But in *ep*. 49.2 to Pammachius (CSEL 54, 351) he referred explicitly to the Roman condemnation.

[62] *Ep*. 49.21 (CSEL 54, 386).

[63] *Ep. extra collectionem* 15.6 (CSEL 82.3, 306); cf. Neumann, *Virgin Mary*, 149–50.

both the virginal conception of Jesus and the *virginitas post partum*. He remained vague on the specific matter of Mary's *virginitas in partu*.

ii. Zeno of Verona

Jerome's reluctance fully to embrace the doctrine of Mary's *virginitas in partu* is yet another indication of the marginal status of this teaching in Christian tradition up to the end of the fourth century. Indeed, the only Western writer prior to Ambrose who manifested clear support for the doctrine was the North Italian bishop Zeno of Verona, who served as bishop from approximately 362 to 380.[64] Zeno is an important figure for several reasons. His discussion of the *virginitas in partu* shows direct dependence on the *Protevangelium of James*, thereby demonstrating the continued influence of that apocryphal text.[65] Zeno was also known to Ambrose, who spoke approvingly of his action in consecrating the virgin Indicia.[66] Moreover, Zeno's interest in the perpetual virginity of Mary was based not only in traditional Christological concerns, but also in an effort to foster ascetic ideals. Thus he marks the beginning of a transition in Western Mariology that was to culminate in the writings of Ambrose.[67]

Zeno's extant corpus consists of a group of ninety-two sermons (or drafts of sermons), the oldest such collection that survives in Latin. While most of the sermons dealt with exegetical topics and appear to have been composed for liturgical feasts, such as the Paschal Vigil, others treated moral or ascetical themes, e.g. *De pudicitia*, *De avaritia*, and *De patientia*. Zeno's discussion of Mary's virginity is found primarily in his Christmas sermons, although important elements also appear in his sermon *De continentia* (*Tract*. II.7).[68]

---

[64] Gordon P. Jeanes, *The Day Has Come! Easter and Baptism in Zeno of Verona* (Alcuin Club Collection, 73; Collegeville, Minn.: The Liturgical Press, 1995), 7–11, has argued that Zeno died *c.*370. But see the comments of Rita Lizzi, 'Ambrose's Contemporaries and the Christianization of Northern Italy', *JRS* 80 (1990), 156–73, who places several sermons in the years 378–9.

[65] Cf. Neumann, *Virgin Mary*, 113: 'The influence of the *Protoevangelium* is evident throughout his tracts and he assumes its narrative of the nativity is known to his hearers.'

[66] See Ambrose, *ep.* 66.1 to Syagrius (CSEL 82.2, 84). Duval, 'L'originalité', 61–4, suggests that Zeno's preaching on virginity was influenced by Ambrose's *De virginibus*, but the influence may go the other way.

[67] According to Campenhausen, it was only in the West (and only at the end of the fourth century) that ascetical concerns merged with Marian doctrines in the teaching of Zeno and Ambrose. See his caustic comment in *Virgin Birth*, 72–3: 'This pretentious theological discovery of a *virginitas* not only *ante* and *post partum*, but also *in partu*, is specially to the credit of Latin theologians.'

[68] I cite Zeno's *tractatus* from Bengt Löfstedt (ed.), *Zenonis Veronensis Tractatus* (CCSL 22; Turnholt: Brepols, 1971). Löfstedt restored the original manuscript order of the sermons, which had been rearranged in the Ballerini edition reprinted in Migne (PL 11).

Jovinian and Marian Heresy

Close attention to Zeno's treatment of the *virginitas in partu* will help to reveal why this doctrine was regarded by Jovinian as not merely novel, but heretical as well.

Zeno's interest in the *virginitas in partu*, as noted above, was motivated by both Christological and ascetical concerns. His ascetical interests are evident in his *Tractatus de continentia*, where he developed at length the contrast between the virgin and the married woman, a theme familiar from many other ascetical treatises: the married woman is concerned to please her husband (cf. 1 Cor 7: 34), but the virgin is completely devoted to God; the married woman wears external ornaments and perfumes, whereas the virgin is distinguished by interior adornment and heavenly scents; the married woman enjoys the lives of her growing children, but the virgin avoids the pains of childbirth and escapes the constant worry over her children's deaths, et cetera.[69] At one point Zeno raised the objection of a hypothetical opponent who questioned his elevation of virginity over marriage: 'But, perhaps, someone will say, "Even the Virgin Mary was married and gave birth." ' To this Zeno responded: 'If there were anyone else like her, I would yield. But she was a virgin after marriage, a virgin after conception, a virgin after her son. Lastly, if there were anything better than virginity, the Son of God could have bestowed this on his mother, to whom he provided that she should possess the surpassing honour of restored virginity (*redivivae virginitatis honore*).'[70] For Zeno, the perpetual virginity of Mary, which was bestowed on her as a special gift by her Son, was evidence of the superiority of virginity over marriage.

More often than not, however, Zeno's attention to Marian virginity seems to be directed primarily by Christological, rather than strictly ascetical, interests. That is, the miraculous character of Jesus' conception and birth—and especially the *virginitas in partu*—was taken by Zeno as evidence of the unique identity of Jesus Christ as the God-Man. Although the Son of God temporarily put aside the 'dignity of his divinity' in the Incarnation, Zeno claimed, he did not lay aside his power: *divinitatis interim dignitate deposita, non tamen potestate*. Like a 'chaste guest' (*hospes pudicus*), Christ 'flowed into the sanctuary of a virginal temple... and prepared for himself a body in the intimate parts of the sacred virgin'.[71] In one of his Christmas sermons Zeno reflected further on the paradoxical implications of the Incarnation in respect to the virginity of Mary:

---

[69] *Tract.* II.7.3 (CCSL 22, 171).
[70] *Tract.* II.7.4 (CCSL 22, 171–2).
[71] *Tract.* II.12.1 (CCSL 22, 185).

What a marvelous thing! Mary conceived by the very one to whom she gave birth; her womb swelled on account of majesty, not on account of semen, and the virgin enclosed the one whom the world and the fullness of the world cannot enclose; [her] members brought forth their own creator, and his own handiwork served as an external garment for its maker. Mary gave birth not in pain, but in joy; a son was born without a father, nor did he come entirely from his mother, for he owed to himself the fact of his conception, and he gave to his mother the fact of his birth. She was the first to be amazed that such a son had come forth from her, nor would she have believed that he was born from her, had she not remained a virgin after the birth, just as she was incorrupt after the conception.[72]

In this remarkable passage Zeno appealed directly to the unique circumstances of Jesus' virginal conception and birth as evidence of the unique character of the child that was born from her. Only a miraculous birth suited a child who was both human and divine.

Zeno's emphasis on the extraordinary nature of Jesus' birth from Mary led him, at times, close to a denial of the actual human birth of Jesus. Zeno was by no means a docetist; he acknowledged that Jesus underwent a 'carnal' nativity from Mary, as well as a spiritual one from God the Father.[73] There is no doubt that Zeno believed the body of Christ which was formed in the womb of Mary consisted of genuine 'flesh': 'Having been fit together into a human being, God was enclosed within a wrapping of flesh (*integumento carnis includitur deus*), and he, who bestows eternity on time, borrowed a human life for a time.'[74] Nevertheless, despite his conviction regarding the genuine corporeality of the body of Christ, Zeno insisted—with unusually graphic precision—on the various ways in which the body of Mary was exempt from the normal corporeal effects of a natural human birth. Mary's entire pregnancy from conception to birth, in Zeno's view, bore witness to the extraordinary character of the child within her.

For example, Zeno stated that Mary 'did not suffer the nausea (*fastidia*) that attends the period of pregnancy, inasmuch as she conceived in herself the Creator of the world'.[75] Furthermore, 'she gave birth not in pain, but in joy' (*parturit non dolore, sed gaudio*). On this occasion Zeno provided intimate details about the birth processes from which the virgin Mary was miraculously spared:

---

[72] *Tract.* II.12.2 (CCSL 22, 185).

[73] *Tract.* II.8.2 (CCSL 22, 176): 'Sed sicut est spiritalis prima [nativitas] sine matre, ita sine patre secunda carnalis.'

[74] *Tract.* II.12.1 (CCSL 22, 185).

[75] *Tract.* I.54.3 (CCSL 22, 128): 'Decem mensium fastidia nescit, utpote quae in se creatorem mundi concepit.'

The pregnant maiden did not groan.... Nor did the child's mother lie pale, enervated in all her intimate parts (*totis... resoluta visceribus*)[76] and exhausted by the burden of such a great birth. The child was not tainted with any impurities (*ullis sordibus delibutus*), either his own or his mother's. For, truly, he who had come to cleanse the human race of its sins, impurities, and stains was unable to have anything unclean around him.[77]

Zeno clearly understood a normal human birth to be an occasion of 'contamination' because of the physical impurities (*sordes*) associated with embodiment, e.g. blood, mucus, and the like. In the case of Jesus' birth, both child and mother were spared these problematic aspects of the flesh. Even the expulsion of the placenta or afterbirth (*purgationes*), Zeno observed, conveyed no harm to mother or child.[78] 'No dressings were applied in the customary way to the young woman who had just given birth because, my brothers, she, who had merited to receive into her womb a son who was the saviour of all souls, was able not to need these things.'[79]

Zeno's argument here is partially reminiscent of that of Origen. As we saw above, Origen emphasized that the virginal conception of Jesus was necessary in order to avoid the contamination or defilement that would have occurred as a result of sexual intercourse. Unlike Origen, however, Zeno focused not only on the virginal conception, but also on the *virginitas in partu*. That is, his concern to exempt Jesus from the characteristic mode of human birth was extended from the moment of Jesus' conception to the moment of his birth. Mary's perpetual virginity—in conception, birth, and after birth—was, for Zeno, the sign that her son was born to free humanity from its sins: 'O great mystery (*sacramentum*)! Mary conceived as an incorrupt virgin; after conception she gave birth as a virgin; after birth she remained a virgin.'[80]

Zeno's account of the birth of Jesus and the *virginitas in partu* of Mary stands in marked contrast to the views of previous Western writers, such as Tertullian, and even to the perspectives of Jerome. In contrast to Tertullian, who seemed to delight in recalling the *immunditia in utero* and the *naturae contumelias* which Christ experienced out of love for the human race, Zeno wished to distance Christ (and his mother) from all of the 'impurities' associated with a real human birth. And in contrast to Jerome, who refused

---

[76] Zeno's term 'viscera', translated here as 'intimate parts', can refer specifically to the uterus. See P. G. W. Glare, *Oxford Latin Dictionary* (Oxford: Clarendon Press, 1982), 2077.
[77] Tr. I.54.4 (CCSL 22, 128–9).
[78] Tr. I.54.4 (CCSL 22, 129): 'Denique purgationes, quae sunt tarditate periculosae, nullo puerum maternorum viscerum prosecutae sunt damno.'
[79] *Tract.* I.54.4 (CCSL 22, 129).   [80] *Tract.* I.54.4 (CCSL 22, 129).

to speculate about Jesus' birth and who dismissed the apocryphal tales as 'mad ravings' (*deliramenta*), Zeno derived his details of Jesus' birth directly from the apocryphal *Protevangelium of James*. In the paragraph following the one just cited, Zeno referred explicitly to the story of the doubting midwife Salome, whose hand was consumed by fire when she attempted to examine Mary after the birth of Jesus. Zeno also preserved a detail from the *Protevangelium*, specifying that Salome's hand was healed after she touched the infant Jesus.[81] There can be no doubt that Zeno's account of the *virginitas in partu* derived ultimately from the apocryphal text.

Under the influence of writings such as the *Protevangelium of James*, Zeno concluded that the divine nature of Christ required that his birth be something out of the ordinary; both child and mother had to be preserved from the 'contamination' associated with natural childbirth. As Zeno put it, even though Christ was born as a human being, he had to be born in an extraordinary way: 'Christ caused himself to be born as a human being,' Zeno asserted, but 'in a manner in which a human being cannot be born.'[82] Though 'humble because of the flesh', he was 'exalted because of the majesty of omnipotence' (*humilis carne, sed excelsus omnipotentiae maiestate*).

Zeno's conclusion helps to explain why the doctrine of the *virginitas in partu* was slow in gaining acceptance in Western Christianity. Zeno's teaching was an innovation within Western Mariology and a significant departure from the approach taken by Tertullian and Jerome. Moreover, it depended explicitly on the witness of apocryphal writings, whose validity was currently being challenged in the West by men such as Filastrius and Jerome. Most troubling of all, from the perspective of some Christians, would have been the Christological implications of the new Marian doctrine. When Jovinian objected to the teaching of Ambrose on Mary's *virginitas in partu* (so we are told by Augustine), he did so explicitly on Christological grounds. That is, the doctrine seemed to imply a denial of the full humanity of Jesus, insofar as it denied a fully human birth of Jesus. The teaching of Zeno, while not technically guilty of the charge of 'docetism', did involve the assertion that both Jesus and his mother were spared certain features of the process of conception and birth that would have produced 'contamination'. Such teaching could easily be interpreted (or misinterpreted) as a heretical denial of Jesus' essential humanity.

---

[81] *Tract.* I.54.5 (CCSL 22, 129): 'Qua tacto infante statim edax illa flamma sopitur.'

[82] *Tract.* I.54.5 (CCSL 22, 129): 'Ita Christus in hominem se fecit nasci, quemadmodum homo non potest nasci.'

iii. Ambrose of Milan

In several ways Ambrose's approach to the doctrine of Mary's *virginitas in partu* differed significantly from that of his North Italian colleague Zeno. Although the notion was present in Ambrose's earliest writings, his expressions of it, at least initially, were more restrained than those of Zeno, and Ambrose never resorted to describing the physical details of Mary's body the way Zeno did. Moreover, unlike Zeno, Ambrose avoided allusions to the sort of apocryphal legends found in the *Protevangelium of James*. Ambrose made no reference to midwives, vaginal exams, or flaming hands.[83] Perhaps most characteristic of Ambrose's Mariology was his peculiar focus on Mary's virginity as a symbol of the virginity of the Church. It was the capacity of Mary to serve as a model of the Church that led Ambrose to his novel perspective on the *virginitas in partu*. These ecclesiological interests also mark a point of contrast and conflict with the concerns of Jovinian.

Ambrose's first reference to the *virginitas in partu* is found in his earliest literary work, the three-book treatise 'Concerning Virgins' (*De virginibus*). *De virginibus* was based on a collection of sermons which Ambrose had delivered and later reworked into a single composition addressed to his sister Marcellina around the year 377. As noted above, in *De virginibus* Ambrose had relied closely on a *Letter to Virgins* by Athanasius. From Athanasius Ambrose took themes that were eventually to become central to his own ascetical theology, especially the use of the Song of Songs to portray the life of the Christian virgin and the use of the virgin Mary as a pattern of the ascetic life of the consecrated virgin. Ambrose urged consecrated virgins to regard the life of Mary as a mirror in which they might behold the very 'image of chastity and model of virtue'.[84] The sublime chastity of Mary was demonstrated in the virginal conception and birth of Jesus: 'What could be more chaste', Ambrose argued, 'than she who gave birth to a body without the contamination of a body?'[85]

Although Ambrose's enthusiasm for Mary as a model of virginal integrity was present in his earliest writings, his explicit development of her *virginitas in partu* evolved only slowly. For example, the notion is first found in *De virginibus* in a passage that did not deal explicitly with Mary, but rather with the virginity and fecundity of the Church:

---

[83] Cf. Neumann, *Virgin Mary*, 138–9, who has observed that Ambrose's most explicit discussions of the doctrine are found only after the condemnation of Jovinian.

[84] *Virg.* 2.6 (Gori 1, 168): 'species castitatis et forma virtutis'. I cite from the critical edition of Franco Gori, *Sant'Ambrogio: Opere morali II/I: Verginità e Vedovanza* (SAEMO 14.1; Milan: Biblioteca Ambrosiana; Rome: Città Nuova Editrice, 1989).

[85] *Virg.* 2.7 (Gori 1, 168): 'quid castius ea, quae corpus sine corporis contagione generavit?'

Thus holy Church is untainted by sexual intercourse (*immaculata coitu*) and yet fruitful in childbirth; she is both a virgin because of her chastity and a mother because of her offspring. She gives birth to us as a virgin made pregnant not by a man, but by the Spirit; she bears us not with bodily pain, but with the joy of angels. She nourishes us not with bodily milk, but with that of the Apostle, with which he nursed the tender age of the people as they were still growing (cf. 1 Cor 3: 2). What married woman, indeed, has more children than Holy Church, who is a virgin in her sacraments, a mother in her people?[86]

Although Ambrose did not explicitly mention Mary in this passage, it is clear that the notion of a virginal conception and birth of Jesus lay behind his exposition of the nature of the Church. Just as the virgin Mary conceived by the power of the Holy Spirit and gave birth to Jesus without the pain of labour, Ambrose suggested, so, too, did the Church give birth to Christians following the Marian model.

Ambrose's reflections on the virginity of Mary and that of the Church became more explicit in his *Exposition on the Gospel of Luke*, composed about ten years after *De virginibus* (386/387), shortly before the outbreak of the Jovinianist controversy. Here Ambrose referred explicitly to the parallel between Mary and the Church when he noted that Mary was both betrothed (*desponsata*) and a virgin (*virgo*) at the time of Jesus' conception and birth. Commenting on the Annunciation scene in Luke 1: 27, where Mary was portrayed as 'a virgin betrothed to a man named Joseph', Ambrose observed:

It is well that she was betrothed but a virgin, for she is a symbol of the Church (*ecclesiae typus*), which is untainted, but married (*inmaculata, sed nupta*). She conceived us as a virgin by the Spirit, she gives birth to us without groaning. And, perhaps, it is for this reason that holy Mary was married to one man, but was filled by another: because the individual churches are filled with the Spirit and grace, but they are joined to the outward form of the temporal bishop.[87]

Here, again, Ambrose showed that his thought about the virginity of Mary naturally tended to coalesce with his thinking about the Church. As in *De virginibus*, the image of childbirth suggested to Ambrose the 'second birth' that Christians received from the womb of 'Mother Church'. The virginal conception and birth of Christ was parallel to—or, in theological terms, was a 'type' of—the baptismal conception and birth of Christians. And just as Mary was married at least in outward appearance (*species*) to Joseph, so the Church is united to the *species* of the bishop.

[86] *Virg.* 1.31 (Gori 1, 132). Gori, 132, n. 110, suggests that *sacramenta* here refers specifically to baptism.

[87] *Luc.* 2.7 (CCSL 14, 33). Hilda Graef, *Mary*, 84–5, has observed that Ambrose was the first author to make explicit the idea of Mary as a 'type' of the Church.

Jovinian and Marian Heresy

Later in the *Exposition on the Gospel of Luke* Ambrose developed further the implications of the virginal birth of Jesus, discussing Luke 2: 21–4 which spoke of Jesus' circumcision and purification. This was the Lukan text, as we saw above, that had led Origen to deny Mary's *virginitas in partu*. Since Luke 2: 23 stated that 'Every male that opens the womb shall be designated as holy to the Lord' (cf. Ex 13: 12), Origen had observed that Christ must have 'opened' the womb of Mary in the process of his birth.[88] Although Ambrose tended to follow Origen's interpretation of Luke very closely, at this point he subtly modified Origen's position on Mary's virginity. The passage must be cited at length because it contains a number of ideas that were crucial to Ambrose's understanding of the *virginitas in partu*:

And so, the child was circumcised. Who was that child, if not the one about whom it was said, 'A child has been born for us, a son has been given to us' (Is 9: 6)? For he was made under the Law, so that he might profit those who were under the Law.... You see that the whole range of the Old Law was a prefiguration of what was to come (*typum futuri*)—for circumcision signifies a cleansing of sins—but since the weakness of the human mind and flesh, being disposed by a sort of desire to sin, is inextricably implicated in vice, the future cleansing of all guilt at the time of the resurrection was prefigured by means of the eighth day of circumcision. For this is [the meaning of] that statement: 'Every male that opens the womb will be called holy to the Lord' (Ex 13: 12). The birth from the virgin (*virginis partus*) was promised in the words of the Law. And he was truly 'holy' because he was untainted. Finally, by the same token, the words that were repeated by the angel declared that he was the one who was signified by the Law: 'For the child to be born will be called holy, the Son of God' (Luke 1: 35). For intercourse with a man did not open the hidden passages of the virgin's womb, but the Holy Spirit poured untainted seed into the inviolable womb. For of all those born of woman, only the Lord Jesus experienced no infection of earthly corruption on account of the novelty of his birth and he repelled it by his heavenly majesty. For if we follow the letter, how could every [firstborn] male be 'holy', when it is clear that many of them were quite wicked? Was Ahab holy? Were the pseudo-prophets holy, upon whom the heavenly fire took vengeance at the prayers of Elijah (cf. 1 Kgs 18: 19–40)? But he was holy, through whom the pious precepts of the divine Law signified the figure of the future mystery, so that he alone might open the hidden womb (*genitale secretum*) of untainted fruitfulness of holy virgin Church in order to generate the people of God. Therefore, he alone opened for himself the womb (*vulvam*). And this was not strange, for he who had said to the prophet, 'Before I formed you in the womb (*in utero*), I knew you and I sanctified you in your mother's womb' (*in vulva matris*; Jer 1: 5)—he who sanctified another's womb so that the prophet might be born—he is the one who opened the womb of his own mother, so that he might come forth untainted.[89]

---

[88] Origen, *Hom. in Lc.* 14.7–8 (SC 87, 226).
[89] *Luc.* 2.55–7 (CCSL 14, 54–6).

Several points must be made about this complex passage.[90] First, like Zeno, Ambrose was directly dependent on Origen's view that the virginal conception of Jesus was necessary so that he might avoid contracting the taint of sin and corruption that would inevitably be transmitted by sexual intercourse.[91] As Ambrose observed, 'intercourse with a man did not open the hidden passages of the virgin's womb (*vulvae virginalis secreta*), but the Holy Spirit poured untainted seed into the inviolable womb' (*inmaculatum semen inviolabili utero spiritus sanctus infudit*). This idea is frequently found in Ambrose's writings, and Augustine later cited this passage to support his own doctrine of the transmission of original sin.[92] Like Origen and the encratite tradition before him, Ambrose could even cite Psalm 50: 7 ('For I was conceived in iniquity, and in sins my mother gave birth to me') as evidence of the universality of human sinfulness that is transmitted by sexual intercourse— a characteristic that Jesus avoided because of his virginal conception.[93] In this respect, Ambrose's Mariology perpetuated the moderate encratite tradition that closely linked sin to sexuality and salvation to sexual purity.

However, even as Ambrose echoed Origen, he subtly modified him on a crucial point that was to have decisive impact on his own Mariology. Rather than interpret the words of Luke 2: 23/Ex 13: 12 ('Every male that opens the womb will be called holy to the Lord') to refer to the physical 'opening' of Mary at the moment of childbirth, as did Origen, Ambrose shifted the reference of the text to the moment of Jesus' conception. Christ was truly 'holy', Ambrose argued, because he was 'untainted'. His being 'untainted' was a result of the infusion of 'untainted seed' into the virgin Mary at the moment of conception, rather than by sexual intercourse: 'For of all those born of woman, only the Lord Jesus experienced no infection of earthly corruption on account of the novelty of his birth and he repelled it by his heavenly majesty.'

---

[90] For the details of this interpretation, I am dependent on the thorough analysis by Neumann, *Virgin Mary*, 113–38.

[91] Cf. Neumann, *Virgin Mary*, 78: 'For Ambrose the virginal generation of Christ is demanded so that He be free of the stain of *original sin*.... The doctor's mind on this point is made up by Origen.'

[92] See Augustine, *Pecc. or.* 41.47 (BA 22, 266); *Jul.* 1.3.10 (PL 44, 645); *C. Jul. op. imp.* 1.66 (PL 45, 1085). On Augustine's (tentative) use of patristic citations in the Pelagian controversy, see Éric Rebillard, 'A New Style of Argument in Christian Polemic: Augustine and the Use of Patristic Citations', *JECS* 8 (2000), 559–78.

[93] For a particularly pointed statement of this view, see Ambrose, *Paen.* 1.3.13 (SC 179, 62): 'Non enim sicut omnes homines ex viri erat et feminae permixtione generatus, sed natus de Spiritu Sancto et Virgine inmaculatum corpus susceperat, quod non solum nulla vitia maculaverant, sed nec generationis aut conceptionis concretio iniuriosa fuscaverat. Nam omnes homines sub peccato nascimur, quorum ipse ortus in vitio est, sicut habes lectum dicente David: *Ecce enim in iniquitatibus conceptus sum, et in delictis peperit me mater mea.*' This passage was to be recalled by Augustine, *C. du. ep. Pel.* 4.11.29 (CSEL 60, 560); *Pecc. or.* 41.47 (BA 22, 264).

To 'open the womb', according to Ambrose's novel interpretation, did not involve any physical 'opening' since Mary was spared the 'corruption' that would have been caused by sexual intercourse or natural childbirth. The text of Luke 2: 23/Ex 13: 12, therefore, referred to the virginal conception of Jesus rather than to his physical parturition. On this point Ambrose intended to modify and to correct Origen's interpretation.[94]

Finally, in this passage, in addition to dispensing with Origen's interpretation of Luke 2: 23/Ex 13: 12 and its testimony against the *virginitas in partu*, Ambrose also invoked the virginity of Mary to illustrate his characteristic concern with the birth of Christians from the 'untainted' womb of the virgin Church: 'But he was holy, through whom the pious precepts of the divine Law signified the figure of the future mystery, so that he alone might open the hidden womb of untainted fruitfulness of holy virgin Church in order to generate the people of God. Therefore, he alone opened for himself the womb.' Here, again, we see that Ambrose's interpretation of the Church as 'untainted' and virginal was profoundly shaped by his view of Mary as an 'untainted' virgin. As Hilda Graef has described his approach, 'everything that is enacted in the Church was first enacted in Mary; Mary is inseparable from the Church and the Church from Mary, for in her womb the mystical body of Christ was formed together with his physical body.'[95] For Ambrose, the notion of Mary as the *ecclesiae typus* involved the claim that the virginal conception and birth of Jesus was both a *symbol* and an effective *source* of the baptismal birth of the Church as the pure body of Christ. In the writings of Ambrose, therefore, the perpetual virginity of Mary had become an essential mechanism in the mystery of salvation.

One dramatic implication of this heady mixture of ecclesiological and Mariological themes in Ambrose's theology is that Mary's physical integrity became for him a powerful symbol of the virginity that ideally should characterize the lives of all Christians. As Ambrose put it in his treatise *De institutione virginis*, composed in 393 in the midst of the Jovinianist controversy, 'Mary is extraordinary, she who raised up the sign (*signum*) of sacred virginity and lifted up the pious standard (*vexillum*) of undefiled integrity for Christ.... All are called to the cult of virginity by the example of holy Mary.'[96] Ambrose's insistence on the necessary absence of sex in the economy of

---

[94] Cf. Neumann, *Virgin Mary*, 133: 'In a word, for Origen the opening of the womb is that of a first-born child at birth; in Ambrose that of a spouse at conception.... This passage is a perfect example of his manner of *correcting* the master; without alluding to an opposite opinion in Origen, he simply omits or contradicts it.'
[95] Graef, *Mary*, 85.
[96] *Inst.* 5.35 (Gori 2, 136).

salvation led directly to his view that virginity was the highest form of the Christian life:

> But, after the Lord entered into this body and joined the Deity to a body without any stain of confusion, this custom characteristic of the heavenly life spread throughout the world and implanted itself in human bodies. It is this that the angels who minister upon the earth declared would come to be, which would offer to the Lord the obedient service of an untainted body (*ministerium domino immaculati corporis*).[97]

Virginity, for Ambrose, had become the paradigm of salvation. The ancient Eve–Mary parallel, which once was used to contrast the disobedience of the first parent with the obedience of Mary, was now mobilized in support of virginity: 'When he was about to bring salvation to the world, the Lord Jesus came through a virgin and cancelled the sin of a married woman (*mulier*) by the birth from a virgin (*virgo*).'[98]

For Ambrose, then, Mariology and soteriology slipped naturally into ascetical theology. Since salvation required that Jesus' mother be a virgin and since Christ's Church was 'a virgin without spot or wrinkle',[99] he regarded the superiority of virginity over marriage as an essential truth of salvation. In a letter written towards the end of his life and directed against followers of Jovinian, who had spread their views to the church at Vercelli, Ambrose stated this point with particular pungency:

> Why should I tell of the great grace of virginity which was worthy of being chosen by Christ so that it might be the bodily temple of God, in which, as we read, dwelt the fullness of the Godhead bodily? A virgin begat the salvation of the world, a virgin brought forth the life of all. Should virginity, then, be abandoned which was of benefit to all in Christ? A virgin carried him whom this world cannot contain or support. And when he was born of Mary's womb, he yet preserved the enclosure of her modesty, and the inviolate seal of her virginity. Thus, Christ found in the virgin that which he wanted to be his own, that which the Lord of all might take for himself. Through a man and a woman flesh was cast out of paradise; through a virgin it was joined to God.[100]

By associating marriage with the fall and by linking virginity with the process of salvation Ambrose drew on the long-standing encratite

---

[97] *Virg.* 1.3.13 (Gori 1, 116); trans. Boniface Ramsey, *Ambrose* (London and New York: Routledge, 1997), 77, slightly altered.

[98] *Exh. virg.* 26 (Gori 2, 218): 'Salutem mundo daturus per virginem venit et mulieris lapsus partu virginis soluit.' Cf. Ambrose, *ep. extra collectionem* 15.3 (CSEL 82.3, 304): 'Per mulierem cura successit, per virginem salus evenit.'

[99] Eph 5: 27, cited in *ep. extra collectionem* 14.36 (CSEL 82.3, 253).

[100] *Ep. extra collectionem* 14.33 (CSEL 82.3, 252); trans. Mary Melchior Beyenka, *Saint Ambrose: Letters* (FC 26; New York: Fathers of the Church, Inc., 1954), 332–3, slightly altered.

tradition.[101] On this foundation he constructed a hierarchy of ascetical merits, and in that hierarchy, crowned by the 'ever-virgin' Mary, married Christians stood on a decidedly lower level than celibates.[102]

Given the novel fusion of ascetical, Christological, and Mariological themes in Ambrose's writings, it is not surprising that his teaching on the *virginitas in partu* became the object of attack by Jovinian. Unfortunately, we do not have enough textual remains of Jovinian's writings to know for certain what precisely he meant when he called the doctrine 'Manichaean'. As Augustine intimated, his charge may have involved simply the accusation of docetism, a reproach that had become traditional since the time of Tertullian. But as I have suggested here, the doctrine of *virginitas in partu* was vulnerable to more than just the charge of attenuating the physical birth of Jesus; it also expressed, in the version of Ambrose, a constellation of ideas that ultimately derived from Origen and the encratite tradition. Ambrose's emphasis on the sexual transmission of human sin, his insistence on the necessary absence of sexual intercourse in the conception of Jesus, and his assimilation of the virgin Mary to the virginal Church were all innovations in the Latin tradition. Moreover, the association of the notion of *virginitas in partu* with the apocryphal literature would not have enhanced its orthodox credentials. Given that the label of 'Manichaean' had become so malleable in the later fourth century and was used to attack a variety of heresies with encratite leanings, it is not impossible that Jovinian's charge against Ambrose reflected this broader anti-heretical use of the term and not simply the accusation of docetism.

Perhaps most offensive to the sensibilities of Jovinian would have been the links Ambrose drew between Marian virginity, baptism, and the superiority of celibacy. As we saw in our initial investigation of his teaching, Jovinian regarded baptism as the ground of salvation for all Christians. The regeneration offered to all Christians through incorporation into the body of Christ completely overrode the relevance of any individual's ascetic merit. Jovinian had also appealed to the notion of the virginity of the Church and argued that all baptized Christians shared in the virginal holiness of the Church.[103] For Ambrose, by contrast, the grace of Christian baptism was inseparably connected with the adoption of celibacy. The waters of baptism were expected 'to

---

[101] This point is well established by Sfameni Gasparro, *Enkrateia e antropologia*, 278–90.

[102] Cf. Campenhausen, *Virgin Birth*, 80, who observes the development in Ambrose's view beyond that of Origen: 'the ascetic consideration of the "flesh" widens into a fundamental reflection on the nature of sin; original sin comes out more clearly and decisively than it had ever done in the thought and doctrine of any eastern Church father. With this the ascetic understanding of Christ's virgin birth gains a directly dogmatic importance that it had hitherto lacked.'

[103] See *Jov.* 1.37 (PL 23, 275), and our discussion above, pp. 30–33, 38, 41–43.

cool the fires of carnal passions', because the Spirit in the baptismal font was the same Spirit that had descended on Mary at the moment of her son's conception.[104] As he observed in an address to the newly baptized, *De mysteriis*: 'If, then, the Holy Spirit coming upon the Virgin effected conception, and accomplished the work of generation, surely there must be no doubt that the Spirit, coming upon the Font, or upon those who obtain baptism, effects the truth of regeneration.'[105] For Ambrose, it was no accident that the primary day for baptism—the Christian *pascha*—was also the privileged day for the consecration of virgins, for 'on this day the Church is accustomed to give birth to many sons and daughters without any pain.'[106]

In the next chapter we shall examine more closely the place of consecrated virgins in Ambrose's ascetical theology. Here it is enough to note that Ambrose's appeal to the virginity of Mary before, during, and after the birth of Jesus served as the basis of a rather different view of the Church from that espoused by Jovinian, one in which virginal integrity was the touchstone of salvation. Like the mother of Jesus, the consecrated Christian virgin escaped the pain of human childbirth 'so that she may receive in her womb (*in utero*) from the Holy Spirit and, made pregnant by God (*deo feta*), give birth to the spirit of salvation'.[107] In Ambrose's vision the virginal Christ, the virgin Mary, the virginal Church, and the consecrated Christian virgin merged into a unity that virtually excluded the average, married Christian. Jovinian's rejection of Ambrose's teaching on Mary's *virginitas in partu* and his accusation of 'Manichaeism', therefore, may have been an expression of his deeper dissatisfaction with the ecclesial implications of the ascetic hierarchy.

---

[104] *Myst.* 3.13 (SC 25bis, 162): 'carnalium refrigeravit incendia passionum'; and the comments of Brown, *Body and Society*, 350–2.
[105] *Myst.* 9.59 (SC 25bis, 192); trans. Roy J. Deferrari, *Saint Ambrose: Theological and Dogmatic Works* (FC 44; Washington, DC: The Catholic University of America Press, 1963), 28.
[106] *Exh. virg.* 7.42 (Gori 2, 232).
[107] *Inst.* 17.109 (Gori 2, 188).

Part III

Jovinian and his Opponents

6

Against Jovinian: From Siricius to Jerome

My arguments in the preceding chapters have stressed the extent to which Jovinian's resistance to the ascetic ideal was in harmony with elements of earlier Christian tradition. His anti-heretical positions echoed those of earlier anti-heretical writers, even as his opponents, most notably Ambrose and Jerome, presented views that reflected the moderate encratite tradition. In this chapter I will shift my attention away from Jovinian himself to examine more closely the perspectives of his first major opponents: Pope Siricius, Ambrose, and Jerome. If my arguments thus far have been correct, then we are faced with an intriguing question. If Jovinian was, in so many respects, representative of an 'orthodox' strand of Christian tradition, then why was he condemned for 'heresy'? In other words, what factors account for the hostile reception of his views by some of the most prominent leaders of the Western Church?

The answer to this question is not a simple one. Although Siricius, Ambrose, and Jerome concurred in their rejection of Jovinian, the three men had rather different perspectives on asceticism and the role it should play in defining authority in the Church. As a result, they each had different reasons for opposing Jovinian and for characterizing his views as 'heresy'. Moreover, the differences in their attitudes towards asceticism led to tensions and, occasionally, overt conflicts among them. As bishops, Siricius and Ambrose tended to approach questions about asceticism from the perspective of the clergy, although, as we shall see, even they did not always see eye to eye. Jerome, by contrast, although he was an ordained presbyter, was often at odds with the resident clergy, whether in Rome or in Bethlehem. Moreover, his hostility towards both Siricius and Ambrose is patent and well-documented. In this chapter I will explore the diverse reasons for each man's opposition to Jovinian, as well as their opposition to each other. Their different views on asceticism and the clerical life reveal some of the different forms that ascetic piety could take in the later fourth century and the variety of conflicts it could generate.[1]

---

[1] Some of the arguments presented here were first articulated in my article, 'Rereading the Jovinianist Controversy: Asceticism and Clerical Authority in Late Ancient Christianity', *JMEMS* 33 (2003), 453–70; reprinted in Dale B. Martin and Patricia Cox Miller (eds.), *The Cultural Turn in Late Ancient Studies: Gender, Asceticism, and Historiography* (Durham and London: Duke University Press, 2005), 119–35. Issues of clerical and ascetical authority have now been more fully explored by Claudia Rapp, *Holy Bishops in Late Antiquity: The Nature of Christian Leadership in an Age of Transition* (Berkeley: University of California Press, 2005).

1. SIRICIUS AND THE DIGNITY OF THE CLERGY

i. Siricius, Asceticism, and the Clerical *Ordo*

At first sight Siricius would not appear to be the most likely candidate to lead the charge against the 'heresy' of Jovinian. Since succeeding Damasus in the papal office in December of 384, he had responded in a decidedly lukewarm manner to the wave of ascetic enthusiasm sweeping through the Western Church. For example, one of his acts in his first year of office had been to preside over the trial and expulsion of Jerome from the city of Rome in the summer of 385.[2] In his Letter 45, composed shortly before he set sail from the port of Ostia, Jerome indicated that he had been the object of accusations of disreputable conduct, stemming from his relationship with the widow Paula.[3] A formal charge had been falsely made, Jerome said, and the assembled clergy (whom Jerome later described as a 'senate of Pharisees') had unanimously passed judgment.[4] Although it seems that the charge of immorality was not substantiated, Jerome apparently was compelled to sign a document agreeing to leave Rome immediately.[5]

One does not have to look very far to discover one source of the Roman clergy's dissatisfaction with Jerome. As we saw in Chapter 2, Jerome had long been inclined to compare the clerical life unfavourably with the life of monks, but during his years in Rome Jerome had surpassed himself in his abuse of the clergy. Only Damasus, it seems, was spared his satire. In his famous Letter 22, for example, Jerome had mercilessly mocked members of the Roman clergy for zealously pursuing wealthy women in search of a handout:

There are others (I am speaking of men of my own order) who are ambitious of obtaining the priesthood and the deaconate, that they may be able to visit women more freely. All they care about is dress: if they are well perfumed, if their shoes are not

---

[2] As J. N. D. Kelly, *Jerome*, 112, has observed, Siricius 'belonged to and had been elected by the clerical establishment which Jerome despised, with the support of the great body of conventional Christians who were the victims of his satire'.

[3] *Ep.* 45.2–3 (CSEL 54, 324–5). For the version of events described in this paragraph, see Kelly, *Jerome*, 112–15, and F. Cavallera, *Saint Jérôme: Sa vie et son oeuvre*, pt. I, ii (Louvain, 1922), 86–8.

[4] Cf. *ep.* 45.6 (CSEL 54, 328): 'infamiam falsi criminis inportarunt.' The expression 'senate of Pharisees' is found in Jerome, *Did. spir.*, pref. (PL 23, 105).

[5] This information is inferred from Jerome, *Ruf.* 3.21 (PL 23, 473), where Jerome reported that Rufinus had threatened to produce documents that revealed the circumstances of his departure from Rome. Pierre Nautin, 'L'excommunication de saint Jérôme', *Annuaire de l'École Pratique des Hautes Études*, Ve section, 80–1 (1972–3), 8, has suggested that the legal grounds for Jerome's expulsion may have been canon 16 of the Council of Nicaea, which prohibited clerics from leaving their dioceses without sufficient cause.

baggy because of a loose fold of leather. Their locks show traces of the curling iron, their fingers gleam with rings, and they take little mincing steps so that the wet streets may not bespatter their feet. When you see such men, look upon them as bridegrooms rather than clergymen. Some have devoted a lifetime of effort to the task of learning the names, the households, and the characters of married women.[6]

Jerome's attacks on the Roman clergy were long remembered, both by his friends and by his enemies. In the heat of the Origenist controversy around the year 400, Rufinus cited the passage above as an example of Jerome's outrageous rhetoric. Rufinus even charged that Jerome's accusations had encouraged pagans to criticize Christianity.[7] At the same time in Gaul, Jerome's ally and fellow-ascetic, Sulpicius Severus, observed that Jerome's writings had incurred hostility because of their abusive treatment of the Roman clergy.[8]

In writings from his Roman period, Jerome also tended to compare the clergy with his female ascetic clientele and to find the former wanting. Summing up the virtues of the virgin Asella, Jerome presented her as a model even for bishops: 'Let widows and virgins imitate her, let wedded wives make much of her, let sinful women fear her, let bishops look up to her.'[9] Such invidious comparisons would certainly have alienated many of the clergy from Jerome's brand of ascetic piety.[10] Whatever the precise accusations made against Jerome in 385, it is not surprising that the clergy would have rallied against him upon the death of his patron Damasus. Although we do not know for certain what role Siricius played in these proceedings, the official measures taken against Jerome by the Roman clergy, as J. N. D. Kelly has observed, 'can scarcely have been taken without [Siricius'] cognizance and consent'.[11]

Jerome's disdain for the clergy, however, may not have been the sole reason for his brusque dismissal from the Roman church. Accusations of sexual immorality were frequently raised against ascetic teachers in this period.

---

[6] *Ep.* 22.28.3–4 (CSEL 54, 185); trans. Mierow, 162. Jerome proceeded to lampoon one elderly cleric who, he says, visited women in order to gossip and receive a hot meal. See also *ep.* 22.16.3.

[7] Rufinus, *Apol.* 2.5 (CCSL 20, 86–7). Rufinus later claimed that the same effect had been caused by Jerome's *Adversus Jovinianum*: *Apol.* 2.38–9 (CCSL 20, 113–14).

[8] Sulpicius Severus, *Dial.* 1.9 (CSEL 1, 161): 'oderunt eum clerici, quia vitam eorum insectatur et crimina'. Letters from Jerome's final year at Rome are filled with negative remarks about the clergy: *ep.* 33.5, 40.2, 45.6.

[9] *Ep.* 24.5 (CSEL 54, 217).

[10] Elsewhere I have contrasted Jerome's appreciation of female asceticism with the very different perspective of Ambrosiaster: 'The Paradise of Patriarchy: Ambrosiaster on Women as (Not) God's Image', *JTS*, n.s. 43 (1992), 447–69.

[11] Kelly, *Jerome*, 112.

We have already seen how such suspicions fuelled the episcopal hostility to Priscillian in these very years; they were also prominent in the concerns about the monastic life expressed in the *Consultationes Zacchaei et Apollonii*. Siricius appears to have shared this more general clerical suspicion of ascetic piety. In the earliest document of his episcopate, a letter written in 385 to Himerius, bishop of Tarragona in Spain, Siricius had issued a series of canons responding to several questions that had been directed to his predecessor Damasus. Siricius' decretal dealt with many topics, including monks and nuns who had abandoned their ascetic resolve and engaged in illicit sexual relationships.[12] His response to the misconduct of professed ascetics was uncompromising:

We direct you to expel these shameless and abominable persons from the company of the monasteries and the congregations of the churches, that they may be thrown into the jails and mourn their terrible crime with constant lamentation and burn with the purifying fire of repentance, so that mercy may help them, at least in death, out of pure compassion, with the grace of communion.[13]

The firmness of Siricius' decree on lapsed ascetics reveals an attitude of suspicion that is borne out in other aspects of his correspondence. From the perspective of the Roman clergy, Jerome seems to have been perceived very much as Priscillian was by many Spanish bishops, that is, as a divisive figure whose ascetical teachings and activities threatened to undermine ecclesiastical order and clerical dignity.[14]

Moreover, it appears that Jerome was not the only prominent ascetic to be shown a cold shoulder by members of the Roman clergy during the episcopate of Siricius. In the middle of the next decade, shortly after the outbreak of the Jovinianist controversy, the Spanish aristocrat Paulinus of Bordeaux (soon to become 'Paulinus of Nola') passed through Rome on the way to his new residence at Nola in Campania. Writing to his Gallic ally, Sulpicius Severus, in the year 396, Paulinus complained that he had recently been treated with contempt by 'those jealous clerics' at Rome, including Siricius. He accused the clergy of 'hating' him and refusing fellowship; he even singled out the 'haughty separation' (*superba discretio*) of Siricius for special complaint.[15] As Dennis Trout has observed, Siricius had several reasons to be disturbed by Paulinus: 'Perhaps Siricius was truly scandalized by the apparent irregularities of Paulinus's presbyteral ordination. Not only had Paulinus, in contravention

---

[12] *Ep.* 1.6.7, and our discussion above, p. 58.

[13] *Ep.* 1.6.7 (PL 13, 1137); trans. Shotwell and Loomis, *See of Peter*, 702.

[14] Henry Chadwick, *Priscillian*, 29–30, has suggested that the original letter of Himerius to Damasus and the response of Siricius may refer obliquely to problems raised by Priscillian.

[15] *Ep.* 5.13–14 (CSEL 29, 33).

of the *cursus* instructions Siricius had issued to Himerius of Tarragona, leapfrogged the lower clerical orders, but he also exemplified the pattern of popular elections and migratory habits that the church labored to restrict.'[16] Paulinus' recent association with Jerome and his ascetic friends at Rome may also have been a matter of concern to Siricius.[17] To the Roman clergy, Paulinus probably appeared to be yet another itinerant, ascetic troublemaker, whose ostentatious piety threatened to disrupt the stability of the Roman church.

A closer examination of the various decrees issued by Siricius confirms Trout's interpretation. Throughout his pontificate Siricius displayed a marked concern to regulate the excesses of ascetic piety and to enhance the dignity of the clergy. Control of access to the clergy, for example, was a prominent concern in Siricius' Letter to Himerius, and in this context he also discussed the ordination of monks to clerical office. This letter is important because it contains the earliest evidence of a papal attempt to impose a clear order of succession in the matter of clerical office; therefore it seems to represent legislation that was of great personal interest to Siricius.[18] In his Letter to Himerius, Siricius presented three possible routes to advancement in church office. He first discussed the case of men who had devoted themselves to the clergy from their youth. Regarding these candidates, Siricius decreed:

Whoever then vows himself to the service of the Church from his infancy should be baptized before the years of puberty and given a share in the ministry of the readers. If he lives honorably from the period of adolescence to his thirtieth year and is content with one wife, one whom he receives as a virgin through the priest with the general benediction, he should be made an acolyte and a subdeacon. If thereafter he maintains the level of his previous continence, he should receive the rank of deacon. If then he performs his ministry commendably for more than five years, he should appropriately be granted the priesthood (*presbyterium*). Finally, after ten more years, he may rise to the episcopal chair, if through all this time he is approved for uprightness of life and faith.[19]

---

[16] *Paulinus of Nola: Life, Letters, and Poems* (Berkeley: University of California Press, 1999), 114.

[17] Paulinus had initiated correspondence with Jerome in 394. See Pierre Nautin, 'Études de chronologie hiéronymienne (393–397): III. Les premières relations entre Jérôme et Paulin de Nole', REAug 19 (1973), 213–39; and Trout, *Paulinus of Nola*, 90–3.

[18] See the full discussion in Alexandre Faivre, *Naissance d'une hiérarchie: Les premières étapes du cursus clérical* (Paris: Éditions Beauchesne, 1977), 313–18.

[19] *Ep.* 1.9.13 (PL 13, 1142–3); trans. Shotwell and Loomis, *See of Peter*, 705. A similar distinction between those who were baptized young and those who were baptized as adults is found in the decretal *Ad Gallos episcopos*, 3.8, a document that has often been attributed to Siricius (*ep.* 10). Recently, however, Yves-Marie Duval has offered persuasive reasons for regarding it as the work of Damasus (with, perhaps, the assistance of Jerome). See Duval, *La décrétale Ad Gallos Episcopos: son texte et son auteur* (Supplements to *Vigiliae Christianae*, 73; Leiden and Boston: Brill, 2005).

Having drawn up this set of regulations, Siricius turned to the case of those candidates for office who were baptized later in life. For these men a similar, though abbreviated, *cursus* was prescribed:

> He who is already of adult years when his change to a better mind prompts him to leave the laity for the sacred army, shall attain the fruit of his desire only upon condition that immediately after his baptism he join the band of readers or exorcists, provided also that he be known to have had or to have but one wife and to have taken her as a virgin. When such a man has been initiated and has served for two years, he shall for the next five years be acolyte and subdeacon and thus be promoted to the diaconate, if during this period he is judged worthy. Then, in the course of time, he may for his deserts win the priesthood and the bishopric, if the choice of the clergy and the people lights upon him.[20]

Siricius' legislation is noteworthy on several counts. It presented for the first time a specific clerical *cursus honorum*, along with a clear notion of 'lower' and 'higher' ranks through which an aspiring cleric had to progress in order to demonstrate his worthiness for office. Moreover, Siricius assumed that the ordinary candidate would be a man who had previously married, although in accordance with 1Timothy 3: 2, he specified that he should have married only once.

We must pause to appreciate the innovative character of Siricius' legislation. In the fourth century spontaneous acclamations of laymen or monks often led to immediate (sometimes even involuntary) ordinations to the priesthood or episcopate.[21] The ordination of Ambrose, who was elected to the bishopric of Milan in 374 directly from secular office and even prior to baptism, was an extreme, though by no means isolated, example.[22] Ambrose himself acknowledged the irregular character of his episcopal election, and, as we shall see shortly, Jerome did not hesitate to use Ambrose's secular past and accelerated ordination against him.[23] Siricius' prescriptions on the course of clerical office were designed specifically to curtail such activities and thereby to strengthen the structure of the various clerical ranks.[24]

---

[20] *Ep.* 1.10.14 (PL 13, 1143); trans. Shotwell and Loomis, *See of Peter*, 705–6.

[21] A good overview in R. Gryson, 'Les elections épiscopales en Occident au IVe siècle', *RHE* 75 (1980), 257–83.

[22] McLynn, *Ambrose*, 44–52. Augustine's installation at Hippo Regius in the winter of 390–1 is another example of what Siricius would have regarded as an irregular ordination. See the discussion in James J. O'Donnell, *Augustine: A New Biography* (New York: HarperCollins, 2004), 25–6.

[23] Ambrose referred to the irregular circumstances of his ordination in *ep. extra collectionem* 14.65 (CSEL 82.3, 269): 'Sed non valuit praescriptio, praevaluit impression.' See also *Off.* 1.4, and my discussion below.

[24] Damasus had also condemned the ordination of laypersons and neophytes to the ranks of the higher clergy, though without the detailed prescriptions of Siricius. See *Ad Gallos episcopos* 5.15 (Duval, *La décrétale*, 42–4).

As for the ordination of men who had previously embraced the monastic life, Siricius allowed that such ordinations were permissible. He insisted, however, that a similar period of testing be imposed on monastic candidates:

> We expect and desire that monks of high reputation for the soberness of their characters and the holy manner of their lives and faith should join the ranks of the clergy. Those under thirty years of age should be promoted through the lower orders, step by step, as time passes, and thus reach the distinction of the diaconate or the priesthood with the consecration of their maturer years. They should not at one bound rise to the height of the episcopate until they have served out the terms (*tempora*) which we have just prescribed for each office.[25]

While Siricius certainly did not exclude monks from holding clerical office, it is clear that the primary purpose of his legislation was to insist that the normal sequence of clerical promotion should be respected, even in the case of monastic candidates. As Philip Rousseau has observed, Siricius' opinion was that 'all clerics, whether or not their background was monastic, must rise through the ranks.'[26]

ii. Siricius and Clerical Sexual Continence

If Siricius did not regard monastic asceticism as a special qualification for membership of the clergy, he did view one form of ascetic behaviour as essential to the clerical office, at least to the higher ranks of deacon, presbyter, and bishop. I refer to the requirement of clerical sexual continence, of which Siricius was a prominent early proponent.[27] Two letters of Siricius contain extensive discussion of sexual continence for the clergy, and it is clear from these letters that Siricius encountered significant resistance from the bishops to whom he addressed his prescriptions. Both Siricius' commitment to the discipline of sexual continence and his difficulty with its enforcement help to explain his role in the Jovinianist controversy. Therefore, we must take a closer look at the emergence of the requirement in the Western Church and the arguments that Siricius advanced for it in his encyclical letters.

---

[25] *Ep.* 1.13.17 (PL 13, 1144–5); trans. Shotwell and Loomis, *See of Peter*, 706.
[26] P. Rousseau, *Ascetics, Authority and the Church in the Age of Jerome and Cassian* (Oxford: Oxford University Press, 1978), 129. Cf. A. Faivre, *Naissance d'une hiérarchie*, 318: 'La principe fondamentale de toute cette legislation sera encore rappelé dans la lettre *Ad diversos episcopos*; il ne faut appeler à l'épiscopat que des clercs préparés par des stages dans les functions inférieures.'
[27] Siricius' requirement involved the practice of sexual continence, not the renunciation of marriage. As we saw above, Siricius assumed that most clerics would be married men, even those committed to the clergy from a young age.

We do not know precisely when a requirement of sexual continence for the higher ranks of the clergy became a general practice in Western Christianity.[28] The earliest evidence of a law prohibiting married clerics from engaging in sex with their wives is found in the canons of a Spanish council held at Elvira around the year 306. Suspicions have been raised, however, regarding the authenticity of some of these canons, including the one on clerical sexual continence.[29] A synod held at Arles in 314 may have ruled on the question as well, although here, too, the authenticity of the relevant canon has been disputed.[30] Only in the later years of the fourth century do we find extensive discussion of the requirement, and the evidence indicates that the matter was hotly disputed, especially outside Italy. The decretal, *Ad Gallos episcopos*, which may have been composed by Damasus in 383–384,[31] stated that 'many bishops' (*multos episcopos*) had regularly ignored ecclesiastical tradition on the matter of clerical sexual continence.[32] The author of this decretal also claimed that he had often spoken on the issue and often been ignored. The same situation is evident in the letters of Siricius, who indicates that some bishops were completely unaware of the requirement and that others, who were aware of it, refused to enforce it.

Siricius' earliest and most extensive discussion of the problem is found in the Letter to Himerius, to which we have already referred. According to Siricius, Himerius had informed him that the 'most holy ranks of the clergy were being trampled and confused'. The reason for this state of affairs was that the ecclesiastical norms regarding sexual continence were being widely violated: 'For we are told that many priests and Levites of Christ, after long years

---

[28] Arguments for the apostolic origins of the requirement founder on the lack of evidence. See, e.g. the studies of Christian Cochini, *Apostolic Origins of Priestly Celibacy*, trans. Nelly Marans (San Francisco: Ignatius Press, 1990); Alfons Maria Stickler, *The Case for Clerical Celibacy: Its Historical Development and Theological Foundations*, trans. Father Brian Ferme (San Francisco: Ignatius Press, 1995); Stefan Heid, *Celibacy in the Early Church: The Beginnings of a Discipline of Obligatory Continence for Clerics in East and West*, trans. Michael J. Miller (San Francisco: Ignatius Press, 2000). While it is reasonable to suggest, as these studies do, that the actual *practice* of priestly celibacy preceded its establishment as *law* in the fourth century, there is no convincing reason to date this practice to the apostolic age.

[29] Can. 3; text in José Vives, *Concilios Visigóticos e Hispano-Romanos* (Barcelona and Madrid: Consejo Superior de Investigaciones Científicas Instituto Enrique Flórez, 1963), 7. For doubts, see Maurice Meigne, 'Concile ou collection d'Elvire?' *RHE* 70 (1975), 361–87; his views are accepted by R. Gryson, 'Dix ans de recherches sur les origines du célibat ecclésiastique', *RTL* 11 (1980), 157–85. For a different view, see Heid, *Celibacy*, 110.

[30] Can. 29 (CCSL 148.25). Canons 24–9 are missing from many of the manuscripts. While Cochini, *Apostolic Origins*, 161–9, is inclined to accept these canons, Heid, *Celibacy*, 112, n. 64, rejects them. See also Roger Gryson, *Les origines du célibat ecclésiastique du premier au septiéme siécle* (Gembloux: Duculot, 1970), 190, who regards canons 24–9 as 'apocryphes'.

[31] See note 19 above.

[32] *Ad Gallos episcopos* 2 (Duval, *La décrétale*, 26).

of consecration, have begotten offspring from their wives as well as in disgraceful adultery and that they are defending their sin on the ground that we read in the Old Testament that priests and ministers were allowed the privilege of begetting children.'[33]

Siricius then proceeded to offer a defence of the requirement of clerical sexual continence and to establish rules for its enforcement. Like his opponents, Siricius took as his starting point the analogy between Old Testament priests and Levites and those of the Christian dispensation, that is, the bishops, presbyters, and deacons. Citing Leviticus 20: 7 ('You must be holy, for I, the Lord your God, am holy'), he appealed to the notion of ritual purity as the basis of the Christian discipline of sexual continence.

In his letter to Himerius, Siricius first responded to the objection of his opponents. He noted that the priests of the Old Testament had to observe a period of sexual continence in order to carry out their sacrifices in the temple: 'Why were the priests bidden to take up their dwelling in the temple, far from their homes, during their year of service? Why but for the purpose that they might have no carnal intercourse even with their wives but in the radiance of an upright conscience offer an acceptable gift unto God?'[34] Once their period of service was complete, Siricius argued, they were allowed to return to their homes and engage in sex with their wives. Such marital relations, he remarked, were allowed only for the sake of procreation 'because it had been commanded that no man from any tribe but that of Levi should be allowed in the ministry of God'.[35] Old Testament priests, as Siricius would have it, were allowed to produce children only because it was necessary to continue the priestly line of Levi. Their participation in marital relations was the exception that proved the rule.

After explaining the exemption offered to priests of the old dispensation, Siricius then turned to the case of Christian priests and Levites. Since Christ has come 'not to destroy the law but to fulfill it' (cf. Mt 5: 17), Siricius argued, perfect sexual continence is now required of the priests who offer sacrifice on behalf of the Church:

And so [Christ] desired that the Church, whose bridegroom he is, should have her visage shining with the splendor of chastity, that in the day of judgment, when he comes again, he might find her without spot or blemish, as he ordained by his apostle (cf. Eph 5:27). Hence all we priests and Levites are bound by the unbreakable law of those instructions to subdue our hearts and bodies to soberness and modesty from the

---

[33] *Ep.* 1.7.8 (PL 13, 1138); trans. Shotwell and Loomis, *See of Peter*, 703.
[34] *Ep.* 1.7.9 (PL 13, 1138); trans. Shotwell and Loomis, *See of Peter*, 703.
[35] Ibid.

day of our ordination, that we may be wholly pleasing to our God in the sacrifices which we daily offer.

Citing Romans 8: 8–9 ('Those who are in the flesh cannot please God. But you are not in the flesh; you are in the Spirit, since the Spirit of God dwells in you'), Siricius concluded: 'And where but in holy bodies, as we read, can the Spirit of God have a dwelling place?'[36]

It is clear that Siricius has based his argument for the requirement of clerical sexual continence on Old Testament regulations regarding ritual purity of priests that were taken and extended to Christian 'priests and Levites'. Such arguments were quite familiar in the church of Rome in the late fourth century. The decretal *Ad Gallos episcopos* had cited the example of Old Testament priests who (it claimed) would spend an entire year in the Temple, 'without once setting foot in their houses', in order to maintain sexual purity.[37] Because bishops, presbyters, and deacons had to be constantly ready to give baptism or offer the sacrifice, it was argued, perpetual sexual continence had to be observed so that the priest of God might be 'constantly pure' (*purgatus perpetuo*).

A similar argument for priestly sexual continence can be found in the writings of Ambrosiaster from approximately the same time period (i.e. the early 380s). Commenting on the prescription of First Timothy 3: 12 ('Let deacons be married only once, and let them manage their children and their households well'), Ambrosiaster provided the following rationale for clerical sexual continence based on Old Testament ritual practice:

The ancient Levites and priests were allowed to have wives for their use because they spent much of their time free from the duties of ministry or priesthood. For there were a large number of priests and a great many Levites, and each one served at the divine ceremonies for a fixed period of time, according to the procedures established by David (cf. 1 Chron 6: 31–53).... Therefore, during the time when they were not required to serve at the altar, they were looking after their households. But whenever the time for their ministry approached, they underwent purification for several days; only then did they go to the Temple to make offering to God.

After citing the example of the Old Testament priests, Ambrosiaster proceeded to explain why this practice of temporary abstinence was no longer practicable among Christian priests:

But now it is necessary that there be seven deacons and a few presbyters, so that there may be two of them in each church, and one bishop in the city. And because of this

---

[36] *Ep.* 1.7.10 (PL 13, 1139); trans. Shotwell and Loomis, *See of Peter*, 703–4.
[37] *Ad Gallos episcopos* 6 (Duval, 32–4): 'Denique, illi qui in templo sacrificia offerebant, ut mundi essent, toto anno in templis solo observationis merito permanebant, domus suas penitus nescientes.' There is no biblical evidence for this assertion.

they all must abstain from intercourse with women, because it is necessary for them to be ready each day (*quotidie*) in the church; nor is it possible for them to find any time during which they might undergo purification after legitimate intercourse, as was the case with the ancient priests.[38]

According to Ambrosiaster, the rationale behind the Christian requirement of perpetual sexual continence was that bishops, presbyters, and deacons were involved in the sacred duties of baptism and eucharist each day. Since the apostle Paul prescribed that even lay persons should abstain from sex in order to be free for prayer (cf. 1 Cor 7: 5), 'how much more is this incumbent on Levites and priests, who have been entrusted with the duty to pray on behalf of the people day and night' (*die noctuque*).[39] All of the clergy, therefore, must be in a constant state of ritual purity.

It is highly likely that similar ideas animated the thought of Siricius on the matter of priestly sexual continence. In 386, the year after writing his Letter to Himerius, a synod of eighty Italian bishops met in Rome. Siricius composed a letter (*ep.* 5) reporting the results of this synod for those bishops who could not be present. Eventually this letter found its way to North Africa, where it was preserved in the records of the Council of Thelepte of 418.[40] In this letter Siricius restated the requirement of sexual continence, echoing the argument of Ambrosiaster that placed emphasis on the *daily* ministrations expected of the clergy:

Moreover, as it is worthy, chaste, and honourable, so we advise: priests and Levites should not have intercourse with their wives, because in their ministry they are occupied with the daily requirements (*quotidianis necessitatibus*) of the ministry. When Paul wrote to the Corinthians, he said: 'Abstain, so that you may be free for prayer' (1 Cor 7: 5). If lay people are commanded to abstain so that their prayers may be heard, how much more should the priest be ready at every moment (*omni momento*), secure in the purity of his clean state, in case he needs to offer sacrifice or to baptize. If he becomes contaminated by carnal concupiscence, what will he do? What excuse will he make? With what shame, in what state of mind will he take up [his service]? By what testimony of conscience, by what merit does he believe that his prayers will be heard, when it has been said: 'To the pure all things are pure, but to the corrupt and unbelieving nothing is pure' (Titus 1: 15)?[41]

---

[38] Ambrosiaster, *Comm. in 1 Tim.* 3: 12–13 (CSEL 81.3, 269); cf. *Quaest.* 127.35–6 (CSEL 50, 414–16) and the discussion of Gryson, *Les origines*, 132–6.

[39] *Comm in 1 Tim.* 3: 12–13 (CSEL 81.3, 269–70).

[40] Text in C. Munier, *Concilia Africae a. 345–a. 525* (CCSL 149, 59–63; PL 13, 1155–62). Cf. Jean Gaudemet, *Les sources du droit d'Église occident du IIe au VIIe siècle* (Paris: Les Éditions du Cerf, 1985), 61, n. 8.

[41] *Ep.* 5.9 (CCSL 149, 61–2; PL 13, 1160–1).

The need to be ready on a daily basis to bestow baptism and to offer the eucharist, Siricius argued, is the primary reason for the celibacy of the clergy. Concerns of ritual purity are plainly paramount.[42]

Siricius' emphasis on the ritual function of clerical celibacy, I would argue, is of one piece with his insistence that the order of clerical promotion should be respected and that monks or neophytes should not be given preferred entry into the clergy. In both instances, Siricius' primary concern was to enhance the stature of the clerical office. While ascetic behaviour in itself did not qualify a man for clerical service, once he entered the clergy he was required to practice one form of renunciation, namely sexual continence for the sake of ritual purity. The intention of Siricius' policy appears to have been twofold: both to bolster the status of the clergy and to distinguish the authority of the clergy from that of lay ascetics. As Peter Brown has observed, Siricius' effort to impose the discipline of 'post-marital celibacy' on the higher clergy was an attempt to create a 'middle party' in the Western Church, somewhere 'between the shrill ascetics and the new men of power, grossly stained by the world'.[43] While clerical celibacy helped to elevate the clergy above the married laity, the link with ritual purity served to distinguish clerical celibacy from the celibacy practised by the lay monastics.

Siricius' concern for the prerogatives of the clergy and his interest in celibacy as a means of enhancing clerical authority were probably factors underlying his opposition to Jovinian. Although we have no evidence that Jovinian opposed the requirement of clerical continence in itself, his defence of the equality of marriage and celibacy would have hampered the efforts of Siricius to impose the discipline, particularly among the more recalcitrant clergy. As we have seen, Siricius' letters show that his rules on clerical celibacy were being widely violated. In Spain, for example, some clergy were unaware of the requirement, while others defended their marital rights by appealing to the example of Old Testament priests.[44] Other opponents of clerical celibacy cited the Pastoral Epistles which specified that clergy ought to have been

---

[42] For a somewhat different view, see Daniel Callam, 'Clerical Continence in the Fourth Century: Three Papal Decretals', *TS* 41 (1980), 3–50, who tries (unsuccessfully, to my mind) to downplay the elements of ritual purity that are present in Siricius' correspondence. Callam also questions the prevalence of daily eucharist in the Western Church: 'The Frequency of Mass in the Latin Church ca. 400', *TS* 45 (1984), 613–50.

[43] Brown, *Body and Society*, 358. For a somewhat different development of this theme, see my essay, 'Clerical Celibacy and the Veiling of Virgins: New Boundaries in Late Ancient Christianity', in William E. Klingshirn and Mark Vessey (eds.), *The Limits of Ancient Christianity: Essays on Late Antique Thought and Culture in Honor of R. A. Markus* (Ann Arbor: The University of Michigan Press, 1999), 139–52.

[44] Siricius, *ep.* 1.7.11 (PL 13, 1140), allowed that a clergyman who lapsed out of ignorance could keep his office as long as he embraced continence thereafter.

married once.[45] We know that Jovinian had pointed to the presence of married apostles and clergy to support his argument for the goodness of marriage.[46] In his *Adversus Jovinianum* Jerome found it necessary to respond to Jovinian's point and to explain why married men were accepted into the clergy, even though they were expected to be sexually continent thereafter. Given the opposition that Siricius had already encountered in his efforts to enforce clerical sexual continence, he probably would have seen Jovinian's views as a source of further damage to the dignity of the clergy.

2. AMBROSE ON PRIESTLY AND VIRGINAL HOLINESS

i. Ambrose on Monasticism and Clerical Life

When we come to Ambrose of Milan, we encounter a vision of asceticism that is similar in some respects to that of Siricius, but one that ultimately moves in a very different direction. Like Siricius, Ambrose showed concern for the dignity of the clergy, and especially for the practice of clerical sexual continence. In his treatise *On Moral Duties* (*De officiis*), much of which was devoted to a discussion of clerical conduct, Ambrose supported the imposition of the requirement of sexual continence in the face of the same kind of opposition that Siricius encountered. Prior to ordination, he argued, only one marriage was to be allowed.[47] After ordination, no sexual intercourse was allowed to ministers:

In quite a number of out-of-the-way places, men who have been exercising a ministry—even, in some cases, the priesthood itself—have fathered children. They defend this behaviour by claiming that they are following an old custom, one which used to obtain when the sacrifice was offered only at lengthy intervals. Yet the fact is that even the ordinary people used to practise continence for a period of two or three days in order to approach the sacrifice in a state of purity, for we read in the Old Testament: 'And he washes his clothes' (Ex 19: 10). If the standard of observance was this scrupulous in the time of the figure, how much greater it should be now, in the time of the truth! Learn, priest and Levite, what it means to wash your clothes: it

---

[45] *Ep.* 5.9 (CCSL 149, 62; PL 13, 1161).
[46] See *Jov.* 1.23 (PL 23, 253) and 1.34 (PL 23, 268–9).
[47] *Off.* 1.248; cf. *ep. extra collectionem* 14.62–3. On this point Ambrose had a long-running conflict with Jerome, who argued that if the first marriage was contracted before baptism, then the second marriage was no impediment to ordination. See Jerome, *ep.* 69.8–9 to Nepotian (CSEL 54, 694–9), with its clear allusion to (and antagonism towards) Ambrose's position.

means displaying a body that is pure (*mundum*), properly prepared for the celebration of the sacraments.[48]

For Ambrose, as for Siricius and Ambrosiaster, the celibacy of bishops, presbyters, and deacons was interpreted as an application of the ritual purity laws of the Old Testament to the new sacraments of the Christian dispensation. Ambrose expected his clergy to exercise a ministry that was 'blameless and beyond reproach, and undefiled by any marital intercourse' (*inoffensum ... et immaculatum ministerium nec ullo coniugali coitu violandum*).[49] Like Siricius, Ambrose regarded sexual chastity (*castimonia*) as essential to the ritual demands of authentic Christian priesthood.[50]

But when we look more closely at Ambrose's conception of the Christian priest, it becomes apparent that his notion of priesthood differed in significant ways from that of Siricius. First, Ambrose did not share Siricius' manifest reservations about the monastic life as a preparation for life in the clergy. On the contrary, Ambrose himself actively supported the monastic movement, even fostering a monastic community on the outskirts of the city of Milan.[51] He also looked with enthusiasm upon those men who left their monastic retreats in order to enter the priesthood or episcopate. For example, in a letter to the church of Thessalonika, written (c.383) to console the people upon the death of their ascetic bishop, Acholius, Ambrose attributed the bishop's virtuous character to his youthful formation in the monastic life:

> Such was this man's life, such his heritage, his way of life, his succession. As a youth he entered a monastery; he was enclosed in a narrow cell in Achaia, while by grace he wandered over the space of many lands. Having been called to the highest priesthood [i.e. the episcopacy] by the people of Macedonia, he was elected by the clergy; and where formerly the faith was weakened through its priest, there, later, through a priest the foundation walls of faith were made firm.[52]

Bishop Acholius had spent his blessed youth, Ambrose recalled, 'in the tabernacle of the God of Jacob, living in a monastery where, to his parents or relatives in search of him, he used to say "Who are my brothers, and who is

---

[48] *Off.* 1.249; text and translation in Ivor J. Davidson, *Ambrose: De officiis* (OECS; Oxford: Oxford University Press, 2001), 260–1.

[49] *Off.* 1.249; trans. Davidson, 261.

[50] A good overview of Ambrose's thought on clerical celibacy can be found in Jean-Paul Audet, *Mariage et célibat dans le service pastoral de l'église: Histoire et orientations*. 2nd edn. (Québec: Éditions des sources, 1999), 165–71; cf. R. Gryson, *Les origines*, 173: 'Chez lui comme chez ses contemporains, c'est l'idée de pureté rituelle qui gouverne sa réflexion en cette matière, non celle de consécration à Dieu.'

[51] Cf. Augustine, *Conf.* 8.6.15 (BA 14, 38): 'Et erat monasterium Mediolanii plenum bonis fratribus extra urbis moenia sub Ambrosio nutritore.'

[52] *Ep.* 51.12 (CSEL 82.2, 66); trans. Beyenka, 205 (slightly altered).

my mother? I do not know my father or mother or brothers, unless they are those who hear the Word and keep it." [53] Unlike Siricius, Ambrose promoted the view that monastic life provided the ideal formation for priestly life.

Ambrose's most well developed reflections on the relationship between the clerical and monastic lives are found in a lengthy letter to the church at Vercelli written in 396, the year before his death. The ostensible occasion for the letter was a disputed episcopal election to the see of Vercelli, which pitted an ascetic Honoratus (Ambrose's preferred candidate) against the people's choice, a wealthy landowner. Complicating the matter was the presence at Vercelli of two former monks from Ambrose's own monastery in Milan, Sarmatio and Barbatianus, who exerted their influence on public opinion by espousing the teachings of Jovinian.[54] In his response Ambrose offered not only an ardent defence of the ascetic ideal, but also a mini-treatise on the proper characteristics of a bishop. As Peter Brown has noted, Ambrose held up to the people of Vercelli the ideal of absolute sexual purity 'in order to persuade them to choose as their leaders and moral guides only men who had maximized their own control of the sexual urge—those who had lived lives of perpetual celibacy'.[55]

In support of his effort to establish an ascetic episcopacy at Vercelli, Ambrose appealed to the example of the famous ascetic Bishop Eusebius of Vercelli, who was among the first bishops to create a monastic community for the local clergy. He presented Eusebius as the model of the monk–bishop, the first to combine 'the restraint of the monastery and the discipline of the Church' (*monasterii continentia et disciplina ecclesiae*):

Eusebius of blessed memory was the first in the lands of the West to bring together these diverse practices, so that living in the city he observed the rules of monks (*instituta monachorum*) and ruled the Church in the temperance of fasting. For one adds much support to the grace of the priesthood, if one binds youth to the pursuit of abstinence and to the guidance of purity, and forbids to them, while living in the city, the customs and way of life of the city.[56]

---

[53] *Ep.* 52.3 (CSEL 82.2, 68); trans. Beyenka, 68 (slightly altered).
[54] *Ep. extra collectionem* 14.7 (CSEL 82.3, 238). On the setting of the letter, see McLynn, *Ambrose*, 285–6; Brown, *Body and Society*, 361–2; and Rita Lizzi, *Vescovi e strutture ecclesiastiche nella città tardoantica: L'Italia Annonaria nel IV–V secolo d.C.* (Como: Edizioni New Press, 1989), 46–50.
[55] Brown, *Body and Society*, 362.
[56] *Ep. extra collectionem* 14.66 (CSEL 82.3, 270). On Eusebius, see Joseph T. Lienhard, 'Patristic Sermons on Eusebius of Vercelli and their Relation to his Monasticism', *RBen* 87 (1977), 163–72; and his *Paulinus of Nola and Early Western Monasticism* (Theophaneia 28; Köln-Bonn: Peter Hanstein Verlag GMBH, 1977), 89–93, 107–10.

Like the ancient 'monastic' heroes—Elijah, Elisha, and John the Baptizer—Bishop Eusebius had prepared himself for exile and other hardships associated with his episcopacy because he had been 'nourished by the life of the monastery'.[57] Monastic renunciation, as Ambrose saw it, provided the ideal preparation for life in the clergy.

Another feature of Ambrose's Letter to the Church of Vercelli that contrasts with the approach of Siricius is the manner in which he simultaneously presented both the life of clerics and that of monks as the highest forms of Christian commitment. Neither way of life was portrayed as superior to the other, but both were proposed as equal and supreme examples of virtue:

> Who doubts that in stricter Christian devotion these two are the more excellent (*praestantiora*): the duties of clerics and the customs of monks (*clericorum officia et monachorum instituta*)? The one is a discipline which trains for courtesy and morality, the other for abstinence and patience; the one as on an open stage, the other in secrecy; the one is observed, the other is hidden from sight.... The one life, then, is in the arena, the other in a cave; the one is opposed to the confusion of the world, the other to the desires of the flesh; the one subdues, the other flees the pleasures of the body; the one more agreeable, the other safer; the one rules over itself, the other restricts itself; yet each way of life denies itself so that it may be Christ's, because to the perfect it was said: 'If anyone wishes to come after me, let him deny himself, take up his cross, and follow me' (Mt 16: 24).[58]

Like Siricius, Ambrose had a strong interest in fostering the life of the clergy and enhancing its stature; unlike Siricius, Ambrose conceived the clerical life in strongly ascetical terms and viewed the monastery as an appropriate training ground for those who wished to hold clerical office.

Perhaps the most striking evidence of Ambrose's interest in fostering the holiness of the clergy by means of ascetic effort can be seen in his appropriation of the notion of the 'Levite', another point at which he differed from Siricius. For Siricius and Ambrosiaster, the term 'Levite' had simply designated the office of deacon. While Ambrose sometimes used the term in this technical sense,[59] he also characterized all New Testament ministers as 'Levites', whether bishops, presbyters, or deacons. Roger Gryson has demonstrated that much of Ambrose's allegorical discussion of the Levites was based

---

[57] *Ep. extra collectionem* 14.71 (CSEL 82.3, 273). On Eusebius's role in the pro-Nicene resistance and his exile to the East, see Daniel H. Williams, *Ambrose of Milan and the End of the Arian-Nicene Conflicts* (OECS; Oxford: Clarendon Press, 1995), 49–68.

[58] *Ep. extra collectionem* 14.71–2 (CSEL 82.3, 273–4); trans. Beyenka, 347–8 (altered).

[59] i.e. 'priest' (*sacerdos*) could refer to either a 'bishop' (*episcopus*) or a 'presbyter' (*presbyter*), whereas 'levite' (*levita*) meant a 'deacon'. See R. Gryson, *Le Prêtre selon saint Ambroise* (Louvain: Édition Orientaliste, 1968), 134–44.

on the writings of Philo and Origen.⁶⁰ But whereas Philo and Origen had tended to identify the Levites with sages who had achieved perfect wisdom, Ambrose saw this perfection of wisdom and virtue embodied in the Christian ministerial priesthood. As Gryson has put it, Ambrose used the Old Testament image of the Levite 'de quoi nourrir sa conception élitiste de la cléricature'.⁶¹ Passages such as Numbers 3: 12 ('I have taken the Levites out of the midst of the children of Israel in place of every firstborn that opens the womb among the children of Israel. They will serve as a redemption-price for the firstborn, and the Levites will be for me') exerted a strong influence on Ambrose's thought. ⁶² The notion of the 'Levite' enabled him to present the Christian clergy as an elite body separated from the laity and consecrated to God's service. Priestly ministry, therefore, required an array of virtues that could be acquired only by serious ascetical effort.

In his treatise *De officiis*, for example, Ambrose reflected at length on the moral qualities expected of the Christian Levite. Like the ancient Levites who were appointed to guard the tabernacle of the covenant and its vessels (Num 1: 49–51), Christian priests were allowed to gaze upon the sacred mysteries and were charged with their protection. Such a privilege required acquisition of the cardinal virtues of wisdom, justice, courage, and self-control.⁶³ Determining one's duty in changing circumstances required constant discernment, Ambrose argued:

This is why the Levite is chosen to guard the sanctuary: he must not be mistaken in his judgement, he must not desert the faith, he must not fear death, and he must not do anything which suggests a lack of temperance; rather, he must by his very appearance give evidence of a seriousness of character. It is seemly that he should keep a firm control not just of his spirit but of his eyes as well; then not even a casual encounter will bring a blush to his sober cheek, for 'he who looks at a woman lustfully has committed adultery with her in his heart'. As we can see, it is not just in the doing of the foul deed that adultery is committed: it is there even in the intention of a look.⁶⁴

The true Levite is the one who has dedicated himself entirely to God, who says to his father and mother, 'I do not know you.'⁶⁵ Like the virgin Mary, the Levites

---

⁶⁰ R. Gryson, 'Les Lévites, figure du sacerdoce veritable, selon saint Ambroise', *ETL* 56 (1980), 89–112; see also Gryson, 'L'interprétation du nom de Lévi (Lévite) chez saint Ambroise', *SacEr* 17 (1966): 217–29.
⁶¹ 'Les Lévites', 112. As Gryson goes on to note, 'La vision qu'Ambroise a de l'Église est infiniment plus "cléricale" que celle d'Origène.'
⁶² Ambrose frequently cited this passage from Numbers. See, e.g. *Off.* 1.250; *ep.* 14.4 (CSEL 82.1, 109); *Cain* 2.2.7 (CSEL 32.1, 383).
⁶³ *Off.* 1.251.   ⁶⁴ *Off.* 1.256; trans. Davidson, 267.
⁶⁵ Deut 33: 9, cited in *Off.* 1.257. Cf. the description of Bishop Acholius cited above, n. 53.

have no guile in their hearts and harbour no deceit within them, but guard his words and ponder them in their hearts.... These are the men who have learned never to put their parents before their duty, the men who detest all who violate chastity, who avenge every outrage to purity, and who have learned to recognize when the time is right for this duty or that, which matters most, and which is right for each specific situation.[66]

Ambrose expected the moral qualities of the clergy to surpass those of the Christian laity and thereby to establish a clear separation between clergy and laity. Commenting on the prohibition of second marriages incumbent on Christian clergy, Ambrose observed: 'For what would be the difference between priest and people if they were bound by the same laws? The life of a priest ought to surpass others as its grace surpasses, and he who binds others by his precepts ought himself to keep the precepts of the law in himself.'[67]

ii. Ambrose and the Consecration of Virgins

If Ambrose's ascetic ideal of the clergy contrasted with that of Siricius, an even greater difference between them existed regarding female asceticism. Just as his approach to the virginity of Mary stressed her absolute and perpetual abstention from all sexual relations, so Ambrose's ascetic vision was shaped by the ideal of an absolute physical *integritas* that was displayed most visibly in the bodies of consecrated virgins.[68] Ambrose was virtually unique among his contemporaries for his deep preoccupation with female virginity, a practice he encouraged throughout his career both in writing and in ritual. The ritual of the *velatio* or veiling of virgins was a novelty in the late fourth century, and it was an exclusively Western practice.[69] Ambrose, in fact, provides some of the most extensive evidence of the practice. Both theologically and liturgically, the consecration of virgins played a central role in Ambrose's understanding of ascetic behaviour. It is necessary, therefore, to take a closer look at his approach to female virginity in order fully to understand his resistance to the teachings of Jovinian.[70]

---

[66] *Off*. 1.258; trans. Davidson, 267.
[67] *Ep. extra collectionem* 14.64 (CSEL 82.3, 269); trans. Beyenka, 345. Cf. Gryson, *Le Prêtre*, 295–317.
[68] On this theme the discussion in Brown, *Body and Society*, 341–65, is indispensable.
[69] Raymond d'Izarny, 'Mariage et consécration virginale au IVe siècle', *La vie spirituelle: Supplément*, 6 (1953), 92–107; René Metz, *La consecration des vierges dans l'église romaine: Étude d'histoire de la liturgie* (Paris: Presses Universitaires de France, 1954), 67–162.
[70] As Ivor Davidson, *Ambrose: De officiis*, 87, has observed, even Ambrose's account of clerical sexual continence has been influenced by his understanding of consecrated virginity: 'No Roman gentleman had ever been bound to such a rigorous commitment; Ambrose requires of his leading men an absolute sexual *integritas*... which traditionally would have been expected only of women.'

Writings from throughout Ambrose's episcopal career provide abundant evidence of his abiding concern with the virginal purity of Christian women. As we have already seen, his earliest literary production was the three-book treatise *De virginibus* (377). This was followed by a series of works on virginity and widowhood: *De virginitate* (probably 378), *De viduis* (378), *De institutione virginis* (393), and *Exhortatio virginitatis* (394).[71] In these writings Ambrose proved to be an indefatigable proponent of sexual continence, and especially perpetual virginity. As he stated in his letter to the church at Vercelli, 'the Church each day proclaims the praise of chastity and the glory of purity (*laudem pudicitiae, gloriam integritatis*) in the sacred lessons and in the sermons of her bishops'.[72] No doubt he had his own sermons and writings in mind when he described the episcopal duty to preach chastity and virginal integrity.

In terms of theology, the public consecration of virgins provided Ambrose with a ready made symbolic language in which he could articulate the superiority of virginity over marriage. The ceremony of virginal consecration was modelled on the veiling that took place at a traditional Roman wedding and marked the moment at which a woman publicly and canonically became a 'bride of Christ'.[73] The rite of consecration was accompanied by prayers and antiphonal chanting of verses taken from the Song of Songs and Psalm 45 (44 in the Vulgate enumeration).[74] For Ambrose, the virgin's status as 'bride of Christ' definitively marked her as superior to women who were married to merely human husbands:

For the first thing that women who are to be married desire more than anything else is that they may boast of the beauty of their bridegroom. In this they inevitably confess that they are not the equals of holy virgins, to whom alone it may justifiably be said: 'More beautiful than the sons of men, grace is poured forth on your lips' (Ps. 45: 2). Who is this bridegroom? He is not one given to base inclinations or proud because of empty wealth, but his 'throne is forever' (Ps. 45: 6) . . . . Notice how much, according to the testimony of divine Scripture (cf. Ps. 45: 13–15), the Holy Spirit has conferred upon you—a kingdom, gold and beauty: a kingdom because you are the bride of the eternal king and because you manifest an unconquerable soul and are not held captive by seductive pleasures but rule them like a queen; and gold, because just as that

---

[71] I have followed the dates given in Gori 1, 62–81.
[72] *Ep. extra collectionem* 14.10 (CSEL 82.3, 240); trans. Beyenka, 324.
[73] The decree *Ad Gallos episcopos* 1.3–4 distinguished between the *virgo velata* and the woman who has made a merely private profession of virginity.
[74] Conclusively demonstrated by Nathalie Henry, 'The Song of Songs and the Liturgy of the *velatio* in the Fourth Century: From Literary Metaphor to Liturgical Reality', in R. N. Swanson (ed.), *Continuity and Change in Christian Worship: Papers Read at the 1997 Summer Meeting and the 1998 Winter Meeting of the Ecclesiastical History Society* (Woodbridge, UK, and Rochester, NY: The Boydell Press, 1999), 18–28.

material is more precious when it is tried by fire, so the charm of the virginal body acquires an increase of loveliness after having been consecrated to the Divine Spirit. As far as beauty is concerned, who can think of a greater comeliness than that of her who is loved by the king, approved by the judge, dedicated to the Lord and consecrated to God, who is always a bride and always unwedded, so that her love is unending and her chastity unharmed.[75]

For Ambrose, a human marriage signified slavery, both to a husband and to the trials of the flesh, 'for even though the marriage bonds are good, they are still bonds'.[76] Virginity, by contrast, meant freedom from earthly entanglements to enjoy the life of angels 'who are not constrained by the nuptial bond'.[77]

Ambrose also developed this rhetorical contrast between human marriage and consecrated virginity by invoking the traditional encratite links between sex and original sin and between salvation and sexual purity. As we saw in the previous chapter, Ambrose had used the familiar Eve–Mary parallel in order to contrast the original sin—which came through a married woman—and the work of salvation—which came through the virgin, Mary.[78] The same dichotomy appeared in his comparison between married persons and consecrated virgins. In his letter to the church at Vercelli, for example, Ambrose presented the original sin as 'pleasure' (*voluptas*) taught to Adam and Eve by the serpent:

Holy Scripture teaches us that pleasure was suggested to Adam and Eve by the crafty enticements of the serpent. If the serpent itself is pleasure, then the passions of pleasure are changeable and slippery, and are infected, as it were, with the poison of corruption (*veneno quodam corruptelarum*). It is certain, then, that Adam, deceived by the desire of pleasure, fell away from the command of God and from the enjoyment of grace. How, then, can pleasure call us back to paradise, when by itself it deprived us of paradise?[79]

In contrast to the lives of married people, marked as they are by sex and sin, the virginal life provided a return to paradise. The virgin could become like Adam and Eve before their fall and before their shame.

---

[75] *Virg.* 1.7.36–7 (Gori 1, 136–8); trans. Ramsey, 83–4. For the contrast between Ambrose's interpretation of Psalm 45 and that of Jerome and Augustine, see my article, 'The Virgin, the Bride, and the Church: Reading Psalm 45 in Ambrose, Jerome, and Augustine', *CH* 69 (2000), 281–303.

[76] *Virgin.* 6.33 (Gori 2, 34): 'Bona igitur vincula nuptiarum, sed tamen vincula'. Cf. *Virg.* 1.9.56 (Gori 1, 154–6); *Exh. virg.* 4.20–4 (Gori 2, 214–16).

[77] *Exh. virg.* 4.19 (Gori 2, 214).

[78] See the texts cited in Chapter 5, note 98.

[79] *Ep. extra collectionem* 14.14 (CSEL 82.3, 242); trans. Beyenka, 326 (slightly altered). As Peter Brown, *Body and Society*, 361, has observed, in this letter '*voluptas* was made to overlap almost entirely with sexual pleasure.'

Addressing himself to virgins in the year 394, Ambrose could exhort them to transcend their sexual nature and to recover the pre-sexual paradise enjoyed by the first human beings, whereas married people continued to wallow in sexual shame:

Show forth that Adam who lived before the sin, that Eve who lived before she drank the slippery poison of the serpent, before they were caught in his snares, when they had no reason to be confused. For in the present, even though marriages are something good, they still contain something that causes married couples to experience shame. Therefore, my daughters, you should be such as Adam and Eve were in paradise. As Scripture says, after Adam was expelled from paradise he knew his wife Eve and she conceived and bore a son (cf. Gen 4: 1).[80]

In a sacred virgin Ambrose believed that he could behold 'the life of angels on earth, which we once lost in paradise'.[81] Her body was the 'enclosed garden' and 'sealed spring' of the Song of Songs (4: 12). The virgin's chastity enabled her to recover what was lost in marriage: 'You are paradise, virgin,' Ambrose admonished, 'Beware of Eve.'[82]

The ritual of virginal consecration, therefore, provided Ambrose both with a privileged occasion on which to declaim the glories of virginal integrity and with a symbolic language in which to exalt the virgin as 'bride of Christ'. But more can be said about the ritual itself, for the ceremony of consecration visually and dramatically enacted the higher status that Ambrose wished to attribute to consecrated women. As noted earlier, Ambrose stated that the Paschal Vigil was widely regarded as the proper time both to bestow baptism and to consecrate virgins. Several other documents suggest that on this occasion the consecrated virgin might have overshadowed (or upstaged) the ordinary baptized Christian. According to *De lapsu virginis*, a text contemporary with the writings of Ambrose, the virgin entered the church in the company of the newly baptized, 'just like a new bride of the King', in order to be veiled at the altar. Upon witnessing her vows, the entire congregation shouted, 'Amen!'[83] Pious and noble women ran to the newly consecrated virgin, eagerly seeking a kiss from her. This document even attested that the consecrated virgin was separated from the rest of the congregation by a wooden railing on which were inscribed the words of 1 Corinthians 7: 34

---

[80] *Exh. virg.* 6.36 (Gori 2, 226). [81] *Inst.* 17.104 (Gori 2, 184–5).
[82] *Inst.* 9.60 (Gori 2, 158).
[83] *Laps. virg.* 5.19–20 (PL 16, 372); trans. by Maureen Tilley, 'An Anonymous Letter to a Woman Named Susanna', in Richard Valantasis (ed.), *Religions of Late Antiquity in Practice* (Princeton, NJ: Princeton University Press, 2000), 222. Once attributed to Ambrose, *De lapsu virginis* is now commonly ascribed to Nicetas of Remesiana.

('The married woman and the virgin differ: the one who is not married thinks about the affairs of the Lord, how she might be holy in body and in soul').[84]

Writing a decade or so after Ambrose, a Pelagian author—probably Pelagius himself—pointed to the ritual of virginal consecration as evidence of the superior status of the consecrated Christian virgin:

> For while the whole multitude of believers receives similar gifts of grace and all rejoice in the same blessings of the sacraments, those to whom you belong have something peculiar to themselves over and above what the rest possess: they are chosen by the Holy Spirit out of the holy and spotless flock of the Church as holier and purer offerings on account of the merits given them for their choice of vocation and are presented at God's altar by his highest priest.... Thus virginity possesses both what others have and what they do not have, since it obtains both common and special grace and also rejoices in the possession of the privilege of a consecration peculiar to itself. Ecclesiastical authority also permits us to call virgins the brides of Christ, since it veils those whom it consecrates to the Lord in the manner of brides, showing in this very special way that those who have shunned partnership of the flesh are destined to enjoy a marriage in the spirit.[85]

The comments of Pelagius indicate the success of Ambrose's initiative in fostering the cult of female virginity through the ritual of the *velatio*. The consecration of the virgin as 'bride of Christ' dramatically enacted, in a conspicuously public manner, the superior status accorded to celibate women.

A final observation can be made about Ambrose's interest in the ritual consecration of the virgin as bride of Christ. Although the consecrated virgin was the primary focus of the ritual of the *velatio*, the consecrating bishop was, in some sense, the liturgical *sine quo non* of the event. In other words, the writings of Ambrose make it abundantly clear that the *velatio* was a decidedly *episcopal* event. According to Ambrose it was the bishop's duty to decide at what age a girl should take the veil and whether or not she had the requisite virtues. The bishop customarily presided at the ceremony, bestowed the veil, pronounced the liturgical benediction, and delivered a sermon of exhortation. The bishop also continued to supervise the consecrated virgin after her veiling and sometimes took responsibility for her welfare after the death of her parents.[86] In essence, the ritual of virginal consecration enabled the bishop to assume the traditional role of the *paterfamilias* by offering the

---

[84] *Laps. virg.* 6.24 (PL 16, 374).

[85] Pelagius, *Virg.* (CSEL 1, 225); trans. B. R. Rees, *The Letters of Pelagius and his Followers* (Rochester, NY: The Boydell Press, 1991), 72. See the similar comments in Pelagius, *Dem.* 19.1. For the attribution to Pelagius, see Robert F. Evans, *Four Letters of Pelagius* (London: Adam and Charles Black, 1968).

[86] Cf. *can.* 31 of the Council of Hippo of 397 (CCSL 149, 42).

virgin as his 'daughter' to Christ as her 'bridegroom'. The analogy was not lost on Ambrose. In *De institutione virginis*, his sermon delivered at the veiling of Ambrosia, Ambrose referred to his namesake as 'she, whom I offer in my office as bishop (*sacerdotali munere*), whom I present with fatherly affection' (*affectu patrio*).[87]

The prominent role of the bishop in the recruitment, veiling, and supervision of consecrated virgins suggests that the ritual of veiling itself may have functioned as a way of enhancing episcopal authority.[88] Unlike Siricius, who had risen to the episcopacy through the ranks of the Roman clergy, Ambrose initially had only secular authority to support his elevation. Although Ambrose eventually achieved extraordinary success as bishop of Milan, he remained defensive about the original circumstances of his ordination. As late as 396, the year before his death, in his letter to the church at Vercelli, we find him protesting that his ordination had occurred under duress, although it was eventually approved by Eastern and Western bishops.[89] Ambrose did not issue such protestations without cause; as we shall see in the next section of this chapter, both Siricius and Jerome strongly disapproved of the elevation of secular leaders to the bishop's chair, and both of them directed their disapproval, albeit indirectly, towards Ambrose himself. Ambrose's enthusiastic support of the cult of female virginity helped to create an alternative source of spiritual authority, one mediated through the office of the Christian bishop.

If Ambrose's zealous promotion of female virginity was, in fact, closely connected with his desire to establish a clerical elite in the Western Church, this helps to explain a curious feature of his ascetical theology, namely his willingness to describe female purity in terms of 'priesthood' (*sacerdotium*) and the consecrated virgin as a 'Levite'. In his *Exhortatio virginitatis*, Ambrose invoked Deuteronomy 33: 8 ('Give to Levi his true ones [*veros eius*] ... Give to Levi his allotments' [*sortes eius*]), a passage he usually reserved for Christian ministers.[90] Those who are 'true' to Levi, Ambrose suggested, are consecrated virgins:

---

[87] *Inst.* 107 (Gori 2, 186). Cf. Pelagius, *Virg.* 1 (CSEL 1, 225), who also speaks of the presentation of the virgin at God's altar *per summum sacerdotem*.

[88] Neil McLynn, *Ambrose*, 60–8, has argued that Ambrose's early promotion of consecrated virginity, reflected already in *De virginibus* of 377, was calculated to consolidate his tenuous position in the see of Milan vis-à-vis the majority of his clergy who were sympathetic to the former bishop, the Homoian Arian Auxentius.

[89] *Ep. extra collectionem* 14.65. Ambrose's apology in this letter may have been a response to Jerome's criticism of his episcopal election. See below, Chapter 6, Section 3.ii.

[90] See *Off.* 1.257, *ep.* 51.1 (CSEL 82.2, 66), *ep.* 17.13 (CSEL 82.1, 127), and the commentary in Davidson, *Ambrose: De officiis*, 689–90. Ambrose's Latin text follows the Septuagint translation of this verse.

What could be truer than uncorrupted virginity, which preserves the seal of chastity and the natural enclosure of purity (*claustrum integritatis genitale*)? But when a young woman loses the flower of her virginity by the act of marriage, she loses what is her own, when something foreign is mixed with her. For the state in which we are born is true, not that into which we change; what we have received from the Creator [is true], not what we have assumed from cohabitation.[91]

Here Ambrose interpreted the purity of the Levite in terms of the preservation of one's 'natural' state, that of virginity. The 'truth' that the virgin displayed was nothing other than her 'uncorrupted' integrity. As Ambrose succinctly put it, 'virginity is truth, corruption is falsehood.'[92]

Ambrose's use of the language of the 'Levite' in reference to both consecrated virgins and the celibate Christian clergy points to the close association in his mind between these two modes of spiritual authority. Ambrose, therefore, had a variety of reasons to oppose the teaching of Jovinian. Jovinian's argument on behalf of the essential equality of all baptized Christians would have seriously undermined Ambrose's notion of the consecrated virgin as the virgin bride of Christ, as well as his sense of the importance of ascetic virtue for the clergy. As we saw in Chapter 1, Jovinian believed that the virginal language of scripture should be applied to 'the whole church of believers', which included married persons as well as widows and celibates as the one virgin Church. If, as I have suggested, the ritual of virginal consecration served to enhance the authority of the bishop, as well as the stature of the consecrated virgin, then Ambrose had further reason to oppose the arguments of Jovinian. By challenging the status of consecrated virgins, Jovinian would have seemed (at least to Ambrose) to have undermined one of the central pillars of episcopal authority, namely the bishop's role in consecrating the 'bride of Christ' herself.

3. JEROME AND THE MAKING OF A HERETIC

The third and most prolific of the opponents of Jovinian was, of course, Jerome. To Jerome we owe most of what remains of Jovinian's writings, quoted

---

[91] *Exh. virg.* 6.35 (Gori 2, 226). Ambrose's word for 'cohabitation' (*contubernium*) was commonly used for sexual relationships between slaves or between a free man and a slave. In this context it is decidedly derogatory.

[92] *Exh. virg.* 7.44 (Gori 2, 234). By 'corruption' Ambrose clearly meant sexual intercourse, even within marriage. In *Exh. virg.* 6.39–41, he argued that no married person could be considered a 'Levite' because married persons sought to please their partners. The Levite, by contrast, belonged solely to Christ and could claim the words of Ps 72[73]: 26, 'The Lord is my portion.'

in copious fragments in his two books, *Adversus Jovinianum*. In addition to this extensive polemic, we have three letters of Jerome written shortly afterwards in response to criticism of his treatise. Jerome's literary presence in the Jovinianist controversy is so overwhelming that we tend to take it for granted. Whom else should we expect to rush to the defence of Christian celibacy than Jerome, the author of the ascetical Letter 22 to Eustochium, the polemical *Contra Helvidium*, and numerous ascetical *vitae*? Such a presumption, however, would be a mistake, for it would lead us to neglect the most obvious—though usually unasked—question: why did Jerome insert himself into the controversy in the first place? Unlike Siricius and Ambrose, Jerome had no pastoral responsibilities in churches threatened by Jovinian's teaching; indeed, Jerome was far away in Bethlehem by the time Jovinian began to preach at Rome. And yet, of all the participants in the debate, only Jerome composed a full-scale polemical treatise, *Adversus Jovinianum*. By doing so he added an essential element to the controversy (indeed, the necessary prerequisite for Jovinian's 'heretical' status), namely the anti-heretical treatise.

What was at stake for Jerome in his engagement with Jovinian? Like Siricius and Ambrose, Jerome had several reasons to oppose Jovinian. Jerome had long been a vociferous and controversial advocate of ascetic renunciation, and his opposition to Jovinian was no doubt motivated by his sincere horror at the spread of Jovinian's teaching. But there were additional factors at work. Since his enforced departure from Rome in 385, Jerome had been alienated from the clerical leaders of the Western Church, Siricius chief among them, and from Ambrose of Milan as well. Jerome desperately needed to rehabilitate his own reputation, especially after his disgraceful exit from Rome eight years earlier. What better way to re-establish himself than to enter Rome again in triumph in the persona of that powerful fiction of late antique Christian literature, the anti-heretical writer?[93] But Jerome also had scores to settle. In the *Adversus Jovinianum* and other writings from this period, we find Jerome not only attacking Jovinian and defending asceticism, but also promoting his own understanding of ecclesiastical authority, specifically against Siricius and Ambrose. Analysis of Jerome's writings reveals a complex web of personal rivalries, literary self-promotion, and conflicting views of asceticism and clerical authority underlying his opposition to Jovinian.

i. Jerome: Against Jovinian

There can be no doubt that in the early 390s Jerome was deeply sensitive to the role that could be played in the Theodosian epoch by the Christian man

---

[93] Cf. Kelly, *Jerome*, 182.

of letters. As Mark Vessey has persuasively argued, already in the mid-380s Jerome had self-consciously fashioned for himself the literary persona of a Christian writer in the image of Origen, that is, as a master of biblical interpretation and ascetic practice.[94] Moreover, in the early 390s, Jerome had begun to reach out again to 'Babylon', that is, to the Christian community at Rome, in an effort to re-establish his literary presence there.[95] For example, shortly before composing *Adversus Jovinianum*, that is, in late 392 or early 393, Jerome had written *De viris illustribus*, a handbook of Christian literary notables and biblical interpreters. The aim of this book had been to demonstrate, especially to learned, pagan critics of Christianity, that the Church had produced its own philosophers, orators, and men of learning. With characteristic immodesty, Jerome included himself prominently in the list of literati; his was the final (and lengthiest) entry among the contemporary authors. Dedicated to Nummius Aemilianus Dexter, former proconsul of Asia and soon-to-be Praetorian Prefect, Jerome's *De viris illustribus* can be read as an effort to inscribe himself into the Christian literary tradition and to gain powerful patronage for this effort.[96]

Similar observations can be made about the *Adversus Jovinianum*. Thanks to the recent comprehensive study by Benoît Jeanjean, *Saint Jérôme et l'hérésie*, it is now possible to view the *Adversus Jovinianum* within the context of a heresiological effort that spanned nearly the entirety of Jerome's literary career, from the *Altercatio Luciferiani et orthodoxi* of 382 to the *Dialogue against the Pelagians* of 415. What emerged throughout these years was the stock portrait of the 'heretic', whose features remained remarkably constant, whether projected on to Jovinian, Rufinus, or Pelagius. By thus portraying his adversaries as 'heretics', Jeanjean has argued, 'Jerome was, in effect, inscribing himself into a heresiological tradition', one that extended back to Justin and Origen in the East, and to Tertullian and Hilary in the West.[97] The creation of this self-conscious literary persona had as much to do with establishing Jerome's own authority in the Western Church as an ascetic teacher and biblical interpreter as it did with refuting Jovinian.

Several features of the *Adversus Jovinianum* support such a reading of the text. First, the treatise itself manifests in its argumentation a number of

---

[94] 'Jerome's Origen: The Making of a Christian Literary *Persona*', *StPatr* 28 (1993), 135–45; id., 'The Forging of Orthodoxy in Latin Christian Literature', *JECS* 4 (1996), 495–513; cf. Brown, *Body and Society*, 366–86.

[95] See *ep.* 45.6 (CSEL 54, 327), where Jerome expressed his desire to leave 'Babylon' for Jerusalem.

[96] For the date of *De viris illustribus*, see Kelly, *Jerome*, 174. Dexter (*PLRE* 1, 251) was the son of Bishop Pacian of Barcelona; he became Praetorian Prefect in 395.

[97] Jeanjean, *Saint Jérôme et l'hérésie* (Paris: Études Augustiniennes, 1999), 11.

the stock features of the heresiological genre. For example, the assimilation of 'heresy' to paganism, and especially to pagan philosophy, was a standard topos in anti-heretical discourse.[98] Jerome employed this stereotype at several points in *Adversus Jovinianum*. For example, he characterized Jovinian as the 'Epicurus of the Christians' and drew a parallel between the name 'Jovinian' and the god 'Jove'.[99] Jerome even created a philosophical origin for Jovinian's proposition that there is one reward in heaven for all who have preserved their baptismal commitment: Stoicism.[100] As we saw in Chapter 1, Jovinian had used a variety of biblical texts to support his view that there were only two classes of Christians, the sheep and the goats or the saved and the damned. But, following the pattern of heresiological writing, Jerome conjured up a philosophical pedigree for Jovinian's position; he traced it to the Stoic view that all sins are equal. As Jerome put it, 'In sexual intercourse and full feeding Jovinian is an Epicurean; in the distribution of rewards and punishments, he all at once becomes a Stoic. He exchanges Jerusalem for Citium, Judea for Cyprus, Christ for Zeno.'[101]

It was also common practice for anti-heretical writers to accuse the 'heretic' of immoral activity and to associate one accused heretic with another known heretic. Jerome accomplished both tasks simultaneously by associating Jovinian with the gnostic Basilides. The passage is worth quoting in full because it brings to light the highly artificial character of Jerome's portrait of Jovinian as 'heretic':

About four hundred years have passed since the preaching of Christ first shone upon the earth. During that time, in which innumerable heresies have rent the robe of Christ, almost all error had proceeded from the Chaldaean and Syriac and Greek languages. [But now] after so many years, Basilides, the teacher of luxury and of all the most wicked embraces, has been transformed into Jovinian, like a second Euphorbus, so that the Latin language might have its own native heresy.[102]

As this passage suggests, Jerome was aware that Jovinian's ideas had not previously been condemned as 'heresy'; like Siricius, then, he believed that Jovinian was propagating a 'new heresy'.[103] In fact, if Jerome composed his

---

[98] This motif goes back to the origins of Christian heresiology. See Le Boulluec, *La notion d'hérésie*, 62, 115, 125–35, 312–24, 469, 472. Jerome's use of the topos is summarized in Jeanjean, *Saint Jérôme et l'hérésie*, 370–4.
[99] *Jov.* 1.1, 2.36, 2.38.   [100] *Jov.* 1.3.
[101] *Jov.* 2.21 (PL 23, 329); cf. Jeanjean, *Saint Jérôme et l'hérésie*, 35–6.
[102] *Jov.* 2.37 (PL 23, 350); cf. *Jov.* 1.40, where Jerome described Jovinian as 'the slave of vices and self-indulgence'. According to Jeanjean, *Saint Jérôme et l'hérésie*, 361, the amalgamation of heresies was the heresiological device which Jerome employed most frequently.
[103] In *ep.* 7.6 (CSEL 82.3, 301) Siricius had characterized Jovinian and his followers as 'auctores novae haeresis et blasphemiae'.

treatise *Adversus Jovinianum* before he was even aware of Jovinian's condemnations at Rome and Milan, as we argued in Chapter 1, then it was all the more critical for him to portray Jovinian as a 'heretic' by employing the standard heresiological topoi. The more salient point, however, is not simply that Jerome employed such arguments in order to characterize Jovinian as a heretic. Rather, as Jeanjean has noted, this portrayal was part of a quite deliberate strategy to portray himself as an arbiter of orthodoxy, that is, as an authority on the subject of asceticism and biblical interpretation. In other words, it was necessary for Jerome to construe Jovinian as 'heretic' in order to portray himself as 'orthodox'.

ii. Jerome: Against Ambrose and Siricius

But even as Jerome was painting the portrait of Jovinian as a purveyor of heresy and himself as a champion of orthodoxy, he also was engaged in a more subtle battle to subvert the authority of the two most prominent leaders of the Western Church, Ambrose and Siricius. Jerome's contentious relationship with Ambrose is a matter that has drawn the attention of numerous scholars, and much still remains to be clarified.[104] Neil Adkin, among others, has detected hostility towards Ambrose in Jerome's writings as early as 384. Jerome's famous Letter 22 to Eustochium, according to Adkin, contains several barbs directed at Ambrose's pompous literary style and excessive reliance on other authors. The reason for this antagonism, Adkin argues, was Jerome's jealousy over Ambrose's superior intellectual gifts and theological achievements.[105] Other scholars have argued that the year 385 marked a decisive turning-point in Jerome's attitude towards Ambrose. Speculating that Ambrose may have been in a position to help Jerome when he was tried

---

[104] Angelo Paredi, 'S. Gerolamo e s. Ambrogio', in *Mélanges Eugène Tisserant*, v (Studi e Testi, 235; Vatican City, 1964), 153–98; Pierre Nautin, 'L'activité littéraire de Jérôme de 387 à 392', *RTP* 115 (1983), 247–59; W. Dunphy, 'On the Date of St. Ambrose's *De Tobia*,' *SacEr* 27 (1984), 29–33; Gérard Nauroy, 'Jérôme, lecteur et censeur de l'exégèse d'Ambroise', in Duval (ed.), *Jérôme entre l'occident et l'orient*, 173–203; Maurice Testard, 'Jérôme et Ambroise: Sur un "aveu" du *De officiis* de l'évêque de Milan', in Duval (ed.), *Jérôme entre l'occident et l'orient*, 227–54; S. M. Oberhelman, 'Jerome's Earliest Attack on Ambrose: *On Ephesians*, Prologue (ML 26:469D–70A)', *TAPA* 121 (1991), 377–401; Neil Adkin, 'Ambrose and Jerome: The Opening Shot', *Mnemosyne*, 46 (1993), 364–76; Neil Adkin, 'Jerome on Ambrose: The Preface to the Translation of Origen's Homilies on Luke', *RBen* 107 (1997), 5–14; Ivor Davidson, 'Pastoral Theology at the End of the Fourth Century: Ambrose and Jerome', *StPatr* 33 (1997), 295–301.

[105] Adkin, 'Ambrose and Jerome', following suggestions by Nautin, 'L'activité littéraire', 258, and Duval, 'L'originalité', 64, n. 270. Adkin's argument has been accepted by Davidson, 'Pastoral Theology', and Andrew Cain, 'In Ambrosiaster's Shadow: A Critical Re-Evaluation of the Last Surviving Letter Exchange between Pope Damasus and Jerome', *REAug* 51 (2005), 257–77.

by the Roman clergy, but that he refused, some believe that Jerome blamed Ambrose for a hand in his expulsion from Rome.[106]

Whatever the ultimate source of Jerome's hostility towards Ambrose, his writings from 386 onwards express increasingly negative opinions about the bishop of Milan. For example, in the Preface to his Commentary on Ephesians, composed in 386, Jerome alluded to several of Ambrose's writings, which he dismissed as a haphazard mixture of scriptural citations and 'worldly eloquence' (*eloquentiam...saecularem*). In contrast to Ambrose's *pompaticum...sermonem*, Jerome presented his own commentaries on books of the Old and New Testaments as the product of careful, rational inquiry.[107] Two years later, in the Preface to his translation of *On the Holy Spirit* by Didymus the Blind—a work which Jerome completed primarily to expose the plagiarisms in Ambrose's work of the same name—Jerome described Ambrose (again not by name) as an 'unsightly little crow' (*informis cornicula*) decked out in the plumage of other birds.[108] Similarly, in the Preface to his translation of Origen's Homilies on Luke, composed in 392, Jerome referred to Ambrose as a 'croaking raven' (*corvum...crocitantem*), who mocked the splendid colours of other birds, 'even though he himself is utterly in the dark' (*cum totus ipse tenebrosus sit*).[109] In the same preface Jerome noted that Paula and Eustochium had recently read a commentary on Luke (certainly that of Ambrose) in which the author 'played in his words and slept in his meanings'.[110] About the same time, in his *Hebrew Questions on Genesis*, Jerome also censured Ambrose's identification of Gog and Magog with the Goths, thereby underscoring Ambrose's inability to read Hebrew.[111] There can be no doubt that Jerome perceived Ambrose to be a rival and that he sought to expose the bishop of Milan as a second-rate thinker and writer. Conversely, Jerome vaunted his own literary achievements, especially in scripture study.

Clear confirmation of this view can be found in the entry on Ambrose in Jerome's *De viris illustribus*, which was composed around 393, shortly before *Adversus Jovinianum*. Here Jerome finally dared to belittle his rival by name: 'Ambrose, bishop of Milan, continues writing down to the present day.

---

[106] This position, first articulated by Paredi, has been strongly maintained by Oberhelman, Nautin, Kelly, and others. See note 104 above.

[107] *Ephes.*, prol. (PL 26, 469–70). Adkin, 'Jerome on Ambrose', sees in these lines a criticism of Ambrose's ignorance of Hebrew.

[108] *Did. spir.*, prol. (PL 23, 107).

[109] *Orig. Luc.*, prol. (PL 26, 230). The latter two allusions to Ambrose in Jerome's prefaces were already exposed by Rufinus, *Apol.* 2.25–6 (CCSL 20, 101–2).

[110] *Orig. Luc.*, prol (PL 26, 230): 'in verbis luderet, in sententiis dormitaret.'

[111] *Qu. Heb. Gen.* 10.21 (CCSL 72, 11). The reference is to Ambrose, *Fid.* (CSEL 78, 105), cited in Oberhelman, 'Jerome's Earliest Attack', 394–5.

Concerning him I postpone judgment in that he is still alive lest I get blamed for flattery, on the one hand, or, on the other, for telling the truth.'[112] Although Jerome here claimed to be refraining from judgement regarding Ambrose's accomplishments as a writer, the meaning of his words is clear enough to anyone familiar with Jerome's previous criticisms of Ambrose's writings. As David Wiesen has observed, 'the sharp contrast drawn between flattery and truth must mean that the truth would be highly uncomplimentary to Ambrose.'[113] Jerome's hostile treatment of Ambrose in *De viris illustribus* and in his earlier writings indicates that in some manner Jerome perceived Ambrose to be a rival, especially in the area of literary accomplishment. While Jerome generally refrained from criticizing Ambrose by name during the latter's lifetime, after Ambrose's death in 397, Jerome proceeded to attack him explicitly.

But Jerome's rivalry with Ambrose was not merely a matter of personal prejudice or even professional jealousy. Jerome differed from Ambrose, and from Siricius as well, in his conception of clerical authority and in his understanding of the role that asceticism should play in defining the proper behaviour of a cleric. Both Siricius and Ambrose, as we have seen, had a high notion of the clerical office, and both of them (though in different ways) sought to enhance the stature of the clergy by encouraging certain types of ascetic behaviour. As bishops, both Siricius and Ambrose had a stake in the maintenance of the clerical order: Siricius sought to uphold it by emphasizing the importance of progressing through the ranks and the adoption of postmarital sexual continence; Ambrose sought to uphold it by emphasizing the importance of sexual purity and the compatibility of the monastic and clerical lives. Jerome, by contrast, although he was an ordained presbyter, seems to have had very little interest in, or even respect for, the clerical office itself. Jerome's radical commitment to the ascetic ideal led him to take an extremely critical perspective on clerical behaviour, especially when that behaviour fell short of his ideal. A closer look at Jerome's perspectives on the clergy and the ascetic life will shed light on his tensions with Ambrose and Siricius, as well as his opposition to Jovinian.

Jerome's thinking on the relationship between monks and clerics underwent significant development, particularly in the years around the composition of *Adversus Jovinianum*.[114] As we saw in Chapter 2, in early writings, such as Letter 14 to Heliodorus (c.376), Jerome emphasized the incompatibility between the

---

[112] *Vir. ill.* 124 (PL 23, 751), trans. Thomas Halton, *Saint Jerome: On Illustrious Men* (FC 100; Washington, DC: The Catholic University of America Press, 1999), 158.

[113] *St. Jerome as a Satirist: A Study in Christian Latin Thought and Letters* (Ithaca, NY: Cornell University Press, 1964), 241.

[114] The main stages have been charted by Philip Rousseau, *Ascetics, Authority, and the Church*, 125–32.

life of monks and that of clerics. While he acknowledged that the clergy had an important role in the life of the Church, specifically for their sacramental ministry, he also expressed fear for the dangers associated with life in the city: 'Therefore, just as he who ministers well acquires for himself a good rank, so he who approaches the chalice of the Lord unworthily shall be guilty of the body and of the blood of the Lord.'[115] Clerical rank did not guarantee that a man was worthy of office, and Jerome seems to have relished exposing those whom he considered unworthy.[116] Throughout his years in Rome, and for a number of years afterwards, Jerome freely expressed contempt for members of the clergy who did not meet his rigorous moral standards.[117]

By the early 390s, however, a change is evident in Jerome's correspondence. In 393 Jerome wrote a letter to Nepotian, nephew of the Heliodorus mentioned above.[118] Heliodorus had ignored the warnings of Jerome's earlier Letter 14 and become bishop of Altinum; his nephew had followed him into ecclesiastical service and, as Jerome reported it, Nepotian had requested that Jerome write a letter 'showing how one who has renounced the service of the world to become a monk or a clergyman may keep the straight path of Christ and not be drawn aside into the haunts of vice'.[119] In Letter 52 to Nepotian, Jerome took it for granted that it was possible for the clergy to live according to the same rigorous standards as monks; in fact, he presented Heliodorus as one who had managed both to achieve monastic perfection and to teach it.[120] Nevertheless, as Jerome undertook the task of describing the duties of the clergy, he could not resist resorting to the same kind of 'caustic digs at priestly cupidity and worldliness, and at stuck-up bishops' that characterized his earlier writings.[121] In other words, Jerome's commitment to the ascetic ideal of the monk remained; only now it had become a criterion for distinguishing the true from the false clergyman.[122]

In Letter 52 to Nepotian, Jerome's ascetic critique of the clergy was evident in numerous ways: he warned Nepotian to avoid clergymen who used their position to acquire wealth (5–6); he cautioned against hypocritical presbyters

---

[115] *Ep.* 14.8.7 (CSEL 54, 57).

[116] An overview of Jerome's satirical treatment of the clergy can be found in Wiesen, *St. Jerome as Satirist*, 65–112.

[117] Oberhelman, 'Jerome's Earliest Attack', 398–401, following Wiesen, *St. Jerome as Satirist*, 95–105, has detected especially harsh criticism of the clergy in the biblical commentaries Jerome composed in the years immediately following his departure from Rome.

[118] For the date, see Nautin, 'Études de chronologie hiéronymienne (393–397): IV. Autres lettres de la période 393–396', *REAug* 20 (1974), 251–3.

[119] *Ep.* 52.1 (CSEL 54, 413).

[120] *Ep.* 52.4 (CSEL 54, 421). See also *ep.* 60.10 (CSEL 54, 559), where Jerome stated that in Heliodorus Nepotian had found 'a monk to imitate and a bishop to venerate'.

[121] Kelly, *Jerome*, 191.

[122] Cf. Rousseau, *Ascetics, Authority, and the Church*, 126: 'It was not necessary to suppose that men would be either monks or clergy: Jerome's distinction now was between clergy who were monks and clergy who were not.'

who preached fasting while enjoying full stomachs; he urged bishops to treat their clergy with honour, rather than lording over them (7); he attacked bishops who expended money on elaborate church buildings while neglecting the poor (10), and so forth. While ostensibly a guide to proper clerical living, Jerome's Letter 52 to Nepotian was also a direct assault on current clerical mores, as he perceived them. Jerome admitted as much in the closing lines of the letter when he informed Nepotian that he expected to arouse criticism. While protesting that he had not directly attacked those who sinned, Jerome acknowledged: 'I have but warned them to sin no more.... If anyone wishes to be angry with me, he will first have to admit that he fits my description.'[123]

Jerome's personal grievances against Ambrose and Siricius and his ascetic ideal of clerical life converged in several writings from the early 390s, including *Adversus Jovinianum*. Ivor Davidson has demonstrated that Letter 52 to Nepotian, composed in 393, contains numerous echoes of Ambrose, *De officiis*, as well as snide swipes at the bishop's rhetorical style and lack of theological preparation for preaching.[124] As Davidson has observed, in *De officiis* Ambrose had referred to his own inadequate training by constantly juxtaposing the words 'to teach' (*docere*) and 'to learn' (*discere*):

Ordinary men must learn beforehand what they are to teach.... In my own case, not even this was allowed. I was snatched into the priesthood from a life spent at tribunals and amidst the paraphernalia of administrative office, and I began to teach you things I had not learnt myself. The result was that I started to teach before I had started to learn. With me, then, it is a matter of learning and teaching all at the same time, since no opportunity was given to me to learn in advance.[125]

As Davidson has noted, in Letter 52 and elsewhere, Jerome similarly played with the pair *discere–docere* in what appears to have been a dig at Ambrose's lack of preparation for the priesthood. In Letter 52 to Nepotian, for example, Jerome told Nepotian to 'learn [from the scriptures] what you are to teach' (*disce, quod doceas*); elsewhere, in a letter to Paulinus of Nola, Jerome complained that too many people 'teach [the scriptures] before they learn' (*docent, antequam discant*).[126]

---

[123] *Ep.* 52.17 (CSEL 54, 440–1).   [124] 'Pastoral Theology', 295–301.
[125] *Off.* 1.3–4; trans. Davidson, 119.
[126] Jerome, *ep.* 52.7.1 (CSEL 54, 426) and *ep.* 53.7.1 (CSEL 54, 453); cited in Davidson, 'Pastoral Theology', 297. The same play on *discere–docere* is found in Siricius, *ep.* 6.3.5 (PL 13, 1166), in a very similar context, i.e. an attack on the practice of ordaining neophytes to the clergy. After citing 1 Tim 3: 6 and complaining that people dared to change the legislation of the apostle, Siricius observed: 'Et qui non didicit, jam docere compellitur. Ita nullus reperitur idoneus clericorum? Nec inter diaconos, nec inter alios clericos invenitur, qui sacerdotio dignus habeatur; sed ad condemnationem Ecclesiae laicus postulatur?' Unfortunately, the date of this letter is uncertain. If Siricius' comment was directed at Ambrose, then Ambrose's remark in *Off.* 1.3–4 may have been a response to Siricius' critique.

Several years later Jerome attacked Ambrose even more aggressively, though again not by name, in his Letter 69 to Oceanus. In the context of complaining about the ordination of neophytes to the clergy and the constant violation of First Timothy 3: 6 ('He must not be a recent convert, or he may be puffed up with conceit and fall into the condemnation of the devil'), Jerome spoke in unmistakable terms about the bishop of Milan: 'There is someone who was yesterday a catechumen and today a bishop; yesterday in the amphitheatre, today in the church; in the evening at the circus, in the morning at the altar; just a little while ago the patron of actors, now the consecrator of virgins!'[127] Jerome's personal animus towards Ambrose has here fused with his convictions about clerical office. Letter 69 suggests that Ambrose's accession to the episcopate was particularly vexing to Jerome. It placed Ambrose in a position of moral and intellectual leadership in the Western Church to which Jerome continued to aspire, and to which he could only aspire.

A similar point can be made about Jerome's relations with Siricius, although here the rivalry had a somewhat different character. As we have seen, Siricius was the Roman bishop who had presided over the trial and expulsion of Jerome from the city of Rome in 385. Obviously, this action (even if only approved, and not actually instigated, by Siricius) would have cast a lasting shadow over relations between the two men. Moreover, we know that Jerome had once hoped to succeed Damasus as bishop of Rome.[128] If so, then it was Siricius who had deprived Jerome of this honour.

But, again, their conflict was not merely a personal one. Even more fundamental were the differences between the two men on the issue of asceticism and its place in the recruitment of the clergy. We have already seen Siricius' reluctance to accept professed monks immediately into the episcopate and his insistence that the usual sequence of clerical promotion should be respected. We have also noted Siricius' assumption that most clergy would be married men, even those who entered the clergy at a young age, although they were expected to practice sexual continence upon ordination. Jerome had a rather different view of the matter. Jerome had a decided preference for monastic clergy; moreover, he believed the preference that many bishops showed in choosing married men for the clergy was simply one more sign of the decadence of the Church.

Jerome made this argument explicitly in several chapters of *Adversus Jovinianum*, where he showed an awareness both of Siricius' legislation on clerical continence and of its rationale.[129] When the apostle Paul prescribed

---

[127] *Ep.* 69.9 (CSEL 54, 698).
[128] See Jerome, *ep.* 45.3 (CSEL 54, 325): 'omnium paene iudicio dignus summo sacerdotio decernebar.'
[129] See *Jov.* 1.34 (PL 23, 268–9), where Jerome referred to the importance of ritual purity and cited several of the same biblical texts that Siricius had invoked. The following quotations in this paragraph are taken from this chapter of *Adversus Jovinianum*.

that the bishop should be a 'man of one wife', Jerome argued (citing 1 Tim 3: 2–4 and Titus 1: 6), he was deliberately diluting the requirements for the new Gentile converts: 'He made the rules for fresh believers somewhat lighter so that they might not shrink in alarm from keeping them.' Since the new converts had just been told that they had to abstain from idolatry and fornication, 'how much more would they have repudiated the obligation of perpetual chastity and continence'. Jerome considered it a regrettable necessity that men of second- or third-rate character (that is, married men) continued to be elected to the episcopate; the problem was that the number of virginal men was not sufficient to provide the necessary number of clergy. The fact that many congregations preferred to elect married men into the clergy, Jerome complained, simply showed that the laity just wished to approve of themselves and, therefore, was further evidence of their inferiority to virgins.

Moreover, Jerome went on to suggest that the fault for choosing married clerics often lay with the bishops themselves, and it is virtually certain that he meant Siricius. 'What I am about to say', Jerome wrote, 'will perhaps offend many. Yet I will say it, and good men will not be angry with me, because they will not feel the sting of conscience.' Jerome observed that bishops often chose clergy based on their wealth or education, or because they are relatives or friends, or (worst of all) because they receive flattery from these episcopal hopefuls. Jerome seems to have had in mind a very specific case, that of Pammachius himself. In one of his letters to Pammachius, written in 394 in the aftermath of the disastrous reception of the *Adversus Jovinianum* at Rome, Jerome mentioned that Pammachius was considered a leading candidate for the episcopate, even though he was still a married layman and a senator. Moreover, Jerome identified Siricius as one of Pammachius' supporters: 'I hear that the enthusiasm of the entire city is aroused on your behalf; I hear that the pontiff and the people are of one mind in this choice. To hold the priesthood is something less than to deserve it.'[130]

It is difficult to read Jerome's comment as anything other than a rebuke, both of Pammachius and of Siricius himself. In 394 Pammachius had not yet adopted the ascetic life, and his wife Paulina was still alive. Jerome himself had remarked in Letter 49 that Pammachius still had it in his power to ascend from the third to the second place, that is, to move from the ranks of the married to that of the sexually continent.[131] For Jerome, it was pre-eminently ascetic virtue, especially celibacy, that made a man suitable for clerical service.

---

[130] *Ep.* 48.4 (CSEL 54, 349). Jerome's allusion to Siricius is overlooked by N. Adkin, 'Pope Siricius' "Simplicity" (Jerome, epist. 127, 9, 3)', *VetChr* 33 (1996), 25–8.
[131] *Ep.* 49.11 (CSEL 54, 366–7).

As he wrote in *Adversus Jovinianum*: 'In every rank and sex, chastity holds the first place. You see, then, that the bishop, presbyter, and deacon are blessed, not because they are bishops, presbyters, or deacons, but only if they possess the virtues that their names and offices imply.'[132]

Clearly, Siricius and the Roman church as a whole preferred a different model of clerical authority, what Peter Brown has described as the 'post-marital' celibacy of the traditional married householder.[133] Jerome's opposition to Siricius, in the very pages of the *Adversus Jovinianum* and in his Letter to Pammachius, indicates that Jerome's entry into the controversy did not involve simply an attack on Jovinian or an effort to rehabilitate his own reputation. The writing of *Adversus Jovinianum* also constituted an implicit challenge to the clerical leadership of the Roman and Milanese churches. For Jerome to trounce Jovinian as a 'heretic' would have been a major step towards establishing himself as a giant in the competitive world of fourth-century ecclesiastical and literary politics.

It is clear that Siricius, Ambrose, and Jerome, though united in their opposition to Jovinian, each had somewhat different reasons for opposing him. The spread of monastic and ascetic piety in the West raised questions and caused conflicts, especially regarding relations between ascetics and the clergy. Siricius, Ambrose, and Jerome had distinctive views on the sources of clerical authority and on the role that ascetic behaviour should play in the establishment of that authority. The largest gap existed between the perspectives of Siricius and those of Jerome: the former focused on strengthening the structures of the clerical office, the latter devoted himself primarily to fostering ascetic practice. Moreover, personal factors seem to have exacerbated the ideological differences, especially in the case of Jerome; his troubled relations with the church at Rome were surely one factor in his intervention against Jovinian.

The differences between Siricius, Ambrose, and Jerome, however, do not represent merely personal idiosyncrasies. Their respective postures also reflect the concerns of different interest groups within the Western Church: the Roman clergy, wealthy ascetic women, powerful bishops, and learned (but powerless) ascetic teachers. All had a stake in the differentiation and distribution of merits based on ascetic practice. It was, perhaps, the very instability of the ascetic project in the West—that is, the volatility produced by these competing interests—that led to Jovinian's condemnation. Too many powerful interests were at stake, especially as ascetic renunciation became increasingly

---

[132] *Jov.* 1.35 (PL 23, 270–1).
[133] See *Body and Society*, 377–8, where Brown used the term to describe the perspective of Ambrosiaster.

tied to the life of the clergy. None of the aforementioned groups could afford to see Jovinian's teaching succeed. All depended on the triumph of the notion that celibacy was superior to marriage. Hence, the condemnation of Jovinian as 'heretic' constituted a critical step in the development of an 'asceticized' clergy in the Western Church.

Finally, Jerome's conflicts with both Siricius and Ambrose reveal something of Jerome's own marginal status within Western Christianity in the 380s and 390s. His vociferous attack on Jovinian, along with his snide digs at Ambrose and Siricius, suggest a man deeply insecure about his own place in the literary and theological context of his day. But if Jerome expected his *Adversus Jovinianum* to establish his pre-eminence as a teacher of ascetic and scriptural orthodoxy, he was to be profoundly disappointed. As we shall see in the next chapter, the reception of Jerome's *Adversus Jovinianum* was nearly unanimously negative. Friends and enemies rushed to repudiate the treatise. In the decade following Jovinian's condemnation it became evident that, although Jovinian's teaching was regarded as 'heresy', Jerome's was not considered 'orthodox'. Soon more moderate voices were heard, seeking a *via media* between Jovinian and Jerome.

7

After Jovinian: Marriage and Celibacy in Western Theology

Jovinian's condemnation in 393 marked the beginning of a new phase in the discussion of marriage and celibacy in Western Christianity. His view of the essential equality of all baptized Christians had been definitively declared to be 'heresy' by the highest officials of the Church. Although Ambrose's letter to the church at Vercelli of 396 showed that Jovinian's ideas continued to circulate for several years, at least in northern Italy, the lack of any episcopal support for his teachings ensured that 'Jovinianism' was not likely to become an organized or influential movement.[1] An imperial decree of 398 appears to have dealt the final blow to the Jovinianist heresy:

> The complaint of the bishops deplores the fact that Jovinian holds sacrilegious meetings outside the walls of the most sacred City. Therefore, we command that the aforesaid person shall be arrested and beaten with leaden whips and that he shall be forced into exile along with the remaining adherents and ministers. He himself, as the instigator, shall be transported with all haste to the island of Boa; the rest, as seems best, provided only that the band of superstitious conspirators shall be dissolved by the separation of exile, shall be deported for life to solitary islands situated at a great distance from each other.[2]

In the face of this combination of ecclesiastical and imperial censures, there could no longer be any question of an open propagation of Jovinian's teachings. After 398 the 'Jovinianists' survived primarily in the imagination of heresiologists.[3]

But that is not the whole story. In the decades following his condemnation we find a number of writers who continued to engage the issues that Jovinian had raised. Although it was now heresy for someone openly to preach the

---

[1] On the lack of support among the *sacerdotes*, see Augustine, *Haer.* 82 (CCSL 46, 337).

[2] *C.Th.* 16.5.53; trans. by Clyde Pharr, *The Theodosian Code and Novels and the Sirmondian Constitutions* (Princeton, NJ: Princeton University Press, 1952), 459–60, slightly altered; text in T. Mommsen, *Theodosiani libri XVI cum constitutionibus Sirmondianis*, i.2 (Zürich: Weidmann, 1971), 873. For the questions surrounding the date and purpose of this decree, see Duval, *L'affaire Jovinien*, 271–2.

[3] Augustine, *Haer.* 82 (CCSL 46, 337); Arnobius the Younger, *Praedest.* 1.82 (PL 53, 615).

equality of marriage and celibacy,[4] many Western Christians remained troubled by the central questions of the Jovinianist debate. Was celibacy superior to marriage, and, if so, what constitutes this superiority? Was it possible to articulate a theological argument for the superiority of celibacy without at the same time condemning or depreciating marriage?

One factor that kept the controversy alive was the negative reception accorded to Jerome's *Adversus Jovinianum*. When it arrived in Rome in 393, the work was widely considered to be an excessive, even heretical, response to Jovinian. Some of Jerome's closest friends were scandalized by his abusive treatment of marriage and demanded that he either explain or recant. The repercussions continued to be felt years later. In the midst of the heated debate over the writings of Origen around the year 400, Rufinus of Aquileia declared that Jerome's books against Jovinian contained teaching that amounted to 'the dogma of the Manichaeans'.[5] A short time later Augustine composed two books, *De bono coniugali* and *De sancta virginitate*, in which he sought to silence the 'chatter and whisperings of certain persons' who boasted that 'Jovinian could not be answered by praising marriage, but only by condemning it'.[6] The allusion to the excesses of Jerome's *Adversus Jovinianum* is palpable, and, as we shall see, Augustine was not alone in his effort to find an alternative to Jerome's *vituperatio* of Christian marriage.

In this chapter I will examine how the issues raised by Jovinian continued to shape Christian discussion of marriage and celibacy in the West in the decade after Jovinian's condemnation. One of the great advances in recent scholarship on late antiquity has been the recognition that debates over one 'heresy' sometimes led naturally into debates over another 'heresy'. Elizabeth Clark, for example, has argued that issues about the body, asceticism, and the afterlife that emerged in the Jovinianist controversy soon spilled over into the Origenist controversy.[7] Similarly, in his recent study of the Jovinianist debate, Yves-Marie Duval has charted the influence of Jovinian's teaching about the power of baptismal regeneration on Pelagius' theory of post-baptismal sinlessness.[8] Although I will draw on these studies, my intention is somewhat different.

---

[4] Vigilantius may have been such a heretic. See Jerome, *Vigil.* 1 (PL 23, 355), who stated that in Vigilantius 'Ioviniani mens prava surrexit'; and my discussion in 'Vigilantius of Calagurris and Victricius of Rouen: Ascetics, Relics, and Clerics in Late Roman Gaul', *JECS* 7 (1999), 401–30.

[5] *Apol.* 2.42 (CCSL 20, 116). [6] *Retract.* 2.22 (CCSL 57, 108).

[7] *The Origenist Controversy: The Cultural Construction of an Early Christian Debate* (Princeton, NJ: Princeton University Press, 1992). Clark has drawn similar connections between issues raised in the Origenist controversy and their later extension into the Pelagian debate: see *Origenist Controversy*, 194–244.

[8] Duval, *L'affaire Jovinien*, 284–365. The central thesis (and subtitle) of Duval's book is that what began in the Jovinianist controversy as 'une crise de la société romaine' (i.e. an argument about marriage and celibacy) became, in the Pelagian controversy, 'une crise de la pensée chrétienne' (i.e. a conflict over the possibility of impeccability).

Rather than trace the influence of Jovinian's teaching in these later controversies, I will examine the manner in which several later Latin writers continued to grapple with the central issues that Jovinian had raised. The excesses of Jerome's *Adversus Jovinianum*, I will argue, created a pressing need for a mediating position, a need that was met by teachers as diverse as Augustine and Pelagius. My aim here is to chart the search for this *via media* in the decade after Jovinian's condemnation.

1. THE ROMAN REACTION

i. Pammachius and Domnio

The Roman nobleman Pammachius was among the first to respond to Jerome's *Adversus Jovinianum*. As we observed in Chapter 1, Pammachius was probably one of the *viri genere optimi* who had first brought Jovinian's writings to the attention of Pope Siricius.[9] But whatever role he may have played in Jovinian's condemnation, it is clear that when Pammachius contacted Jerome regarding the reception of the *Adversus Jovinianum* at Rome, he did so as a critic of the treatise. Although the initial letter of Pammachius is no longer extant, we can reconstruct the main lines of his criticism from the two letters Jerome sent to him in response. One letter was a lengthy apology for the *Adversus Jovinianum* (*ep.* 49), the other was a brief cover letter that accompanied the longer treatise (*ep.* 48).[10] In Letter 48 Jerome stated that Pammachius had taken care to withdraw the exemplars of the *Adversus Jovinianum* from circulation, although he also noted that this effort had been to no avail, since both his enemies and his admirers had been eager to copy the treatise.[11] Jerome also challenged Pammachius to produce a better exposition of the Apostle Paul's discussion of marriage and virginity, if he rejected Jerome's defence. Jerome even claimed to have spoken more moderately about marriage than Paul did, and he cited previous commentators in his defence.[12]

Jerome's two letters to Pammachius must be read together with his Letter 50 to Domnio. Domnio was another friend of Jerome's who also served as a

---

[9] See Siricius, *ep.* 7.5 (CSEL 82.3, 300), and the comment of Jerome, *ep.* 49.2 (CSEL 54, 351): 'denique idcirco te post dominum faciente damnatus est quod ausus sit perpetuae castitati matrimonium conparare.'
[10] I have followed the enumeration of these letters in the CSEL edition. In the edition of Vallarsi, reprinted in PL and translated in the NPNF² series, the order of letters 48 and 49 is reversed.
[11] *Ep.* 48.2 (CSEL 54, 347). [12] *Ep.* 48.3 (CSEL 54, 349).

depository of his books at Rome.[13] Like Pammachius, Domnio had been shocked by the contents of the *Adversus Jovinianum*. He had copied out the most offensive passages and sent them to Jerome demanding either an explanation or a retraction.[14] Jerome's lengthy apology to Pammachius in Letter 49 probably was meant to serve as a response to both men, for in it Jerome cited numerous passages from *Adversus Jovinianum* and attempted to interpret them in such a way as to absolve himself of accusations of heresy. In other words, Letter 49 to Pammachius appears to contain Jerome's responses to the offensive passages that had been culled from his writings by Domnio.

According to Jerome's apology, the central objection of his critics was that he had been 'excessive' (*nimius fuerim*) in his praise of virginity and in his depreciation of marriage.[15] On the basis of Jerome's response, it appears that these complaints came from two groups of people. Some, such as Pammachius and Domnio, accepted the superiority of virginity over marriage and rejected Jovinian's teaching, but still believed that Jerome had gone too far in his denunciation of marriage. Others, however, agreed with Jovinian's equation of marriage and celibacy. Jerome seems to be especially disturbed that Jovinian's supporters included some celibate clergy and monks:

If worldly men take offense at the notion that they are on a lower level than virgins, I am amazed that clerics, monks, and continent [married men] do not praise that which they do. They separate themselves from their wives in order to imitate the chastity of virgins, but they wish for married people to be what virgins are. Either they should be joined to their wives, whom they have renounced, or, if they abstain, they will confess (even in their silence) that what they have chosen over marriage is the better thing.[16]

It is not surprising that Jerome would have been concerned about the presence of celibate clergy, monks, and married men among Jovinian's supporters. He had spent much of the *Adversus Jovinianum* satirizing the alleged immorality of Jovinian and his followers. If Jovinian's supporters turned out to be devoted ascetics, this would certainly have undermined a central feature of Jerome's argument.

Moreover, Jerome's comments in Letter 49 suggest that some of his critics may have accused him of 'Manichaeism' because of his excessively pessimistic

---

[13] For Domnio's role in the circulation of Jerome's writings at Rome, see *ep.* 47.3 (CSEL 54, 346) and *ep.* 48.4 (CSEL 54, 349). In the latter Jerome referred to Domnio as *sancto patri*, which suggests that he may have been a clergyman; *pace* Duval, *L'affaire Jovinien*, 249, who refers to Domnio as 'qui n'était ni clerc ni moine'.

[14] *Ep.* 50.3 (CSEL 54, 391): 'excerpta de volumine per ordinem digressisti poscens, ut vel emendarem vel exponerem'.

[15] *Ep.* 49.2 (CSEL 54, 351).   [16] *Ep.* 49.2 (CSEL 54, 352).

evaluation of marriage. At one place, for example, he complained: 'While I fight on one side, I am wounded on the other; and, to speak more directly, while I enter into hand-to-hand combat with Jovinian, I am stabbed in the back by Manichaeus.'[17] In his defence Jerome cited a passage from the preface of *Adversus Jovinianum* in which he had explicitly repudiated the teaching of Marcion, Manichaeus, Tatian, and the Encratites. It is evident from the character of Jerome's defence that his two books *Adversus Jovinianum* were regarded by some readers as a heretical condemnation of marriage. Hence his apology to Pammachius included repeated assertions that he nowhere condemned marriage, although he valued celibacy more highly.[18] The charge of 'Manichaeism', which may have first been adumbrated by Jovinian himself, remained a live issue; it was later to be revived by Rufinus, though in a different context and for a different motive.

How legitimate were these complaints about Jerome's *Adversus Jovinianum*? In other words, how close did he come to condemning marriage? The question is difficult to answer directly because Jerome offered different evaluations of marriage in his treatise, and he was not always consistent. In fact, Jerome stated that he had been charged with presenting 'contrary opinions' (*diversas sententias*), and he indirectly acknowledged the validity of the charge when he said to Pammachius that his critics should interpret 'those statements that seemed to be harsh' (*ea, quae videbantur dura*) in the light of his more positive statements.[19] Moreover, Jerome also attempted to excuse his inconsistencies and exaggerations by appealing to the rhetorical character of the *Adversus Jovinianum*. He claimed that the work had been written 'γυμναστικῶς' rather than 'δογματικῶς', that is, with the aim of vanquishing his opponent, not instructing his readers. Jerome stated that he had presented any arguments that would help him to win his case, whether or not he actually believed them. In his defence he cited the example of previous Christian polemicists, who (he claimed) 'sometimes are forced to say, not what they think, but what is necessary'. Jerome even suggested that the apostle Paul had done something similar when he cited passages from the Old Testament taken out of context.[20]

Even allowing for rhetorical exaggeration and dissimulation, it is clear that Jerome had uttered certain statements in *Adversus Jovinianum* that exposed

---

[17] Ibid.
[18] See also the close of *ep.* 50.5 (CSEL 54, 394), where Jerome insisted, 'non damno nuptias, non damno coniugium.'
[19] *Ep.* 49.12 (CSEL 54, 367). The charge of inconsistency in *Adversus Jovinianum* was also pressed against Jerome by Rufinus when he criticized the extreme positions that Jerome had taken. See *Apol* 2.43 (CCSL 20, 116).
[20] *Ep.* 49.13 (CSEL 54, 369).

him to legitimate suspicions of heresy. For example, although in one place Jerome could imply that marriage was something 'good',[21] for the most part he portrayed marriage merely as a lesser evil than fornication, something that was permitted only to avoid a worse evil. Commenting on the words of 1 Corinthians 7: 1 ('It is good for a man not to touch a woman'), Jerome had stated: 'If it is good not to touch a woman, it is bad (*malum*) to touch one, for there is no opposite of goodness but badness. But if it is bad and the evil is pardoned, the reason for the concession is to prevent worse evil.'[22] Since Paul allowed marriage only because fornication was worse, Jerome argued, marriage is, in some sense, not truly in accord with the apostle's will.[23]

Similarly, when Jerome came to interpret Paul's dictum that 'it is better to marry than to burn' (1 Cor 7: 9), he noted that by comparing marriage with burning Paul had implied that marriage was not actually good:

The reason why it is better to marry is because it is worse to burn. Take away the fire of lust, and he will not say, 'it is better to marry'.... If marriage is good in itself, do not compare it with fire, but simply say 'it is good to marry'. I am suspicious of the 'good' of that thing which the greatness of another evil compels to be the lesser evil. What I want is not a lesser evil (*levius malum*), but a good that is simply good in itself.[24]

It has long been recognized that Jerome drew these interpretations of Paul directly from the Montanist writings of Tertullian.[25] By relying so closely on a writer whose orthodoxy was questionable and by speaking of marriage as merely a 'lesser evil' than fornication, rather than a positive good in itself, Jerome had exposed himself to accusations of condemning marriage.

Nor were these the only instances of Jerome's hostility to marriage in the *Adversus Jovinianum*. On the subject of second marriages, Jerome allowed that such unions were permissible, but he characterized the remarried woman as a prostitute. Remarriage was allowed, he argued, but only because 'it is more tolerable for a woman to prostitute herself to one man than to many.'[26] Noting that a twice-married widow was not permitted to be enrolled in the order of widows, Jerome suggested that perhaps such a woman was unworthy

---

[21] *Jov.* 1.13 (PL 23, 243): 'Tantum est igitur inter nuptias et virginitatem, quantum inter non peccare, et bene facere; imo, ut levius dicam, quantum inter bonum et melius.'
[22] *Jov.* 1.7 (PL 23, 229).
[23] *Jov.* 1.8 (PL 23, 231): 'In voluntate promeremur, in venia abutimur.'
[24] *Jov.* 1.9 (PL 23, 233).
[25] F. Schultzen, 'Die Benützung der Schriften Tertullians De monogamia und De ieiunio bei Hieronymus', *Neue Bücher für Deutsche Theologie*, 3 (1894), 485–502. Duval, *L'affaire Jovinien*, 112–207, has now provided an exhaustive account of the sources of the *Adversus Jovinianum*, especially Jerome's use of Tertullian and Origen.
[26] *Jov.* 1.14 (PL 23, 244): 'tolerabilius est uni homini prostitutam esse, quam multis.'

Marriage and Celibacy in Western Theology 249

to receive the eucharist as well.[27] Such an opinion should not be too surprising, for in *Adversus Jovinianum* Jerome maintained that 'in view of the purity of the body of Christ, all sexual intercourse is unclean'.[28] According to Jerome's interpretation, 1 Corinthians 7: 5, where Paul recommended temporary sexual abstinence for the sake of prayer, applied also to reception of the eucharist.[29] Perhaps the clearest example of Jerome's deep antipathy to sex and marriage can be seen in his comment on the contrast between the (virginal) apostle John and the (married) apostle Peter. According to the Gospel of John, it was prophesied that Peter was to be a martyr (cf. Jn 21: 18–19), whereas it was rumoured that John would not die (cf. Jn 21: 22–3). For Jerome, this passage signified that 'virginity does not die, and the defilement of marriage (*sordes nuptiarum*) is not washed away by the blood of martyrdom'.[30]

Jerome's abusive rhetoric had got him into trouble before. This time, however, even supporters of the ascetic and monastic lives were disturbed by his teachings. In his Letter 50 to Domnio, Jerome spoke at length about a specific monk at Rome who was attacking both Jovinian and Jerome. Domnio had informed him that the young monk—someone whom Jerome had known personally during his previous stay in Rome—had engaged in public disputation with Jovinian.[31] According to Domnio, the monk was a former lawyer who had vanquished Jovinian in debate, but who had also severely criticized Jerome's writings for their denunciation of marriage. The identity of this monk has long been a matter of speculation. In 1943 Georges de Plinval suggested that the unnamed monk was none other than the heresiarch Pelagius, who was to give rise twenty years later to the 'Pelagian' heresy.[32] Robert F. Evans considerably strengthened the case of Plinval, and it has been accepted by numerous scholars.[33] In 1980, however, Yves-Marie Duval

---

[27] Ibid.
[28] *Jov.* 1.20 (PL 23, 249): 'quod ad munditias corporis Christi, omnis coitus immunda sit.'
[29] *Jov.* 1.7 (PL 23, 230): 'Oro te, quale illum bonum est, quod orare prohibet? quod corpus Christi accipere non permittit?'
[30] *Jov.* 1.26 (PL 23, 258): 'Ex quo ostenditur virginitatem non mori, nec sordes nuptiarum abluere cruore martyrii.' This passage was later cited by Rufinus as an example of Jerome's excess.
[31] *Ep.* 50.4.
[32] *Pélage: Ses écrits, sa vie et sa réforme. Étude d'histoire littéraire et religieuse* (Lausanne: Librairie Payot, 1943), 47–55.
[33] *Pelagius: Inquiries and Reappraisals* (New York: Seabury, 1968), 26–42. Accepting this identification: Kelly, *Jerome*, 187–8; Otto Wermelinger, *Rom und Pelagius: Die theologische Position der römischen Bischöfe im pelagianischen Streit in den Jahren 411–432* (Stuttgart: A. Hiersemann, 1975), 46; B. R. Rees, *Pelagius: A Reluctant Heretic* (Woodbridge and Rochester, NY: The Boydell Press. 1988), 4–5.

published a lengthy article challenging this identification.³⁴ The question of the identity of the unnamed monk need not detain us here. For now it is enough to note that the criticisms issued by Pammachius, Domnio, and the unnamed monk reflect sentiments that seem to have been widespread in the church at Rome in the mid-390s. While Jovinian's refusal to grant that virgins were superior to married people may have been regarded as 'heresy', Jerome's excessive hostility to marriage was considered equally problematic. The need for a more balanced discussion of marriage and celibacy, therefore, remained high on the agenda of Western Christian theology.

ii. The *Consultationes Zacchaei et Apollonii*

One document that responded to this need was the little-known Latin dialogue, *Consultationes Zacchaei et Apollonii*. This apologetic treatise, as we saw in Chapter 2, contained several descriptions of the monastic life, as well as responses to Christian criticisms of monks. In the course of his discussion of the ascetic life, the anonymous author of the *Consultationes* also attended to the question of marriage and its relation to the ideal of celibacy. The date and provenance of the *Consultationes* have been a matter of debate.³⁵ Most recently M. A. Claussen has provided very persuasive reasons for locating the text in Rome or Italy in the immediate aftermath of Jovinian's condemnation, that is, in c.394.³⁶ Building on the work of Jean-Louis Feiertag, Claussen argued that the author of the *Consultationes* sought deliberately to correct the excesses of Jerome's *Adversus Jovinianum* and to present a more moderate view of marriage, one that would unite Christians at Rome during the pagan revivals of the early 390s. As Claussen has written:

> The form of ascetic Christianity advocated by people like Jerome, Ambrose and Cassian was—its attraction to Paula, the Melanias and others notwithstanding—simply too extreme to appeal to most Romans. Our author quite clearly presents other options. His Christianity is not divided between the saved ascetics and a

---

³⁴ 'Pélage est-il le censeur inconnu de l'*Adversus Iovinianum* à Rome en 393? Ou: du "portrait-robot" de l'hérétique chez s. Jérôme', *RHE* 75 (1980), 525–57. Duval returned to the question in 'Pélage en son temps: Données chronologiques nouvelles pour une présentation nouvelle', *StPatr* 38 (2001), 95–118, esp. 105–13.

³⁵ P. Courcelle, 'Date, source et genèse des "Consultationes Zacchaei et Apollonii"', *RHR* 146 (1954), 174–93, argued that the text should be placed in North Africa immediately after the sack of Rome in 410. Jean-Louis Feiertag placed it in Italy or Gaul shortly after 410: *Les Consultationes Zacchaei et Apollonii: Étude d'histoire et de sotériologie* (Fribourg: Éditions Universitaires, 1990), 143–5; also SC 401, 16–31.

³⁶ 'Pagan Rebellion and Christian Apologetics in Fourth-Century Rome: The *Consultationes Zacchaei et Apollonii*', *JEH* 46 (1995), 589–614.

damned remainder. Rather, he presents a whole series of possible Christian *conversationes*, from that of the honest householder who believes, fears, and loves God, to the way of the *solus* living in the desert battling demons, all of which ensure salvation. Although he himself clearly favours the ascetic *via*, he allows Christians marriage, wealth, land, possessions, children, status and all the other necessary accoutrements of Roman life. He seeks, in other words, to moderate the way Christianity is portrayed, and thus to broaden its appeal.[37]

Claussen's argument is surely correct. There are numerous places in the *Consultationes* where the anonymous author provided clear alternatives to Jerome's interpretation of the value of marriage and celibacy. While Claussen presented his case briefly and Feiertag stated his tentatively, I would like to provide a more detailed argument for seeing the author of the *Consultationes* in direct conflict with Jerome.[38]

Immediately after discussing the problem of wealth and arguing that the possession of wealth was not in itself sinful,[39] the author of the *Consultationes* turned to the issue of marriage and wrote:

But honorable marriages do not displease God, nor does a moderate love of the dignified marriage bed (*sollemnis tori modesta dilectio*) when used for the procreation of children. As scripture says, 'For this reason a man will leave his father and mother and will cleave to his wife, and the two will become one flesh' (Gen 2: 24); and again, 'What God has joined, man should not separate' (Mt 19: 6). That is why clothing should be dedicated to neatness, not to luxury. And, according to the apostle, all food that is sold in the marketplace is without fault (cf. 1 Cor 10: 25) because, as the same apostle says, 'But the kingdom of God is not food and drink, but righteousness and peace in the Holy Spirit' (Rom 14: 17). It is the excessive use (*nimietas usus*) of the two things that is dangerous, as the Lord warns, 'Be on your guard so that your hearts are not weighed down with wine and drunkenness' (Lk 21: 34).[40]

For the author of the *Consultationes*, a life of dramatic ascetic renunciation was not required of all Christians. For the 'average' (*mediocres*) it was sufficient to observe the precepts of moderation and sobriety. They, too, would receive the promise of eternal life, even if they failed to achieve the highest status.

---

[37] Claussen, 'Pagan Rebellion', 614.
[38] Cf. Feiertag, *Consultationes*, 106: 'Il faudra voir ici, sinon une volonté de "corriger" la position de Jérôme, du moins une insertion de l'auteur anonyme dans les discussions qui agitaient les milieux ascétiques italiens, romains et milanais en particulier, autour des theses de Jovinien à la fin du 4e s.'
[39] According to *Zacch*. 3.1.12, the harsh sayings of Jesus directed against the wealthy, e.g. Luke 6: 24 and Luke 18: 24, condemned only an excessive desire for wealth and the accumulation of wealth unjustly.
[40] *Zacch*. 3.1.13 (SC 402, 168–70).

The author of the *Consultationes* has directly engaged one of the central issues debated by Jovinian and Jerome: do forms of ascetic behaviour, such as celibacy, gain for the Christian a greater reward in heaven? In opposition to Jovinian, the anonymous author did not hesitate to answer in the affirmative, but his tone and approach also differed dramatically from that of Jerome. Rather than engage in polemic against the married state, our author emphasized that even the lowliest Christians will be saved: 'for if the loftiest splendour does not lift them up to the brightest stars of the future kingdom, nevertheless their sins will not completely overwhelm those who are the least.'[41] This, he argued, is the meaning of the apostle's dictum, 'All those who believe in me will not be put to shame' (Rom 9: 33; 10: 11).

Moreover it should be noted that the author of the *Consultationes* has interpreted this saying from Romans in a manner that would have been entirely acceptable to Jovinian, namely by emphasizing the ultimate saving power of faith and baptismal regeneration. Commenting on the Pauline texts just cited, our author observed: 'This means that no power will separate them from Christ once a pure faith has joined them to him, and those who reject actions that are difficult or impossible because of the labour involved, or who fear to undertake them because they are great and arduous, will be saved by the integrity of the saving sign.'[42]

In the *Consultationes Zacchaei et Apollonii* we find the author attempting to strike a delicate balance between Jovinian and Jerome. While accepting the view of Jerome on the superiority of celibacy over marriage, our author echoed the teaching of Jovinian on the ultimate saving power of faith and baptism. Like Augustine in the next decade, the author of the *Consultationes* appears to have been intent on defending the acceptability of 'Christian mediocrity', even as he supported asceticism.[43]

Several chapters later the author of the *Consultationes* addressed the question again from the point of view of the scriptural grounds of the preference for celibacy. After accepting the argument of Zacchaeus that sexual continence and renunciation of the world merited a greater reward in heaven, Apollonius asked his mentor to provide him with 'a clear command (*praeceptum*) of continence and virginity in the same authorities of the scripture'.[44] Specifically, he wondered, why does scripture contain the command to procreate, and yet elsewhere suggests that marriage will produce labour without fruit

---

[41] *Zacch.* 3.1.16 (SC 402, 170): 'si inter illa futura regni clarissima sidera splendor eximius non attollit, exiguous delicta non opprimant.'

[42] *Zacch.* 3.1.17 (SC 402, 172).

[43] I borrow the expression from R. A. Markus, *End of Ancient Christianity*, 45–62, who used it to describe Augustine's response to the debate between Jovinian and Jerome.

[44] *Zacch.* 3.5.2 (SC 402, 194).

(cf. Gen 3: 17–18)?[45] The answer of Zacchaeus, expressing the opinion of the author of the *Consultationes*, articulated a careful and nuanced response to the primary issue between Jovinian and Jerome. Once again, his approach to marriage and celibacy differed significantly from the harsh rhetoric of the *Adversus Jovinianum*.

Zacchaeus' first argument involved a discussion of the Genesis creation stories. Like Jovinian, the author of the *Consultationes* stressed that the marital relationship and procreation originated in a divine command that was given 'from the beginning' (*a principio*):

> From the beginning it was said to Adam, 'It is not good that the man should be alone' (Gen 2: 18); soon thereafter the decree of procreation followed, 'Increase and multiply, and fill the earth' (Gen 1: 28). But the woman, who was created for him and from him, was a solace to him before she was a wife, up until the time when their disobedience made them exiles from paradise, whereas their obedience had kept them within paradise. After their departure from this blessed state, the man who had been expelled knew his wife, as the book of Genesis teaches, 'And Adam knew his wife Eve, and she conceived and bore a son' (Gen 4: 1). Therefore, their marriage (*nuptiae*) occurred prior to the labour that was imposed on them, and they entered into union (*conventus*) before they experienced the thorns and thistles. Then followed the difficult conditions (*taedia*) of procreation, and another decree preceded the woman's giving birth: 'In pain and grief you will bear children' (Gen 3: 16). The children, as we have seen, once they were created, suffered all sorts of troubles and sorrows. That is why the apostle proclaimed: 'They will experience trials in the flesh' (1 Cor 7: 28).[46]

The author of the *Consultationes* has staked out a careful position on an issue that frequently appeared in early Christian discussions of marriage. Indeed, it is the question that regularly surfaced in anti-encratite polemics: should human sexual relations be considered strictly a post-lapsarian phenomenon, inevitably tainted by connection with the 'original' sin? Jerome, as we have seen, was fond of citing Gen 4: 1 to make the point that Adam and Eve did not engage in sexual relations until after they had been expelled from paradise.[47] He stated this position emphatically in *Adversus Jovinianum*: 'Regarding Adam and Eve, it must be said that before the offense they were virgins in paradise, but after their sin and as soon as they left paradise, their marriage

---

[45] *Zacch.* 3.5.3 (SC 402, 194). Apollonius appears to allude to Gen 2: 24 and Matt 19: 6, cited previously by Zacchaeus in *Zacch.* 3.1.13.

[46] *Zacch.* 3.5.4–6 (SC 402, 196). Contrast with Jerome, *ep.* 22.19.1–3 (CSEL 54, 168), who cites several of the same biblical texts used in the *Zacch.* 3.5.4–9 (SC 402, 196–8): Gen 1: 28, Eccl 3: 5, and Zach 9: 16.

[47] *Ep.* 22.19 (CSEL 54, 169). See above, pp. 165–6.

began.'[48] For Jerome, sex and procreation were irrevocably associated with sin and punishment.

By contrast, the author of the *Consultationes*, while acknowledging that Genesis 4: 1 stated that the first children of Adam and Eve were born after the fall and therefore were liable to the punishments of sin, was careful to point out that the marriage of Adam and Eve had begun prior to the fall. Moreover, by citing the verses of Genesis 2: 18 and 1: 28, he emphasized the essential and original goodness of marriage and sexual union, despite the negative effects of the first sin. Although our author mentioned the pain of labour imposed in childbirth (cf. Gen 3: 16), he insisted that sex and marriage remained untainted by sin. Immediately following the passage just cited we read: 'Nevertheless, the beds of married people are not without honour, nor is the immaculate couch without fruit (cf. Heb 13: 4): do they not produce saints as their offspring?'[49]

In addition to stressing the original grounding of marriage and procreation in the divine decree, the author of the *Consultationes* took another position that differed dramatically from that of Jerome. Rather than contrast 'chastity' (*castitas*) with 'marriage' (*nuptiae*) to the detriment of the latter, as did Jerome,[50] the *Consultationes* held that chastity itself is found in marriage, as well as in sexual continence and virginity:

And that which is praised in virginity belongs to marriage, although continence has a higher reward and virginity is more exalted. The former cannot fear being something less, nor should the latter show contempt because it is greater. But, according to a catholic interpretation, honourable marriages receive their distinctive praises of chastity, those who are abstinent acquire the merit of continence, and the reward of virginity is bestowed on those who remain untouched. This is not to condemn what is good, but to encourage what is better.[51]

In contrast to Jovinian, the author of the *Consultationes* clearly maintained a threefold hierarchy of rewards in heaven: virginity, sexual continence, and marital chastity, each receiving a distinct, and successively lower, reward. But, unlike Jerome, our anonymous author held that married people were also capable of 'chastity' (*castitas*) and that their marital lives were genuinely good.[52]

---

[48] *Jov.* 1.16 (PL 23, 246).

[49] *Zacch.* 3.5.6 (SC 402, 196). Feiertag, *Consultationes*, 242, sees here an echo and modification of Jerome, *Jov.* 1.27, where Jerome held that women will be saved by bearing children, only if the children remain virgins (cf. 1 Tim 2: 15).

[50] See *Jov.* 1.16 (PL 23, 245–6): 'non quoque debemus...docere castitatem semper operi nuptiarum fuisse praelatam'. I am dependent for this point on Feiertag, *Consultationes*, 243–4.

[51] *Zacch.* 3.5.6–8 (SC 402, 196–8).

[52] The question whether the word 'chastity' (*castitas*) should be applied to sexual relations within marriage was explicitly treated (and answered negatively) in the Pelagian treatise *De castitate* 2.1–2 (PLS 1, 1465–6). This radical Pelagian author considered any sexual expression to be devoid of 'chastity'.

There is another point of contrast to be noted between the *Consultationes Zacchaei et Apollonii* and the *Adversus Jovinianum*, one that shows the author of the *Consultationes* directly contradicting Jerome. Immediately following the passage just cited, the author of the *Consultationes* began to discuss several of the classic biblical passages that Jerome had used to exalt celibacy: Matthew 19: 12, with its praise of eunuchs 'who have made themselves eunuchs for the sake of the kingdom of heaven'; Isaiah 56: 5, which promised to eunuchs a reward better than that bestowed on the sons and daughters; 1 Corinthians 7: 26, which stated that it is good 'on account of the pressing necessity' (*propter instantem necessitatem*) for a man to remain as he is; and Revelation 14: 4, which describes those who follow the Lamb wherever he goes as virgins, 'who have not defiled themselves with women'.[53] Commenting on this assortment of ascetic 'proof-texts' our author concluded:

Therefore, it is reasonable to prefer the better things, but those which are lower (*humiliora*) are not bad. Nor does it signify that there is any defect (*delictum*) in marriage, but as you recognized a little while ago, continence is advised on account of the necessity of the imminent end (*propter instantis finis necessitatem*), lest according to the gospel there be 'woe to those who are pregnant and nursing' (Mt 24: 19).[54]

Characteristically, the author of the *Consultationes* acknowledged the preference for asceticism that could be read in the texts, but chose to emphasize that a recommendation of celibacy did not entail a condemnation of marriage.

A rather different approach was taken by Jerome in *Adversus Jovinianum*. Commenting on the very same dossier of ascetic texts—including the pericope from Matthew 19, Isaiah 56: 5, 1 Corinthians 7: 26, and Matthew 24: 19—Jerome had offered a rather different reading of the biblical evidence:

What is this 'necessity' that seeks the freedom of virginity by spurning the conjugal bond? 'Woe to those who are pregnant and nursing on that day' (Mt 24: 19). We do not have here a condemnation of harlots or brothels, about whose damnation there is no doubt. What is condemned is the swelling womb, the wailing infant, and the fruits and works of marriage! 'Since it is good for a man to be as he is' (1 Cor 7: 26). If it is good for a man to remain as he is, it is bad for a man not to remain as he is![55]

Given the parallel collection of biblical citations, there can be no doubt that the author of the *Consultationes* had before him Jerome's *Adversus Jovinianum*. Therefore, our anonymous author's emphasis on marriage as a genuine *bonum* and his claim that there is no 'defect' (*delictum*) in marriage must have

---

[53] *Zacch.* 3.5.10–13 (SC 402, 198–200). Cf. Jerome, *Jov.* 1.12 (PL 23, 239).
[54] *Zacch.*3.5.14 (SC 402, 200).   [55] *Jov.* 1.12 (PL 23, 239).

been a direct response to Jerome's description of marriage as a *malum* and 'the fruits and works of marriage' as worthy of condemnation.

In sum, the *Consultationes Zacchaei et Apollonii* articulated the same type of concerns expressed by the original critics of Jerome's *Adversus Jovinianum*, that is, by Pammachius, Domnio, and the anonymous monk at Rome. While clearly stating his opposition to the positions held by Jovinian, the author of the *Consultationes* deliberately distanced himself from the excesses of Jerome. Acknowledging the superiority of celibacy and the existence of a hierarchy of ascetic merits, the anonymous author also emphasized the goodness of marriage and the reality of salvation for all ranks of Christians, including the *mediocres*. It is evident, then, that the condemnation of Jovinian in 393 did not by any means signal a general approval of Jerome's teaching. Although in his apologetic Letter 49 Jerome had claimed that one had to stand either with Jovinian or with himself, the reality was rather different.[56] As the evidence of the *Consultationes* indicates, it was quite possible to stand neither with Jovinian nor with Jerome. In the following sections of this chapter, we shall see that there were at least two other Western theologians—Pelagius and Augustine—who chose to take this middle path between Jerome and Jovinian.

2. FRIENDS AND ENEMIES OF JEROME

i. Rufinus, Sulpicius, and Vigilantius

The reception of the *Adversus Jovinianum* was to remain a troubling issue for Jerome over the next two decades. Initially, however, he may have experienced some respite. In his apology to Pammachius, Jerome did not explicitly retract any statements of the *Adversus Jovinianum*, but he did emphasize the more 'orthodox' aspects of his treatise and acknowledged its rhetorical excesses. Moreover, it was probably to Jerome's benefit that another controversy followed closely on the heels of the condemnation of Jovinian, thus diverting attention, at least initially, away from the scandal of the *Adversus Jovinianum*. In the same year that Jerome composed his apologetic letter to Pammachius (394), Bishop Epiphanius of Salamis sent a letter to Bishop John of Jerusalem attacking the teachings of Origen.[57] Thus began the 'Origenist Controversy',

---

[56] Cf. *ep.* 49.2 (CSEL 54, 351): 'aut mea sententia sequenda est aut Ioviniani.'

[57] Epiphanius' letter was translated in Jerome, *ep.* 51. See Clark, *Origenist Controversy*, 94–104, who plausibly suggests that the debate between Jerome and Jovinian may have influenced Epiphanius' attack on Origen in 394. In his letter to John of Jerusalem, Epiphanius had argued that Origen's theory of the pre-existence of souls impugned the value of sex and marriage: Jerome, *ep.* 51.4 (CSEL 54, 402–3).

and, for the moment, Jerome was spared further defence of his treatise. In letters to Furia and Paulinus of Nola, written in 394–5, Jerome could recommend the reading of his *Adversus Jovinianum* without any apparent embarrassment.[58]

By the early years of the fifth century, however, Jerome's treatise was again subjected to public recrimination at Rome. Rufinus of Aquileia, a long-time friend of Jerome and prominent ascetic teacher, had fallen out with him over the question of Origen's writings. In 397 Rufinus had returned to Italy from his monastery in Palestine, eventually settling at Aquileia in 399. Rufinus' decision to translate Origen's *De principiis* in 398 provoked further conflict with Jerome, and the two men then exchanged a series of polemical tracts. In his *Apology against Jerome*, issued circa 400, Rufinus again raised for public scrutiny the issue of Jerome's attack on marriage in the *Adversus Jovinianum*.[59] Rufinus observed that Jerome's books against Jovinian 'had been read by a great many people, and almost everyone was offended by them'.[60] He noted that Jerome was widely considered to have fallen prey to 'the most foul lust of detraction' (*foedissimam obtrectandi libidinem*). Rufinus also asserted that some of Jerome's comments in *Adversus Jovinianum* had amounted to the 'dogma of the Manichaeans', and he pointed to Jerome's statement about the 'defilement' (*sordes*) of marriage and the blood of martyrdom as a prime example. Rufinus' references to Jerome show that the issue of Jerome's 'condemnation' of marriage did not die in the mid-390s. Although Rufinus raised the issue largely with the aim of discrediting Jerome personally, his comments indicate that the *Adversus Jovinianum* was still a target for derision in the early fifth-century West.

The same impression is given by Sulpicius Severus in his discussion of Jerome in the *Dialogues*, composed in Gaul shortly after Rufinus' apology (403–4).[61] Sulpicius shared Jerome's enthusiasm for asceticism, and, especially, Jerome's antagonism towards a lax clergy. Although Sulpicius regretted Jerome's wholesale repudiation of the writings of Origen, he inserted into his *Dialogues* the following defence of Jerome as a 'man most catholic and deeply learned in the sacred law':[62]

---

[58] *Ep.* 54.18 to Furia; *ep.* 58.6 to Paulinus.

[59] For the dates I have followed C. P. Hammond, 'The Last Ten Years of Rufinus' Life and the Date of his Move South from Aquileia', *JTS*, n.s. 27 (1977), 372–427.

[60] *Apol.* 2.42 (CCSL 20, 116): 'iam a plurimis legerentur et offenderentur pene omnes.' Rufinus made the same point in *Apol.* 2.48 (CCSL 20, 120).

[61] For the dates, see Clare Stancliffe, *St. Martin and His Hagiographer: History and Miracle in Sulpicius Severus* (Oxford: Clarendon Press, 1983), 71–85.

[62] *Dial.* 1.7 (CSEL 1, 159): 'vir maxime catholicus et sacrae legis peritissimus.' Sulpicius also defended Origen by claiming that he had been guilty of *error*, but not of *haeresis*.

The heretics hate him because he does not cease to attack them; the clerics hate him because he assails their life and crimes. But it is plain that all good men admire him and love him, whereas those who regard him as a heretic are crazy. To speak truly, the man's knowledge is catholic, his teaching sound. He is always reading, always in his books. Day and night he does not rest; he is always either reading or writing something.[63]

Sulpicius' defence of Jerome is illuminating because it shows that Jerome was a controversial figure in early fifth-century Gaul, and even regarded by some as a 'heretic'. One of the characters in Sulpicius' dialogue, named appropriately the 'Gaul' (*Gallus*), at the mention of Jerome's name referred to Jerome's abusive treatment of monks in 'a certain book of his'. This allusion to Jerome's Letter 22 reflects the discomfort that even some ascetics felt about Jerome's polemical style. The very fact that Sulpicius found it necessary to defend Jerome is an index of the degree to which some clergy in Gaul had taken offence at the monk of Bethlehem.[64]

Another reminder of Jerome's hostility to marriage would have emerged in his conflict with Vigilantius, which spanned the years 395–406. Vigilantius was a priest from Gaul who served as a letter carrier for Paulinus of Nola. He is an interesting figure because he had personal contact with Jerome, Paulinus of Nola, Sulpicius, and probably Rufinus as well. In 395 Vigilantius visited Jerome in Bethlehem, where, it appears, he earned Jerome's enmity by raising the embarrassing question of his reliance on the writings of Origen.[65] On this trip he probably also spent some time with Rufinus and Melania at their monasteries on the Mount of Olives, and it is possible (as Jerome himself later suggested) that Rufinus might have turned Vigilantius' opinions against him.[66] When Vigilantius returned to Italy, he continued to spread rumours of Jerome's sympathy for Origen, to which Jerome replied in Letter 61 (396). In the summer of 396 Paulinus sent Vigilantius to Sulpicius with a letter (*ep.* 5), and we then lose sight of him for eight years. When Vigilantius reappeared

---

[63] *Dial.* 1.9 (CSEL 1, 161). In *Dial.* 1.21 Sulpicius again mentioned Jerome's attacks on the clergy.

[64] On the controversies with Jerome as background to Sulpicius' *Dialogues*, see Stancliffe, *St. Martin*, 297–312.

[65] Jerome, *ep.* 61.3 (CSEL 54, 580).

[66] See Jerome, *Ruf.* 3.19 (SC 303, 264–6), and discussion in Clark, *Origenist Controversy*, 36. For Vigilantius' visit to Rufinus, see P. Nautin, 'Études de chronologie hiéronymienne (393–397). III: Les premières relations entre Jérôme et Paulin de Nole', *REAug* 19 (1973), 231–3. Nautin argued persuasively that since Vigilantius had carried a letter from Paulinus to Jerome in Bethlehem, he probably also had conveyed one to Melania in Jerusalem, since she was a relative of Paulinus.

in Gaul in the year 404, he had become an outspoken critic of the cult of relics and a proponent of a married clergy.[67]

Jerome's letters and his polemical *Contra Vigilantium* are our primary sources for the teaching and activity of Vigilantius. It is difficult to tell from Jerome's account how many of Jovinian's opinions Vigilantius may have shared. In *Contra Vigilantium* Jerome stated that 'in Vigilantius the depraved mind of Jovinian has arisen,' but Jerome may simply be employing the traditional anti-heretical device of associating one known 'heretic' with another.[68] But regardless of Vigilantius' connection with Jovinian, the appearance of Jerome's attack on Vigilantius in 406 would have been a reminder to Western Christians, especially in Gaul, of Jerome's previous excursions on marriage and celibacy. *Contra Vigilantium* was one of Jerome's most distasteful productions. In this work, as J. N. D. Kelly has noted, Jerome 'surpassed himself ... in sheer coarseness and personal insinuation.'[69] Like the observations of Rufinus and Sulpicius, Jerome's conflict with Vigilantius would have recalled to Western readers the unhappy memory of the *Adversus Jovinianum*.

ii. Pelagius and the 'Pelagian' Tradition

The comments of Rufinus and Sulpicius, together with the polemics of Vigilantius, provide a helpful backdrop to the writings of Pelagius. They show that the issues raised by Jovinian were still very much alive at Rome in the early fifth century and that Jerome's *Adversus Jovinianum* was still considered problematic. Pelagius had resided at Rome since at least 390 and had moved in some of the same circles as had Jerome.[70] He must have been familiar with both the condemnation of Jovinian and the controversy surrounding the *Adversus Jovinianum*. Pelagius composed his Commentary on the Pauline Epistles and most of his ascetical treatises between the years 405 and 410, and in the former work he referred to Jovinian by name on four occasions. Moreover, Pelagius was a friend of Paulinus of Nola and probably

---

[67] Jerome, *ep.* 109 to Riparius of 404, spoke only about the critique of relics, but Vigilantius' opposition to clerical celibacy was discussed in the *Contra Vigilantium* of 406. On the circumstances affecting the development of Vigilantius' polemic, see Hunter, 'Vigilantius', 410–29.

[68] *Vigil.* 1 (PL 23.355): 'in isto Ioviniani mens prava surrexit'.

[69] *Jerome*, 289. Cf. H. Crouzel, 'Chronologie proposée de prêtre commingeois Vigilance de Calagurris (Saint-Martory)', *BLE* 73 (1972), 265, who refers to the work as 'une des plus violentes polémiques du moine de Bethléhem'.

[70] Much of what we know of Pelagius' biography is summarized in Yves-Marie Duval, 'Pélage en son temps', cited above n. 34. See also Flavio G. Nuvolone, 'Pélage et Pélagianisme', *DSp* 12 (1986), 2895–902.

knew Rufinus as well. As Peter Brown has observed, Pelagius appears to have gravitated towards the circles that were already hostile to Jerome, that is, 'the friends of Rufinus and the friends of the friends of Rufinus'.[71] The writings of Pelagius, as I will argue here, can plausibly be read as an effort to negotiate a position somewhere between Jovinian and Jerome on the issue of marriage and celibacy.

Pelagius' ascetical teaching can be found primarily in his Commentary on the Pauline Epistles and in several letters of spiritual direction: *Epistula ad Claudiam sororem de virginitate*, *Epistula ad Celantiam*, and *Epistula ad Demetriadem*.[72] In an essay first published nearly forty years ago, Peter Brown offered the following assessment of the relation between Pelagius' ascetical theology and the teaching of Jovinian:

> The heresy of Jovinian shows that a crisis in the associations surrounding baptism was imminent. Jovinian would argue that the sanctity conferred by baptism was sufficient to keep the Christian, thereafter, safe from sin; above all, that this rite fused the Christian community into a single group, in such a way as to make unnecessary the distinction between a 'perfect' ascetic life and a less perfect life of the married laity. Pelagian enthusiasts will merely stand Jovinian's views on their head—by making the ascetic life obligatory for all baptized Christians, in a similar, drastic *reductio ad unum*.[73]

Brown's account provides a helpful starting point for our investigation of Pelagius. At the heart of Pelagius' ascetical vision lay the notion that 'righteousness' (*iustitia*) was required of all Christians, regardless of their marital status. Righteousness was the foundational Christian virtue, and without it salvation was not possible.

For Pelagius, 'righteousness' was defined as 'not to sin', which, in turn, was defined as, 'to keep the commandments of the law', both those commandments which demanded the avoidance of evil acts and those which demanded

---

[71] 'The Patrons of Pelagius: The Roman Aristocracy Between East and West', in his *Religion and Society in the Age of Saint Augustine* (London: Faber and Faber, 1972), 211. There is, however, no conclusive evidence that Pelagius had met Rufinus, although they had mutual friends (e.g. Paulinus of Nola) and Pelagius had read Rufinus' translation of Origen's Commentary on Romans and his translations of the *Sentences of Sextus*. See the discussion in Evans, *Pelagius: Inquiries and Reappraisals*, 18–20.

[72] While considerable uncertainty has surrounded the writings that can be reliably attributed to Pelagius, there is a broad consensus that these four texts are authentic. See Robert F. Evans, *Four Letters of Pelagius* (New York: The Seabury Press, 1968), 13–31; F. G. Nuvolone, 'Pélage', 2898–902; B. R. Rees, *Pelagius: A Reluctant Heretic* (Rochester, NY: The Boydell Press, 1988), 133–4; Eligius Dekkers, *Clavis patrum latinorum*. 3rd edn. (Turnhout: Brepols, 1995), 251–5; and Duval, *L'affaire Jovinien*, 288. For continued doubts on the matter, see Sebastian Thier, *Kirche bei Pelagius* (PTS 50; Berlin and New York: Walter de Gruyter, 1999), 26–30.

[73] 'Pelagius and his Supporters: Aims and Environment', in his *Religion and Society*, 203.

the performance of good acts.[74] Righteousness, he argued, was required of all Christians, whether they were virgin, widowed, or married. As Pelagius put it in his Letter to Celantia: 'And so his twofold and contrary commandment, that is, prohibitive and imperative, has been imposed on all with equal force of law; the virgin, the widow, the wife are not exempt from this law: in any vocation whatever, in any station whatever, it is an equal sin either to commit deeds which are prohibited or to fail to do deeds which are commanded.'[75]

Robert Markus has aptly summarized Pelagius' emphasis on the common requirements of the Christian life incumbent on all the baptized: 'Like Jovinian before him, Pelagius rejected the "double standard" of the ordinary Christian and the ascetic elite. Unlike Jovinian, he sought to close the gap between the two not by rehabilitating "ordinary" Christianity, but by demanding perfection of all, virgin or married, lay or cleric.'[76]

Pelagius' emphasis on the perfection required of all Christians, however, did not lead him to reject altogether the notion of a hierarchy of ascetic practice. He fully embraced the view that virginity, sexual continence (for the widowed or married), and marriage were three distinct modes of life, which merited different rewards in heaven.[77] Addressing himself to a consecrated virgin, for example, Pelagius could speak of the 'peculiar merit' that accrued to those who had received virginal consecration in the Church: 'For while the whole multitude of believers receives similar gifts of grace and all rejoice in the same blessings of the sacraments, those to whom you belong have something peculiar to themselves over and above what the rest possess.'[78] And in what may have been a comment directed against the teaching of Jovinian, Pelagius noted that 'whoever thinks chastity a matter for small reward or none at all is either ignorant of the labour involved or is unwilling to incur it. Hence it is that those men are always belittling chastity who either do not possess it or are forced to possess it against their will.'[79]

---

[74] *Virg.* 6 (CSEL 1, 230–1): 'Iustitia ergo non aliud est quam non peccare, non peccare autem est legis praecepta servare. Praeceptorum autem observatio duplici genere custoditur, ut nihil eorum quae prohibentur facias, et cuncta quae iubentur implere contendas.'

[75] *Cel.* 5 (CSEL 56.1, 333); trans. B. R. Rees, *The Letters of Pelagius and his Followers* (Woodbridge, UK and Rochester, NY: Boydell, 1991), 130. On the common requirements of the Christian life, see also *Virg.* 11.3 (CSEL 1, 241); *Dem.* 10.1 (PL 30, 26), 24.3 (PL 30, 40).

[76] *End of Ancient Christianity*, 41.

[77] *Dem.* 17.2 (PL 30, 33): 'In the kingdom of heaven there are different dwelling-places in accordance with the merits of individuals; for diversity in works makes for diversity of rewards, and a man will shine there in glory as much as he has shone here in holiness'; trans. B. R. Rees, *Letters*, 54.

[78] *Virg.* 1 (CSEL 1, 225); trans. B. R. Rees, *Letters*, 72.

[79] *Virg.* 3 (CSEL 1, 227); trans. B. R. Rees, *Letters*, 73.

Pelagius' support of the ascetic hierarchy resulted in explicit opposition to Jovinian at several points, both in his Pauline commentary and in his Letter to Celantia. In the former work, while commenting on 2 Corinthians 9: 6 ('The one who sows sparingly will also reap sparingly') he observed: 'This passage makes against Jovinian because it shows that there are grades of merits.'[80] Similarly, in his commentary on 1 Corinthians 3: 8 ('Each will receive wages according to the labour of each'), Pelagius succinctly noted: 'Against Jovinian, who supposes that there is one reward for all in the kingdom of God.'[81] Sometime later in his Letter to Celantia, Pelagius summarized Paul's approach to marriage and celibacy as a mean between Jovinian and the Manichees: 'The rule of the apostolic doctrine neither makes works of continence equal to those of marriage with Jovinian nor does it condemn marriage with the Manichaean. So the vessel of election and master of the gentiles follows a moderate, middle path between either extreme, in this way conceding a remedy for incontinence and at the same time encouraging continence to seek its reward.'[82]

There can be no doubt that Pelagius opposed Jovinian's effort to equate the merits of celibates and married Christians. He fully endorsed the notion that sexual continence (and fasting) gained for the Christian a higher reward in heaven. In this regard Pelagius stood on the side of Jerome in the controversy with Jovinian.

Nevertheless, when one takes a closer look at Pelagius' teaching on the function of ascetic practice in the Christian life, it becomes clear that he cannot simply be placed on the 'side' of Jerome in the ascetic debates. Both in the Pauline commentary and in his ascetical letters Pelagius offered a rationale for ascetic behaviour that differed significantly from that of Jerome. For example, one finds in Pelagius no trace of that disparagement of sex that characterized the writings of Jerome. Unlike Jerome, he never spoke of any 'defilement' (*sordes*) attaching to conception or birth. Moreover, because of his own strongly anti-Manichaean assumptions about human nature,

---

[80] *Exp. 2 Cor.* 9: 6 (Souter, 281). I cite Pelagius' Pauline commentary from the edition of Alexander Souter, *Pelagius's Expositions of the Thirteen Epistles of St. Paul. II: Text and Apparatus Criticus* (TaS 9; Cambridge: Cambridge University Press, 1926). Other references to Jovinian in the Pauline commentary are found at *Exp. Phil.* 3: 19 (Souter, 409) and *Exp. 1 Thess.* 2:3 (Souter, 421). The former passage alludes to Jovinian's (alleged) opposition to fasting and the latter to his 'impurity' (*inmunditia*).

[81] *Exp. 1 Cor.* 3: 8 (Souter, 142). Souter, however, placed these words in brackets, indicating that they were omitted from significant manuscripts.

[82] *Cel.* 28.2 (CSEL 56.1, 352); trans. B. R. Rees, *Letters*, 141–2. It is well established that Pelagius' theology was deeply shaped by anti-Manichaean concerns. See Torgny Bohlin, *Die Theologie des Pelagius und ihre Genesis* (Uppsala: A.-B. Lundequistska Bokhandeln/Wiesbaden: Otto Harrassowitz, 1957), 12–45.

Pelagius rejected any attempt to link the sin of Adam with an effect in the human body, such as sexual desire or *concupiscentia*. As Theodore de Bruyn has observed, 'when Pelagius discusses the question of the transmission of sin he is silent about those effects of the fall which are conveyed irrespective of choice from one generation to the next—ignorance, weakness, mortality, concupiscence—and he repudiates any notion of the transmission of guilt.'[83]

Furthermore, because Pelagius had a relatively benign view of sex as a 'natural' phenomenon, he never presented sexual continence as an end in itself, but always as a means to achieve the detachment from worldly affairs that would make it easier to obey the divine commandments. Pelagius articulated this idea with particular clarity in his letter 'On Virginity':

There are three types of virtue through which one gains possession of the heavenly kingdom: the first is purity (*pudicitia*), the second is contempt of the world (*mundi contemptus*), and the third is righteousness (*iustitia*). First of all, then, purity is sought so that contempt of the world may be acquired more easily, since those who are not held in the bonds of marriage can more easily despise the world. But contempt of the world is demanded so that righteousness may be maintained, for those who are embroiled in desires for worldly goods and in the business of mundane pleasures can fulfill the demands of justice only with difficulty.[84]

For Pelagius sexual continence and fasting served a purely instrumental function. The purpose of abstinence from sex or food was to detach a person's desires from worldly goods so that they could be redirected towards the pursuit of virtue. Therefore, ascetical practices were meant to be 'an aid towards sanctity, not the perfect accomplishment of it'.[85] The problem with marriage, as Pelagius saw it, was that the responsibilities of raising children and maintaining a household inevitably involved a person in 'worldly' concerns that made it more difficult to obey all the demands of charity that pertain to the gospel. Since these demands fell equally upon the married and the unmarried, it was expedient, in Pelagius' view, to forgo marriage in favour of virginity.[86]

This understanding of asceticism guided Pelagius' interpretation of the crucial text of 1 Corinthians 7. Both in his Pauline commentary and in his ascetical letters, Pelagius found what he called a 'moderate, middle path' in

---

[83] *Pelagius's Commentary on St Paul's Epistle to the Romans* (OECS; Oxford: Clarendon Press, 1993), 23.
[84] *Virg.* 5 (CSEL 1, 229–30).
[85] *Cel.* 22 (CSEL 56.1, 347): 'haec enim virtus adiumentum est, non perfectio sanctitatis.'
[86] *Virg.* 11.3. The 'instrumental' character of virginity and continence in Pelagius' teaching is clearly recognized by Carlo Tibiletti, 'Teologia pelagiana sul celibato/matrimonio', *Aug* 27 (1987), 488–9.

the teaching of the apostle.[87] To be sure, Pelagius saw marriage as a 'remedy' (*remedium*) conceded by the apostle to those too weak to undertake the higher path of sexual continence. The medicinal metaphor underlined the character of incontinence as a disease that required the curative skill of an experienced spiritual physician like Paul.[88] Pelagius could also echo the teaching of Origen (apparently via Jerome) in stressing the role of sexual abstinence in facilitating prayer. In his comments on 1 Corinthians 7: 5, for example, Pelagius (like Jerome) cited Exodus 19: 15, where Moses required three days of abstinence prior to the revelation on Mount Sinai, together with 1 Samuel 21: 4–5, where the priest Ahimelech allowed David and his men to eat the holy bread only because they had been sexually abstinent for three days.[89] Pelagius, like Origen and Jerome, connected these texts to the reception of the eucharist by married persons, to whom Paul had recommended temporary sexual abstinence.

But despite his preference for celibacy, Pelagius offered a much more moderate appraisal of married life than did Jerome. First, unlike Jerome, Pelagius clearly stated that marriage was not to be regarded as a 'sin' (*peccatum*), although he admitted that married persons would find it considerably more difficult than celibates to fulfil all the precepts of the gospel. Commenting on 1 Corinthians 7: 28 ('But if you have taken a wife you have not sinned'), Pelagius remarked: 'Since you have free will, if you do not wish to be greater, you may be less; marriage is not a sin, although because of their concern for the world those who are married are barely able to fulfil the law.'[90] From Pelagius' point of view, 'worldly concern' (*sollicitudo mundi*) made it

---

[87] *Cel.* 28 (CSEL 56.1, 352): 'temperatus incedit ac medius.' My interpretation of Pelagius here differs from that of Duval, 'Pélage', 107–8, who emphasizes the rigorism in Pelagius' interpretation of 1 Cor 7: 'On verra que la rigueur de Pélage n'est pas moindre que celle de Jérôme.... Vers 405, où se situent donc, selon moi, tous ces écrits, Pélage ne me semble aucunement un opposant à Jérôme, ni un adversaire de son *Contre Jovinien*.' See his similar comments in *L'affaire Jovinien*, 297: 'L'attaque contre Jovinien est à peine moins violente que celles d'Ambroise ou de Jérôme.' Pelagius' attack on Jovinian, in my view, was considerably *less* violent than that of Ambrose or Jerome. For a more accurate appraisal, see Robert Markus, 'Augustine's *Confessions* and the Controversy with Julian of Eclanum: Manicheism Revisited', in B. Bruning, M. Lamberigts, J. Van Houtem (eds.), *Collectanea Augustiniana: Mélanges T.J. Van Bavel* (Leuven: Leuven University Press, 1990), 919: 'To Pelagius, there was not much to chose between Jerome and the Manichees; and here Augustine could sympathise with his Pelagian opponents.' For a similar stress on the moderation of Pelagius in comparison to Jerome, see Thier, *Kirche bei Pelagius*, 155–6.

[88] *Exp. 1 Cor.* 7: 2–3 (Souter, 159): 'quo modo si peritus medicus inquieto aegro et neganti se posse a pomis omnibus abstinere, saltem minus pernitiosa concedat.'

[89] *Exp. 1 Cor.* 7: 4–5 (Souter, 161–2); cf. Jerome, *Jov.* 1.20 (PL 23, 249); *ep.* 49.15 (CSEL 54, 377); Origen, *Fr. 34 in 1 Cor.* 7: 5 (*JTS* 9 [1908], 502); the parallels are noted by Clark, *Reading Renunciation* 280–1. See also *Cast.* 5.2–3 (PLS 1, 1472–3).

[90] *Exp. 1 Cor.* 7: 28 (Souter, 166).

more difficult for married persons to achieve a state of righteousness; the virgin, by contrast, was able 'to fulfil greater justice with less labour'.[91] Marriage itself, however, was not regarded as an evil, nor were married Christians excluded from the possibility of perfection; indeed, the novelty of Pelagius' ascetical theology was precisely that married people were subject to the same requirement of perfect righteousness as celibates.[92] This, Pelagius asserted, was the meaning of Paul's description of the Church as 'without spot or wrinkle' (Eph 5: 27): it referred to the common perfection achieved by virgins, widows, and married women.[93]

Pelagius' moderation is also evident in the practical guidance he offered to married people on how to achieve perfection in the married state. In his letter to the matron Celantia, for example, Pelagius attempted to lead the ascetically inclined woman to embrace her commitment to her husband and family along with her devotion to Christ. He urged her to set aside a place in the household where she could retreat for quiet prayer and reading, 'as if to a harbour out of a great storm of cares and there, in the peace of inner seclusion, calm the turbulent waves of thoughts outside'. This temporary respite from household cares was meant to enhance (not to detract from) Celantia's fulfilment of her familial duties: 'Nor do we say this with the purpose of detaching you from your family; rather our intention is that in that place you may learn and meditate as to what kind of person you ought to show yourself to your own kin.'[94] Similarly, Pelagius argued, the apostle Paul had recommended temporary sexual abstinence to married couples as a way to test the strength of their self-control in a gradual manner, so that they did not rashly embrace perpetual continence.[95] Pelagius' comment was a pointed rebuke of Celantia, who had adopted celibacy without the consent of her husband. It is difficult to imagine Jerome speaking with such equanimity on the matter of conjugal, familial, and spiritual responsibilities, but such a balanced perspective seems to have come naturally to Pelagius.

Another difference between Pelagius and Jerome can be seen in their rival interpretations of 1 Corinthians 7: 26 where Paul stated, 'On account of the pressing necessity (*propter instantem necessitatem*), it is good for a man to

---

[91] *Exp. 1 Cor.* 7: 28 (Souter, 167): 'ut minore labore maiorem possitis implere iustitiam.'

[92] In his Letter to Demetrias, written several years after the Pauline commentary, Pelagius referred to marriage as one of the 'intermediate' things (*media*), like meat and wine; they were neither forbidden nor recommended, but simply 'allowed' (*conceduntur*). See *Dem.* 9.2 (PL 30, 25).

[93] *Virg.* 11.3 (CSEL 1, 241); *Dem.* 24.3 (PL 30, 40). As Thier, *Kirche bei Pelagius*, 155, has argued, for Pelagius the difference between marriage and virginity was more 'quantitative', whereas for Jerome it was more 'qualitative'.

[94] *Cel.* 24 (CSEL 56.1, 350); trans. B. R. Rees, *Letters*, 140. It is significant that Pelagius offered the same advice to the virgin Demetrias: *Dem.* 23.

[95] *Cel.* 29 (CSEL 56.1, 353).

remain as he is.' As we saw above, in *Adversus Jovinianum* Jerome had invoked this passage to argue that marriage was 'condemned' as 'evil' (*malum*): 'What is this "necessity" that seeks the freedom of virginity by spurning the conjugal bond? . . . We do not have here a condemnation of harlots or brothels, about whose damnation there is no doubt. What is condemned is the swelling womb, the wailing infant, and the fruits and works of marriage. . . . If it is good for a man to remain as he is, it is bad for a man not to remain as he is.'[96]

Pelagius' interpretation of 1 Corinthians 7: 26, by contrast, was at once more moderate and more nuanced than that of Jerome: ' "On account of the pressing necessity." That is, concern for the present life, which can be a great obstacle to righteousness, and by which those who are joined in marriage are especially implicated. "It is good for a man to remain as he is." There is a twofold good: he avoids the cares of the world and he awaits the reward of virginity.'[97]

Unlike Jerome, Pelagius did not regard sex or procreation as, in themselves, deficient or sinful. For Pelagius, marriage represented an inferior choice of life because it involved a person in 'worldly cares' that made it more difficult to fulfil all the precepts of the law. In continence, by contrast, 'the body is freed of conjugal use, the soul is freed of concern for worldly things, while the whole person is freed for divine service.'[98] Hence the apostle Paul encouraged more prudent Christians to choose the better path and to avoid becoming involved in transient, worldly affairs.[99]

On the whole, then, Pelagius offered an account of marriage and celibacy that preserved the ascetic hierarchy (contra Jovinian) and yet treated marriage without rancour or contempt (contra Jerome). The apostle Paul (in Pelagius' reading) sought to encourage continence without condemning marriage: 'He preaches chastity and abstinence in such a way that he does not condemn either nature or creatures. He encourages the stronger to follow one path, while he allows the weaker to follow another.'[100] Had not the apostle taught that a married woman who achieved righteousness was 'happy' (*beata*), even though the widow was 'happier' (*beatior*), and the virgin 'happiest of all' (*beatissima*)?[101] Pelagius' response to the Jovinianist controversy, while opposed to Jovinian's teaching on the equality of marriage and celibacy, also

---

[96] *Jov.* 1.12 (PL 23, 239). The passage is cited in full in the main text at note 55 above.
[97] *Exp. 1 Cor.* 7: 26 (Souter, 166). [98] *Exp. 1 Cor.* 7: 34 (Souter, 169).
[99] *Exp. 1 Cor.* 7: 38 (Souter, 170): 'unde prudentibus semper meliora et perfectiora sectanda sunt, quia nec in saecularibus et [in] caduis norunt mediocribus esse contenti.'
[100] *Exp. 1 Tim.* 4: 2 (Souter, 489). Cf. Pelagius' comment at *Exp. Eph.* 5: 29 (Souter, 378): 'non nuptias quidem damnat, sed ad continentiam cohortatur.'
[101] *Exp. 1 Cor.* 7: 40 (Souter, 170).

offered an important corrective to the excesses of Jerome's *Adversus Jovinianum*. It is difficult to believe that Pelagius did not intend his position to be a subtle rebuke of Jerome, especially because he explicitly sought to establish a middle way between Jovinian and those, like the Manichees, who would condemn marriage.[102]

We have, perhaps, indirect support for this last point in the fact that Pelagius did eventually criticize Jerome's teaching on marriage several years after the composition of his Pauline commentary and ascetical treatises. In the year 414, as Jerome began to compose his Commentary on Jeremiah, he mentioned that he was being harassed by a new critic in Palestine, one who was reviving Rufinus' old accusations against him. Jerome explicitly mentioned that the new critic—whom he described as 'a very stupid dolt weighed down with Scottish porridge'—had objected to his use of Origen in his Commentary on Ephesians and to his abusive treatment of marriage in *Adversus Jovinianum*.[103] The new critic, of course, was Pelagius, who had been resident in Palestine since at least 413,[104] and he appears to have borrowed the criticisms from Rufinus' *Apology against Jerome*, composed more than a decade earlier. According to arguments advanced by Yves-Marie Duval, Jerome had first accused Pelagius of reviving Jovinian's second proposition by teaching the possibility of living a sinless life; Pelagius, in turn, responded by recalling the old accusations against Jerome issued by Rufinus.[105] Even if Pelagius' attack on Jerome's teaching was a defensive reaction, it is unlikely that he would have criticized the excesses of Jerome's *Adversus Jovinianum* unless he had actually found the treatise offensive. Pelagius' criticisms of Jerome in 414, therefore, provide additional support for the argument we have advanced here: that Pelagius sought a *via media* between Jovinian and Jerome in his teachings on marriage and celibacy.

Finally, Pelagius' mediating position on the topic of marriage is noteworthy because it gave rise to two contrasting views among his so-called 'Pelagian' disciples. His insistence on the goodness and integrity of human nature was capable of inspiring a rather positive appreciation of conjugal life, such as that advanced by his supporter Bishop Julian of Eclanum. After the condemnation of Pelagius for heresy in 418, Julian attacked Augustine's theology of original sin precisely because of its 'Manichaean' depreciation of marriage. As Mathijs Lamberigts has observed: 'For Julian, *concupiscentia* is not a deficiency of

---

[102] See *Cel.* 28.2 (CSEL 56, 352), cited above n. 82.
[103] *Jer.* 1, Pref. 3–4 (CSEL 59, 4): 'stolidissimus et scottorum pultibus praegravatus'.
[104] Nuvolone, 'Pélage', 2895–6.
[105] Duval, 'Pélage est-il le censeur inconnu', 550–5; 'Pélage en son temps', 108–10. In *L'affaire Jovinien*, 327–57, Duval has carefully sifted the evidence of Jerome's encounter with Pelagius in Palestine. For a somewhat different view of the same evidence, see Evans, *Pelagius*, 26–42.

nature but rather a quality thereof, a sentiment or feeling.... In addition, Julian considers sexual *concupiscentia* to be the divinely willed means *par excellence* for the realization of a successful sexual union, a natural prerequisite for procreation.'[106] In Julian, Pelagius' defence of nature became a defence of marriage and sexuality.

Conversely, Pelagius' emphasis on the possibility of sinlessness and the capability of all human beings to achieve perfection led other disciples to take a more radical stance towards the Christian life. The author of the Pelagian tract, *De castitate*, attributed to the 'Sicilian Anonymous' by Gerald Bonner, took just such an approach, arguing that perfect discipleship, as defined by Jesus, was incompatible with married life.[107] Ironically, this 'Pelagian' author managed to combine Pelagius' account of the integrity of human nature with Jerome's interpretation of 1 Corinthians 7.[108] The result was an ascetic tirade that rejected all sex as 'defiling', even within marriage; not surprisingly, the author of *De castitate* also explicitly attacked the views of Jovinian.[109] Like many figures in the history of Christian thought, therefore, Pelagius inspired followers who carried aspects of his teaching to extremes that he himself would not have endorsed.[110]

---

[106] 'A Critical Evaluation of Critiques of Augustine's View of Sexuality', in Robert Dodaro and George Lawless (eds.), *Augustine and His Critics: Essays in Honour of Gerald Bonner* (London and New York: Routledge, 2000), 177. On the debate between Augustine and Julian, see Peter Brown, 'Sexuality and Society in the Fifth Century A.D.: Augustine and Julian of Eclanum', in E. Gabba (ed.), *Tria Corda: Scritti in onore di Arnaldo Momigliano* (Como: Edizioni New Press, 1983), 49–70; Elizabeth A. Clark, 'Vitiated Seeds and Holy Vessels: Augustine's Manichean Past', in her *Ascetic Piety and Women's Faith: Essays on Late Ancient Christianity* (Lewiston, NY/Queenston, Ontario: Edwin Mellen Press, 1986), 291–349; Philip L. Barclift, 'In Controversy with Saint Augustine: Julian of Eclanum on the Nature of Sin', *RTAM* 58 (1991), 5–20. On Julian, the essential study is now that of Josef Lössl, *Julian von Aeclanum: Studien zu seinem Leben, seinem Werk, seiner Lehre und ihrer Überlieferung* (Leiden and Boston: Brill, 2001).

[107] *Cast.* 7.1. Similarly extreme views on marriage are also found in the *Opus imperfectum in Matthaeum*, now thought to be a Pelagian writing; see the discussion in Fredric W. Schlatter, 'The Pelagianism of the Opus imperfectum in Matthaeum', *VC* 41 (1987), 267–85, especially 279–82.

[108] For the influence of Pelagius, see *Cast.* 3.5 (PLS 1, 1467–8): 'For no one is born corrupt nor is anyone stained by corruption before the lapse of an appointed period of time.' For the influence of Jerome, see *Cast.* 10.2 (PLS 1, 1479): 'Again, when you say that it is good for a man not to touch his wife, by this you clearly prove that it is bad if he does touch her, since the only opposite to good is evil.'

[109] Cf. *Cast.* 10.5 (PLS 1, 1482): 'Alioquin totiens inmundus erit, quotiens incontinentiae fuerit sorde pollutus.' For the attacks on Jovinian, see *Cast.* 10.8 (PLS 1, 1483) and 16 (PLS 1, 1498). On the social context of *De castitate*, see Michael R. Rackett, 'Anxious for Worldly Things: The Critique of Marriage in the Anonymous Pelagian Treatise *De Castitate*', *StPatr* 33 (1997), 229–35.

[110] As Gerald Bonner, 'Pelagianism and Augustine', *AugStud* 23 (1992), 39, has observed, 'in his uncompromising asceticism, [the Sicilian Anonymous] goes further than Pelagius, but his attitude reflects a very real tendency in Pelagianism: a rejection of any compromise in Christian living. The Pelagians were not monks; but their program, if it had been carried through uncompromisingly, would have turned the entire Christian Church into a monastery.' Overall, however, the author of *De castitate* showed much greater affinities with Jerome than with Pelagius himself.

3. SUBVERTING THE ASCETIC HIERARCHY: AUGUSTINE OF HIPPO

The final opponent of Jovinian (and Jerome) to be considered here is the famous North African bishop, Augustine of Hippo. Augustine's entry into the Jovinianist controversy, like that of Pelagius, occurred about a decade after Jovinian's condemnation at Rome. Around the year 404 Augustine composed two small treatises, one titled 'The Good of Marriage' (*De bono coniugali*), the other 'On Holy Virginity' (*De sancta virginitate*).[111] Looking back on these works in his *Retractationes* of 427, Augustine observed that the 'heresy of Jovinian' was the immediate occasion for his writing:

The heresy of Jovinian, by equating the merit of consecrated virgins and conjugal continence, was so influential in the city of Rome that even some consecrated women, about whose incontinence there had been no previous suspicion, were precipitated into marriage, it was said, especially by the following argument: he kept urging them saying: 'Are you, then, better than Sara, better than Susanna or Anna?' and by mentioning other women, highly praised according to the testimony of Holy Scripture, to whom they could not think themselves superior or even equal. In this way, too, he shattered the holy celibacy of holy men by reminding them of and comparing them with fathers and husbands.

Although the church at Rome had responded faithfully and forcefully to 'this monster', Augustine stated, nevertheless 'these arguments of his, which no one dared to defend openly, had survived in the chatter and whisperings of certain persons. Therefore, it was still necessary to oppose the secretly spreading poisons with all the power which the Lord gave me, especially since they were boasting that Jovinian could not be answered by praising marriage, but only by censuring it.'[112]

Augustine's statement shows the importance of the Jovinianist controversy as the context for his own treatises on marriage and celibacy, but it also conceals as much as it reveals. In recent decades a strong consensus has emerged among Augustinian scholars that Augustine's two treatises were directed not only against Jovinian, but also against Jerome. His reference to

---

[111] Rather than the traditional date of 401, I have adopted the revised date of 404 proposed by Pierre-Marie Hombert, *Nouvelles recherches de chronologie augustinienne* (Paris: Études Augustiniennes, 2000), 105–36. For my arguments in support of Hombert's chronology, see 'Augustine, Sermon 354A: Its Place in His Thought on Marriage and Sexuality', *AugStud* 33 (2002), 40–4.

[112] *Retract.* 2.22 (CCSL 57, 107–8); trans. Mary Inez Bogan, *Saint Augustine: The Retractations* (FC 60; Washington, DC: The Catholic University of America Press, 1968), 164, slightly altered.

those who responded to Jovinian by censuring marriage was, of course, a not-too-subtle allusion to the *Adversus Jovinianum*. As Robert Markus has observed regarding Augustine's aims in the two treatises: 'The memory of Jerome's notorious and ill-fated attack on Jovinian was fresh in Augustine's mind.... Augustine's rehabilitation of the married state is a thinly veiled answer to Jerome's denigration (*vituperatio*) of it: his covert work *Against Jerome*.'[113] Markus is certainly correct. As I will argue below, there are numerous places in *De bono coniugali* and *De sancta virginitate* where it is clear that Augustine wished to contradict and to correct the perspectives of the *Adversus Jovinianum*.

Before turning to those two treatises, however, it is necessary to say a word about Augustine's earlier discussions of marriage and celibacy. For *De bono coniugali* and *De sancta virginitate* were not Augustine's first excursions on this subject, nor were these writings his first encounter with Jerome. In earlier treatises against the Manichees Augustine had first attempted to formulate an orthodox Christian understanding of marriage and celibacy, and in his earlier correspondence with Jerome over the interpretation of Paul's Letter to the Galatians, Augustine had first broached the issue of the apostle's teaching on marriage. Both Augustine's previous anti-Manichaean polemics and his previous conflict with Jerome shed light on the arguments developed in the two treatises of 404.

i. Against the Manichaeans

Like Ambrosiaster, Pelagius, and other Western writers (including Jovinian), Augustine was deeply preoccupied with refuting the Manichaean heresy. Because he had spent nearly a decade in the sect himself, Augustine felt a particular need to counteract his earlier enthusiasm by preaching and writing on behalf of catholic Christianity. In his early anti-Manichaean writings, Augustine closely followed traditional anti-heretical arguments, especially those that had been formulated by previous opponents of Marcionite and encratite asceticism. For example, in his two books, *De moribus ecclesiae catholicae* and *De moribus Manichaeorum*, begun at Rome in 388 and completed the following year in Africa, Augustine attacked the Manichees for their ascetic rigour: 'Why do you maliciously claim that the faithful who have been renewed in baptism ought no longer to beget children, or to possess lands or

---

[113] *End of Ancient Christianity*, 45. See also Émile Schmitt, *Le mariage chrétien dans l'oeuvre de saint Augustin: Une théologie baptismale de la vie conjugale* (Paris: Études Augustiniennes, 1983), 68; Goulven Madec, *Introduction aux 'Révisions' et à la lecture des oeuvres de saint Augustin* (Paris: Études Augustiniennes, 1996), 74; Duval, *L'affaire Jovinien*, 275–6.

houses or money?'[114] Citing Paul's discussion in 1 Corinthians 7, Augustine noted that the Apostle had expressed a preference for celibacy but allowed marriage: 'Does it not seem to you that he has both pointed out to the strong what is most perfect, and permitted to the weaker what is next best?' That which is 'next best' to the highest good, Augustine observed, is 'conjugal chastity to avoid the ravages of fornication'.[115] Like Clement of Alexandria before him, Augustine underscored Paul's claim in 1 Corinthians 7: 14 that 'the unbelieving husband is sanctified in the believing wife, and the unbelieving wife is sanctified in the believing husband.' Paul's word is proof, he argued, that 'those who are united in conjugal chastity are sanctified by each other, should one of them be an unbeliever, and that the children born of them are also sanctified.'[116]

In a similar vein, in *Contra Adimantum*, another anti-Manichaean work composed around the year 392, Augustine again invoked Paul, as well as Jesus, to demonstrate that the Old and New Testaments stood in fundamental agreement in their approval of sex and marriage. Augustine cited Matthew 19: 3–9, where Jesus appealed to Genesis 1: 27 and 2: 24 to endorse the permanence of marriage; he also recalled the final verses of Ephesians 5, where the author also quoted Genesis 2: 24 and referred the text to the 'great mystery' (*sacramentum... magnum*) of Christ and the Church. Since both Jesus and Paul quoted the Old Testament with approval, Augustine argued, there could be no ultimate contradiction between the Old and the New Testaments in regard to marriage: 'All things both in the Old and in the New Testament have been written and transmitted by one Spirit.'[117] This too, as we have seen, was an argument used by previous anti-heretical writers. Against the claims of radical ascetics, Augustine followed the orthodox tradition and emphasized the essential unity between the two testaments.

Augustine's most extensive discussion of marriage prior to the treatises of 404 is found in his lengthy anti-Manichaean treatise *Contra Faustum*. Faustus, a Manichaean bishop who had once made a friendly impression upon the young Augustine, had raised the question of marriage primarily by attacking the conjugal morality of the mothers and fathers of the Old Testament. The Old Testament, Faustus charged, is rife with stories of polygamy, incest, and

---

[114] *Mor. eccl.* 1.35.78 (PL 32, 1343); trans. Donald A. Gallagher and Idella J. Gallagher, *The Catholic and Manichaean Ways of Life* (FC 56; Washington, DC: The Catholic University of America Press, 1965), 59.
[115] *Mor. eccl.* 1.35.79 (PL 32, 1344): 'huic autem summo coniugalis castitas proxima est, ne homo fornicatione vastetur.'
[116] Ibid.; cf. Clement, *Strom.* 3.6.47 (Stählin-Früchtel, 2, 217). Augustine repeated the argument in *Bon. coniug.* 11.13.
[117] *Adim.* 3 (CSEL 25.1, 121).

concubinage. Either the stories are false, in which case the Old Testament is to be rejected as untrue; or the stories are true, in which case the patriarchs and matriarchs are guilty of sin. 'In either case', Faustus taunted, 'the crime is equally detestable, for vicious conduct and falsehood are equally loathsome.'[118]

In response to Faustus' critique, Augustine defended the sexual lives of the Old Testament saints with a twofold argument. On the one hand, he argued that their behaviour was necessary to produce the line of descendants that would lead to Christ. Because the Old Testament fathers acted as they did out of obedience to a divine command, they should not be considered guilty of immorality. On the other hand, Augustine suggested, stories that appeared to be unedifying could be interpreted symbolically as prophecies of the coming of Christ and the Church: 'The whole kingdom of the Hebrews was like a great prophet, corresponding to the greatness of the one prophesied.'[119] Both of these readings of the Hebrew Scriptures will reappear in modified form in *De bono coniugali* and *De sancta virginitate*, as Augustine sought to rehabilitate the sanctity of the Old Testament saints, while simultaneously maintaining the superiority of celibacy.

It is significant that much of Augustine's early discussion of marriage took place in the context of his anti-Manichaean writings. Although his own conversion to orthodox Christianity, at least as presented in the *Confessions*, took the form of an embrace of the ascetic life, and especially sexual continence, Augustine's early theology of marriage was shaped largely by his ongoing polemic against the Manichees.[120] As a result, by the early 400s, when he entered the debate between Jovinian and Jerome, Augustine was predisposed to defend the goodness of marriage and procreation against all criticism. In *De bono coniugali* and *De sancta virginitate* Augustine offered an innovative and relatively moderate appraisal of marriage that drew on his previous anti-Manichaean writings, especially *Contra Faustum*. Although he

---

[118] *Faust.* 22.5 (CSEL 25.1, 595). On Augustine's earlier relations with Faustus, see *Conf.* 5.3.3—7.13.

[119] *Faust.* 22.24 (CSEL 25.1, 619). Augustine had first articulated this twofold reading of the supposed immorality of the Hebrew saints in *Doct. chr.* 3.10.14—3.22.32 (BA 11/2, 254–80). See also *Conf.* 3.7.12–13, and my fuller discussion in 'Reclaiming Biblical Morality: Sex and Salvation History in Augustine's Treatment of the Hebrew Saints', in Paul M. Blowers, Angela Russell Christman, David G. Hunter, and Robin Darling Young (eds.), *In Dominico Eloquio. In Lordly Eloquence: Essays on Patristic Exegesis in Honor of Robert Louis Wilken* (Grand Rapids, MI/Cambridge, UK: William B. Eerdmans, 2002), 317–35.

[120] See *Conf.* 8.11.25–30 for Augustine's struggle to accept the admonitions of 'Lady Continence'. For an overview of Augustine's teaching on marriage against the Manichees, see Schmitt, *Le mariage chrétien*, 19–41.

rejected the views of Jovinian, Augustine's antipathy to Manichaeism also led him to criticize Jerome's excessively negative view of marriage.

ii. Against Jerome

Augustine's previous conflicts with Jerome also left their mark on the two treatises of 404. Augustine had first approached Jerome by letter in 395 with criticisms of his biblical translations and commentaries, and they engaged in contentious correspondence on these matters over the next ten years. One of the major issues between them was Jerome's interpretation of Galatians 2: 11–14, the story of Paul's rebuke of Peter at Antioch. Because Jerome could not accept that the two most important leaders of the early Christian church could be in real conflict, he had attempted to circumvent the obvious meaning of Galatians and to argue that the story of the conflict at Antioch was, in fact, an elaborate subterfuge perpetrated by Paul. As Jerome put it in his Commentary on the Letter to the Galatians: 'Paul employed the same strategy of pretence that Peter had, when he "resisted Peter to his face" (cf. Gal 2: 11).... He was not rebuking Peter, so much as correcting those on whose behalf Peter had conducted his pretence.'[121]

In several letters to Jerome, written between 395 and 405, Augustine repeatedly objected to Jerome's view that either of the apostles might have lied. In Augustine's view, once the possibility of falsehood was admitted in the scriptures, 'not one bit of those books will remain'. If the biblical authors were capable of lying, he argued, anytime a person found the testimony of scripture to be difficult to understand or to follow, he would have recourse to 'this most destructive principle of interpretation' (*eadem perniciosissima regula*).[122] For the purpose of my argument here, it is significant that Augustine noted the dangerous implications of Jerome's approach to Galatians for an interpretation of Paul's teaching on marriage in 1 Corinthians 7. As Augustine wrote in Letter 28:

If the apostle Paul was lying when he rebuked Peter... what will we respond when wicked people arise who forbid marriage, as Paul himself predicted that they would? What will we do when they say that the whole passage, where the apostle spoke about strengthening the right of marital unions, is a falsehood, which Paul fabricated, not

---

[121] *Gal.* 1.2 (PL 26, 367). For an overview of the conflict between Jerome and Augustine on this point, see R. Hennings, *Der Briefwechsel zwischen Augustinus und Hieronymus und ihr Streit um den Kanon des alten Testament und die Auslegung von Gal. 2, 11–14* (Leiden: Brill, 1994), 121–30.
[122] *Ep.* 28.3.3 (CSEL 34.1, 108).

because he really believed it, but in order to placate those men who would have raised a disturbance because of the love of their wives?[123]

The danger of Jerome's approach, as Augustine argued in 395, is that someone who wished to reject Paul's teaching on the permissibility of marriage could simply claim that Paul did not really mean what he said when he approved of marriage.

We find an even more direct statement of this view among the newly discovered sermons of Augustine edited by François Dolbeau. In Sermon 162C on Galatians 2, Augustine explicitly linked the interpretation of verses 28 and 38 of 1 Corinthians 7 to the interpretation of the conflict between Peter and Paul at Antioch. Once again Augustine argued that allowing the possibility of deliberate deception in scripture could lead to erroneous teachings on marriage:

What are we to do, when I say to someone, 'It is good to marry, but it is better not to marry, as the apostle Paul wrote' (cf. 1 Cor 7: 28, 38)? What if someone who condemns marriage (*damnator nuptiarum*) then replies to me: 'Paul most certainly did condemn marriage; but he was only pretending when he wrote this, since the truth itself could not be borne by the weak. It is because continence can only be undertaken with great hardship that he said, "It is good to marry". In fact, he knew that it is bad to marry.'[124]

Augustine's primary aim both in Letter 28 to Jerome and in Sermon 162C was to defend the truth of the scriptures and, specifically, the veracity of the apostle Paul. But it is clear that the question of the reliability of Paul's teaching on marriage was also at stake. This sermon, as Pierre-Marie Hombert has recently argued, was probably written a year or two after *De bono coniugali* and *De sancta virginitate*.[125] It indicates that the issue how to read Paul's teaching on marriage in 1 Corinthians 7 and the issue whether an apostle was capable of deliberate deception were closely linked in Augustine's mind, both before and after the composition of his treatises on marriage and virginity.

Augustine's comment in the Dolbeau sermon raises the intriguing possibility that Jerome might have been the *damnator nuptiarum* whose approach to Galatians 2 led to an erroneous reading of 1 Corinthians 7. Support for this view can be found in Augustine's Letter 82 to Jerome written around the same time as Sermon 162C (405). Here Augustine suggested that Jerome's approach

---

[123] *Ep.* 28.3.4 (CSEL 34.1, 108–9).
[124] *Ser.* 162C.14 (Dolbeau 10; Mainz 27). The text has been published in F. Dolbeau, *Augustin d'Hippone: Vingt-six sermons au people d'Afrique* (Paris: Études Augustiniennes, 2001), 45–56, quotation at 54–5.
[125] Although Dolbeau suggested a date of 397 for Sermon 162C, Hombert, *Nouvelles recherches*, 347–54, has argued for the year 405.

to Pauline interpretation was potentially more dangerous than that of the Manichees. Whereas the Manichees claimed that the text of Paul's epistles had suffered scribal corruption, Augustine observed, Jerome presented the more pernicious view that Paul had actually *intended* to deceive:

> The Manichees maintain that many parts of the divine scriptures are false, because they cannot twist them to a different meaning, but their detestable error is refuted by the perfect clarity of scriptural expression. And yet even they do not attribute falsehood to the apostolic writers, but to some supposed corrupters of the text.... Does your holy Prudence not understand what an avenue we open to their malice if we say, not that the apostolic writings were falsified by others, but that the apostles themselves wrote falsehood?[126]

Augustine's Letter 82 shows that he remained deeply troubled by Jerome's willingness to attribute falsehood and dissimulation to the apostles. This letter, composed shortly after Augustine wrote his two treatises on marriage and virginity, did not explicitly mention the issue of Paul's teaching about marriage in 1 Corinthians 7, but, given that Augustine had explicitly connected the topics both in Letter 28 and in Sermon 162C, it is reasonable to assume that he had this in mind in Letter 82.

Augustine's debate with Jerome over the interpretation of Galatians 2 left its clear imprint on his discussion of marriage and celibacy in the treatises on marriage and virginity of 404. There are several passages in *De sancta virginitate* that directly recall the discussion of the veracity of the apostle Paul and his teaching on marriage in 1 Corinthians 7. At one point, while commenting on 1 Corinthians 7: 28, Augustine observed: 'First of all, therefore, and above all, let those who choose virginity hold it as absolutely beyond question that holy scripture contains no lies, and hence that statement also was true: "And if you have married, you have not committed a sin, and if a virgin marries, she does not commit a sin."'[127] It is critical, Augustine insisted, that the text of 1 Corinthians 7: 28 be taken in its plain and most literal sense: 'In a matter of such importance, what would we do if it were not clear and certain that chaste marriages should not be condemned, not less than it is clear and certain that holy scripture cannot lie?'[128]

Several lines later Augustine again raised the issue of the veracity of scripture, this time in connection with 1 Corinthians 7: 38:

---

[126] *Ep.* 82.6 (CSEL 34.2, 356); trans. W. Parsons, *St. Augustine: Letters* (FC 12; New York: Fathers of the Church, 1951), 394 (partially altered).

[127] *Virg.* 18.18 (CSEL 41, 251); trans. Ray Kearney, *Augustine: Marriage and Virginity* (WSA 1/9; Hyde Park, NY: New City Press, 1999), 77–8.

[128] *Virg.* 20.20 (CSEL 41, 254); trans. Kearney, 79.

Since people are being urged to aspire to such a splendid gift, not because of a merely human opinion, but on the authority of divine scripture, we must act in a careful and thorough manner, so that no one will think that the divine scripture contains lies. Those who would persuade sacred virgins to maintain that way of life by condemning marriage are really discouraging them rather than encouraging them. For how can they be sure that the text, 'and he who does not marry does better' (1 Cor 7: 38), is true, if they think that what was written immediately before it, 'He who marries his virgin does well' (1 Cor 7: 38), is not true? But if they believe the scripture without question when it speaks of the good of marriage, they will find security in that absolutely trustworthy authority of the heavenly speech, and will hurry on with enthusiasm and confidence to what it says about their own superior good.[129]

It is clear that in *De sancta virginitate* Augustine remained concerned with the issue raised in his correspondence with Jerome. Interpretations of scripture, such as Jerome's, that attributed mendacity or duplicity to the biblical authors remained anathema to Augustine, as did any suggestion that marriage was not good.

Moreover, Augustine had good reason to broach this subject in *De sancta virginitate*, for Jerome had advanced exactly such readings of Paul in *Adversus Jovinianum*. Commenting on 1 Corinthians 7: 28, for example, Jerome had argued that when Paul said, 'and if a virgin marries, she has not sinned,' he immediately followed it with the words, 'but they will experience distress in the flesh'. The purpose of Paul's addendum, Jerome suggested, was to negate his previous concession, so that he would not appear to be encouraging marriage.[130] Several lines later Jerome made the same point about 1 Corinthians 7: 38. When Paul wrote that 'he who marries his virgin does well', Jerome argued, he immediately added, 'and he who does not marry does better'. Jerome suggested that Paul negated his affirmation of marriage by adding the negative comparison with virginity: 'the apostle diminishes that good and obscures it by comparison with what is better.'[131]

Augustine's discussion of 1 Corinthians 7: 28 and 7: 38 in *De sancta virginitate* appears to be a direct response to Jerome's discussion of the same verses in *Adversus Jovinianum*. Whereas Jerome had attempted to turn the first and second parts of these verses against each other in favour of virginity, Augustine insisted that both halves of verses 28 and 38 must be true in order to preserve the veracity of the apostle. Augustine's interpretation of these verses clearly demonstrates that he had the excesses of the *Adversus Jovinianum* in view and that his earlier debate with Jerome was still informing

[129] *Virg.* 21.21 (CSEL 41, 255); trans. Kearney, 79–80, altered.
[130] *Jov.* 1.13 (PL 23, 240).
[131] *Jov.* 1.13 (PL 23, 242). Duval, *L'affaire Jovinien*, 137–40, has observed that Jerome's interpretation is dependent on Origen.

his thought. Jerome's willingness to allow some dissimulation on Paul's part in Galatians 2: 14–17 and his restrictive interpretation of Paul's teaching on marriage in 1 Corinthians 7 were both examples of interpretive practices that, in Augustine's view, undermined the truth of the scriptures and led to pernicious teaching about marriage.[132]

iii. The Good of Marriage

This brings us to the centrepiece of Augustine's response to Jovinian and Jerome, the treatises *De bono coniugali* and *De sancta virginitate*. We do not know whether there was a specific event that served as a catalyst for the composition of these two works.[133] According to the *Retractationes*, Augustine composed his treatise *De opere monachorum* because of 'violent quarrels' (*tumultuosa certamina*) caused by the establishment of the first monasteries at Carthage.[134] Since *De opere monachorum* appears in the *Retractationes* immediately before *De bono coniugali* and *De sancta virginitate*, it is possible that these controversies may have influenced Augustine's decision to write on marriage and virginity at this time. The chronological studies of Pierre-Marie Hombert have shown that Augustine devoted a number of sermons in the years 403–404 to the subject of marriage, which suggests that the topic may have been a matter of some urgency to him.[135] Moreover, in the same years Augustine continued to write polemical treatises against the Manichees in which he defended marriage against the Manichaean critique.[136] All of these factors, in addition to his ongoing debate with Jerome, seem to have led Augustine to engage directly the topic of marriage and celibacy and to construct his own alternative to the positions of Jovinian and Jerome.

Like Pelagius and the author of the *Consultationes*, Augustine attempted to strike a balance between Jovinian's equation of marriage and celibacy and

---

[132] Jerome explicitly argued in favour of falsehood in *Jov.* 1.34 (PL 23, 268–70), where he suggested that Paul's prescription that the bishop should be a 'man of one wife' was merely a concession for new converts and not a true expression of the apostle's preferences regarding the clergy. In *ep.* 49.13 (CSEL 54, 370), Jerome argued that his own words should not be taken at face value and that dissimulation was an acceptable method of argumentation in the biblical writers, including Paul.

[133] Cf. Madec, *Introduction*, 74: 'Ainsi ne connaît-on pas la circonstance précise qui a provoqué la redaction du *De bono coniugali*.' I have suggested several possibilities in my article, 'Augustine, Sermon 354A,' cited above n. 111.

[134] *Retract.* 2.21 (CCSL 57, 107).

[135] I have discussed Hombert's evidence in 'Augustine, Sermon 354A', 52–4.

[136] Augustine's debate with Felix the Manichaean has been precisely dated to 7 and 12 December 404. In *Fel.* 1.7–8 Augustine discussed marriage while commenting on 1 Tim 4: 1–5. See also *Secund.* 2 and 21–2, which probably dates from these years.

Jerome's denigration of marriage. Against Jovinian, Augustine offered several explanations to account for the 'superiority' of celibacy over marriage. In *De sancta virginitate*, for example, he argued that all the good features of marriage—the procreation of children, marital fidelity, and the sacramental sign—are temporal values that do not last into eternity. By contrast, virginal integrity and sexual continence involve 'a participation in the life of angels and a foretaste of perpetual incorruption in the corruptible flesh'.[137] Augustine also attempted to uphold the superiority of celibacy by noting that, according to the apostle Paul, the married person is concerned about worldly things (cf. 1 Cor 7: 33–4), whereas the virgin is potentially undivided.[138] Because of their more intense commitment to Christ, virgins could 'follow the Lamb wherever he goes' (Rev 14: 4); as a result, they were capable of experiencing a more intense degree of joy in the next life than other Christians: 'The special joys of Christ's virgins are not the same as those of non-virgins, even if the latter belong to Christ; others have joys, but none of them have this kind.'[139] Ultimately, for Augustine, the 'superiority' of celibacy over marriage lay in the capacity of a celibate Christian to love God more wholeheartedly, whereas married persons were always divided in their attentions and affections.[140]

In *De bono coniugali* and *De sancta virginitate* Augustine also attempted to refute Jovinian's appeal to the married saints of the Old Testament as evidence of the equality of marriage and celibacy. Augustine's response involved transposing his defence of the patriarchs from the anti-Manichaean context of *Contra Faustum* into the new context of his debate with Jovinian. Augustine shared Jovinian's esteem for the Hebrew saints, but he argued that the particular merit of Abraham and the others was that they engaged in sex purely out of obedience to the divine command:

In the times when the mystery of our salvation was still hidden under the veil of prophetic symbols ... they entered into marriage because of the duty to continue the human race. They did not do this under the domination of lust, but in response to their sense of duty. If they had been offered the same alternative as is offered today with the revelation of the New Testament, when the Lord says, 'Let the one who can accept it' (Mt 19: 12), they would have accepted it with joy.[141]

---

[137] *Virg.* 12.13 (CSEL 41, 245): 'angelica portio est et in carne corruptibili incorruptionis perpetua meditatio.' Cf. *Bon. conjug.* 8.8 (CSEL 41, 198): 'sic et mortalis ista generatio, propter quam fiunt nuptiae, destruetur; ob omni autem concubitu inmunitas et hic anglica meditatio est et permanet in aeternum.'

[138] *Virg.* 13.13—14.14. In *Bon. conjug.* 11.13, however, Augustine acknowledged that married people also think about the Lord, but do so less than virgins.

[139] *Virg.* 27.27 (CSEL 41, 264).

[140] See *Virg.* 11.11 and 54.55.

[141] *Bon. conjug.* 13.15 (CSEL 41, 207–8).

Marriage and Celibacy in Western Theology 279

Augustine's point is twofold. On the one hand, the married saints of the Old Testament possessed continence as an internal, spiritual disposition (*habitus*).[142] Therefore, their marital lives were motivated by obedience, not by lust. They were, in Augustine's view, 'continent' in spirit, if not in body.[143] On the other hand, historical circumstances have changed, and now, the propagation of children no longer serves any necessary function in the history of salvation. Therefore, in the present dispensation even those who marry solely for the sake of producing children are not equal to the Old Testament saints: 'In the present even the desire for children is carnal, whereas in the past it was spiritual, because it accorded with the sacred mystery (*sacramentum*) of that time.'[144] Since there is no longer any spiritual need to produce children, Augustine argued, the only reason to marry is a lack of self-control.[145] Hence, against Jovinian, Augustine insisted that the moral excellence of the Old Testament saints could not be used as evidence of the equality of marriage and celibacy, for marriage and procreation now play a fundamentally different role in the history of salvation than they did before the coming of Christ. While marriage remains something good, in the present time celibacy is better, since it is better not to make use of something for which there is no longer any need.[146]

Nevertheless, despite his rejection of Jovinian, Augustine displayed equally strong opposition to positions taken by Jerome in *Adversus Jovinianum*. We have already discussed his 'correction' of Jerome's interpretation of 1 Corinthians 7: 28 and 7: 38. Throughout *De bono coniugali* and *De sancta virginitate*, Augustine emphasized, contra Jerome, that marriage was a genuine *bonum* (albeit a lesser one than celibacy), and not merely a *levius malum*, as Jerome had put it. Perhaps the most explicit example of this is found in *De bono coniugali*, where Augustine commented on the text of Hebrews 13: 4 ('Let marriage be held in honour by all, and let the marriage bed be undefiled'):

---

[142] Cf. *Bon. conjug.* 21.25 (CSEL 41, 218–19).

[143] In *Bon. conjug.* 13.15 Augustine argued that the married saints of the Old Testament were superior even to celibate Christians. The reason is that it is more difficult to make use of marriage while retaining the disposition of continence than it is to renounce the use of marriage altogether. See also *Bon. conjug.* 19.22.

[144] *Bon. conjug.* 17.19 (CSEL 41, 212–13).

[145] Cf. *Bon. conjug.* 10.10 (CSEL 41, 202): 'unde mihi videtur hoc tempore solos eos, qui se non continent, coniugari oportere secundum illam eiusdem apostoli sententiam: *quodsi se non continent, nubant: melius est enim nubere quam uri.*'

[146] Cf. *Bon. conjug.* 9.9 (CSEL 41, 200): 'ac per hoc bonum est nubere, quia bonum est procreare, matrem familias esse; sed melius est non nubere, qui melius est ad ipsam humanam societatem hoc opere non egere.'

We do not call marriage 'good' merely because it is good in comparison with fornication. In that case, they would be two evils, one of which was worse.... No, marriage and fornication are not two evils, one of which is worse, but marriage and continence are two goods, one of which is better. In the same way health and sickness in this life are not two evils, one of which is worse, but earthly health and immortality are two goods, one of which is better. Likewise, knowledge and illusion are not two evils, with illusion being worse, but knowledge and love are two goods, with love being better. For 'knowledge will end', the apostle says, although in the present it is still necessary, whereas 'love will never fail' (1 Cor 13: 8).[147]

For Augustine the proper analogy between marriage and celibacy was the behaviour of Martha and Mary. While Mary chose the 'better part' by sitting at the Lord's feet (cf. Luke 10: 42), what Martha did by attending to the needs of the saints was not bad, even though Mary had to forgo the lesser good in order to achieve the greater one.[148] Like Pelagius and the author of the *Consultationes*, Augustine went out of his way to correct Jerome's teaching on marriage as a 'lesser evil' and to insist on its genuine goodness.[149]

Augustine, however, went further than Pelagius or Jerome's other critics towards undermining the very utility of an ascetic hierarchy based on degrees of sexual renunciation. Moreover, he did so in ways that show further confrontation with specific arguments of the *Adversus Jovinianum*. For example, both in *De bono coniugali* and in *De sancta virginitate* Augustine observed that there were virtues of greater value than sexual continence: obedience and readiness for martyrdom are two that he names.[150] To take the latter example, a virtue such as readiness for martyrdom will remain hidden (even to the one who possess it) unless it is tested by actual persecution. Since it is possible that a virgin may not be ready for martyrdom and that a married person may be, Augustine argued, no virgin could ever legitimately consider herself to be superior to a married person. In other words, although he upheld the superiority of celibacy over marriage in theory, Augustine rejected its application to any particular persons in practice. As a result, Augustine urged all Christians to meditate on the fact that they do not know the limits of their own virtues, nor do they know the hidden and, perhaps, superior virtues that other people may possess.[151]

---

[147] *Bon. conjug.* 8.8 (CSEL 41, 198).   [148] *Bon. conjug.* 8.8 (CSEL 41, 199).

[149] Augustine also went beyond any of his contemporaries by differentiating the threefold good of marriage: *proles, fides,* and *sacramentum*, that is, the procreation of children, conjugal fidelity, and the sacramental bond. See Philip Lyndon Reynolds, *Marriage in the Western Church: The Christianization of Marriage During the Patristic and Early Medieval Periods* (Leiden: E. J. Brill, 1994), 241–311; and my discussion in 'Augustinian Pessimism? A New Look at Augustine's Teaching on Sex, Marriage and Celibacy', *AugStud* 25 (1994), 153–77.

[150] *Bon. conjug.* 23.29–30 (obedience); *Virg.* 46.46 (readiness for martyrdom).

[151] See *Virg.* 47.47 for an important statement of this point.

Augustine's choice of readiness for martyrdom as an example of a virtue that was superior to sexual continence was probably not accidental. Not only did he have at hand the example of a specific North African martyr who was a married woman (Crispina), but the linkage of marriage and martyrdom also served as a response to one of Jerome's more outrageous statements.[152] In *Adversus Jovinianum* Jerome had compared the married apostle Peter to the virgin apostle John and declared that 'virginity does not die, and the defilement of marriage is not washed away by the blood of martyrdom.'[153] By asserting that readiness for martyrdom was a virtue superior to sexual continence, and, moreover, by using this as grounds for asserting the potential superiority of a married person over a celibate, Augustine had subtly subverted Jerome's disdainful dismissal of the apostle Peter.[154]

There is another point at which Augustine's theology of marriage and celibacy radically destabilized the ascetic hierarchy maintained by Jerome. In *De sancta virginitate* Augustine raised the question of the proper interpretation of the hundredfold, sixtyfold, and thirtyfold harvest spoken of in the Parable of the Sower. While Jerome could confidently assert that the thirtyfold referred to marriage, the sixtyfold to widowhood, and the hundredfold to virginity, Augustine was not so certain.[155] He pointed to the tradition received from Cyprian which identified martyrdom with the hundredfold fruit.[156] He also mentioned the interpretation of Jerome and several variations on it. But Augustine's preference was to leave the question undecided: 'Since there are many gifts of divine grace and since one is greater and better than another... we do best to believe that there are too many gifts to be distributed into three categories.'[157] Given the wide variety of possible gifts, given the fact that some people have received few (but greater) gifts and that other people have received many (but lesser) gifts, and given that the advantages of the better gifts are not for this life only but for eternity—given all these possible

---

[152] In *Virg.* 44.45 Augustine had noted that the virgin might not yet be a 'Thecla', whereas the married woman might already be a 'Crispina'. According to P. G. Walsh, Crispina, who may have been a native of his hometown of Thagaste, was 'one of Augustine's heroines'. See *Augustine: De bono coniugali. De sancta virginitate* (OECT; Oxford: Clarendon Press, 2001), 130, n. 131. Walsh cites Augustine's comments at *Psal.* 120.13 and *Psal.* 137.3. See also Augustine, *ser.* 354.5 (PL 39, 1565), where he compared the virgin martyr Agnes with the married martyr Crispina.

[153] *Jov.* 1.26 (PL 23, 258).

[154] In *Bon. conjug.* 21.26 (CSEL 41, 221) Augustine argued that just as John's celibacy was not superior to Abraham's married life (since Abraham possessed continence *in habitu*), so Peter's patient endurance of martyrdom was not necessarily superior to John's (since John possessed such patience *in habitu*), even though John did not experience martyrdom. Therefore, the martyr, the virgin, and the married man were 'equal' in virtue.

[155] See *Jov.* 1.3 (PL 23, 223–4).

[156] *Virg.* 45.46 (CSEL 41, 290); cf. Cyprian, *Hab. virg.* 21, and our discussion above, p. 122.

[157] *Virg.* 45.46 (CSEL 41, 290).

variations in divine gifts, Augustine concluded: 'who among us would dare to decide among them as to their equality or the extent of their inequality?'[158] The only certainty that Augustine was willing to hazard was this: 'No one, in my opinion, should dare to consider virginity superior to martyrdom, and no one should doubt that martyrdom is a gift that remains hidden if there is no test to bring it to light.'[159]

Finally, there is one further point at which Augustine's discussion reflects a sympathy with Jovinian's way of thinking rather than Jerome's. Early on in *De bono coniugali* Augustine raised the question of the possibility of Adam and Eve engaging in sexual relations before their fall and expulsion from Eden. The question is a significant one because it touched on one of the central tenets of encratite Christianity: should human sexual activity be considered a result or symptom of the 'original sin'? Biblical interpreters had long been struck by the gap between God's original command, 'Increase and multiply', issued in Genesis 1: 28, and the fact that there is no explicit mention of sex and procreation until after the fall. That is, only in Genesis 4: 1 do we read: 'Adam knew his wife Eve, and she conceived and bore Cain.' Some commentators dealt with this conundrum by interpreting Genesis 1: 28 to refer to an originally spiritual creation or to some non-sexual form of 'increase' and 'multiplication'.[160] In the *Confessions* and in his early commentaries on Genesis, Augustine followed this line of thought, preferring to give the text a purely allegorical reading.[161] Others, such as Jerome, used Genesis 4: 1 to characterize sexuality as a purely post-lapsarian condition.

By the time he composed *De bono coniugali* and *De sancta virginitate*, however, Augustine had begun to grow dissatisfied with a non-literal reading of Genesis 1: 28. As Elizabeth Clark has demonstrated, Augustine moved away from his own earlier spiritual interpretation towards 'an earthier, more literal reading' largely under the influence of the debate between Jerome and Jovinian.[162] Although the evidence is not entirely conclusive, Clark has

---

[158] *Virg.* 46.46 (CSEL 41, 291); trans. Kearney, 99.
[159] *Virg.* 46.47 (CSEL 41, 292).
[160] A good summary of the Christian exegetical tradition on Gen 1: 28 can be found in Jeremy Cohen, *'Be Fertile and Increase, Fill the Earth and Master It': The Ancient and Medieval Career of a Biblical Text* (Ithaca and London: Cornell University Press, 1989), 235–70.
[161] e.g. in *Conf.* 13.24.37 Augustine took Gen 1: 28 to refer to the human mind's ability to generate a multiplicity of concepts to express a single thought or to the mind's ability to give an obscure text a plurality of meanings.
[162] Clark, 'Heresy, Asceticism, Adam and Eve: Interpretations of Genesis 1–3 in the Later Latin Fathers', in her *Ascetic Piety and Women's Faith*, 353–85; see also Susan E. Schreiner, 'Eve, the Mother of History: Reaching for the Reality of History in Augustine's Later Exegesis of Genesis', in Gregory A. Robbins (ed.), *Genesis 1–3 in the History of Exegesis: Intrigue in the Garden* (Lewiston, NY and Queenston, Ontario: Edwin Mellen Press, 1988), 135–86.

suggested that Jovinian may have taught that Adam and Eve could, theoretically, have had sinless intercourse in Eden.[163] Her argument is quite plausible, especially given the fact that both Ambrosiaster and the author of the *Consultationes Zacchaei et Apollonii* advanced a similar argument against Jerome.

In any case, it is clear that by 404 Augustine was willing to entertain the possibility of sinless sex in Eden in a manner that he did not in his earlier writings. In *De bono coniugali* Augustine presented three possible interpretations of Genesis 1: 28, including the literal, sexual one, although he declined to rule in favour of any of them. While Augustine's full embrace of the literal meaning of 'Increase and multiply' did not emerge until he composed his *Literal Commentary on Genesis* shortly after *De bono coniugali*, Clark is surely correct to see the Jovinianist controversy leading him in this direction. By 404 Augustine had begun to realize that an orthodox Christian approach to marriage required an acceptance of the original, created goodness of the body and sexuality. Only such a theology could provide sufficient safeguards against encratite and Manichaean heresy.[164]

In sum, Augustine's response to the Jovinianist controversy was similar in many ways to that of Pelagius and the author of the *Consultationes Zacchaei et Apollonii*. All three authors appear to have deliberately distanced themselves from the positions of both Jovinian and Jerome. While upholding some form of the ascetic hierarchy and acknowledging the superiority of celibacy over marriage (against Jovinian), each maintained that marriage was something genuinely good (against Jerome). If, on some level, they all regarded Jovinian as a 'heretic', it does not appear that they would have considered Jerome to be purely 'orthodox'. The efforts of these three authors to 'correct' Jerome, while at the same time confuting Jovinian, demonstrate the extent to which 'heresy' and 'orthodoxy' on the matter of marriage and asceticism were still very much under construction in the late fourth and early fifth centuries.

Augustine's response to Jovinian and Jerome, however, remained exceptional. Whereas Pelagius had, in a sense, relativized the ascetic hierarchy by insisting on the requirement of perfect righteousness for all Christians, Augustine issued a more fundamental challenge to the hierarchy itself. By introducing virtues that were superior to sexual continence (e.g. readiness for martyrdom) and by emphasizing that it was impossible to know if one possessed such virtues, Augustine had introduced a note of radical instability into the discussion of marriage and celibacy. While acknowledging the

---

[163] Clark, 'Heresy, Asceticism', 361, cites *Jov.* 1.29, where Jerome responded to the contention that the first parents 'could have had union without sin'.

[164] Cf. Clark, 'Heresy, Asceticism', 371, who notes Augustine's influence on both Thomas Aquinas and Martin Luther.

theoretical superiority of celibacy over marriage, Augustine simultaneously undermined the *practical* validity of this hierarchy, since no individual celibate could ever claim superiority over any individual married person. Augustine's subversion of the ascetic hierarchy seems to have been motivated primarily by his desire to call celibate Christians to acknowledge the fragility of their virtue and to adopt a genuine attitude of humility. On this point he clearly shared common ground with Jovinian.[165]

Finally, even as they rejected Jovinian's teaching on the equality of marriage and celibacy, Augustine, Pelagius, and the author of the *Consultationes* each preserved some features of his thought. The author of the *Consultationes* emphasized faith and baptismal regeneration as the foundation of salvation for all Christians in a manner that recalled several of the propositions of Jovinian. Pelagius, likewise, echoed the optimism of Jovinian's belief that a sinless life after baptism was within the reach of all Christians.[166] And Augustine undermined the ascetic hierarchy in a form that mirrored the intentions, if not all of the arguments, of Jovinian. Augustine's defence of marriage, like Jovinian's, drew on the long tradition of anti-heretical discourse, and his emphasis on humility undermined discriminations within the Church based on ascetic practice. In this sense, one could say that each of these opponents of Jovinian perpetuated elements of his 'heresy' even as they repudiated it.

---

[165] Cf. Jovinian's appeal to consecrated virgins, cited in *Jov.* 1.5 (PL 23, 228): 'Do not be proud! You belong to the same Church as those who are married.'

[166] Essential on this topic is Duval, *L'affaire Jovinien*, 285–313.

Conclusion

This book has been largely a study of contexts. I have attempted to shed new light on Jovinian and his teaching by relating him to a variety of contexts: the rise of a Christian aristocracy in the fourth century (Chapter 2); the development of an anti-heretical tradition in the first three centuries (Chapter 3); the proliferation of this heresiological discourse in the fourth century (Chapter 4); and the history of Marian theology, especially on the matter of Mary's perpetual virginity (Chapter 5). Moreover, I have attempted to distinguish the different approaches to marriage, celibacy, and clerical life evinced by Jovinian's opponents (Chapter 6) and to highlight the ways in which at least one of these opponents, Jerome, became the object of criticism and accusations of heresy (Chapter 7). If there is a single conclusion to be derived from my study, it is that Jovinian stood much closer to the centre of the Christian tradition than previous critics have recognized; certainly he was closer to early Christian 'orthodoxy' than his condemnation for 'heresy' would suggest. Not only did he have clear anti-heretical intentions, but he also shared many arguments and tactics with previous anti-heretical writers.

But to succeed in placing Jovinian closer to the 'centre' of Christian discourse is simultaneously to 'de-centre' some major figures in the Christian tradition, and my study has raised some questions about the ascetical theologies of Ambrose and Jerome and their relation to the prior tradition. Jerome's deep dependence on the Montanist writings of Tertullian, as well as the extensive influence of Origen, led him to adopt a posture towards marriage that many, if not most, of his contemporaries found scandalous. Similarly, Ambrose's attraction to the ideal of virginal integrity, also influenced by a heavy dose of Origen's theology, caused him to adopt a Marian doctrine (*virginitas in partu*) that had only a fragile basis in earlier Christian tradition. In different ways, both Jerome and Ambrose represented the survival of the ancient encratite tradition, at least in its moderate form. Both strongly associated sex with original sin and linked salvation to sexual purity. If Ambrose and Jerome were the only evidence, one might conclude that the condemnation of Jovinian marked the triumph of encratism and the demise of earlier orthodoxy.

Fortunately, there were other voices in the mix, and, as I argued in Chapter 7, the responses of Augustine, Pelagius, and other critics of Jerome point towards a different resolution to the Jovinianist controversy. Although they rejected Jovinian's equation of marriage and celibacy, these writers also repudiated the excesses of Jerome's *Adversus Jovinianum*. Jerome's concept of marriage as merely a *levius malum* was discarded, as was the notion of an inevitable 'defilement' (*sordes*) or corruption attached to sexual intercourse. Augustine and the other opponents of Jerome insisted on the original, created goodness of human sexuality, thus repudiating a central tenet of encratite Christianity. Moreover, Augustine's development of the 'three goods' of marriage—offspring (*proles*), fidelity (*fides*), and sacrament (*sacramentum*)—entered into the mainstream of the Western theological tradition and provided an essential bulwark against the currents of encratism that had troubled (and continued to trouble) the Christian conscience.[1] While Jovinian's condemnation stood firm, his resistance to the exaltation of asceticism found confirmation in unexpected places, such as in Augustine's subversion of the ascetic hierarchy. Like many heresies, the teaching of Jovinian survived, *mutatis mutandis*, in the formation of a 'new orthodoxy'.

Ironically, it was Augustine, who spoke so forcefully about 'the good of marriage' against Jerome, who also provided the Christian tradition with the most lasting variant of ancient encratism. In the decades following the composition of *De bono coniugali* and *De sancta virginitate*, Augustine continued to speculate on the creation of the first human beings and the nature of the sin that so disrupted human history. Eventually the moderate character of his response to Jovinian was overshadowed (though never completely obscured) by his reflections on the inherited nature of sin and its pernicious effects on human sexual desire (*concupiscentia carnis*). Even as Augustine insisted on the original place of sex in God's providential plan, he came to believe that the sin of Adam and Eve had irrevocably damaged human beings in their ability to function as sexual persons. As Augustine engaged in debate first with Pelagius and then with Bishop Julian of Eclanum, he persistently emphasized the impotence of the human will, which, apart from God's grace, was incapable of controlling even the human body.[2] By stressing the damage

---

[1] The sensitive discussion of Carol Harrison is a good antidote to the many modern misrepresentations of Augustine's thought on marriage: *Augustine: Christian Truth and Fractured Humanity* (Oxford: Oxford University Press, 2000), 158–93. For a similarly nuanced account of Augustine's views on monasticism, see Conrad Leyser, *Authority and Asceticism from Augustine to Gregory the Great* (Oxford: Clarendon Press, 2000), 3–32.

[2] Brown, *Body and Society*, 402–27, provides an excellent overview of the debate with Julian. See also his 'Sexuality and Society in the Fifth Century A. D.: Augustine and Julian of Eclanum', in E. Gabba (ed.), *Tria Corda: Scritti in onore di Arnaldo Momigliano* (Como: Edizioni New Press, 1983), 49–70.

done to human nature by the primeval sin and by insisting on the 'sinful' character of sexual concupiscence, Augustine transmitted to future generations a new version of the encratite tradition.[3]

The eventual course of Augustine's development, however, should not blind us to the significance of his treatises *De bono coniugali* and *De sancta virginitate*, nor lead us to neglect the other moderate voices that were raised in the Jovinianist controversy. Jovinian's concern about the dangers of certain ascetic teachings clearly resonated with many other Western Christians, even with those who did not share his rejection of the ascetic hierarchy. The many critical responses to Jerome's *Adversus Jovinianum* attest to the desire of Western Christians to find a more moderate approach to the issue of marriage and celibacy. While Jovinian's condemnation signalled the emergence of a 'new orthodoxy' in the Western Church and an official embrace of the notion that celibacy was superior to marriage, the Jovinianist controversy allowed a number of different voices to emerge: Ambrosiaster, Pelagius, the author of the *Consultationes Zacchaei et Apollonii*, Rufinus, Vigilantius, Augustine, and other opponents of Jerome echoed, in varying degrees, the concerns of Jovinian. If this book has allowed these voices, as well as that of Jovinian, to be heard more clearly, then it has served its purpose.

---

[3] On the encratite elements in Augustine's teaching on the transmission of original sin, see Pier Franco Beatrice, *Tradux peccati: Alle fonti della dottrina agostiniana del peccato originale* (Milan: Vita e Pensiero, 1978).

References

1. English Translations of Ancient Sources

Atkinson, James, *The Christian in Society* (Luther's Works, 44; Philadelphia: Fortress Press, 1966).

Barkley, Gary Wayne, *Origen: Homilies on Leviticus 1–16* (FC 83; Washington, DC: The Catholic University of America Press, 1990).

Beyenka, Mary Melchior, *Saint Ambrose: Letters* (FC 26; New York: Fathers of the Church, Inc., 1954).

Bogan, Mary Inez, *Saint Augustine: The Retractations* (FC 60; Washington, DC: The Catholic University of America Press, 1968).

Brakke, David, *Athanasius and the Politics of Asceticism* (OECS; Oxford: Clarendon Press, 1995).

Bruyn, Theodore de, *Pelagius's Commentary on St Paul's Epistle to the Romans* (OECS; Oxford: Clarendon Press, 1993).

Chadwick, Henry, *Saint Augustine: Confessions* (Oxford and New York: Oxford University Press, 1991).

Charlesworth, J. H., *The Odes of Solomon* (Oxford: Clarendon Press, 1973).

—— *The Old Testament Pseudepigrapha*, 2 vols. (Garden City, NY: Doubleday, 1985).

Clark, Elizabeth A., and Hatch, Diana F., *The Golden Bough. The Oaken Cross: The Virgilian Cento of Faltonia Betitia Proba* (AAR Texts and Translations, 5; Chico, CA: Scholars Press, 1981).

Clarke, G. W., *The Octavius of Marcus Minucius Felix* (ACW 39; New York, NY and Paramus, NJ: Newman Press, 1974).

Davidson, Ivor J., *Ambrose: De officiis* (OECS; Oxford: Oxford University Press, 2001).

Davis, Raymond, *The Book of Pontiffs* (Translated Texts for Historians; Liverpool University Press, 1989).

Deferrari, Roy J., *Saint Ambrose: Theological and Dogmatic Works* (FC 44; Washington, DC: The Catholic University of America Press, 1963).

Duff, J. Wight, and Duff, Arnold M., *Minor Latin Poets* (LCL; Cambridge, Mass: Harvard University Press, 1968).

Ehrman, Bart D., *The Apostolic Fathers*, 2 vols. (LCL 24–5; Cambridge, Mass.: Harvard University Press, 2003).

Evans, Ernest, *Tertullian's Treatise on the Incarnation* (London: SPCK, 1956).

Finn, Thomas M., *Early Christian Baptism and the Catechumenate: Italy, North Africa, and Egypt* (MFC 6; Collegeville, Minn.: The Liturgical Press, 1992).

Gallagher, Donald A., and Gallagher, Adella J., *The Catholic and Manichaean Ways of Life* (FC 56; Washington, DC: The Catholic University of America Press, 1965).

Grant, Robert M., *Theophilus of Antioch: Ad Autolycum* (OECT; Oxford: Clarendon Press, 1970).

Greer, Rowan A., *Origen* (CWS; New York: Paulist Press, 1979).
Halton, Thomas P., *Saint Jerome: On Illustrious Men* (FC 100; Washington, DC: The Catholic University of America Press, 1999).
Hanson, Craig, L., *The Iberian Fathers* (FC 99; Washington, DC: The Catholic University of America Press, 1999).
Hennecke, Edgar, and Schneemelcher, Wilhelm (eds.), *New Testament Apocrypha*, Revised English trans. R. McL. Wilson, 2 vols. (Cambridge: James Clarke & Co./Louisville, Ky: Westminster/John Knox, 1992).
Hill, Charles Leander, *Melanchthon: Selected Writings* (Minneapolis, Minn.: Augsburg, 1962).
Hock, Ronald F., *The Infancy Gospel of James and Thomas* (Santa Rosa, CA: Polebridge Press, 1995).
Hritzu, John N., *Saint Jerome: Dogmatic and Polemical Works* (FC 53; Washington, DC: The Catholic University of American Press, 1965).
Kearney, Ray, *Augustine: Marriage and Virginity* (WSA 1/9; Hyde Park, NY: New City Press, 1999).
Keenan, Angela Elizabeth, *Saint Cyprian: Treatises* (FC 36; New York: Fathers of the Church, 1958).
Krabbe, M. K., *Epistula ad Demetriadem De Vera Humilitate* (Washington, DC: The Catholic University of America Press, 1965).
Le Saint, William P., *Tertullian: Treatises on Marriage and Remarriage* (ACW 13; New York, NY and Ramsey, NJ: Newman Press, 1951).
—— *Tertullian: Treatises on Penance: On Penitence and On Purity* (ACW 28; New York: Newman Press, 1959).
Lienhard, S.J., Joseph T., *Origen: Homilies on Luke. Fragments on Luke* (FC 94; Washington, DC: The Catholic University of America Press, 1996).
Lutz, Cora E., 'Musonius Rufus: The Roman Socrates', *Yale Classical Studies* 10 (1947), 3–147.
Meyer, Robert T., *St. Athanasius: The Life of Antony* (ACW 10; Westminster, Md.: The Newman Press, 1950).
—— *Palladius: The Lausiac History* (ACW 34; Westminster, Md.: The Newman Press, 1965).
Mierow, Charles Christopher, *The Letters of St. Jerome* (ACW 33; New York: Newman Press, 1963).
Nardeau, Ray, 'The Progymnasmata of Aphthonius in Translation', *Speech Monographs*, 19 (1952), 264–85.
Oulton, John Ernest Leonard, and Chadwick, Henry, *Alexandrian Christianity* (LCC; Philadelphia: Westminster Press, 1954).
Parsons, W., *St. Augustine: Letters* (FC 12; New York: Fathers of the Church, 1951).
Pharr, Clyde, *The Theodosian Code and Novels and the Sirmondian Constitutions* (Princeton, NJ: Princeton University Press, 1952).
Ramsey, Boniface, *Ambrose* (London and New York: Routledge, 1997).
Rees, B. R., *The Letters of Pelagius and his Followers* (Rochester, NY: The Boydell Press, 1991).
Rolfe, John C., *Ammianus Marcellinus: Res gestae*, 3 vols. (LCL; Cambridge, Mass.: Harvard University Press, 1937–1950).

Scheck, Thomas P., *Origen: Commentary on the Epistle to the Romans. Books 6–10* (FC 104; Washington, DC: The Catholic University of America Press, 2002).
Schoedel, William R., *Athenagoras: Legatio and De Resurrectione* (OECT; Oxford: Clarendon Press, 1972).
—— *Ignatius of Antioch: A Commentary on the Letters of Ignatius of Antioch* (Philadelphia: Fortress Press, 1985).
Sellew, Philip, *The Hundredfold Reward: Martyrdom and Sexual Renunciation in Christian North Africa* (WGRW; Atlanta: SBL/Leiden: Brill, forthcoming).
Shotwell, James T., and Loomis, Louise Ropes, *The See of Peter* (New York: Columbia University Press, 1927; reprint New York: Octagon Books, 1965).
Sowards, J. K., *Erasmus: Literary and Educational Writings*, iii (CWE 25; Toronto: University of Toronto Press, 1985).
Tanner, Norman P., *Decrees of the Ecumenical Councils*, ii, *Trent to Vatican II* (London and Washington, DC: Sheed & Ward and Georgetown University Press, 1990).
Teske, Roland J., *Answer to the Pelagians*, ii (WSA I/24; Hyde Park, NY: New City Press, 1998).
Tilley, Maureen, 'An Anonymous Letter to a Woman Named Susanna', in Richard Valantasis (ed.), *Religions of Late Antiquity in Practice* (Princeton, NJ: Princeton University Press, 2000), 218–29.
Unger, Dominic J., with further revisions by John J. Dillon, *St. Irenaeus of Lyons: Against the Heresies*, i (ACW 55; New York, NY, and Mahwah, NJ: The Newman Press, 1992).
Veilleux, Armand, *Pachomian Koinonia*, i. *The Life of Saint Pachomius and his Disciples* (Cistercian Studies, 45; Kalamazoo, Mich.: Cistercian Publications, 1980).
Walsh, P. G., *Augustine: De bono coniugali. De sancta virginitate* (OECT; Oxford: Clarendon Press, 2001).
Waszink, J. H., *Quinti Septimi Florentis Tertulliani De anima* (Amsterdam: J.M. Meulenhoff, 1947).
Whittaker, Molly, *Tatian: Oratio ad Graecos and Fragments* (OECT; Oxford: Clarendon Press, 1982).
Williams, Frank, *The Panarion of Epiphanius of Salamis*, 2 vols. (NHMS 35–6; Leiden: Brill, 1987, 1994).
Williamson, G. A., *Eusebius: The History of the Church from Christ to Constantine* (Minneapolis, Minn.: Augsburg Publishing House, 1975).
Wood, Simon P., *Clement of Alexandria: Christ the Educator* (FC 23; New York: Fathers of the Church, 1954).
Yarbrough, O. Larry, 'Canons from the Council of Gangra', in Vincent L. Wimbush (ed.), *Ascetic Behavior in Greco-Roman Antiquity: A Sourcebook* (Minneapolis, Minn.: Fortress Press, 1990), 448–55.

2. Modern Sources

Adkin, Neil, 'Ambrose and Jerome: The Opening Shot', *Mnemosyne*, 46 (1993), 364–76.
—— 'Pope Siricius' "Simplicity" (Jerome, epist. 127, 9, 3)', *VetChr* 33 (1996), 25–8.

—— 'Jerome on Ambrose: The Preface to the Translation of Origen's Homilies on Luke', *RBen* 107 (1997), 5–14.
Aldama, José A. de, 'La condenación de Joviniano en el sínodo de Roma', *EphMar* 13 (1963), 107–19.
Allison, Dale, *Jesus of Nazareth: Millenarian Prophet* (Minneapolis, Minn.: Fortress Press, 1998).
Arjava, Antti, *Women and Law in Late Antiquity* (Oxford: Clarendon Press, 1996).
Audet, Jean-Paul, *Mariage et célibat dans le service pastoral de l'église: Histoire et orientations*. 2nd edn. (Québec: Éditions des sources, 1999).
Barclift, Philip L., 'In Controversy with Saint Augustine: Julian of Eclanum on the Nature of Sin', *RTAM* 58 (1991), 5–20.
Barnard, L. W., 'The Heresy of Tatian—Once Again', *JEH* 19 (1968), 1–10.
Barnes, T. D., 'Christians and Pagans in the Reign of Constantius', in A. Dihle (ed.), *L'Église et l'empire au IVe siècle* (Entretiens sur l'antiquité classique 34; Geneva: Vandoeuvres, 1989), 302–37.
Bassler, Jouette M., *1 Timothy. 2 Timothy. Titus* (Nashville: Abingdon Press, 1996).
Bauer, Walter, *Orthodoxy and Heresy in Earliest Christianity*, edited by Robert Kraft and Gerhard Krodel (Philadelphia: Fortress Press, 1971).
Beatrice, Pier Franco, *Tradux peccati: Alle fonti della dottrina agostiniana del peccato originale* (Milan: Vita e Pensiero, 1978).
—— 'Le tuniche di pelle: Antiche letture di Gen. 3, 21', in U. Bianchi (ed.), *La tradizione dell'Encrateia: Motivazioni ontologiche e protologiche* (Rome: Edizioni dell'Ateneo, 1985), 433–82.
Beduhn, Jason, 'The Battle for the Body in Manichaean Asceticism', in Richard Valantasis and Vincent Wimbush (eds.), *Asceticism* (New York: Oxford University Press, 1995), 513–19.
Behr, John, *Asceticism and Anthropology in Irenaeus and Clement* (OECS; Oxford: Clarendon Press, 2000), 162–3.
Berg, Beverly, 'Alcestis and Hercules in the Catacomb of the Via Latina', *VC* 48 (1994), 219–34.
Beskow, Per, 'The Theodosian Laws against Manichaeism', in P. Bryder (ed.), *Manichaean Studies: Proceedings of the First International Conference on Manichaeism* (Lund: Plus Ultra, 1988), 1–11.
Bianchi, Ugo, 'La tradition de l'*enkrateia*: motivations ontologiques et protologiques', in U. Bianchi (ed.), *La tradizione dell'enkrateia: Motivazioni ontologiche e protologiche* (Rome: Edizioni dell'Ateneo, 1985), 293–315.
Birley, A. R., 'Magnus Maximus and the Persecution of Heresy', *BJRL* 66 (1982–3), 13–43.
Bohlin, Torgny, *Die Theologie des Pelagius und ihre Genesis* (Uppsala: A.-B. Lundequistska Bokhandeln/Wiesbaden: Otto Harrassowitz, 1957).
Bolgiani, Franco, 'La tradizione eresiologica sull'encratismo, i. La notizie di Ireneo', *Atti dell'Accademia delle scienze di Torino*, 91 (1956–7), 343–419.
Bonner, Gerald, 'Pelagianism and Augustine', *AugStud* 23 (1992), 33–51.

Boyarin, Daniel, *A Radical Jew: Paul and the Politics of Identity* (Berkeley: University of California Press, 1994).
Brakke, David, *Athanasius and the Politics of Asceticism* (OECS; Oxford: Clarendon Press, 1995).
Brandenburg, Hugo, 'Bellerophon christianus?' *RQ* 63 (1968), 49–86.
—— *Ancient Churches of Rome from the Fourth to the Seventh Century: The Dawn of Christian Architecture in the West*, trans. Andreas Kropp (Turnhout: Brepols, 2005).
Braun, René, *'Deus Christianorum': Recherches sur le vocabulaire doctrinal de Tertullien* (Paris: 1962).
—— 'Tertullien et l'exégèse de I Cor 7', in J. Fontaine and C. Kannengiesser (eds.), *Epektasis: Mélanges patristiques offerts au Cardinal Jean Daniélou* (Paris: Beauchesne, 1972), 21–8.
Brochet, J., *Saint Jérôme et ses ennemis* (Paris, 1905).
Broudéhoux, Jean-Paul, *Mariage et famille chez Clément d'Alexandrie* (Paris: Beauchesne, 1970).
Brown, Peter, *Religion and Society in the Age of Saint Augustine* (London: Faber and Faber, 1972).
—— 'The Diffusion of Manichaeism in the Roman Empire', in his *Religion and Society*, 94–118.
—— 'Aspects of the Christianization of the Roman Aristocracy', in his *Religion and Society*, 161–82.
—— 'Pelagius and his Supporters: Aims and Environment', in his *Religion and Society*, 183–207.
—— 'The Patrons of Pelagius: The Roman Aristocracy between East and West', in his *Religion and Society*, 208–26.
—— 'Sexuality and Society in the Fifth Century A.D.: Augustine and Julian of Eclanum', in E. Gabba (ed.), *Tria Corda: Scritti in onore di Arnaldo Momigliano* (Como: Edizioni New Press, 1983), 49–70.
—— *The Body and Society: Men, Women, and Sexual Renunciation in Early Christianity* (New York: Columbia University Press, 1988).
—— 'Christianization and Religious Conflict', in Averil Cameron and Peter Garnsey (eds.), *The Late Empire A.D. 337–425* (CAH 13; Cambridge: Cambridge University Press, 1998), 632–4.
Brown, Raymond, Donfried, Karl P., Fitzmyer, Joseph A., and Reumann, John (eds.), *Mary in the New Testament* (Philadelphia: Fortress Press, 1978).
Budzin, Allan J., 'Jovinian's Four Theses on the Christian Life: An Alternative Patristic Spirituality', *Toronto Journal of Theology*, 4 (1988), 44–59.
Burrus, Virginia, 'Ascesis, Authority, and Text: The Acts of the Council of Saragossa', *Semeia* 58 (1992), 95–108.
—— *The Making of a Heretic: Gender, Authority, and the Priscillianist Controversy* (Berkeley: University of California Press, 1995).
Cain, Andrew, 'In Ambrosiaster's Shadow: A Critical Re-Evaluation of the Last Surviving Letter Exchange between Pope Damasus and Jerome', *REAug* 51 (2005), 257–77.

Callam, Daniel, 'Clerical Continence in the Fourth Century: Three Papal Decretals', *TS* 41 (1980), 3–50.
—— 'The Frequency of Mass in the Latin Church ca. 400', *TS* 45 (1984), 613–50.
Cameron, Alan, 'Rutilius Namatianus, St. Augustine, and the Date of the *De reditu*', *JRS* 57 (1967), 31–9.
Callam, Daniel, *Claudian: Poetry and Propaganda at the Court of Honorius* (Oxford: Clarendon Press, 1970).
—— 'The Last Pagans of Rome', in W. V. Harris (ed.), *The Transformations of Vrbs Roma in Late Antiquity* (Journal of Roman Archaeology, Supplementary Series 33; Portsmouth, R. I., 1999), 109–21.
Cameron, Averil, 'How to Read Heresiology', *JMEMS* 33 (2003), 471–92; reprinted in Dale B. Martin and Patricia Cox Miller (eds.), *The Cultural Turn in Late Ancient Studies: Gender, Asceticism, and Historiography* (Durham, NC: Duke University Press, 2005), 193–212.
Campenhausen, Hans von, 'Polykarp von Smyrna und die Pastoralbriefe', in his *Aus der Frühzeit des Christentums* (Tübingen: J. C. B. Mohr, 1963), 197–252.
—— *The Virgin Birth in the Theology of the Ancient Church*, trans. Frank Clarke (Studies in Historical Theology, 2; London: SCM, 1964).
Cavallera, Ferdinand, *Saint Jérôme: Sa vie et son oeuvre*, Première partie, t. ii (Louvain: Spicilegium Sacrum Lovaniense, 1922).
Chadwick, Henry, 'Some Reflections on the Character and Theology of the Odes of Solomon', in P. Granfield and J. Jungmann (eds.), *Kyriakon: Festschrift Johannes Quasten*, i (Münster: Aschendorff, 1970), 266–70.
—— *Priscillian of Avila: The Occult and the Charismatic in the Early Church* (Oxford: Clarendon Press, 1976).
—— *The Church in Ancient Society: From Galilee to Gregory the Great* (New York and Oxford: Oxford University Press, 2001).
Charlesworth, J. H., 'The Odes of Solomon—Not Gnostic', *CBQ* 31 (1969), 357–69.
Chastagnol, A., 'Le sénateur Volusien et la conversion d'une famille de l'aristocratie romain au Bas-Empire', *Revue des études anciennes*, 58 (1956), 241–53.
—— *La Préfecture urbaine à Rome sous le Bas-empire* (Paris: Presses universitaires de France, 1960).
Clark, Elizabeth A., *Ascetic Piety and Women's Faith: Essays on Late Ancient Christianity* (Lewiston/Queenston: The Edwin Mellen Press, 1986).
—— 'Ascetic Renunciation and Feminine Advancement: A Paradox of Late Ancient Asceticism', in her *Ascetic Piety and Women's Faith*, 175–208.
—— 'Authority and Humility: A Conflict of Values in Fourth-Century Female Monasticism', in her *Ascetic Piety and Women's Faith*, 209–28.
—— 'Vitiated Seeds and Holy Vessels: Augustine's Manichean Past', in her *Ascetic Piety and Women's Faith*, 291–349.
—— 'Heresy, Asceticism, Adam and Eve: Interpretations of Genesis 1–3 in the Later Latin Fathers', in her *Ascetic Piety and Women's Faith*, 353–85.
—— *The Origenist Controversy: The Cultural Construction of an Early Christian Debate* (Princeton, NJ: Princeton University Press, 1992).

Clark, Elizabeth A., 'The Lady Vanishes: Dilemmas of a Feminist Historian after the "Linguistic Turn"', *CH* 67 (1998), 1–31.

—— *Reading Renunciation: Asceticism and Scripture in Early Christianity* (Princeton, NJ: Princeton University Press, 1999).

Clark, E. Gillian, 'Women and Asceticism in Late Antiquity: The Refusal of Status and Gender', in R. Valantassis and V. Wimbush (eds.), *Asceticism* (New York: Oxford University Press, 1995), 33–48.

Clarke, G. W., 'The Date of the Oration of Tatian', *HTR* 60 (1967), 123–36.

Clausi, Benedetto, 'La parola stravolta: Polemica ed esegesi biblica nell'*Adversus Iovinianum* di Gerolamo', in Marcello Marin and Mario Girardi (eds.), *Retorica ed esegesi biblica: Il rilievo dei contenuti attraverso le forme* (Bari: Edipuglia, 1996), 87–126.

—— 'Storia sacra e strategia retorica: Osservazioni sull'uso dell' "*exemplum*" biblico nell'*Adversus Iovinianum* de Gerolamo', *Cristianesimo nella Storia* 16 (1995), 475–84.

Claussen, M. A., 'Pagan Rebellion and Christian Apologetics in Fourth-Century Rome: The *Consultationes Zacchaei et Apollonii*', *JEH* 46 (1995), 589–614.

Cochini, Christian, *Apostolic Origins of Priestly Celibacy*, trans. Nelly Marans (San Francisco: Ignatius Press, 1990).

Cohen, Jeremy, '*Be Fertile and Increase, Fill the Earth and Master It*': *The Ancient and Medieval Career of a Biblical Text* (Ithaca and London: Cornell University Press, 1989).

Cooper, Kate, 'Insinuations of Womanly Influence: An Aspect of the Christianization of the Roman Aristocracy', *JRS* 82 (1992), 150–64.

—— *The Virgin and the Bride: Idealized Womanhood in Late Antiquity* (Cambridge, Mass.: Harvard University Press, 1996).

Cothenet, Edouard, 'Le Protévangile de Jacques: origine, genre et signification d'un premier midrash chrétien sur la Nativité de Marie', *ANRW* II.25.6 (1988), 4252–69.

Courcelle, Pierre, 'Date, source et genèse des "Consultationes Zacchaei et Apollonii"', *RHR* 146 (1954), 174–93.

—— *Late Latin Writers and their Greek Sources*, trans. Harry E. Wedeck (Cambridge: Harvard University Press, 1969).

Coyle, J. Kevin, 'Empire and Eschaton', *Église et Théologie*, 12 (1981), 36–41.

Croke, Brian, and Harries, Jill (eds.), *Religious Conflict in Fourth Century Rome* (Sydney: Sydney University Press, 1982).

Crouzel, Henri, 'La théologie mariale d'Origène', in Crouzel (ed.), *Origène: Homélies sur. s. Luc* (SC 87; Paris, 1962), 11–64.

—— *Virginité et mariage selon Origène* (Paris: Desclée de Brouwer, 1963).

—— 'Les critiques adressées par Méthode et ses contemporains à la doctrine origénienne du corps ressuscité', *Greg* 53 (1972), 679–716.

—— 'Chronologie proposée de prêtre commingeois Vigilance de Calagurris (Saint-Martory)', *BLE* 73 (1972), 265–6.

—— *Origen: The Life and Thought of the First Great Theologian*, trans. A. S. Worrall (San Francisco: Harper and Row, 1989).

Cullman, O., 'Infancy Gospels', in Edgar Hennecke and Wilhelm Schneemelcher (eds.), *New Testament Apocrypha*, i., 2nd edn., trans. R. McL. Wilson (Louisville, Ky: Westminster/John Knox Press, 1992), 370–4.

Curran, John, *Pagan City and Christian Capital: Rome in the Fourth Century* (Oxford: Clarendon Press, 2000).

Daniélou, Jean, *A History of Early Christian Doctrine Before the Council of Nicaea*, iii. *The Origins of Latin Christianity*, trans. David Smith and John Austin Baker (Philadelphia: Westminster Press, 1977).

Davidson, Ivor, 'Pastoral Theology at the End of the Fourth Century: Ambrose and Jerome', *StPatr* 33 (1997), 295–301.

Davis, Stephen J., *The Cult of Saint Thecla: A Tradition of Women's Piety in Late Antiquity* (OECS; Oxford: Clarendon Press, 2001).

Dechow, Jon F., *Dogma and Mysticism in Early Christianity* (PMS 13; Macon, GA: Mercer University Press, 1988).

—— 'Origen and Corporeality: The Case of Methodius' *On the Resurrection*', in Robert J. Daly (ed.), *Origeniana Quinta* (Louvain: Peeters Press, 1992), 509–18.

Dekkers, Eligius, *Clavis patrum latinorum*. 3rd edn. (Turnhout: Brepols, 1995).

Deléani, Simone, 'Présence de Cyprien dans les oeuvres de Jérôme sur la virginité', in Yves-Marie Duval, (ed.), *Jérôme entre l'occident et l'orient* (Paris: Études Augustiniennes, 1988), 61–82.

Deming, Will, *Paul on Marriage and Celibacy: The Hellenistic Background of 1 Corinthians 7* (Cambridge: Cambridge University Press, 1995).

Dibelius, Martin, and Conzelmann, Hans, *The Pastoral Epistles: A Commentary on the Pastoral Epistles* (Philadelphia: Fortress Press, 1972).

Dolbeau, François, *Augustin d'Hippone: Vingt-six sermons au people d'Afrique* (Paris: Études Augustiniennes, 2001).

Drijvers, J. W., 'Virginity and Asceticism in Late Roman Elites', in J. Bolk and P. Mason (eds.), *Sexual Asymmetry: Studies in Ancient Society* (Amsterdam: J. C. Gieben, 1987), 241–73.

—— 'The Acts of Thomas,' in Edgar Hennecke and Wilhelm Schneemelcher (eds.), *New Testament Apocrypha*, ii. *Writings relating to the Apostles, Apocalypses, and Related Subjects*, 2nd edn., trans. R. McL. Wilson (Louisville, Ky: Westminster/John Knox Press, 1992), 322–39.

Dudden, F. Holmes, *The Life and Times of St. Ambrose*, 2 vols. (Oxford: Clarendon Press, 1935).

Dungan, David, *The Sayings of Jesus in the Churches of Paul* (Philadelphia: Fortress Press, 1971).

Dunphy, W., 'On the Date of St. Ambrose's *De Tobia*', *SacEr* 27 (1984), 29–33.

Duval, Yves-Marie, 'Bellérophon et les ascètes chrétiens: "Melancholia" ou "otium"?' *Caesarodunum*, 2 (1968), 183–90.

—— 'Sur une page de saint Cyprien chez saint Ambroise: *Hexameron* 6,8,47 et *De habitu virginum* 15–17', *REAug* 16 (1970), 25–34.

—— 'L'originalité du *De virginibus* dans le mouvement ascétique occidental: Ambroise, Cyprien, Athanase', in Yves-Marie Duval (ed.), *Ambroise de Milan: XVIe Centenaire de son election épiscopale* (Paris: Études Augustiniennes, 1974), 9–66.

Duval, Yves-Marie, 'L'influence des écrivains africains du IIIe siècle sur les écrivains chrétiens de l'Italie du nord dans la seconde moitié du IVe siècle', *Antichità Altoadriatiche*, 5 (1974), 191–225.

—— 'Le problématique de la Lettre aux vierges d'Athanase', *Mus* 88 (1975), 405–33.

—— 'Pélage est-il le censeur inconnu de l'*Adversus Iovinianum* à Rome en 393? Ou: du "portrait-robot" de l'hérétique chez s. Jérôme', *RHE* 75 (1980), 525–57.

—— 'Traces de lecture de *Peri Archôn* d'Origène avant le depart de Rome de Jérôme en 385', in Yves-Marie Duval (ed.), *Jérôme entre l'occident et l'orient* (Paris: Études Augustiniennes, 1988), 139–51.

—— 'Pélage en son temps: Données chronologiques nouvelles pour une presentation nouvelle', *StPatr* 38 (2001), 95–118.

—— *L'affaire Jovinien: D'une crise de la sociètè romaine à une crise de la pensée chrétienne à la fin de IVe et au début de Ve siècle* (Rome: Institutum Patristicum Augustinianum, 2003).

—— *La décrétale Ad Gallos Episcopos: son texte et son auteur* (Supplements to *Vigiliae Christianae* 73; Leiden and Boston: Brill, 2005).

Eck, W., 'Das Eindringen des Christentums in den Senatorenstand bis zu Konstantin d. Gr.', *Chiron* 1 (1971), 381–406.

Elm, Susanna, '*Virgins of God*': *The Making of Asceticism in Late Antiquity* (Oxford: Clarendon Press, 1994).

—— Rebillard, Éric, and Romano, Antonella, (eds.), *Orthodoxy, Christianity, History* (Rome: École Française de Rome, 2000).

Elze, Martin, *Tatian und seine Theologie* (Göttingen: Vandenhoek and Ruprecht, 1960).

Evans, Robert F., *Four Letters of Pelagius* (New York: The Seabury Press, 1968).

—— *Pelagius: Inquiries and Reappraisals* (New York: The Seabury Press, 1968).

Faivre, Alexandre, *Naissance d'une hiérarchie: Les premières étapes du cursus clérical* (Paris: Beauchesne, 1977).

Feiertag, Jean-Louis, *Les Consultationes Zacchaei et Apollonii: Étude d'histoire et de sotériologie* (Fribourg: Éditions Universitaires, 1990).

Ferrua, Antonio, *The Unknown Catacomb: A Unique Discovery of Early Christian Art*, trans. Iain Inglis (Florence: Nardini, 1990).

Finn, Thomas M., 'Ritual Process and the Survival of Early Christianity: A Study of the Apostolic Tradition of Hippolytus', *Journal of Ritual Studies*, 3 (1989), 69–89.

—— *From Death to Rebirth: Ritual Conversion in Antiquity* (New York: Paulist Press, 1997).

Fisch, Thomas, and Hunter, David G., 'Echoes of the Early Roman Nuptial Blessing: Ambrosiaster, *De peccato Adae et Evae*', *Ecclesia Orans*, 11 (1994), 225–44.

Fitzmyer, Joseph M., *The Gospel According to Luke* (AB 28A; Garden City, NY: Doubleday, 1985).

Fontaine, Jacques, 'L'aristocratie occidentale devant le monachisme au IVème et Vème siècles', *Revista di storia e letteratura religiosa*, 15 (1979), 28–53.

Franzmann, Majella, *Jesus in the Manichaean Writings* (London and New York: T & T Clark, 2003).

Frazee, Charles A., 'Anatolian Asceticism in the Fourth Century: Eustathios of Sebastea and Basil of Caesarea', *Catholic Historical Review*, 66 (1980), 16–33.
Fredouille, Jean-Claude, *Tertullien et la conversion de la culture antique* (Paris: Études Augustiniennes, 1972).
Gaca, Kathy L., *The Making of Fornication: Eros, Ethics, and Political Reform in Greek Philosophy and Early Christianity* (Berkeley: University of California Press, 2003).
Gaudemet, Jean, *Les sources du droit d'Église occident du IIe au VIIe siècle* (Paris: Les Éditions du Cerf, 1985).
Glare, P. G. W., *Oxford Latin Dictionary* (Oxford: Clarendon Press, 1982).
Goehring, James E., 'Hieracas of Leontopolis: The Making of a Desert Ascetic', in his *Ascetics, Society, and the Desert: Studies in Early Egyptian Monasticism* (Harrisburg, PA: Trinity Press International, 1999), 110–33.
Gordini, Gian Domenico, 'L'opposizione al monachesimo a Roma nel IV secolo', in M. Fois, V. Monachino, and F. Litva (eds.), *Dalla chiesa antica alla chiesa moderna* (Rome: Università Gregoriana Editrice, 1983), 19–35.
Gougaud, L., 'Les critiques formulées contre les premiers moines d'occident', *Revue Mabillon*, 24 (1934), 145–63.
Graef, Hilda, *Mary: A History of Doctrine and Devotion* (London and New York: Sheed and Ward, 1963).
Grant, Robert M., 'The Textual Tradition of Theophilus of Antioch', *VC* 6 (1952), 146–59.
—— 'The Date of Tatian's Oration', *HTR* 46 (1953), 99–101.
—— 'The Heresy of Tatian', *JTS*, n.s. 5 (1954), 62–8.
—— 'Tatian (or. 30) and the Gnostics', *JTS*, n.s. 15 (1964), 65–9.
Gregg, Robert C., 'Die Ehe: Patristische und reformatorische Fragen', *ZKG* 96 (1985), 1–12.
Grubbs, Judith Evans, '"Pagan" and "Christian" Marriage: The State of the Question', *JECS* 2 (1994), 361–412.
—— *Law and Family in Late Antiquity: The Emperor Constantine's Marriage Legislation* (Oxford: Clarendon Press, 1995).
Gryson, Roger, 'L'interprétation du nom de Lévi (Lévite) chez saint Ambroise', *SacEr* 17 (1966): 217–29.
—— *Le Prêtre selon saint Ambroise* (Louvain: Édition Orientaliste, 1968).
—— *Les origines du célibat ecclésiastique du premier au septième siècle* (Gembloux: J. Duculot, 1970).
—— 'Les elections épiscopales en Occident au IVe siècle', *RHE* 75 (1980), 257–83.
—— 'Les Lévites, figure du sacerdoce veritable, selon saint Ambroise', *ETL* 56 (1980), 89–112.
—— 'Dix ans de recherches sur les origines du célibat ecclésiastique', *RTL* 11 (1980), 157–85.
Gundry-Volf, Judith M., 'Controlling the Bodies: A Theological Profile of The Corinthian Sexual Ascetics (1 Cor 7)', in R. Bieringer (ed.), *The Corinthian Correspondence* (Leuven: Peeters Press, 1996), 519–41.
Haller, Wilhelm, *Iovinianus: Die Fragmente seiner Schriften, die Quellen zu seiner Geschichte, sein Leben und seine Lehre* (TU 17.2; Leipzig: J.C. Hinrichs, 1897).

Hammond, C. P., 'The Last Ten Years of Rufinus' Life and the Date of his Move South from Aquileia', *JTS*, n.s. 27 (1977), 372–427.

Harnack, Adolf, 'Geschichte der Lehre von der Seligkeit allein durch den Glauben in der alten Kirche', *ZTK* 1 (1891), 82–178.

—— *History of Dogma*, trans. Neil Buchanan (New York: Dover Publications, 1961).

Harries, Jill, '"Treasure in Heaven": Property and Inheritance Among Senators of Late Rome', in Elizabeth M. Craik (ed.), *Marriage and Property* (Aberdeen: Aberdeen University Press, 1984), 54–70.

—— and Croke, Brian (eds.), *Religious Conflict in Fourth Century Rome* (Sydney: Sydney University Press, 1982).

Harrison, Carol, *Augustine: Christian Truth and Fractured Humanity* (Oxford: Oxford University Press, 2000).

Hedrick, Charles W., *History and Silence: Purge and Rehabilitation of Memory in Late Antiquity* (Austin, Texas: University of Texas Press, 2000).

Heggelbacher, Othmar, 'Beziehungen zwischen Ambrosiaster und Maximus von Turin?', *FZPhTh* 41 (1994), 5–44.

Heid, Stefan, *Celibacy in the Early Church: The Beginnings of a Discipline of Obligatory Continence for Clerics in East and West*, trans. Michael J. Miller (San Francisco: Ignatius Press, 2000).

Helmbold, Andrew K., 'Gnostic Elements in the "Ascension of Isaiah"', *NTS* 18 (1972), 222–7.

Hennings, R., *Der Briefwechsel zwischen Augustinus und Hieronymus und ihr Streit um den Kanon des alten Testament und die Auslegung von Gal. 2, 11–14* (Leiden: Brill, 1994).

Henry, Nathalie, 'The Song of Songs and the Liturgy of the *velatio* in the Fourth Century: From Literary Metaphor to Liturgical Reality', in R. N. Swanson (ed.), *Continuity and Change in Christian Worship* (Woodbridge, UK, and Rochester, NY: The Boydell Press, 1999), 18–28.

—— 'A New Insight into the Growth of Ascetic Society in the Fourth Century AD: The Public Consecration of Virgins as a Means of Integration and Promotion of the Female Ascetic Movement', *StPatr* 35 (2001), 102–9.

Hombert, Pierre-Marie, *Nouvelles recherches de chronologie augustinienne* (Paris: Études Augustiniennes, 2000).

Hopkins, Keith, 'Elite Mobility in the Roman Empire', *Past and Present*, 32 (1965), 12–26.

Humphress, Caroline, 'Roman Law, Forensic Argument and the Formation of Christian Orthodoxy (III–VI Centuries)', in Susanna Elm, Éric Rebillard, and Antonella Romano (eds.), *Orthodoxy, Christianity, History* (Rome: École Française de Rome, 2000), 125–47.

Humphries, Mark, *Communities of the Blessed: Social Environment and Religious Change in Northern Italy, AD 200–400* (OECS; Oxford: Oxford University Press, 1999).

Hunt, Emily J. *Christianity in the Second Century: The Case of Tatian* (London and New York: Routledge, 2003).

Hunter, David G., 'Preaching and Propaganda in Fourth Century Antioch: John Chrysostom's *Homilies on the Statues*', in David G. Hunter (ed.), *Preaching in the Patristic Age: Studies in Honor of Walter J. Burghardt, S.J.* (New York: Paulist Press, 1989), 119–38.

—— '*On the Sin of Adam and Eve*: A Little-known Defense of Marriage and Childbearing by Ambrosiaster', *HTR* 82 (1989), 283–99.

—— 'The Paradise of Patriarchy: Ambrosiaster on Woman as (Not) God's Image', *JTS*, n.s. 43 (1992), 447–69.

—— 'Helvidius, Jovinian, and the Virginity of Mary in Late Fourth-Century Rome', *JECS* 1 (1992), 47–71.

—— 'Augustinian Pessimism? A New Look at Augustine's Teaching on Sex, Marriage and Celibacy', *AugStud* 25 (1994), 153–77.

—— 'Clerical Celibacy and the Veiling of Virgins: New Boundaries in Late Ancient Christianity', in William E. Klingshirn and Mark Vessey (eds.), *The Limits of Ancient Christianity: Essays on Late Antique Thought and Culture in Honor of R. A. Markus* (Ann Arbor: The University of Michigan Press, 1999), 139–52.

—— 'Vigilantius of Calagurris and Victricius of Rouen: Ascetics, Relics, and Clerics in Late Roman Gaul', *JECS* 7 (1999), 401–30.

—— 'The Virgin, the Bride, and the Church: Reading Psalm 45 in Ambrose, Jerome, and Augustine', *CH* 69 (2000), 281–303.

—— '*Acts of Thomas*: Scene One', in Richard Valantassis (ed.), *Religions of Late Antiquity in Practice* (Princeton, NJ: Princeton University Press, 2000), 207–17.

—— 'Augustine, Sermon 354A: Its Place in His Thought on Marriage and Sexuality', *AugStud* 33 (2002), 39–60.

—— 'Reclaiming Biblical Morality: Sex and Salvation History in Augustine's Treatment of the Hebrew Saints', in Paul M. Blowers, Angela Russell Christman, David G. Hunter, and Robin Darling Young (eds.), *In Dominico Eloquio. In Lordly Eloquence: Essays on Patristic Exegesis in Honor of Robert Louis Wilken* (Grand Rapids, MI/Cambridge, UK: William B. Eerdmans, 2002), 317–35.

—— 'Rereading the Jovinianist Controversy: Asceticism and Clerical Authority in Late Ancient Christianity', *JMEMS* 33 (2003), 453–70; reprinted in Dale B. Martin and Patricia Cox Miller (eds.), *The Cultural Turn in Late Ancient Studies: Gender, Asceticism, and Historiography* (Durham and London: Duke University Press, 2005), 119–35.

—— 'Fourth-Century Latin Writers: Hilary, Victorinus, Ambrosiaster, Ambrose', in Frances Young, Lewis Ayres, and Andrew Louth (eds.), *The Cambridge History of Early Christian Literature* (Cambridge: Cambridge University Press, 2004), 302–17.

Issakson, Abel, *Marriage and Ministry in the New Temple* (Lund: Gleerup, 1965).

Izarny, Raymond d', 'Mariage et consécration virginale au IVe siècle', *La vie spirituelle: Supplément*, 6 (1953), 92–107.

Jacobs, Andrew S., 'The Disorder of Books: Priscillian's Canonical Defense of Apocrypha', *HTR* 93 (2000), 135–59.

Janssen, L. F., '"Superstitio" and the Persecution of Christians', *VC* 33 (1979), 131–59.

Jeanes, Gordon P., *The Day Has Come! Easter and Baptism in Zeno of Verona* (Alcuin Club Collection, 73; Collegeville, Minn.: The Liturgical Press, 1995).

Jeanjean, Benoît, *Saint Jérôme et l'hérésie* (Paris: Études Augustiniennes, 1999).

Jeffers, James S., *Conflict at Rome: Social Order and Hierarchy in Early Christianity* (Minneapolis, Minn.: Fortress Press, 1991).

Jensen, Anne, 'Faltonia Betitia Proba—eine Kirchenlehrerin der Spätantike', in H. Pissarek-Hudelist and L. Schottroff (eds.), *Mit allen Sinnen glauben: feministische Theologie unterwegs* (Gütersloh: Gütersloher Verlag-Haus Mohn, 1991), 84–94.

Johnson, Mark, 'Pagan-Christian Burial Practices of the Fourth Century: Shared Tombs?', *JECS* 5 (1997), 37–59.

Jones, A. H. M., 'The Social Background of the Struggle between Paganism and Christianity', in A. Momigliano (ed.), *The Conflict between Paganism and Christianity in the Fourth Century* (Oxford: Clarendon Press, 1963), 17–37.

—— *The Later Roman Empire 284–602: A Social Economic and Administrative Survey* (Norman, OK: University of Oklahoma Press, 1964).

Jouassard, G., 'La personnalité d'Helvidius', *Mélanges J. Saunier* (Lyons, 1944), 139–56.

Kaestli, Jean-Daniel, 'L'Utilisation des Actes apocryphes des apôtres dans le manichéisme', in M. Krause (ed.), *Gnosis and Gnosticism* (Leiden: Brill, 1977), 107–16.

Kantorowicz, E. H., 'On the Golden Marriage Belt and the Marriage Rings of the Dumbarton Oaks Collection', *DOP* 14 (1960), 1–16.

Karris, Robert J., 'The Background and Significance of the Polemic of the Pastoral Epistles', *JBL* 92 (1973), 549–64.

Kelly, J. N. D., *Jerome: His Life, Writings and Controversies* (New York: Harper & Row, 1975).

Knight, Jonathan, *Disciples of the Beloved One: The Christology, Social Setting, and Theological Context of the Ascension of Isaiah* (JSPSup 18; Sheffield: Sheffield Academic Press, 1996).

Koch, Hugo, *Virgo Eva—Virgo Maria: Neue Untersuchungen über die Lehre von der Jungfrauschaft unde der Ehe Mariens in der ältesten Kirche* (Berlin and Leipzig: Walter de Gruyter, 1937).

Koester, Helmut, *Ancient Christian Gospels: Their History and Development* (Philadelphia: Trinity Press International, 1990).

—— *Introduction to the New Testament*, ii. *History and Literature of Early Christianity*, 2nd edn. (New York and Berlin: W. de Gruyter, 2000).

Kopecek, Thomas, 'Curial Displacements and Flights in Later Fourth Century Cappadocia', *Historia*, 23 (1974), 319–42.

Krautheimer, Richard, *Rome: Profile of a City, 312–1308* (Princeton, NJ: Princeton University Press, 1980).

Labriolle, Pierre de, 'Rutilius Claudius Namatianus et les moines', *REL* 6 (1928), 30–41.

Lamberigts, Mathijs, 'A Critical Evaluation of Critiques of Augustine's View of Sexuality', in Robert Dodaro and George Lawless (eds.), *Augustine and His Critics: Essays in Honour of Gerald Bonner* (London and New York: Routledge, 2000), 176–97.

Laporte, Jean, 'From Impure Blood to Original Sin', *StPatr* 31 (1997), 438–44.
Laurence, Patrick, *Jérôme et le nouveau modèle feminin* (Paris: Études Augustiniennes, 1997).
Le Boulluec, Alain, *La notion d'hérésie dans la littérature grecque IIe–IIIe siècles*, 2 vols. (Paris: Études Augustiniennes, 1985).
Leroux, J. M., 'Monachisme et communauté chrétienne d'après saint Jean Chrysostome', in *Théologie de la vie monastique* (Paris: Aubier, 1961), 143–90.
—— 'Saint Jean Chrysostome et le monachisme', in Charles Kannengiesser (ed.), *Jean Chrysostome et Augustin* (Paris: Beauchesne, 1975), 125–44.
Leyser, Conrad, *Authority and Asceticism from Augustine to Gregory the Great* (Oxford: Clarendon Press, 2000).
Lienhard, Joseph T., 'Patristic Sermons on Eusebius of Vercelli and their Relation to his Monasticism', *RBen* 87 (1977), 163–72.
—— *Paulinus of Nola and Early Western Monasticism* (Theophaneia 28; Köln–Bonn: Peter Hanstein Verlag GMBH, 1977).
Lieu, Samuel N. C., 'An Early Byzantine Formula for the Renunciation of Manichaeism: the *Capita VII Contra Manichaeos* of (Zacharias of Mitylene)', *JAC* 26 (1983), 152–218.
—— *Manichaeism in the Later Roman Empire and Medieval China: A Historical Survey* (Manchester: Manchester University Press, 1985).
—— 'Some Themes in Later Roman Anti-Manichaean Polemics: I–II', *BJRL* 68 (1986), 434–72; 69 (1986), 235–75.
Lilla, Salvatore, *Clement of Alexandria: A Study in Christian Platonism and Gnosticism* (Oxford: Clarendon Press, 1971).
Lizzi, Rita, *Vescovi e strutture ecclesiastiche nella città tardoantica: L'Italia Annonaria nel IV–V secolo d.C.* (Como: Edizioni New Press, 1989).
—— 'Ambrose's Contemporaries and the Christianization of Northern Italy', *JRS* 80 (1990), 156–73.
Lössl, Josef, *Julian von Aeclanum: Studien zu seinem Leben, seinem Werk, seiner Lehre und ihrer Überlieferung* (Leiden and Boston: Brill, 2001).
Lüdemann, Gerd, *Heretics: The Other Side of Early Christianity*, trans. J. Bowden (London: SCM Press, 1996).
Lyman, J. Rebecca, 'Ascetics and Bishops: Epiphanius on Orthodoxy', in Susanna Elm, Éric Rebillard, and Antonella Romano (eds.), *Orthodoxy, Christianity, Heresy* (Rome: École Française de Rome, 2000), 149–61.
McClure, Judith, 'Handbooks Against Heresy in the West, from the Late Fourth to the Late Sixth Centuries', *JTS*, n.s. 30 (1979), 186–97.
MacDonald, Dennis R., *The Legend and the Apostle: The Battle for Paul in Story and Canon* (Philadelphia: Westminster Press, 1983).
McLynn, Neil, *Ambrose of Milan: Church and Court in a Christian Capital* (Berkeley: University of California Press, 1994).
MacMullen, Ramsey, *Christianizing the Roman Empire. A.D. 100–400* (New Haven and London: Yale University Press, 1984).

Madec, Goulven, *Introduction aux 'Révisions' et à la lecture des oeuvres de saint Augustin* (Paris: Études Augustiniennes, 1996).

Maier, Harry O. 'The Topography of Heresy and Dissent in Late-Fourth-Century Rome', *Historia*, 44 (1995), 232–49.

—— 'Heresy, Households, and the Disciplining of Diversity', in Virginia Burrus (ed.), *A People's History of Christianity*, ii. *Late Ancient Christianity* (Minneapolis, Minn.: Fortress Press, 2005), 213–33.

Malbon, Elizabeth Struthers, *The Iconography of the Sarcophagus of Junius Bassus* (Princeton, NJ: Princeton University Press, 1990).

Markus, Robert A., 'Paganism, Christianity and the Latin Classics in the Fourth Century', in J. W. Binns (ed.), *Latin Literature of the Fourth Century* (London and Boston: Routledge and Kegan Paul, 1974), 1–21.

—— *The End of Ancient Christianity* (Cambridge: Cambridge University Press, 1990).

—— 'Augustine's *Confessions* and the Controversy with Julian of Eclanum: Manicheism Revisited', in B. Bruning, M. Lamberigts, and J. Van Houtem (eds.), *Collectanea Augustiniana: Mélanges T.J. Van Bavel* (Leuven: Leuven University Press, 1990), 913–25.

Martin, Dale B., *Inventing Superstition: From the Hippocratics to the Christians* (Cambridge, Mass.: Harvard University Press, 2004).

—— and Miller, Patricia Cox (eds.), *The Cultural Turn in Late Ancient Studies: Gender, Asceticism, and Historiography* (Durham, NC and London: Duke University Press, 2005).

Martini, Coelestinus, *Ambrosiaster: De auctore, operibus, theologia* (Rome: Pontificium Athenaeum Antonianum, 1944).

Matthews, John, *Western Aristocracies and Imperial Court A.D. 364–425* (Oxford: Clarendon Press, 1975).

—— 'The Poetess Proba and Fourth-Century Rome: Questions of Interpretation', in Michel Christol, et al. (eds.), *Institutions, société et vie politique dans l'empire romain au IVe siècle ap. J.-C.* (Paris: École Française de Rome, 1992), 277–304.

Mees, M., 'Clemens von Alexandrien über Ehe und Familie', *Aug* 17 (1977), 113–31.

Meigne, Maurice, 'Concile ou collection d'Elvire?' *RHE* 70 (1975), 361–87.

Merkt, A., 'Wer war der Ambrosiaster? Zum Autor einer Quelle des Augustinus—Fragen auf eine neue Antwort', *Wissenschaft und Weisheit*, 59 (1996), 19–33.

Metz, René, *La consecration des vierges dans l'église romaine: Étude d'histoire de la liturgie* (Paris: Presses Universitaires de France, 1954).

Micaeli, C., 'L'influsso di Tertulliano su Girolamo: le opere sul matrimonio et le seconde nozze', *Aug* 19 (1979), 415–29.

Mueller, J. R., 'The Temple Scroll and the Gospel Divorce Texts', *Revue de Qumran*, 10 (1979–81), 247–56.

Nagel, Peter, 'Die apokryphen Apostelakten des 2. und 3. Jahrhunderts in der manichäischen Literatur', in Karl-Wolfgang Tröger (ed.), *Gnosis und Neues Testament* (Gütersloh, 1973), 148–82.

Nauroy, Gérard, 'Jérôme, lecteur et censeur de l'exégèse d'Ambroise', in Duval (ed.), *Jérôme entre l'occident et l'orient*, 173–203.

Nautin, Pierre, 'L'excommunication de saint Jérôme', *Annuaire de l'École Pratique des Hautes Études*, Ve section, 80–1 (1972–3), 7–37.
—— 'Études de chronologie hiéronymienne (393–397): III. Les premières relations entre Jérôme et Paulin de Nole', *REAug* 19 (1973), 213–39.
—— 'Études de chronologie hiéronymienne (393–397): IV. Autres letters de la période 393–396', *REAug* 20 (1974), 251–84.
—— 'L'activité littéraire de Jérôme de 387 à 392', *RTP* 115 (1983), 247–59.
Neumann, Charles William, *The Virgin Mary in the Works of Saint Ambrose* (Paradosis 17; Fribourg: The University Press, 1962).
Nolan, John Gavin, *Jerome and Jovinian* (Washington, D.C.: The Catholic University of America Press, 1956).
Novak, David M., 'Constantine and the Senate: An Early Phase of the Christianization of the Roman Aristocracy', *Ancient Society*, 10 (1979), 271–310.
—— 'Anicianae domus culmen, nobilitatis culmen', *Klio*, 62 (1980), 473–93.
Nuvolone, Flavio G., 'Pélage et Pélagianisme', *DSp* 12 (1986), 2895–902.
Oberhelman, S. M., 'Jerome's Earliest Attack on Ambrose: *On Ephesians*, Prologue (ML 26:469D–70A)', *TAPA* 121 (1991), 377–401.
O'Donnell, James J., *Augustine: A New Biography* (New York: HarperCollins, 2004).
Oppel, John, 'Saint Jerome and the History of Sex', *Viator*, 24 (1993), 1–22.
Orbe, Antonio, 'El pecado original y el matrimonio en la teología del s. II', *Greg* 45 (1964), 449–500.
Pagels, Elaine, 'Adam and Eve, Christ and the Church: A Survey of Second-Century Controversies Concerning Marriage', in A. H. B. Logan and A. J. M. Wedderburn (eds), *The New Testament and Gnosis: Essays in Honor of R. Mcl. Wilson* (Edinburgh: T & T Clark, 1983), 146–75.
Palanque, Jean-Rémy, *Saint Ambroise et l'empire romaine* (Paris: Boccard, 1933).
Paredi, Angelo, *Saint Ambrose: His Life and Times*, trans. M. Joseph Costelloe (Notre Dame, Indiana: University of Notre Dame Press, 1964).
—— 'S. Gerolamo e s. Ambrogio', in *Mélanges Eugène Tisserant*, v (Studi e Testi, 235; Vatican City, 1964), 153–98.
Paschoud, François, *Roma Aeterna: Études sur le patriotisme romain dans l'occident latin à l'époque des grandes invasions* (Rome, 1967).
Patterson, Lloyd G., 'Who Are the Opponents in Methodius' *De resurrectione*?', *StPatr* 19 (1989), 121–9.
—— *Methodius of Olympus: Divine Sovereignty, Human Freedom, and Life in Christ* (Washington, D.C.: The Catholic University of America Press, 1997).
Peterson, William L., 'Tatian's Diatesseron', in H. Koester, *Ancient Christian Gospels: Their History and Development* (Philadelphia: Trinity Press International, 1990), 403–30.
Petitmengin, Pierre, 'Saint Jérôme et Tertullien', in Yves-Marie Duval (ed.), *Jérôme entre l'occident et l'orient* (Paris: Études Augustiniennes, 1988), 43–59.
Pietri, Charles, *Roma Christiana: Recherches sur l'Église de Rome, son organization, sa politique, son idéologie de Miltiade à Sixte III (311–440)* (Rome: École Française de Rome, 1976).

Pietri, Charles, 'Evergétisme et richesses ecclésiastiques dans l'Italie du IVe à la fin du Ve s.: l'exemple romaine', *Ktema*, 3 (1978), 317–37.

—— 'Le mariage chrétien à Rome', in Jean Delumeau (ed.), *Histoire vécue du peuple chrétien* (Paris: Privat, 1979), 105–31.

Plinval, Georges de, *Pélage: Ses écrits, sa vie et sa réforme: Étude d'histoire littéraire et religieuse* (Lausanne: Librairie Payot, 1943).

Plumpe, Joseph C., 'Some Little-Known Early Witnesses to Mary's *virginitas in partu*', *TS* 9 (1948), 567–77.

Pourkier, Aline, *L'hérésiologie chez Épiphane de Salamine* (Paris: Beauchesne, 1992).

Quacquarelli, Antonio, *Il triplice frutto della vita cristiana: 100, 60 e 30* (Rome: Coletti Editore, 1953).

Quispel, Gilles, 'L'Evangile selon Thomas et les origins de l'ascèse chrétienne', in his *Gnostic Studies*, ii (Leiden: Nederlands Historisch-Archaeologisch Instituut te Istanbul, 1975), 98–112.

—— 'The Study of Encratism', in U. Bianchi (ed.), *La tradizione dell'enkrateia: Motivazioni ontologiche e protologiche* (Rome: Edizioni dell'Ateneo, 1985), 35–82.

Rackett, Michael R., 'Anxious for Worldly Things: The Critique of Marriage in the Anonymous Pelagian Treatise *De Castitate*', *StPatr* 33 (1997), 229–35.

Rahner, Karl, '*Virginitas in partu*: A Contribution to the Problem of the Development of Dogma and of Tradition', in his *Theological Investigations*, iv (Baltimore: Helicon Press, 1966), 134–62.

Ramsey, Boniface 'Almsgiving in the Latin Church: The Late Fourth and Early Fifth Centuries', *TS* 43 (1982), 226–59.

Rapp, Claudia, *Holy Bishops in Late Antiquity: The Nature of Christian Leadership in an Age of Transition* (Berkeley: University of California Press, 2005).

Rebillard, Éric, 'A New Style of Argument in Christian Polemic: Augustine and the Use of Patristic Citations', *JECS* 8 (2000), 559–78.

Reekmans, L., 'La *dextrarum iunctio* dans l'iconographie romaine et paléochrétienne', *Bulletin de l'Institut historique belge de Rome*, 31 (1958), 23–95.

Rees, B. R., *Pelagius: A Reluctant Heretic* (Woodbridge and Rochester, NY: The Boydell Press. 1988).

Reitzenstein, Richard, 'Eine frühchristliche Schrift von den dreierlei Früchten des christlichen Lebens', *ZNW* 15 (1914), 60–90.

Reynolds, Philip Lyndon, *Marriage in the Western Church: The Christianization of Marriage During the Patristic and Early Medieval Periods* (Leiden: E. J. Brill, 1994).

Rice, Eugene F., *Saint Jerome in the Renaissance* (Baltimore, Md.: Johns Hopkins University Press, 1985).

Rocca, Giancarlo, 'La perpetua verginità di Maria nelle lettere di s. Ignazio di Antiochia', *EphMar* 25 (1975), 397–414.

—— *L'Adversus Helvidium di san Girolamo nel contesto della letteratura ascetico-mariana del secolo IV* (New York: Peter Lang, 1998).

Rouselle, Aline, *Porneia: On Desire and the Body in Antiquity* (Oxford: Blackwell, 1988).

Rousseau, Philip, *Ascetics, Authority, and the Church in the Age of Jerome and Cassian* (Oxford: Oxford University Press, 1978).

Salzman, Michele, *On Roman Time: The Codex Calendar of 354 and the Rhythms of Urban Life in Late Antiquity* (Berkeley: University of California Press, 1990).

—— 'Competing Claims to "Nobilitas" in the Western Empire of the Fourth and Fifth Centuries', *JECS* 9 (2001), 359–85.

—— *The Making of a Christian Aristocracy: Social and Religious Change in the Western Roman Empire* (Cambridge, Mass.: Harvard University Press, 2002).

Sampley, J. Paul, *'And the Two Shall Become One Flesh': A Study of Traditions in Ephesians 5:21–33* (Cambridge: Cambridge University Press, 1971).

Sanders, E. P., *Jesus and Judaism* (Philadelphia: Fortress Press, 1985).

Schenk, W., 'Die Briefe an Timotheus I und II und an Titus (Pastoralbriefe) in der neueren Forschung (1945–1985)', *ANRW* ii.25.4 (1987), 3405–6.

Schlatter, Fredric W., 'The Pelagianism of the Opus imperfectum in Matthaeum', *VC* 41 (1987), 267–85.

Schmitt, Émile, *Le mariage chrétien dans l'oeuvre de saint Augustin: Une théologie baptismale de la vie conjugale* (Paris: Études Augustiniennes, 1983).

Schoedel, William R., *A Commentary on the Letters of Ignatius of Antioch* (Hermeneia; Philadelphia: Fortress Press, 1985).

Schreiner, Susan E., 'Eve, the Mother of History: Reaching for the Reality of History in Augustine's Later Exegesis of Genesis', in Gregory A. Robbins (ed.), *Genesis 1–3 in the History of Exegesis: Intrigue in the Garden* (Lewiston, NY and Queenston, Ontario: Edwin Mellen Press, 1988), 135–86.

Schultzen, F., 'Die Benützung der Schriften Tertullians De monogamia und De ieiunio bei Hieronymus', *Neue Bücher für Deutsche Theologie*, 3 (1894), 485–502.

Schüssler Fiorenza, Elisabeth, *In Memory of Her: A Feminist Theological Reconstruction of Christian Origins* (New York: Crossroad, 1983).

Sfameni Gasparro, Giulia, *Enkrateia e antropologia: Le motivazioni protologiche della continenza e della verginità nel cristianesimo dei primi secoli e nello gnosticismo* (Rome: Institutum Patristicum Augustinianum, 1984).

—— 'Asceticism and Anthropology: *Enkrateia* and "Double Creation" in Early Christianity', in Vincent L. Wimbush and Richard Valantasis (eds.), *Asceticism* (New York and Oxford: Oxford University Press, 1995), 127–46.

Shanzer, Danuta, 'The Anonymous *Carmen contra paganos* and the Date and Identity of the Centonist Proba', *REAug* 32 (1986), 232–48.

—— 'The Date and Identity of the Centonist Proba', *RechAug* 27 (1994), 75–96.

Shotwell, James T., and Loomis, Louise Ropes, *The See of Peter* (New York: Columbia University Press, 1927; reprint New York: Octagon Books, 1965).

Sivan, Hagith, 'On Hymens and Holiness in Late Antiquity: Opposition to Aristocratic Female Asceticism at Rome', *JAC* 36 (1993), 81–93.

—— 'The Cento of Proba and Aristocratic Conversion in the Fourth Century', *VC* 47 (1993), 140–57.

Smid, H. R., *Protevangelium Jacobi: A Commentary* (Apocrypha Novi Testament, 1; Assen: Van Gorcum, 1965).

Smith, Jonathan Z., *Drudgery Divine: On the Comparison of Early Christianities and the Religions of Late Antiquity* (Chicago: University of Chicago Press, 1990).

Snyder, H. Gregory, 'Pictures in Dialogue: A Viewer-Centered Approach to the Hypogeum on Via Dino Compagni', *JECS* 13 (2005), 349–86.

Souter, Alexander, *A Study of Ambrosiaster* (TaS 7.4; Cambridge: Cambridge University Press, 1905).

Stancliffe, Clare, *St. Martin and His Hagiographer: History and Miracle in Sulpicius Severus* (Oxford: Clarendon Press, 1983).

Sterk, Andrea, *Renouncing the World Yet Leading the Church: The Monk–Bishop in Late Antiquity* (Cambridge, Mass. and London: Harvard University Press, 2004).

Stickler, Alfons Maria, *The Case for Clerical Celibacy: Its Historical Development and Theological Foundations*, trans. Father Brian Ferme (San Francisco: Ignatius Press, 1995).

Stroumsa, G., 'Monachisme et Marranisme chez les Manichéens d'Egypte', *Numen* 2 (1982): 184–201.

—— 'The Manichaean Challenge to Egyptian Christianity', in B. Pearson and J. Goehring (eds.), *The Roots of Egyptian Christianity* (Philadelphia: Fortress Press, 1986), 307–19.

—— 'Aspects of Anti-Manichaean Polemics in Late Antiquity and Under Early Islam', *HTR* 81 (1988), 37–58.

Testard, Maurice, 'Jérôme et Ambroise: Sur un "aveu" du *De officiis* de l'évêque de Milan', in Duval (ed.), *Jérôme entre l'occident et l'orient*, 227–54.

Theissen, Gerd, *Social Reality and the Early Christians*, trans. M. Kohl (Minneapolis, Minn.: Fortress Press, 1992).

Thier, Sebastian, *Kirche bei Pelagius* (PTS 50; Berlin and New York: Walter de Gruyter, 1999).

Tibiletti, Carlo, 'Teologia pelagiana sul celibato/matrimonio', *Aug* 27 (1987), 487–507.

Tissot, Yves, 'L'Encratisme des Actes de Thomas', *ANRW* II.25.6 (1988), 4415–30.

Treggiari, Susan, *Roman Marriage: Iusti Coniuges from the Time of Cicero to the Time of Ulpian* (Oxford: Clarendon Press, 1991).

Trevett, Christine, *Montanism: Gender, Authority and the New Prophecy* (Cambridge: Cambridge University Press, 1996).

Trout, Dennis, *Paulinus of Nola: Life, Letters, and Poems* (Berkeley: University of California Press, 1999).

—— 'The Verse Epitaph(s) of Petronius Probus: Competitive Commemoration in Late-Fourth-Century Rome', *New England Classical Journal*, 28 (2001), 157–76.

Valli, Francesco, *Gioviniano: Esame delle fonti e dei frammenti* (Urbino: Università di Urbino, 1953).

Van den Hoek, Annawies, *Clement of Alexandria and his Use of Philo in the Stromateis* (Leiden: Brill, 1988).

Van Gennep, Arnold, *The Rites of Passage*, trans. Monika Vizedom and Gabrielle Caffee (Chicago: The University of Chicago Press, 1960).

Verner, David C., *The Household of God: The Social World of the Pastoral Epistles* (SBL Dissertation Series, 71; Chico, CA: Scholars Press, 1983).

Vessey, Mark, 'Jerome's Origen: The Making of a Christian Literary *Persona*', *StPatr* 28 (1993), 135–45.
—— 'The Forging of Orthodoxy in Latin Christian Literature', *JECS* 4 (1996), 495–513.
Vogels, H., 'Ambrosiaster und Hieronymus', *RBen* 66 (1956), 14–19.
Weitzmann, Kurt (ed.), *Age of Spirituality: Late Antique and Early Christian Art* (New York: Metropolitan Museum, 1979), 282–3.
Wendland, P., *Quaestiones Musonianae: De Musonio Stoico Clementis Alexandrini aliorumque auctore* (Berlin, 1886).
Wermelinger, Otto, *Rom und Pelagius: Die theologische Position der römischen Bischöfe im pelagianischen Streit in den Jahren 411–432* (Stuttgart: A. Hiersemann, 1975).
Wharton, Annabelle, 'Ritual and Reconstructed Meaning: The Neonian Baptistery in Ravenna', *The Art Bulletin*, 69 (1987), 358–75.
Wiesen, David S., *St. Jerome as a Satirist: A Study in Christian Latin Thought and Letters* (Ithaca, NY: Cornell University Press, 1964).
Wilken, Robert Louis, *The Christians as the Romans Saw Them* (New Haven and London: Yale University Press, 1984.
Williams, Daniel H., *Ambrose of Milan and the End of the Arian-Nicene Conflicts* (OECS; Oxford: Clarendon Press, 1995).
Williams, G., 'Some Aspects of Roman Marriage Ceremonies and Ideals', *JRS* 48 (1958), 16–29.
Williams, Michael Allen, *Rethinking 'Gnosticism': An Argument for Dismantling a Dubious Category* (Princeton, NJ: Princeton University Press, 1996).
Wisse, F., 'Gnosticism and Early Monasticism in Egypt', in B. Aland (ed.), *Gnosis: Festschrift für Hans Jonas* (Göttingen: Vandenhoeck & Ruprecht, 1978), 431–40.
Yarnold, Edward, *The Awe-Inspiring Rites of Initiation: The Origins of the RCIA*, 2nd edn. (Collegeville, Minn.: The Liturgical Press, 1994).
Young, Frances, *From Nicaea to Chalcedon* (London: SCM Press, 1983).

Index

Acholius, bishop of Thessalonika 220–1, 223 n. 65
Acts of Andrew 139 n. 33, 151
Acts of John 114, 139, 151
Acts of Paul and Thecla 94, 114, 115, 139
Acts of Peter 139, 151
Acts of Thomas 94, 105 n. 52, 114, 139, 151
Adkin, Neil 234, 235 n. 107, 240 n. 130
Albina 76–8
Aldama, José de 16 n. 5
Allison, Dale 88 n. 2
Ambrose, bishop of Milan 59 n. 28, 66, 77 n. 91, 135–6, 170, 207, 285
    attacked by Jerome 234–6, 238–42
    baptismal catecheses 44–50
    on clerical celibacy 219–20
    on consecration of virgins 32–3, 224–9
    influenced by Athanasius 188
    influenced by Cyprian 121
    influenced by Origen 123
    influenced by Zeno of Verona 192 n. 66
    on monasticism and clergy 220–4
    on objections to asceticism 60–1
    ordination 212
    and Priscillian 135, 136
    source for Jovinian's teaching 20–4
    on virginity of Mary 22–4, 171–2, 197–204
    on virgins as 'Levites' 229–30
Ambrosiaster 131, 209 n. 10, 222, 241 n. 133
    and anti-Manichaean legislation 142 n. 41
    on asceticism 159–70
    on nuptial blessing 154–5 n. 101
    on *Patriciani* 152 n. 91
    and priestly celibacy 216–17
Ammianus Marcellinus 65–6, 74 n. 83
Anastasius I, bishop of Rome 144
Anicii 64, 66
    adoption of asceticism 80–82
Apelles 181–2, 186–7
Aphthonius of Antioch 28–9
apocrypha
    criticized by heresiologists 151–2
    and Encratism 114, 151–2
    rejected by Jerome 190
    used by Priscillian 136, 139–40
    and virginity of Mary 171, 175–81
Apologists 97–101

Arbogastes 20
Arcadius, emperor 55, 69, 71, 143
Aristides of Athens 98–9
Arjava, Antti 77
Arles, council of 214
Ascension of Isaiah 151 n. 86, 173, 176–8, 187
Asella 77, 209
Athanasius, bishop of Alexandria 55–6, 131–3, 142, 188, 197
Athenagoras of Athens 99
Audet, Jean-Paul 220 n. 50
Augustine, bishop of Hippo 27 n. 39, 45, 66, 105 n. 53, 111 n. 79, 159–60, 188 n. 50, 212 n. 22, 243 n. 3
    against the Manichaeans 270–3, 277
    on Ambrose and monasticism 220 n. 51
    and the *Anicii* 66, 81
    on influence of Jovinian 18, 244
    on Jovinian's criticism of Ambrose 23–4, 171, 196, 203
    on Jovinian's use of scripture 34 n. 58
    on Manichaean use of apocrypha 139 n. 33
    on Manichaeans at Rome 144–5
    opposition to Jerome on Galatians 273–7
    opposition to Jerome on marriage 277–84
    on original sin 185, 196, 200, 286–7
    on *Patriciani* 152 n. 91
    on Priscillian 140
    and Rutilius Namatianus 54 n. 8
    on three goods of marriage 286

Baptism
    in *Consultationes Zacchaei et Apollonii* 252, 284
    in Jovinian's theology 9, 26, 30–1, 35–8, 41–50, 203
    in Pelagius' theology 260
    and removal of original sin 122, 184
    requires clerical sexual continence 162, 216–19
    and 'second birth' of Church 198, 201, 203–4
    and sexual renunciation 114–15, 119–20, 122, 203–4
    and virginal consecration 204, 227
Barbatianus 59 n. 28, 221

Index

Barclift, P. 268 n. 106
Barnard, L. W. 102 n. 43, 103 n. 45
Barnes, T. D. 63 n. 41, 64 n. 45
Baronius, Caesar 7–8, 16
Bassler, Jouette 93 n. 19
Bassus, Junius 64–5, 67
Bauer, Walter 12
Beatrice, Pier Franco 110 n. 73, 287 n. 3
Beduhn, Jason 142 n. 39
Behr, J. 106 n. 56
Berg, Beverley 68 n. 60
Beskow, Per 143
Bianchi, U. 90 n. 8, 102 n. 39, 104 n. 51, 110 n. 73
Birley, A. R. 135 n. 14
Blesilla 62
Bohlin, T. 262 n. 82
Bolgiani, Franco 102 n. 39
Bonner, Gerald 268 n. 110
Boyarin, D. 89 n. 6
Brakke, David 56 n. 14, n. 15, 132–3, 188 n. 48
Brandenburg, H. 53 n. 5, 82 n. 113
Braun, R. 116 n. 94, 118 n. 100
Broudéhoux, Jean-Paul 107 n. 58
Brown, Peter
  on Ambrose and virginity 204 n. 104, 221, 224 n. 68, 226 n. 70
  on Ambrosiaster 161–2
  on asceticism 2 n. 1
  on Christian aristocracy 63 n. 41, 68 n. 60
  on Christian imperial legislation 11 n. 21
  on clerical celibacy 218, 241
  on Clement 113
  on Jerome 232 n. 94
  on Jovinian 83 n. 118, 260
  on Julian of Eclanum 268 n. 106, 286 n. 2
  on Manichaeism 141 n. 37
  on 'New Prophecy' 117 n. 95
  on Origen 123 n. 117, 126 n. 131
  on Paul 89 n. 7
  on Pelagius 260
  on *pneuma* 106 n. 55
  on Tatian 103 n. 47, 114 n. 84
Budzin, Allan J. 10–11 n. 20, 30 n. 49
Burrus, Virginia 73 n. 8, 136 n. 17, 137 n. 21, 138 n. 27, n. 29

Cain, Andrew 161 n. 127, 234 n. 105
Callam, Daniel 218 n. 42
Cameron, Alan 20 n. 19, 53 n. 4, 54 n. 8, 66 n. 51
Cameron, Averil 11 n. 21, 147 n. 67, n. 69, 149 n. 75
Campenhausen, Hans von 93, 174 n. 8, n. 9, 180, 184 n. 34, 187 n. 47, 192 n. 67, 203 n. 102
Cavallera, Ferdinand 9, 208 n. 3
Chadwick, Henry
  on Ambrosiaster 160 n. 118
  on *Odes of Solomon* 175 n. 12
  on Priscillian 30 n. 48, 135–9, 210 n. 14
Charlesworth, J. H. 175 n. 12, 176 n. 14
Chastagnol, A. 64 n. 45, 77 n. 94
Chrysostom, John 54 n. 10, 55 n. 12, 58 n. 22, 66, 166
Clark, Elizabeth A. 75 n. 87, 79 n. 101, 268 n. 106
  on asceticism and exegesis 110 n. 70, 126 n. 133, 165 n. 147, 264 n. 89, 282–3
  on *De laudibus Christi* 68 n. 62, 69, 70 n. 67, 71 n. 72
  on female asceticism 79 n. 101, 80
  on Origenism 123 n. 115, 155, 157 n. 107, 244, 256 n. 57, 258 n. 66
Clark, Gillian 79 n. 101
Clarke, G. W. 103 n. 45
Claussen, M. A. 58 n. 24, 59 n. 25, n. 27, n. 28, 250–1
Clement of Alexandria
  affinities with Jovinian 128–9, 159, 165–6, 169
  discussion of marriage and celibacy 105–13
  on Marcion and philosophy 156
  on original sin 110–11, 154
  on remarriage 99 n. 34
  superiority of marriage over celibacy 111–13
  on Tatian 104, 107–11
  use of Pastoral Epistles 96
  use of scripture 107–10
  on Valentinus 102
  on *virginitas in partu* 179–80, 185 n. 40, 187
Clement of Rome 91–2
clergy
  and Ambrosiaster 159–60, 162, 170
  conflict with ascetics 55–8, 60, 133–4, 210–11
  criticized by Jerome 32, 56–7, 208–9, 236–8, 239–42
  criticized by Jovinian 17, 30
  as 'Levites' 222–4, 229–30
  and Manichaeans 144
  opposition to Jovinian 16–18, 73–4
  and Priscillian 135

310

Index

clergy (*cont.*)
  and sexual continence 35, 161–2, 213–19
  support of Jovinian 18, 246
  rejection of Jerome 208, 256–9
  viewed by Ambrose 219–24
  viewed by Siricius 211–13
Clausi, Benedetto 27 n. 40, 28 n. 42
Cochini, C. 214 n. 28
Cohen, Jeremy 165 n. 146, 166, 282 n. 160
Consultationes Zacchaei et Apollonii
  on monastic life 58–60, 210
  opposition to Jerome 250–6
Conzelman, H. 93 n. 19, 94 n. 23
Cooper, Kate 11, 29, 83
Cothenet, Edouard 177 n. 17, 178
Courcelle, Pierre 129 n. 139, 250 n. 35
Coyle, J. Kevin 98 n.
Crouzel, Henri 123 n. 117, 124 n. 122, 125 n. 124, n. 125, n. 128, 126 n. 132, 157 n. 108, 184 n. 34, 185 n. 39, n. 40, 186 n. 43, n. 46, 259 n. 69
Cullman, O. 177 n. 17
Curran, John 11, 64 n. 43, 65 n. 49, 70–1
Cyprian, bishop of Carthage 115, 120–2, 129, 281

Damasus, bishop of Rome 32, 55 n. 11, 68, 74 n. 83, 239
  and Ambrosiaster 160–1, 234 n. 105
  author of *Ad Gallos episcopos* 211 n. 19, 212 n. 24
  on clerical continence 214
  and Priscillian 135–7, 139, 210 n. 14
Daniélou, Jean 115 n. 88, 118 n. 100
Davidson, Ivor 220 n. 48, n. 49, 223 n. 64, 224 n. 70, 229 n. 90, 234 n. 104, 238
Davis, Stephen J. 94 n. 21
De centesima, sexagesima, tricesima 114–15
Dechow, Jon 148 n. 72, 157 n. 108
Deléani, Simone 121 n. 109
Demetrias 33, 81–3, 265 n. 92
Deming, W. 89 n. 6
devil 108, 122, 239
  in Encratite theology 149, 151–2
  in Jovinian's second proposition 35–8
  and Jovinian's fourth proposition 41–2
  in Priscillian's theology 138–9
  renunciation at baptism 45–7
Dexter, Nummius Aemilianus 37, 232
Diatesseron 104 n. 50, 115
Dibelius, M. 93 n. 19, 94 n. 23
Diocletian, emperor 142, 163
Dionysius, bishop of Corinth 68, 96–7

d'Izarny, Raymond 224 n. 69
docetic, docetism
  accusation against Priscillian 136
  attacked by Ignatius of Antioch 173
  linked to encratism 110–11
  taught by Manichaeans 23, 163
  and *virginitas in partu* 175–7, 181–7, 196, 203
Dolbeau, F. 274
Domnio 18, 24, 191, 245–6, 249–50
Drijvers, J. W. 64 n. 44, 114 n. 85
Dungan, David 88 n. 4
Dunphy, W. 234 n. 104
Duval, Yves-Marie 11 n. 22, 53 n. 5, 244
  on Ambrose's influence on Augustine and Jerome 188 n. 50
  on Ambrose's influence on Zeno of Verona 192 n. 66
  on Ambrose's use of Cyprian 121 n. 110, 188 n. 49
  on Augustine and Jovinian 270 n. 113
  on authorship of *Ad Gallos episcopos* 211 n. 19
  on date of Jovinian's condemnation 17 n. 5
  on Domnio 246 n. 13
  on imperial condemnation of Jovinian 243 n. 2
  on Jerome's use of Origen 123 n. 116, 126 n. 133, 248 n. 25, 276 n. 131
  on Jerome's use of Tertullian 120 n. 108, 167 n. 153, 248 n. 25
  on Jovinian's writings 19 n. 17
  on Pammachius and Jerome 26 n. 36
  on Pelagius 249–50, 259 n. 70, 260 n. 72, 264 n. 87, 267, 284 n. 166

Easter Vigil 45–6; *see also* Paschal Vigil
Eck, W. 64 n. 44
Elm, Susanna 12 n. 26, 133 n. 5, 134 n. 50, 147 n. 66
Elvira, council of 214
Elze, Martin 103 n. 47
Encratite, Encratism 88 n. 2, 89 n. 6, 90
  accusations against Jerome 247, 285
  adopted by Augustine 286–7
  in Ambrose 200–3, 226–7, 285
  in apocryphal Acts 114–15
  attacked by Ambrosiaster 159, 163–9
  attacked by Epiphanius and Filastrius 146–55, 158–9
  attacked by Irenaeus 101–2
  attacked in Pastoral Epistles 94–7

Index

confused with Manichaeism 141–46
  in Cyprian 120–2, 127–8
  espoused by Pinytos of Cnossos 96–7
  in fourth-century monastic teachers 131–4
  'moderate' version 106 n. 57, 115
  opposed by Augustine 282–3
  opposed by Clement of Alexandria 106–13
  opposed by *Consultationes Zacchaei et Apollonii* 253–4
  in Origen 123–8, 184–6
  in Priscillian 135–41
  taught by Tatian 101–5
  in Tertullian 116–20, 127–8
  and *virginitas in partu* 178–9
Epiphanius, bishop of Salamis
  on goodness of sex 153–4, 256 n. 57
  opposition to Encratism 105 n. 53, 148–54
  opposition to Hieracas 131–3
  opposition to Manichaeans 146, 153 n. 93
  opposition to Origen 155–8
Epistle to Diognetus 99
Erasmus, Desiderius 6, 159
Eugenius, emperor 20–1
Eusebius, bishop of Caesarea 96–7, 100 n. 36, 102 n. 38, n. 43, 117 n. 95
Eusebius, bishop of Vercelli 221–2
Eustathius, bishop of Sebaste 133–4, 140
Evans, Robert F. 228 n. 85, 249, 260 n. 72, 267
Evans Grubbs, Judith 11, 100

Faivre, A. 211 n. 18, 213 n. 26
fasting
  in Ambrosiaster 161
  and ascetic life 57, 62, 87, 158, 221 238
  forbidden on Sundays 135
  Jovinian's teaching on 17, 21, 50
  in Jovinian's third proposition 39–41
  by Manichaeans 30 n. 48, 145–6
  Pelagius' teaching on 262–3
  as preparation for baptism 43, 45–6
  and prophecy 117
  as punishment for Manichaeans 144
  in teaching of Priscillian 137 n. 25
Feiertag, Jean-Louis 59, 250–1, 254 n. 49, n. 50
Ferrua, Antonio 67 n. 59, 68 n. 60
Filastrius, bishop of Brescia
  on apocryphal Acts 139 n. 33, 196
  on Encratism and Manichaeism 105 n. 53, 150–3, 154–5
  on heresy 148
  on Origen 158 n. 113
  on Priscillian and Manichaeism 140–1, 146–7
Filocalus, Furius Dionysius 68
Finn, Thomas M. 43 n. 84, 44 n. 85, 45 n. 88, n. 89, n. 90, n. 91, 46 n. 95, 47 n. 96, 49 n. 103, 50
Fisch, Thomas 164 n. 143
Fitzmyer, J. A. 88 n. 1
Fontaine, Jacques 52 n. 3, 118 n. 100
Franzmann, Majella 23 n. 29
Frazee, Charles A. 133 n. 9
Fredouille, Jean-Claude 116 n. 94

Gaca, Kathy L. 103 n. 47, 107 n. 58
Gangra, council of 133–4, 136
Gasparro, Giulea Sfameni 90 n. 8, 92, 97, 102 n. 39, 115 n. 89, 118 n. 100, 164 n. 140, 203 n. 101
Gaudemet, J. 217 n. 40
Goehring, James 132 n. 1, 141 n. 37
Gnosticism 93–4, 101–2, 105–6
Gordini, Gian Domenico 10, 52 n. 3
Gospel of Thomas 88 n. 1, 115
Graef, Hilda 174 n. 8, 198 n. 87, 201
Grant, Robert M. 100 n. 35, n. 36, 102 n. 40, 103 n. 44, n. 45
Gratian, emperor 51, 55 n. 11, 136, 142
Gregg, Robert 7 n. 7
Gregory I, bishop of Rome 147
Gryson, Roger 162 n. 132, 212 n. 21, 214 n. 29, n. 30, 217 n. 38, 220 n. 50, 222–24
Gundry-Volf, Judith M. 89 n. 5

Haller, Wilhelm 8–9, 19, 27, 31 n. 50, 36
Hammond, C. P. 257 n. 59
Harnack, Adolf von 8–9
Harries, Jill 52 n. 1, 66 n. 51, n. 54, n. 55, 75–6
Harrison, Carol 286 n. 1
Hatch, Diane F. 68 n. 62, 69–71
Hedrick, Charles W. 20 n. 19, 52 n. 1
Heggelbacher, O. 160 n. 118
Heid, Stefan 10 n. 20, 16 n. 4, 214 n. 28, n. 29, n. 30
Heliodorus, Letter to 56–7, 236–7
Helmbold, Andrew K. 176 n. 14
Helvidius 166–7, 172, 188–90
Hennings, R. 273 n. 121
Henry, Nathalie 32, 225 n. 74
Hieracas 130–3, 140, 151 n. 86
Himerius, bishop of Tarragona 58, 210–11, 214–15
Hippolytus of Rome 50 n. 108, 96 n. 25, 105 n. 53

Hombert, Pierre-Marie 269 n. 111, 274, 277
Household codes 90–1
Humphress, Caroline 144
Humphries, Mark 150 n. 84
Hunt, Emily 103 n. 44, 105 n. 52
Hunter, David G. 54 n. 10, 105 n. 52, 159 n. 114, 160 n. 118, 164 n. 143, 165 n. 146, 168 n. 158, 172 n. 2, 207 n. 1, 209 n. 10, 218 n. 43, 226 n. 75, 244 n. 4, 269 n. 111, 272 n. 119, 277 n. 133, n. 135, 280 n. 149
Hydatius, bishop of Merida 136

Ignatius, bishop of Antioch 90 n. 10, 92–3, 173
Innocent I, bishop of Rome 81
Irenaeus, bishop of Lyons
  against Tatian and Encratism 101–2, 103 n. 44, 104 n. 50, 105, 113, 128
  on Eve-Mary parallel 174
  influence on Methodius 156, 159
  on Jesus' birth 181 n. 27
  on 'three-fold fruit' 122 n. 113
  on sin of Adam and Eve 111 n. 79
  use of Pastoral Epistles 96
Issakson, Abel 88 n. 4
Ithacius, bishop of Ossonuba 136

Jacobs, Andrew 139 n. 32
Janssen, L. 98 n.
Jeanes, Gordon P. 192 n. 64
Jeanjean, Benoît 232–4
Jeffers, James 92 n. 14
Jerome
  against Helvidius 188–90
  as anti-heretical writer 231–4
  on clergy and monastic life 236–8
  conflict with Ambrose 219 n. 47, 231, 234–6, 238–9, 242
  conflict with Siricius 231, 239–42
  expulsion from Rome 208–10, 231
  hostility towards clergy 56–8, 208–9, 231
  on Jovinian's four propositions 30–43
  letter to Heliodorus 56–7, 236–7
  letters to Pammachius 17, 24–6, 245–50
  on monastic life 59 n. 27, 60–3, 77
  negative reception of *Adversus Jovinianum* 244–50
  opposed by Ambrosiaster 161–70
  opposed by Augustine 269–70, 273–84
  opposed by *Consultationes Zacchaei et Apollonii* 250–56
  opposed by Pelagius 259–67
  opposed by Rufinus 257
  opposed by Vigilantius 258–9
  on Petronius Probus 66 n. 53
  on Priscillian 135
  as source for Jovinian's teaching 15, 19–20, 24–30
  use of Cyprian 120–1
  use of Origen 123, 126 n. 133
  use of Tertullian 120
  on *virginitas in partu* 171, 187, 190–2
Jesus
  cited by Ambrosiaster 166
  cited by Augustine 271
  cited by Clement of Alexandria 107–9
  cited by Cyprian 121
  cited by Epiphanius 153
  cited by Hieracas 132–3
  cited by Jovinian 40–2
  cited in *Consultationes Zacchaei et Apollonii* 251
  miraculous birth of 22–4, 172–204
  teaching on marriage 87–90
  see also virginal conception
Johnson, Mark 68 n. 60
Jones, A. H. M. 64 n. 42
Jouassard, G. 188 n. 51
Jovinian
  affinities with Clement of Alexandria 128–9
  anti-heretical interests 29–30, 141, 146
  and baptism 30–1, 35–8, 41–50
  and Church 38, 42–3
  ecclesiastical condemnation 16–17
  and female asceticism 31–3
  four propositions 26, 30–43
  imperial condemnation 243
  parallels with Epiphanius and Filastrius 158–9
  popularity at Rome 17–18
  popularity with pagans 19–20, 27–8
  and Roman aristocracy 71–4, 83
  similarity to Ambrosiaster 169–70
  use of scripture 19, 21–2, 29, 33–5, 36–8, 39–41
  on virginity of Mary 22–4, 171, 187
  writings 19, 26–7
Julian, bishop of Eclanum 16, 23, 27, 267–8, 286
Juliana, Anicia 81–2
Julius Cassian 94 n. 21, 101, 106, 110–11, 118 n. 100, 124, 155
Justin Martyr 99, 173–4

Index

Kaestli, Jean-Daniel 114 n. 85
Kantorowicz, E. H. 70 n. 68
Karris, Robert J. 93 n. 18
Kelly, J. N. D. 17 n. 5, 20–1, 24 n. 33,
  30–1, 36, 208 n. 2, n. 3, 209, 231 n.,
  232 n. 96, 235 n. 106, 237 n. 121,
  249 n. 33, 259
Knight, Jonathan 177 n. 16
Koch, Hugo 174 n. 10
Koester, Helmut 93 n. 17
Krautheimer, R. 65 n. 47

Lamberigts, Mathijs 264 n. 87, 267–8
Laporte, Jean 185 n. 37
Laurence, P. 120 n. 108
Le Boulluec, Alain 12, 100 n. 36, 102 n. 39,
  103 n. 43, 233 n. 98
Lefort, Louis-Théodore 188 n. 48
Leo I, bishop of Rome 82, 144
Levites 214–17, 222–4, 229–30
  see also priesthood
Leyser, Conrad 286 n. 1
Lienhard, Joseph T. 186 n. 45, 221 n. 56
Lieu, Samuel 133 n. 5, 137 n. 21, 141 n. 37,
  n. 38, 144 n. 54, 145 n. 58, n. 61, 146
Lilla, Salvatore 106 n. 54
Lizzi, Rita 192 n. 64, 221 n. 54
Lössl, J. 268 n. 106
Lüdemann, Gerd 92 n. 17, 96 n. 24, n. 26
Luther, Martin 6–7, 283 n. 164
Lyman, J. Rebecca 147

MacDonald, Dennis R. 94
McClure, Judith 147 n. 65
McLynn, Neil 21 n. 21, 61 n. 32, 212 n. 22,
  221 n. 54, 229 n. 88
MacMullen, R. 64 n. 42
Madec, G. 270 n. 113, 277 n. 133
Maier, Harry O. 73
Malbon, Elizabeth Struthers 65
Manichaeans, Manichaeism
  Ambrosiaster's discussion of 163–4
  asceticism of 141–2, 145–6, 169
  associated with Hieracas 132–3
  attacked by Epiphanius and
    Filastrius 146–53, 158
  attacked by Pelagius 262, 264 n. 87
  Augustine accused of 267–8
  Augustine's attack on 270–3, 277–8, 283
  Augustine's descriptions of 144–5
  confusion with Encratites 142–4
  Helvidius' argument against 189 n. 55
  imperial legislation against 142–4

Jerome accused of 29–30, 244, 246–7, 257,
  275–7
Jovinian's accusations against 22–4,
  29–30, 39 n. 73
persecuted by popes 144
persistence in Rome 144–5
Priscillian accused of 135–41
use of apocryphal Acts 114, 151
use of private space 73
and *virginitas in partu* 22–4, 171, 203–4
Marcella 61, 76, 77, 161
Marcion
  attacked by Ambrosiaster 163
  attacked by Clement of Alexandria 105–6,
    111, 156
  attacked by Irenaeus 101–2
  attacked by Origen 125, 186–7
  attacked by Tertullian 116, 181–2
  attacked by Theophilus of Antioch 100
  and Pastoral Epistles 93–4
  and Tatian 102–5
  influence on Tertullian 118 n. 100
Markus, Robert A. 12 n. 25, 51–2, 68 n. 62,
  252 n. 43, 261, 264 n. 87, 270
Martin, Dale B. 98 n., 207 n.
Martini, C. 160 n. 117
Mary (mother of Jesus) *see* virginal
  conception (of Jesus); *virginitas in
  partu; virginitas post partum*
Matthews, John 20 n. 19, 51 n. 1, 65–6,
  69 n. 63
Maximus, emperor 135–6
Mees, M. 107 n. 58
Meigne, M. 214 n. 29
Melancthon, Philip 7
Melania, the elder 80, 258
Melania, the younger 78
Merkt, A. 160 n. 118
Methodius, bishop of Olympus 156–7
Metz, R. 224 n. 69
Micaeli, C. 120 n. 108, 167 n. 153
Miltiades, bishop of Rome 144
Monasticism
  Ambrose's support of 219–24
  criticism of 52–63
  and Hieracas 131–2
Montanism 117
  see also 'New Prophecy'
Mueller, J. R. 88 n. 4
Musonius Rufus 28–9, 106

Nagel, Peter 114 n. 85
Namatianus, Rutilius Claudius 53–4, 60

Nauroy, G. 234 n. 104
Nautin, Pierre 17 n. 6, 208 n. 5, 211 n. 17, 234 n. 104, n. 105, 235 n. 106, 237 n. 118, 258 n. 66
Nepotian 219 n. 47, 237–8
Neumann, Charles W. 16 n. 4, 24 n. 32, 190–2, 197 n. 83, 200 n. 90, n. 91, 201 n. 94
'New Prophecy' 117, 119–20
see also Montanism
Nolan, John Gavin 10, 19 n. 16
Novak, D. M. 63 n. 41, 64 n. 43, n. 44, 65 n. 50
Novatian 120, 150 n. 80, 187
Nuvolone, F. G. 259 n. 70, 260 n. 72, 264 n. 104

Oberhelman, S. M. 234 n. 104, 235 n. 106, n. 111, 237 n. 117
Odes of Solomon 105 n. 52, 175–8, 187
O'Donnell, James J. 212 n. 22
Oppel, John 6
Orbe, Antonio 111 n. 79
Origen of Alexandria
  attacked by Epiphanius 147, 155–8
  attacked by Filastrius 147, 158 n. 113
  fourth-century debates over 244, 256–8
  as 'moderate encratite' 115, 123–9
  on 'Levites' 223
  used by Ambrose 199–201
  used by Jerome 123, 126 n. 133, 232, 248 n. 25, 267, 276 n. 131
  used by Pelagius 264
  on virginal conception 184–6, 195
  on *virginitas in partu* 184, 186–7
original sin
  Ambrose's teaching on 199–203, 226
  Ambrosiaster's teaching on 164–9
  Augustine's teaching on 267, 282–3, 286–7
  Clement of Alexandria's teaching on 110–11
  in *Consultationes Zacchaei et Apollonii* 253–4
  Origen's teaching on 184–5
  Priscillian's teaching on 138–9
  Tatian's teaching on 103–4

Pachomius 55
Pacian, bishop of Barcelona 37–8, 44, 47–8, 232 n. 96
Pagels, Elaine 94–5 n. 23
Palladius, bishop of Helenopolis 78, 80
Pammachius
  adoption of ascetic life 60
  candidate for episcopacy 240–1
  correspondence with Jerome 24–6, 170 n. 161, 191, 245–7
  opposition to *Adversus Jovinianum* 245–7
  opposition to Jovinian 16–18, 72
Paredi, A. 17 n. 5, 234 n. 104, 235 n. 106
Paschal Vigil 192, 227; *see also* Easter Vigil
Pastoral Epistles
  opposition to encratism 92–7, 102
  used by Clement of Alexandria 108–10, 113
  used by Epiphanius 153
  used by Irenaeus 96
  used by Jerome 239–40
  used by Jovinian 21, 29, 34–5, 39–41, 128–9
  used by opponents of clerical continence 218–19
Patterson, Lloyd 156 n. 106, 157 n. 108
Paul (apostle)
  cited by Ambrosiaster 166–7, 217
  cited by Augustine 271–8
  cited by Clement of Alexandria 107–10, 112 n. 80
  cited by Hieracas 132
  cited by Jerome 239–40, 247–9
  cited by Jovinian 21, 34–5, 41
  cited by Origen 124–7
  cited by Pelagius 262–6
  cited by Priscillian 137, 139
  cited by Tatian 103–4, 108
  cited by Tertullian 116–18
  teaching on marriage 88–96
  see also Pastoral Epistles
Paula
  ascetic renunciation of 76, 78
  education 80
  friend of Jerome 16, 208
  mother of Blesilla 62
  reading of Ambrose 235
Paulinus, bishop of Nola 60, 71 238, 257
  on almsgiving and ascetic renunciation 79
  and Pelagius 259–60
  and Vigilantius 258–9
Pelagius
  and anonymous Roman monk 249–50
  on consecration of virgins 228–9
  correspondent with Demetrias 81
  opposition to Jerome 259–68
  on possibility of sinlessness 244–5
Peterson, William L. 104 n. 50
Petitmengin, P. 120 n. 108
Pietri, Charles 24 n. 33, 61 n. 34, 79 n. 98, 162 n. 130

Index

Pinytos, bishop of Cnossos 96–7
Plinval, Georges de 249
Plumpe, Joseph C. 173 n. 6
Pourkier, A. 149 n. 76
Praetextatus, Vettius Agorius 74 n. 83
priesthood
   Ambrose's teaching on 219–24
   incompatible with monastic life 55–8
   Jerome's perspectives on 208–9, 236–41
   requires sexual continence 161–2, 213–18
   Siricius' legislation on 211–13
   of virgins 229–30
   see also clergy; Levites
Priscillian, bishop of Avila 30 n. 48, 210 n. 14
   on celibacy 135–41
   treatment by Filastrius 150–2
   use of apocrypha 114, 139–40, 151
Proba, Anicia Faltonia 68–72, 80–2
Proba, Faltonia Betitia 68–72
Probus, Sextus Claudius Petronius 65–7, 69, 71 n. 73
Protevangelium of James
   cited by Origen 185–7
   influence on Zeno of Verona 192, 196
   rejected by Jerome 190
   on *virginitas in partu* 177–81, 196–7

Quacquarelli, Antonio 122 n. 113
Quispel, Gilles 102 n. 39, 104 n. 50, 105 n. 52, 115 n. 88
Quodvultdeus, bishop of Carthage 45

Rackett, Michael R. 268 n. 109
Rahner, Karl 172 n. 3
Ramsey, Boniface 79 n. 99, 203 n. 97, 227 n. 75
Rapp, Claudia 207 n. 1
Rebillard, Éric 200 n. 92
Reekmans, L. 70 n. 68
Rees, B. R. 249 n. 33, 260 n. 72
Reitzenstein, R. 114, n. 86
Reynolds, Philip L. 280 n. 149
ritual purity 215–18, 220, 239 n. 129
Rocca, Giancarlo 173 n. 6, 188 n. 51, 189 n. 53, n. 55, 191 n. 60
Rome, synod of 217
Rousseau, Philip 56 n. 17, 213, 236 n. 114, 237 n. 122
Rufinus of Aquileia
   connection with Pelagius 259–60, 267
   connection with Vigilantius 258–9
   opposition to Jerome 208 n. 5, 209, 235 n. 109, 244, 247 n. 19, 249 n. 30, 256–7, 267

Salome 178, 196
Salzman, Michele 3 n. 3, 52 n. 2, 63 n. 41, 64 n. 45, 68, 71 n. 74, 73 n. 82, 75 n. 84, 79 n. 100, 83
Sampley, J. Paul 91 n. 13
Saragossa, council of 135–6
Sarmatio 59 n. 28, 221
Satornilus 151, 153 n. 93, n. 94; *see also* Saturninus
Saturninus 101–2, 151; *see also* Satornilus
Schlatter, F. 268 n. 107
Schmitt, Émile 270 n. 113, 272 n. 120
Schoedel, William R. 92, n. 15, n. 16, 99 n. 33, 173
Schreiner, Susan 282 n. 162
Schüssler Fiorenza, Elisabeth 90 n. 11
Schultzen, F. 248 n. 25
Sellew, Philip 114 n. 86, 115 n. 87
Shanzer, Danuta 69
Siricius, bishop of Rome
   anti-Manichaean activities 144
   attacked by Jerome 239–42
   legislation on clerical celibacy 213–19
   legislation on clerical promotion 211–13
   legislation on lapsed monks 58, 210
   opponent of Jerome 208–9
   opponent of Jovinian 16–20, 22, 24, 72
   and Priscillian 135–6
   snub of Paulinus of Nola 210–11
Sivan, Hagith 63 n. 40, 69 n. 65, 77–8, 82
Smid, H. R. 177 n. 17
Smith, Jonathan Z. 6 n. 4
Snyder, H. Gregory 68 n. 60
Souter, A. 160, 263 n. 80, n. 81
Stancliffe, Clare 257 n. 61
Sterk, Andrea 133 n. 9, 134
Stickler, Alfons Maria 214 n. 28
Stoic, Stoicism 28, 106, 233
Stroumsa, G. 141 n. 37, n. 38, 142 n. 39
Sulpicius Severus 59 n. 25, 136 n. 18, 209–10, 256–9
Symmachus, Q. Aurelius 145

Tatian
   attacked by Clement of Alexandria 106–13
   influence on *De centesima* 114–15
   interpretation of Paul 103–4, 108–9
   Irenaeus' attack on 101–2
   teaching on creation and fall 102–5
   opposed by Epiphanius 148–50, 158–9
   rejected by Jerome 29, 247
Tertullian
   cited by Helvidius 189

Tertullian (cont.)
   influence on Jerome 120, 167 n. 153, 170, 190, 248, 285
   influenced by Theophilus of Antioch 100
   on marriage and celibacy 116–20, 127–9
   opposition to Marcion 102 n. 42
   opposition to *virginitas in partu* 181–4
   on remarriage 99 n. 34
   use of Pastoral Epistles 96
Testard, M. 234 n. 104
Theissen, Gerd 90 n. 9
Thelepte, council of 217
Theodoret, bishop of Cyrus 56 n. 14
Theodosian Code 8 n. 11
   anti-Manichaean legislation 22 n. 28, 142–4
   condemnation of Jovinian 243
   on monks 54–5, 74 n. 83
Theodosius I, emperor 20, 22 n. 28, 37, 51, 55, 142–3
Theodosius II, emperor 81
Theophilus, bishop of Antioch 99–100, 111 n. 79
Thier, Sebastian 260 n. 72, 264 n. 87, 265 n. 93
Tibiletti, Carlo 263 n. 86
Tissot, Y. 114 n. 85
Treggiari, Susan 70 n. 70
Trevett, C. 117 n. 95
Trout, Dennis 60 n. 30, 66–7, 79, 210–11

Valens, emperor 54–5, 142
Valentinian I, emperor 54, 55 n. 11, 142
Valentinian II, emperor 55, 135 n. 14, 142–3
Valentinus (Gnostic teacher) 94, 101–2, 105, 181–2
Valli, Francesco 9–10, 16 n. 3, 17 n. 5, 19 n. 17, 24 n. 33, 27, 31 n. 50, 36 n. 65
Van den Hoek, Annawies 106 n. 54
velatio, *see* veiling of virgins
veiling of virgins 32–3, 81, 135, 224–30
Verner, David 94 n. 23
Vessey, Mark 218 n. 43, 232
Via Latina (catacomb) 67–8

Vigilantius of Calagurris 244 n. 4, 258–9, 287
Vincent of Lérins 16, 27 n. 40
virginal conception (of Jesus)
   in Ambrose 197–203
   and baptism 119
   in Origen 184–5
   in second-century writers 172–4, 178
   in Tertullian 181–2
   in Zeno of Verona 193–6
virginitas in partu
   in Ambrose 197–204
   in *Ascension of Isaiah* 176–7
   in Clement of Alexandria 179–80
   in Jerome 190–2
   Jovinian's denial of 17 n. 7, 22–4, 171
   in *Odes of Solomon* 175–6
   opposed by Origen 184–6
   opposed by Tertullian 181–4
   in *Protevangelium of James* 177–9
   in Zeno of Verona 192–6
virginitas post partum
   defended by Jerome 190–2
   opposed by Helvidius 188–9
   in Origen 184–6
Vogels, A. 161

Walsh, P. G. 281 n. 152
Weitzmann, K. 70 n. 68
Wermelinger, O. 249 n. 33
Wharton, Annabel 47 n. 97
Wiesen, David S. 236, 237 n. 116, n. 117
Wilken, Robert Louis 98 n., 272 n. 119
Williams, Daniel H. 222 n. 57
Williams, G. 70 n. 68
Williams, Michael Allen 93 n. 20, 102 n. 40
Wisse, F. 142 n. 39

Yarnold, Edward 49
Young, Frances 147, 160 n. 118

Zeno, bishop of Verona
   baptismal sermons 44, 47, 50
   on *virginitas in partu* 192–6